THE UNIVERS
WINCH

michael jordan, inc.

D1344596

NOT TO BE REMOVED
FROM THE LIBRARY

WITHDRAWN FROM
THE LIBRARY
UNIVERSITY OF
WINCHESTER

SUNY series on Sport, Culture, and Social Relations

C. L. Cole and Michael A. Messner, editors

# michael jordan, inc.

Corporate Sport, Media Culture,
and Late Modern America

**David L. Andrews, editor**

STATE UNIVERSITY OF NEW YORK PRESS

cover photograph: Dale Cotton

Published by
STATE UNIVERSITY OF NEW YORK PRESS, ALBANY

© 2001 State University of New York

Printed in the United States of America

For information, address State University of New York Press
90 State Street, Suite 700, Albany, NY 12207

Production and book design, Laurie Searl
Marketing, Anne M. Valentine

Library of Congress Cataloging-in-Publication Data

Michael Jordan, Inc.: corporate sport, media culture, and late modern America / edited by David L. Andrews.
      p. cm.—(SUNY series on sport, culture, and social relations)
Includes bibliographical references and index.
ISBN 0-7914-5025-2 (alk. paper)—ISBN 0-7914-5026-0 (pb : alk. paper)
      1. Sports—Anthropological aspects—United States. 2. Jordan, Michael, 1963—Influence. 3. Mass media and sports—Social aspects—United States. I. Andrews, David L., 1962- II. Series.

GV706.2.M53 2001
306.4'83'0973—dc21                                                    00-054794

10  9  8  7  6  5  4  3  2  1

# Contents

## part III Jordan and Identity Politics

## part IV Jordan and the Global Marketplace

## part V Jordan and Critical Pedagogy

# From Paul Robeson to Althea Gibson to Michael Jordan: Images of Race Relations and Sport

I was told when I was a kid, well we want you to go and meet Paul Robeson. Paul Robeson was right up there with W. E. B. Dubois. I don't know
of any other black athlete who was seen in the way Paul Robeson is. This
kind of quintessential scholar-athlete.
      —Gerald Early, *The Journey of the African-American Athlete*

Any player who can take the beating Robeson has taken from you, giving as good as he's gotten and without squealing, is not black. He's a white
man! Now go back out there and play like hell—and give him a break.
      —Harry Edwards, *Paul Robeson: The Great Forerunner*

Long before Michael Jordan dazzled the world with his bald head, creative
dunks, and million-dollar status, the athletic experience for African Americans was resisted, limited, and pioneering (Ross 1999; Smith 1999). Much
attention has centered on the plights of Jack Johnson, Joe Louis, Jesse Owens,
and Jackie Robinson. In terms of women, Althea Gibson and Wilma
Rudolph dominate the integration discourse in the context of race and
sport. One name routinely omitted within discussions of sport is that of Paul
Robeson (Brown 1997). Before becoming renowned for his artistic achievements in both music and theatre, and prior to being widely pilloried for his
forthright commitment to worker's rights and international socialism,
Robeson was the quintessential student and athlete: he epitomized what I call
the "scholar-baller." This nomenclature derives from Robeson's outstanding
career in and outside the classroom while at Rutgers College (now Rutgers
University). Having received an academic scholarship to attend Rutgers, he
was elected to Phi Kappa Beta in his junior year and selected valedictorian
in his senior year. Robeson also excelled in the college sports arena, earning
twelve varsity letters in basketball, baseball, football, and track. He was also
named an All-American in football in 1917 and 1918. Evidently, Robeson
was the prototypical African American "scholar-baller," whose academic and

sporting achievements were realized in the face of both pre–Civil Rights institutional discrimination and physical intimidation. Moreover, as Harry Edwards, the renowned scholar-activist, articulated:

> Paul Robeson was not simply an extraordinarily gifted intellect, but a man of great passions as well. In his athletic career—as in all other sectors of his life—he never lost sight of the fact that intellectuality devoid of passion results in technocratic sterility, while passion divorced from intellectuality inevitably leads to chaos. Therefore, any portrayal of the man and the significance of his deeds that did not encompass both would be to separate the shadow from the act, to emphasize the words while ignoring what is being said. (1976, 25)

As such, Robeson—the early twentieth-century African American icon whose remarkable achievements, commitments, and demeanor brought him a degree of popular renown unprecedented in an era whose race relations were captured, and indeed defined, by the brutalizing racism of D. W. Griffith's *Birth of a Nation*—represents an interesting early twentieth-century counterweight to the social derivation and influence of the Michael Jordan phenomenon described within this anthology.

While perhaps polar opposites in terms of displaying their personal political commitments, there exist numerous parallels between Robeson and Jordan, in terms of the superior nature of their achievements. As Edwards stated, "If Aliens came down to earth, and asked to see the most extraordinary human being in existence, I would show them Michael Jordan. A team of physicists, chemists and scientists can't explain his athletic performances" (Edwards 1999b). Elsewhere, Edwards is in a less celebratory mode when describing the social legacy of the "Be Like Mike" ethos as it pertains to the implicit encouragement of black sports participation:

> It would appear, then, that not only the past history and contemporary circumstances but the future prospects of the Black athlete and the Black masses are inextricably intertwined and interdependent. And from this undeniable fact there is no escape for either—by way of sports or any other route. As things now stand, the overwhelming majority of young Blacks who seek to fill the shoes of O. J., Dr. J., Reggie J., and "Magic" J. in all likelihood will end up with no "J" at all—no job whatsoever that they are competent to do in a highly technological modern society. Thus, big-name athletes who tell Black kids to "practice and work hard and one day you can be just like me" are playing games with the future of Black society. (Edwards 1980, 242)

Herein, Edwards implicitly points to the need to problematize Jordan's black male body in terms of its social and economic import. This is because, as Kelley (1997, 44) succinctly noted, the imaged identities of African

American sportstars, such as that of Jordan, "have created a world where young black males do nothing but play." Several respected scholars in various disciplines have also added the black athlete and Michael Jordan to their cultural critique. Michael Eric Dyson's (1993, 74) analysis shows connection between Robeson and Jordan: "His body is still the symbolic carrier of racial and cultural desires to fly beyond limits and obstacles, a fluid metaphor of mobility and ascent to heights of excellence secured by genius and industry." Others question the passive objectification and feminization of Jordan's black male body (Boyd 1997a; 1997b; Coakley 1998; Carby 1998; hooks 1994; Stewart 1998). Evidently, the visual politics of the black male athlete operate at both ends of the spectrum: fearless but childish; success and failure; greedy but grateful; and strong but weak. These binaries must be challenged, and this anthology interrogates precisely such notions: Jordan-mania is deconstructed like never before.

While it is useful to contrast Robeson and Jordan it would be remiss not to acknowledge that the struggle has indeed changed for the African American athlete. As eloquently articulated by Edwards: "The struggle is different now. Michael Jordan does not want to be on the team—he wants to own the team" (Edwards 1999a). While entry barriers to football and basketball are plentiful for the black male athlete, covert forms of racism are manifested in the corporate world, the media, and the twenty-first-century society. Most black athletes will never come close to being Director of Operations for a professional sports team, which Jordan recently became. Moreover, mass and print media continue to passively endorse the racial stigmas and stereotypes of black men as hyper-sexual, immoral, and irresponsible (Harrison 1998c; Hutchinson 1996; Lucas 1999; White and Jones, 1999). These residual racist ideologies have encouraged the American public's pseudo-scientific beliefs (evidence speaks to more differences within the races than between them) pertaining to African Americans as "natural" black athletes who can jump out of the gym; soar like a bird; run like horses; and are genetic freaks of nature. Clearly, the racism that continues to envelop the African American athlete is not to be taken lightly, thus the need for the type of theoretical and textual analysis of contemporary representations and experiences of race, gender, and athleticism exemplified within this anthology.

ESPN's NBA analyst David Aldridge commented on the retirement of Michael Jordan by expressing that he felt that Michael Jordan changed race relations. I agree, but have one major revision and correction to this statement. Michael Jordan changed race relations for basketball and sporting fans that previously resisted African American achievement in sports and the commercial sphere. By contrast, Paul Robeson changed race relations in a broader sense, not only through sport, film, and media, but through his politics, language, and scholarship. While we should be cautious of the temptation to juxtapose one black athlete to another (good black, bad black binary), contrasting the space and bodies of these two icons makes for a good contrast and compare exercise. Robeson in Jordan's shoes (so to speak) would truly be a figure bigger than life. Jordan in Robeson's shoes would have progressive politics of that time moving at a slower pace. But let's be fair to both men. America is a country that still fears (on a daily basis) the black male body, and the consumption of Jordan has done little to change stereotypes and attitudes of racist and conservative people of black masculinity outside of the sporting arena and gladiator type spaces. Consuming a Robeson image and all the complexities that come with it does exactly what cultural studies set out to do—remove the *center* and cultivate a dialogue on race, class, gender, and image that challenges systemic thought, perception, and reality. This process will not come easily. With the dominance of African American women in the Women's National Basketball Association (Sheryl Swoopes, Lisa Leslie, Cynthia Cooper, Teresa Witherspoon) and track and field (Marion Jones), racial explanations will come with the existing social constructs of gender ideology for the sisters as well. In terms of the black male, cultural studies can help his athletic, aesthetic, and eclectic reality. The hip hop and rap genre sound bite phrase "Ballin like Jordan" must be defined and re-defined. It must mean more than the character "Shorty," in the movie *Sunset Park* (1992), articulated to his girlfriend, "I love you more than all my Michael Jordan possessions." In other words, links must be made with black athletes on the continuum and timeline prior to Robeson and after Jordan. "Ballin like Jordan" could mean making a career transition like Isiah Thomas (previously part-owner of an NBA team, now head coach of the Indiana Pacers) or Eric Dickerson (Monday Night Football sideline analyst). "Ballin like Jordan" could also mean staying in school and graduating with a psychology or history degree and then becoming a lottery pick (Tim Duncan of the San Antonio Spurs, Grant Hill of the Orlando Magic respectively). This is not to judge different paradigms, they are equally valid to the social and historical identities of African American athletes (Latrell Sprewell, Allen Iverson, or Randy Moss). Questions that should surface in the twenty-first century include finding out what happens to black sports stars after their playing days? How tight is the "glass ceiling" in terms of leadership and power roles in the hierarchy of sports? Will mainstream white Americans consume a highly intellectual, physically aesthetic, warrior-type scholar image in the years to come? Clearly, blacks can be experiencing the "Jordan effect" of acceptance in sports. Can African Americans broaden this "Jordan effect" to education, medicine, law, and business in terms of human respect? With the image of the African American male athlete so visible and images of Robeson and Jordan so connected *and* disconnected, the timing of *Michael Jordan, Inc.* could not be better to help begin to answer these questions.

C. KEITH HARRISON

## Note

The title of this foreword is borrowed from the Curt Flood Art Gallery housed in the Paul Robeson Center at the University of Michigan.

## References

Boyd, T. (1997a). *Am I black enough for you? Popular culture from the `hood and beyond.* Bloomington: Indiana University Press.

———. (1997b). *Out of bounds: Sports, the media, and the politics of identity.* Bloomington: Indiana University Press.

Brown, L. (1997). *The young Paul Robeson: On my journey now.* Boulder: Westview Press.

Carby, H. (1999). *Race men.* Cambridge: Harvard University.

Coakley, J. (1998). *Sport in society.* Boston: McGraw-Hill.

Dyson, M. (1993). *Reflecting black: African-American cultural criticism.* Minneapolis: University of Minnesota.

Early, G. (1996). *The Journey of the African-American Athlete.* HBO Sports.

Edwards, H. (1976). "Paul Robeson: His political legacy to the twentieth-century gladiator." In *Paul Robeson: The Great Forerunner*, 17–25.

——— (1980). *The struggle that must be: An autobiography.* New York: Macmillan.

——— (1999a). "An end of the golden age of black athlete participation." Keynote lecture and paper presented at San Diego State University, San Diego, California.

——— (1999b). Roundtable discussion at Saginaw Valley State University, Saginaw, Michigan.

hooks, b. (1994). "Feminism Inside: Toward a Black Body Politic." In *Black Male: Representations of Masculinity in Contemporary American Art*, T. Golden, 127–140.

Harrison, C. K. (1998). "The Assassination of the Black Male Image in Sport," *Journal of African American Men* 2(3):45–56.

Hutchinson, O. (1996). *The assassination of the black male image.* New York: Simon & Schuster.

Kelley, R. (1997). *Yo mama's disfunktional!: Fighting the culture wars in urban America.* Boston: Beacon Press.

Lucas, S. (1999). "Who's your daddy? Fatherhood, race, and the home run chase." Paper presented at the Annual Meeting of the North American Society for the Sociology of Sport. November 3–6, 1999, Cleveland, Ohio.

Ross, C. (1999). *Outside the lines: African Americans and the integration of the National Football League.* New York: NYU press.

Shakur, T. (1999). *The rose that grew from concrete.* New York: MTV Books/Pocket Books.

Smith, E. (1999). "Race matters in the National Basketball Association," *Marquette Sports Law Journal* 9(2):239–252.

Stewart, J. (1998). *Paul Robeson: Artist and citizen.* New Brunswick: Rutgers University Press.

White, J., and J. Jones. (1999). *Black man emerging: Facing the past and seizing a future in America.* New York: Routledge.

## Introduction

# Michael Jordan Matters

## David L. Andrews

Michael Jordan's entry into American popular consciousness can be traced to his successful—though by no means unparalleled—collegiate basketball career at the University of North Carolina. From this now distant beginning (largely etched into collective memory by the regular replaying of his winning shot in the 1982 NCAA Championship game) Jordan has emerged as a vivid emblem of late-twentieth-century sporting culture: an embodied fusion of sporting mastery and commercial maximization. In terms of the former, Jordan's stellar basketball career encompassed: six NBA championships with the Chicago Bulls; ten seasons as the NBA's leading scorer; two Olympic gold medals (one *Dream Team*); a plethora of individual records, awards, and accolades; a highly publicized retirement from basketball and brief flirtation with baseball; and, an equally high profile return to the NBA, culminating in a storybook ending to an imperious playing career. In tandem with his playing exploits, Jordan also nurtured a ground-breaking and even more lucrative career within the commercial sphere, which has included: a revolutionary endorsement contract signed with Nike; annual versions of the Air Jordan shoes; numerous Nike advertising campaigns penetrating the United States and the rest of the globe; a vast portfolio of prestigious corporate endorsements; and, latterly, elevation to the corporate executive and ownership ranks (both of Nike's Jordan brand and the Washington Wizards NBA franchise), and the enduring threat of another return to the basketball court.

In the accumulated wake of these highly visible triumphs and achievements, the mass media has largely narrated the Jordan story in terms of a heroic transcendental sporting and commercial odyssey. Indeed, none other than Henry Louis Gates even anointed Jordan "a twentieth century sports hero . . . [with only] . . . plausible competition from Babe Ruth and Muhammad Ali," and "the greatest pitchman of all time" (1998, 48). By its very nature such aggrandizing hyperbole diminishes the political import of public individuals, by simplifying their sociostructural derivation and influence. For instance, as we bask in the glow of Michael Jordan's preeminence, it is easy to overlook (indeed the commercial media encourages us to do so) that not only is he one of the most celebrated individuals in America, Jordan is also a member of one of the nation's most historically oppressed and reviled populations (African American males). Discerning the mechanisms and motives responsible for this apparent contradiction reveals much about American culture at the turn of the twenty-first century. So, this anthology is intended as an intervention into the process whereby Michael Jordan—as an important vehicle for critical cultural analysis—has been lost to the trivializing excesses of the promotional culture that dominates and defines contemporary existence (Wernick 1991). As such, and paraphrasing Cornel West (1994), this anthology represents both an intellectual expression of, and a political commitment to, the fact that Michael Jordan *matters*.

Despite Jordan's contemporaneous cultural centrality, and belying mainstream America's deep rooted anti-intellectualism, *Sports Illustrated* poured scorn on the very sensible idea of students taking a course on "Michael Jordan: Pop Culture Icon of the Late 20th Century" (Whiteside 1995); something developed to great effect by Kaufman (1997). Unlike *Sports Illustrated,* ESPN's production staff recognized plainly Jordan's broader import, as evidenced by the manner which they introduced him as "ESPN's Athlete of the Twentieth Century" (ABC, December 26, 1999). In an unexpectedly adroit and incisive filmed segment, ESPN focused as much on Jordan's cultural and temporal significance, as it did on his peerless exploits on the basketball court. Unfortunately such contemplative reportage is all too rare, since the incestuous nature of the contemporary media has spawned a mass culture industry, centered on Jordan, that oscillates between the sycophantic and the sensationalist (for example see Esquinas 1993; Greene 1992; Greene 1995; Johnson 1998; Smith 1992; Smith 1995; for informative exceptions see Halberstam 1999, and the routinely overlooked Naughton 1992). More surprisingly is the fact that Jordan has figured so negligibly within the ever expanding field of popular cultural studies. Indeed, up to this point, the Jordan phenomenon has provided the focus for only three culturally focused discussions (see Dyson 1993; Gates 1998; LaFeber 1999). More frequently, Jordan has been the focus of passing or tangential references within critical scholarly works focusing on *broader* social and cultural issues (see Boyd 1997a, 1997b; Goldman and Papson 1998; Hall 1993; hooks 1994; 1995; Lull 1995; Marqusee 1999; Ritzer 1993; Twitchell 1996; Willis 1991).

In light of the relative academic disregard that has greeted Jordan, it should be pointed out that this anthology is not a piece of intellectualizing for its own sake, myopically designed to redress the Jordan balance. Nor is it, on the other hand, a flimsily disguised celebratory account of Jordan's status as a popular hero. Rather, this anthology brings together a selection of chapters that use Michael Jordan as a vehicle for developing progressive understandings of the *broader* social, economic, political, and technological concerns that frame contemporary culture. It seeks to make sense of a celebrated figure, whose public existence graphically exteriorizes a late capitalist order defined by the convergence of corporate and media interests.

As the epitome of contemporary celebrityhood, Jordan is an embodied exaltation of the twinned discourses of late modernity: neo-liberal democracy and consumer capitalism (Marshall 1997). The neo-liberal order that engulfed much of the globe in the second half of the twentieth century: incorporates a political system preoccupied with "the personal, the intimate, and the individual" (Marshall 1997, xiii); encourages an equally solipsistic regime of economic [re]production, consumer capitalism; both of which are nurtured by the celebrity culture emanating from that supreme technology of hyper-individualization, commercial television. This anthology is underpinned by the belief that Jordan's continuing odyssey enunciates the rhythms and regimes of this late capitalist order, in a manner that renders Michael Jordan a key locus for critical contemporary cultural analysis. Hence, both individually and in aggregate, the chapters gathered together in this anthology examine Michael Jordan as a cultural product "constituted with and constitutive of a larger context of relationships" characteristic of the American condition at the turn of the twenty-first century (Grossberg 1997, 257). In other words—and in the tradition of a Marxist historical materialism founded on the notion that "even the most abstract categories . . . are by the very definiteness of the abstraction a product of historical conditions as well, and are fully applicable only to and under those conditions" (Marx, in McLellan 1977, 355)—herein the general may be realized through the particular: that Michael Jordan *matters* is exhibited through the explication of particular Michael Jordan *matters*.

Following McDonald and Birrell's (1999) energizing appeal to interrogate contemporary sport culture, both collectively and in isolation, the proceeding chapters engage Jordan as one of sport culture's most insightful

> vantage points from which to observe, critique, and intervene in the complex and contradictory interactions of the power lines of ability, age, race, class, nationality, gender, and sexuality . . . [these chapters] . . . provide

interventions into the dynamics of power, revealing what might have been
obscured, while placing events and celebrities within their particular historical and political contexts. (McDonald and Birrell 1999, 295–296)

In light of this directive, and in order to critically contextualize Jordan's commodified being, the chapters that comprise this anthology are divided into
five parts, each of which focuses on a foundational pillar of contemporary
cultural existence.

Part I: Jordan and the Celebrity Economy provides an introduction to
late capitalism's pervasive and invasive cult of celebrity, so epitomized by
Michael Jordan. Norman Denzin (re)presents Jordan as the ultimate celebrity-athlete functioning within today's mass mediated market place. Denzin
illustrates how, from the outset of his career in the NBA, the aggressive brand-
ing of Jordan turned him into a sign of himself through seductively conflat-
ing his imaged identity with that of established entities within the global
corporate American order. Bringing the discussion up to date, Denzin goes
on to show how the subsequent globalization of Jordan's celebrityhood has
contributed to the emergence of a televisually based transnational racial
order, prefigured on the production and circulation of universalizing, nonthreatening—and thereby highly marketable—representations of black ethnic
otherness. Edward Armstrong locates the derivation and influence of Jordan's
celebrity more explicitly within the hypercommodified logics of postmodern
society. This is achieved through his imaginative use of Jordan's uniform number as his vehicle of analysis. Armstrong's semiotic framework provide a fruitful entrée into a wide range of issues pertaining to the commodification and
spectacularization of contemporary sport. Perhaps most interestingly,
Armstrong points to the teleological nature of contemporary celebrity,
whereby—and invoking Denzin's argument—Jordan's uniform number
becomes a de facto sign of the commodified and simulated reality that
informs his very public being.

In Part II: Jordan and Corporate Culture, the notion of Jordan's aggressively commodified being is developed by focusing on the mantras and
mechanisms underpinning his most fruitful and innovative corporate connection: that being the revolutionary association with Nike Inc., responsible
for reconfiguring the culture and economics of American professional sport.
Douglas Kellner identifies the Jordan/Nike nexus (captured by the Air Jordan
campaign) as being emblematic of the media-led transformation of sport into
an entertainment-oriented mass spectacle designed to promote the market
values, products, and identities that propel consumer capitalism. This initiates
a discussion of (Air) Jordan's relationship to the complexities and contradictions implicit within the increasingly commercialized, raced spectacle that

colors American culture. However, Kellner also elucidates how, by association, the "unholy alliance" between Nike and Jordan taints him with the
detritus of postindustrial corporate capitalism, particularly that derived from
the practices of targeting underprivileged consumers in so-called developing
nations, while exploiting poorly regulated workers in the developing world.
C. L. Cole further problematizes the Jordan/Nike nexus in her broad-rang-
ing discussion of American Jordan as a nationally representative figure.
Focusing on Nike's P.L.A.Y. campaign (within which Jordan played a central
role), Cole illustrates how Jordan's identity is imagined as an embodiment of
the abstract values, beliefs, and principles through which particular American
knowledges and configurations of power are mobilized. As such, Cole
unequivocally contextualizes Jordan within the political culture of late modern America.

Developing from Cole's discussion, Part III: Jordan and Identity Politics
focuses more specifically on the cultural politics imbued within two facets of
Jordan's commodified identity. David Andrews revisits some of the issues raised
in earlier chapters within his genealogy of Jordan's racial identity. While routinely characterized as an expression of racial transcendence, Andrews corroborates Cole's argument when identifying Jordan as a cultural site around which
particular neoconservative racial ideologies have been embodied and authorized. As such, Andrews uses Jordan's fluctuating racial identity to illustrate the
socially constructed nature, and inherent dynamism, of racial classifications.
While the racial question is tackled within numerous chapters throughout the
book, Mary McDonald keys on the media's representation of Jordan's sexuality: an implicit aspect of popular portrayals of African American otherness, but
something hitherto largely overlooked by Jordan scholars. McDonald evidences how, in his carefully crafted public persona as the consummate family
man, Jordan's demure and implacably responsible heterosexual masculinity
provides a commercially valorized counterpoint to more routine depictions of
African American males as irresponsibly individualistic hypersexual beings.
Once again, McDonald grounds an aspect of the Jordan phenomenon within
its broader cultural context, this time within the "family values" politics that
continue to permeate post-Reaganite America.

Part IV: Jordan and the Global Marketplace demonstrates the global reach
and influence that has accompanied the concerted commodification of Jordan.
Carrington, Andrews, Jackson, and Mazur engage Jordan as one of the coterie
of American cultural exports to the rest of the world, whose presence necessarily contributes to the reconstitution of local understandings, identities, and
experiences. In effect, the authors use Jordan to explore the relationship
between global media products and the cultural contingencies of three distinct

local contexts (Poland, New Zealand, and the United Kingdom). Wilson and Sparks provide an ethnographically grounded examination of the consumption of images of African American basketball players (epitomized by Jordan) among youth populations drawn from two Canadian cities, and from contrasting ethnic backgrounds. Among other significant issues, their findings speak to a subject raised by Carrington within the previous chapter, namely, the practice of incorporating African American sport stars such as Jordan within the vernacular cultures of the black diaspora. Thus, the authors provide further empirical support for Carrington's suggestive observation, while revealing much about the climate of race relations within contemporary Canada.

Lastly, Part V: Jordan and Critical Pedagogy reflects on what can be learned from Jordan's most visible and invasive of imaged personas. In his now seminal piece, Dyson demonstrates Jordan's function as a public pedagogue whose career authorizes and educates the populace as to the productive and disenabling potentialities of athletic, African American, and commercial cultures. Dyson concludes that despite the deleterious effects of Jordan's appropriation by the forces and sensibilities of corporate capitalism, the physical exploits of his "big black body" nonetheless represents a compelling exposition of black culture's continued disposition toward practices of improvisational ingenuity as sources of collective identification and resilience. In the final chapter, Hoechsmann reflects on Dyson's articulation of Jordan as a "supremely instructive figure for out times," from the vantage point of the post-retirement world, and with specific reference to the complexities of young people's consumption of Jordan's commodified being. So, Hoechsmann challenges educators to engage critically, and thereby expose, the role of iconic figures such as Jordan as powerful ideational forces, which inform significantly the attitudes and experiences of young people within contemporary cultures of consumption.

# References

Andrews, D. L. (1996). "The fact(s) of Michael Jordan's blackness: Excavating a floating racial signifier," *Sociology of Sport Journal* 13(2):125–158.

———. (1998). "Excavating Michael Jordan: Notes on a critical pedagogy of sporting representation." In *Sport and postmodern times*, ed. G. Rail, 185–220. New York: State University of New York Press.

Anon. (1995). "Newsweek Poll: How well do the following people represent American ideals in the way they live their lives?" *Newsweek* (July 10), 30.

Boyd, T. (1997a). "The day the niggaz took over: Basketball, commodity culture, and black masculinity." In *Out of bounds: Sports, media, and the politics of identity*, ed. A. Baker and T. Boyd, 123–142. Bloomington: Indiana University Press.

Boyd, T. (1997b). *"Am I black enough for you?" Popular culture from the 'hood and beyond.* Bloomington: Indiana University Press.

Castle, G. (1991). "Air to the throne," *Sport,* (January), 28–36.

Cole, C. L., and D. L. Andrews. (1996). "'Look—it's NBA *show time!*':Visions of race in the popular imaginary," *Cultural studies: A research volume* 1:141–181.

Dyson, M. E. (1993). "Be like Mike-Michael Jordan and the pedagogy of desire," *Cultural studies,* 7(1):64–72.

Esquinas, R. (1993). *Michael & me: Our gambling addiction . . . my cry for help.* San Diego: Athletic Guidance Center Publishing.

Gates, H. L. (1998). "Annals of marketing: Net worth," *The New Yorker* (June 1) 48–61.

Giroux, H. A. (1994). *Disturbing pleasures: Learning popular culture.* New York: Routledge.

Goldman, R., and S. Papson. (1998). *Nike culture.* London: Sage.

Greene, B. (1992). *Hang time: Days and dreams with Michael Jordan.* New York: Doubleday.

———. (1995). *Rebound: The odyssey of Michael Jordan.* New York: Viking.

Grossberg, L. (1997). *Bringing it all back home: Essays on cultural studies.* Durham: Duke University Press.

Halberstam, D. (1991). "A hero for the wired world: In the satellite age, Michael Jordan has become the global hero of a global show," *Sports Illustrated* (December 23), 76–81.

———. (1999). *Playing for keeps: Michael Jordan and the world he made.* New York: Random House.

Hall, R. E. (1993). "Clowns, buffoons, and gladiators: Media portrayals of African-American men." *Journal of Men's Studies* 1(3):239–251.

hooks, b. (1994). "Feminism inside: Toward a black body politic." In *Black male: Representations of masculinity in contemporary American art,* ed. T. Golden, 133–134. New York: Whitney Museum of American Art.

———. (1995). *Art on my mind: Visual politics.* New York: The New Press.

Johnson, R. S. (1998). "The Jordan effect: The world's greatest basketball player is also one of its great brands. What is his impact on the economy?" *Fortune* (June 22), 124–126, 130–132, 134, 138.

Kaufman, P. (1997). "Michael Jordan meets C. Wright Mills: Illustrating the sociological imagination with objects from everyday life." *Teaching Sociology* 25:309–314.

Kellner, D. (1991). "Reading images critically: Toward a postmodern pedagogy." In *Postmodernism, feminism, and cultural politics: Redrawing educational boundaries,* ed. H. A. Giroux, 60–82. Albany: State University of New York Press.

LaFeber, W. (1999). *Michael Jordan and the new global capitalism.* New York: W. W. Norton.

Lull, J. (1995). *Media, communication, culture: A global approach.* Oxford, England: Polity Press.

Marqusee, M. (1999). *Redemption song: Muhammad Ali and the spirit of the sixties.* London: Verso.

Marshall, P. D. (1997). *Celebrity and power: Fame in contemporary culture*. Minneapolis: University of Minnesota Press.

McDonald, M. G., and S. Birrell. (1999). "Reading sport critically: A methodology for interrogating power," *Sociology of Sport Journal* 16(4):283–300.

McLellan, D. (1977). *Karl Marx: Selected writings*. Oxford: Oxford University Press.

Naughton, J. (1992). *Taking to the air: The rise of Michael Jordan*. New York: Warner Books.

Putnam, P. (1995). "Rivers of dollars flow with Jordan," *The Observer* (April 9), 15.

Ritzer, G. (1993). *The McDonaldization of society: An investigation into the changing character of contemporary social life*. Thousand Oaks: Pine Forge Press.

Rowe, D. (1999). *Sport, culture, and the media: The unruly trinity*. Buckingham: Open University Press.

Smith, S. (1992). *The Jordan rules: The inside story of a turbulent season with Michael Jordan and the Chicago Bulls*. New York: Simon & Schuster.

———. (1995). *Second coming: The strange odyssey of Michael Jordan—from courtside to home plate and back again*. New York: HarperCollins.

Snider, M. (1996). "Michael Jordan's bigger than basketball; he's a pop icon," *USA Today* (July 19), 3D.

Twitchell, J. B. (1996). *Adcult, USA: The triumph of advertising in American culture*. New York: Columbia University Press.

Wernick, A. (1991). *Promotional culture: Advertising, ideology, and symbolic expression*. London: Sage.

West, C. (1994). *Race matters*. Boston: Beacon Press.

Whiteside, K. (1995). "Inside the NBA," *Sports Illustrated*, April 10, 92.

Willis, S. (1991). *A primer for daily life*. London: Routledge.

# part I

# JORDAN

## and the Celebrity Economy

# 1

# Representing Michael

## Norman K. Denzin

It could easily be a matter of timing, where society was looking for something positive. It could easily be a sport that was gradually bursting out into global awareness at a time when I was at the top. And then there's the connections that I've had with corporate America since I started with Coca-Cola and then went to Nike, which has gone totally global.

—Michael Jordan

I really felt that I wanted to instill some positive things back to the game. You know, there's a lot of negative things that have been happening to the game, and I guess in terms of me coming back, I came back with the notion, you know, Magic Johnson and the Larry Birds and the Dr. Js—all those players paved the road for a lot of the young guys, and the young guys are not taking care of their responsibilities in terms of maintaining that love for the game, you know, and not let it waste to where it's so business-oriented that the integrity of the game's going to be at stake.

—Michael Jordan

Mentally, I'm exhausted. I know from a career standpoint, I've accomplished everything I could as an individual. Right now I just don't have the mental challenges that I've had in the past to proceed as a basketball player. This is a perfect time for me to walk away from the game. And I'm at peace with that.

—Michael Jordan

So he is gone, Air Jordan the NBA basketball star has flown away. Only his image remains, Michael Jordan, an empire of signs (Gates 1998, 61), the ultimate celebrity-athlete. The man who became a sign of himself. His job today is to care for that empire, to be the man behind that black man who is not really black in the Wieden and Kennedy Nike ads (Gates 1998, 60). This is Michael the image, in part it is that grin, and the shaved head and the gold earring. But there is more, for this is the Michael who has become "the object of allure, the sign of black urban manhood, supple, smooth, commanding, powerful, and hip" (Gates 1998, 58).

Those who become signs of themselves function as commodities in today's mass media marketplace. Their celebrityhood is commodified, turned into an object that endorses another object. And Michael has become a sign attached to the leading brands of the day: Nike, Coca-Cola, McDonald's, Quaker Oats, Wilson, CBS SportsLine, Sara Lee, Jordan brand apparel, Ball Park Franks, Hanes underwear, General Motors, Chevrolet, Rayovac, Bijan (the Michael Jordan fragrance), MCI, Wheaties, MJ's sports videos ("Come Fly With Me").

MJ is the ultimate pitchman. In his representations he is seen as embodying the "attributes of a quintessential champion: will and perseverance, and discipline and excellence" (Elliott 1999, 66). For all of this he is paid well. He earned more than $42 million in 1998 in product endorsements (Elliott 1999), and his total income in 1997 was estimated to be in excess of $70 million (Gates 1998, 60). This is one version of the so-called "Jordan Factor" (Gates 1998, 51; and below). Irony of ironies, he broke the rules. He is a black professional basketball player who was not from one of the major media markets, neither New York nor Los Angeles (Elliott 1999). But he has become something more than Michael the NBA all-star. He no longer has to be in a sports setting. "Michael Jordan the brand is much bigger than Michael Jordan the basketball player" (Elliott 1999, 66). He has transcended his sport. He is now famous for being famous, like Elizabeth Taylor, Muhammad Ali, or one of the Beatles (Elliott, 1999). Forty years from now we will be able to "envision Jordan flying through the air, dunking a basketball" (Elliott 1999, 66).

Jordan and David Falk (his agent) learned how to turn Michael into a product, into a sign of himself. They reversed the usual direction of the commodity sign, that logic that connects celebrities to products. Under the conventional model, meaning, emotion, imagery, and product identification move from the celebrity to the product to the consumer (Gates 1998, 52). Michael and Falk altered this model. Falk and Jordan placed the commodity (Coca-Cola, Nike) in front of the image of MJ. This representation then joined Michael to the commodity and, in turn, to the consumer, to wit: Air Jordan–Michael Jordan–consumer.

Here is how it happened. It started with shoes. Falk describes what he did in Jordan's rookie year: "I asked all the shoe companies to make a presentation to us and explain what they would do to market Michael. Nike turned out to be the keenest suitor, but they refused to call it the 'Michael Jordan line' . . . . I came up with the idea of calling the shoe Air Jordan" (Falk quoted in Gates 1998, 52). The result was a $2.5 million contract over five years plus royalties, with Falk demanding that "the company spend at least a million dollars on promotion, and so guarantee his client that measure of commercial exposure" (Gates 1998, 53). Falk went next to the national executives of McDonald's and Coca-Cola, inviting them to formulate specific plans for marketing Michael. Thus did global corporate America become a pitchman for MJ.

This is not just any old version of corporate America. Nike, McDonald's, and Coca-Cola are universally recognized brand names, their products have planet-wide appeal. This appeal and recognition naturally carries over to the celebrity who endorses the product. Hence, we have another version of the "Jordan Factor." By endorsing Coke, McDonald's, and Nike, Jordan became a universal signifier of these products, and they of him (Gates 1998, 52).

Together, these two sign systems, Jordan and Coke, or Jordan and McDonald's, reinforced one another; each took on the positive characteristics of the other: authentic, the real thing, young, warm, friendly, reliable, wholesome, American, family-minded (Gates 1998, 53). Thus did the mystique of Michael become transcendant. He was larger than the thing itself, larger than Coke, or Nike, or the NBA, or the Chicago Bulls, and now you had to read the thing itself back through the presence of Michael. And in this way the NBA perpetuated its new star system: Michael and the Bulls (his supporting cast), Penny Hardaway and the Orlando Magic, Grant Hill and the Detroit Pistons, Karl Malone and the Utah Jazz (Gates 1998, 52).

Michael and the Bulls. 1998 version. A motley crew. An international cast, the global NBA, a player from every major continent: Luc Longley from Australia, Toni Kukoc from Eastern Europe, MJ and little brother Scottie Pippen (Tonto) from the South, another country in America, Ron Harper from Chicago, cross-dressing, orange-haired, tattooed, trash-talking, "bad-as-I-wanna-be" Dennis Rodman from Detroit, the straight-arrow white guys, Steve Kerr, Scott Burrell et al.; Phil Jackson, spiritual adviser, Chief Sitting Bull from South Dakota. A supporting cast of journeymen, except for Scottie and Dennis and Phil. The ordinariness of these niche players served to define MJ's specialness, his brilliance. Gates suggests that a kind of division of labor operated for the 1998 Bulls, "with Rodman's freakishness helping to secure Michael's normality" (1998, 61). Nothing new here, the deviant defines what is normal, and in the NBA, as elsewhere, nobody is too deviant, if they show up, score points, and help win games.

Falk and Jordan trumped the race card, because, as Falk understood, "Celebrities aren't black. People don't look at Michael as being black. They accept that he's different because he is a celebrity" (Falk quoted in Gates 1998, 54). If Michael was allowed to make race a non-issue, it was perhaps because he was the "right, best athlete for us now, for this relatively serene and altogether prosperous fin de siecle, when the United States rules alone, as much superculture as superpower" (Deford 1999, 4). Michael hit it on the head, when he said (as quoted above) society was looking for something positive, and I fit the bill.

Michael understands this very well. He is a man fitted for this historical moment. He is a black man who is not black. He was at the top when the NBA went international. He has shaped the ideals and standards that will define the sport for at least the next decade, perhaps forever. Furthermore, the global awareness of the NBA intersected directly with the globalization of corporate America in the nineties. Cable and satellite communication systems crisscrossed the planet. Global (and regional) sports television linked each major continent, from Europe to Asia, to North and South America, South Africa, Australia, and beyond. The NBA and Michael were everywhere. And Michael and Falk saw this coming; indeed, they helped make it happen. The audience was huge, and just keeps getting bigger. In turn, the internationalization of Nike, Coke, and McDonald's overlapped with the rise of the sign of MJ. And this sign of MJ was one that would sell globally, the gentle, kind, warm, dependable, wholesome, authentic, family man; the man for all seasons.

Those who control the media control a society's discourses about itself. A majority of Americans know and understand the American racial order through media representations of the black ethnic other. For these individuals, there is no empirical world beyond the worlds of the "small screen" (Gray 1995, 8). With only slight exaggeration it can be argued that the most significant feature of the contemporary American racial order is the one given in the professional sporting arena, the worlds of the national basketball (NBA) and football (NFL) associations. Within the confines of the NBA and the NFL black and white men battle one another. Television is the apparatus that produces and interprets these sporting spectacles. These spectacles are commercial productions, sponsored by the NBA and the NFL and the major athletic shoe corporations, Nike and Reebok.

Thus, at this level, race in America today is largely a matter of advertising, commercials, and the media. The key racial moments (NBA and NFL playoffs, Rodney King, Hill-Thomas Hearings, Simpson trial, Los Angeles riots) of the last two decades have been media events, staged by and interpreted on television. Of course each storied version of the American racial order contains a kernel of utopian fantasy. In these idealized worlds black and white Americans can happily interact within a racially unified culture where the facts of bigotry, racism, and discrimination are, if not absent, at least easily negotiated.

The black other occupies a complex site, a place where fears, desires, and repressed dreams are lodged. The black body is a site of spectacle, its blackness, as Herman Gray (1995, 165) argues, a potential measure of evil, and menace. And so the media constantly seek new ways of containing blackness, including nostalgic (and critical) re-readings of the racial past (Dr. J and NBA history); the normalization of exceptional blackness as it does service for whites (Air Jordan); and blackness as spectacle, e. g., the NBA playoffs (Gray 1995). Each of these strategies makes and remakes the signs of blackness, constantly folding blackness into the existing repressive systems of gender, and class.

Network (and Rupert Murdoch—Fox, SKY) television represents an American and transnational racial order based on a politics of cultural differ-ence. This discourse reifies and essentializes racial (and gender) differences, creating a series of cultural oppositions, pitting the black, ethnic male against a mainstream, white American or European other. This discourse continues to privilege full assimilation into the American (and increasingly internation-al) racial order as the proper end point for all minority group members.

Black media personalities such as Michael Jordan, Spike Lee, Arsenio Hall, Oprah Winfrey, and Bill Cosby "focus, organize, and translate blackness into commodifiable representations and desires that [can] be packaged and marketed across the landscape of American popular culture" (Gray 1995, 68). Modifying Gray (1995, 97), we are witnessing the "'African Americanization' of global popular culture." And Michael Jordan is leading the way (see Gates 1998; Halberstam 1999; and LaFeber 1999).

In their multiple treatments of blackness, sporting television operates as an internal "Orientalizing" agency for the larger global culture. Michael Jordan and the NBA are everywhere present, translating blackness, into a nonthreatening Reaganesque masculinity for male youth in New Zealand, Poland, Great Britain, Canada, and Japan. Television, hand-in-hand with the NBA and Nike, is the institutional apparatus which describes, teaches, and authorizes a particular view of the emerging international racial order. As the site of our collective (and repressed) unconscious, Nike television is the place where the new American and then world racial order will be first imagined, then created, and then played out. It is no longer appropriate to study this racial order outside of its media representations.

Following arguments developed by Jean-Paul Sartre (1981, ix) it is pos-sible to read this world racial order through the figure of one man, Michael Jordan (MJ). Sartre would call Jordan a universal singular, a single instance of more universal social experiences. Sartre reminds us that every person "is summed up and for this reason universalized by his [her] epoch, and he [she] in turn resumes it by reproducing him [her]self in it as singularity. Universal by the singular universality of human history, singular by the universalizing singularity of his [her] projects, he [she] requires examination from both ends" (Sartre 1981, ix).

Michael Jordan sums up his epoch, the most widely recognized professional athlete in the world today. A universal singular, this wife (Juanita), these three children, this now dead father (daddy), this mother, two brothers and two sisters who worked, while growing up, at Hardee's and McDonald's, and drove buses to earn money. No other NBA player has surpassed Jordan's achievements, no other player makes the money he does with commercial endorsements. To read race and postindustrial America through Jordan (and Nike) is to examine how this man mastered his sport by being subservient to his master's rules. Jordan (with Nike and its P.L.A.Y. program) embodies the cultural logic of a transnational capitalism. Thus, we can read this global order through the texts that define Jordan.

### Reading Michael Jordan

Underneath and stitched into those cultural formations called Michael Jordan is an old-fashioned, modernist conception of play, game, and competition in American culture (see Oriard 1991, ix). This model conceptualizes play as a natural, free, spontaneous activity. But central to this notion is its opposite, the idea that play is work, hard work. And central to this understanding is the argument that play-as-work is paid labor; professional sporting performers get paid well for doing their work well. But then skilled players have to work hard at the work of play. This Jordan does well, "I tell my wife that what I do for a living is a game" (Jordan in Vancil 1995, 49).

"I'm back. More rare Air." So announced Jordan in 1995 (Vancil 1995), and thus did Jordan on Jordan, Nike, and the Air Jordan Flight club return; but had they ever really left? Michael Jordan's/The Restaurant continued to do well on 500 North LaSalle, Chicago. The Chicago Bulls won the 1996, 1997, and 1998 NBA championships. In 1998 MJ became only the third player in NBA history to win the NBA Most Valuable Player Award five times. The Bulls lost ten games in the 1996 season and the next year Michael asked for $18 million to play for the Bulls, and he made $34 million in 1998.[1] Maybe life is just a game.

Elaborating Oriard (1991), Jordan embodies this conception of life as a game, the game of life, knowing how to play (and work) at the game (Jordan in Vancil 1995, 87). Jordan does for postmodern America what it has never

been able to do for itself, that is "satisfactorily ground American social reality in a . . . satisfying integration of work and play" (Oriard 1991, 484). And
Jordan does more than this. Andrews (1996) demonstrates that MJ enacts a
racially neutered identity, a black version of a white cultural model, an understated racial identity that privileges his superlative basketball skills. In his own
words, "I've been trying to have people view me more as a good person than
a good black man" (Jordan in Beahm 1994, 126).

This framework helps secure Jordan's place in an American, but increasingly global, mass-mediated culture. He is the racially neutral NBA superstar,
everybody's All-American, white America's solution to the race problem.
According to the media, no NBA star worked harder in the summer of the
1995–1996 season, "coming out of retirement to rebuild a former winner
into a world champ" (Seymour 1996).

American mass culture is rooted in a conspicuous playfulness. This playfulness commodifies performers, audiences, the sporting experience, and
media events, turning them into spectacles of display for entertainment purposes. These carnival-like events have little to do with the drama and rhetoric of play as pure, natural activity.

Of course Jordan defines sport-as-spectacle, witness Air Jordan. But with
that devilish grin, that wink of the eye, Michael tells us that he knows he is
pulling our leg, he knows, and we know, that this is just pure fun. And then,
there is a little of the business self in Michael. "My mother would say, 'I think
you should get more money son. I think you should hold out and get what
you're worth.' That's the business side of my mother. And I have some of that,
too" (Jordan in Vancil 1995, 87). But this business sense will not interfere, as
it has for the younger players, with the integrity of the game.

So this American sporting culture needs players like Michael Jordan. His
modernist view of play allows the culture to maintain a rhetoric of play and
sport that is separate from the understanding that the game is commodified
experience, a media hype. Michael Jordan embodies a conservative, personal
rhetoric of play and competition. This rhetoric values sport as an emblem of
hard work, moral character, heroism, and teamwork.[2] Success is more than
winning: "When the One Great Scorer comes to write against your name He
marks—not that you won or lost—but how you played the game" (Grantland
Rice, quoted in Oriard 1991, ix).

Michael Jordan rewrites what the One Great Scorer will write against
his name, for Michael not only played the game better than anyone else, but
he and his team won six NBA championships. This sporting ethos and his
accomplishments place him outside and above a new generation of NBA

stars. These new stars, as Cole and Andrews (1996) note, celebrate postmodernist conceptions of sport-as-a-commodity, the athlete as a media celebrity. They are NBA stars who act like spoiled celebrities. They have lost touch with the pure and innocent past of the NBA, that pastoral time when the game was played for the sheer love of competition and self-pride.

Michael embodies these beliefs from sport's pastoral past. They define who he is to himself and to his fans. These beliefs lead him to compete with himself and with the rules of game, impersonal rules that define winners and losers. These rules define the prideful dimensions of his playing self. This playing self does this for a living, knowing of course that it is a game: "It's a game on the basketball court and it's a game off the court" (Jordan in Vancil 1995, 49).

But in the moment of the game, in the moment of the play, Jordan experiences and expresses character, being a positive person, being honest, hardworking, committed, disciplined, well trained. He has submitted to the rules of competition, competing, any game will do, cards, golf, basketball. But he hasn't gone too far: "I've never known competing to be a major problem. I don't believe I've ever heard of Competitor's Anonymous.[3] I know that I'm not at a point in my life where I'm jeopardizing my family's standard of living with any gambling that I might do. I am nowhere near that. It's just a game, a game that I want to win" (Jordan in Vancil 1995, 76).

## Winning for Daddy

And so on that Sunday in 1996 when he won the fourth championship, we all watched. George Vecsey (1996, B-5), a fan of James Joyce, pointed out that it was Bloomsday, it was Father's Day, a day for family. "I won for Daddy," MJ tearfully told a worldwide viewing audience. He couldn't hit a jump shot, he cried like a baby (Araton 1996, B-13) and wrapped his arms around that tattooed body of Dennis Rodman with the orange-colored hair, and said, we'll be back next year.

On America's Father's Day he won one for his dead daddy, and everybody without a daddy felt deep inside his feelings, that emptiness that can not be filled. So he is all too human, this superstar, and in the end he would praise his wife (Araton 1996, B-13), "When I didn't feel like getting up . . . she set the alarm and made sure I got up," and applauded his "Tonto-like" little brother Scottie, and then listed the names of other, less famous teammates, Jud Buechler, Steve Kerr, Randy Brown (Araton 1996, B-13). A man for all seasons, a superstar with everyday values, the stuff of Capra films and Norman

Rockwell paintings, those lasting values so deep and so dear to capitalism. He set a goal, to come back better than ever, to win a fourth NBA championship. His goals became ours. We all want to be comeback artists, who doesn't need a second chance? So we won when he won. He did it for us. And who can ever forget the last twenty seconds of Game 6 of the 1998 NBA Championship? Another Sunday, June 14, 1998, close to another Father's Day and another Bloomsday. The Jazz are up by one, 85-86. We are headed to Game 7. Malone has the ball. All he has to do is let the clock run out. Everybody in the world but Malone sees Jordan coming around from behind, his eye on the ball. Malone is dribbling, suddenly Jordan swats the ball out of Malone's hand and dribbles upcourt. He pulls up short, nineteen feet from the basket, and lets fly. There are 5.2 seconds left. Nothing but air. Bulls lead, 87-86. The Jazz had one last shot, and Stockton took it, a three-pointer that missed. Series over. Bulls win Championship number Six!!! (see Taylor 1999, 118).

So in his return in 1995, just as in his leaving in 1999, Jordan would restore a sense of justice and balance to the American sporting order. Race would be back in its proper place, repressed and so visible that it had become invisible. With Jordan's return and then his retirement the natural order of the game of basketball has been restored, the integrity of the game no longer an issue. MJ saved basketball for America, and in so doing saved America from itself, for the time being from itself at least.

But there is one slight hitch. Goffman (1967, 44) argues that through ritual "societies everywhere . . . mobilize their members as self-regulating participants in social encounters . . . individuals are taught to be perceptive, . . . to have pride, honor, and dignity . . . to have tact and a certain amount of poise." These things must be built into persons "if practical use is to be made of them as interactants . . . it is these elements that are referred to in part when one speaks of universal human nature" (Goffman 1967, 44-45).

Michael Jordan has more than his share of these human-attributes. The universal human nature he announces is one, like Goffman's, that erases race. And this seems to be the last requirement of a global capitalism: cultural differences disappear, to be replaced by a universal, circumspect human nature that knows its place in the order of things. Is this how we want our heroes to be?

## Notes

1. His 1998 salary was the highest one-year salary in the NBA. His average salary during his first five years with the Bull was $800,000 (Burns 1999, 10).

2. Nike and the appalling labor conditions in its Indonesian sweatshops has caused Jordan some trouble on this point (Strom 1996, C1). Confronted with these facts Jordan replied, "I don't know the complete situation. Why should I? I'm trying to do my job. Hopefully, Nike will do the right thing" (Strom 1996, C-6). Jordan's decision to not be more visible in social or political causes has come under considerable criticism, but also defended by others (see Gates 1998, 57–58).

3. Of course MJ is referring to Gambler's Anonymous, and clearly distancing himself from this twelve-step group, and from the charges that his gambling, "the most objectionable of all recreational vices" (Oriard 1991, xii), and the most negative form of gaming, is out of control (see Gates 1998, 57).

# References

Andrews, D. L. (1996). "The fact(s) of Michael Jordan's blackness: Excavating a floating racial signifier," *Sociology of Sport Journal* 13(2):125–158.

Araton, H. (1996). "Jordan puts his family first," *New York Times*, June 18, B13.

Beahm, G. (1994). *Michael Jordan: A shooting star*. Kansas City: Andrews and McMeel.

Burns, M. (1999). "Jordanalia: Michael Inc," *Sports Illustrated,* January 20, 8–13. (Special Collector's Edition: Michael Jordan: A Tribute).

Cole, C. L., and D. L. Andrews. (1996). "'Look—It's NBA *ShowTime!*':Visions of race in the popular imaginary," *Cultural Studies: A Research Volume* 1:141–181.

Deford, F. (1999). "A man for his time," *Sports Illustrated,* January 20, 4–7. (Special Collector's Edition: Michael Jordan: A Tribute).

Elliott, S. (1999). "Markets from Gatorade to Nike try to decide if they will still like Michael Jordan when he retires," *New York Times,* January 13, C6.

Gates, H. L. Jr. (1998). "Annals of marketing: Net worth," *The New Yorker,* (June 1) 48–61.

Goffman, E. (1967). *Interaction ritual.* New York: Doubleday.

Gray, H. (1995). *Watching race: Television and the struggle for blackness.* Minneapolis: University of Minnesota Press.

Halberstam, D. (1999). *Playing for keeps: Michael Jordan and the world he made.* New York: Random House.

Jordan, M. (1995). "Interview." *CNN News,* March 19, 1995.

LaFeber, W. (1999). *Michael Jordan and the new global capitalism.* New York: W .W. Norton & Company.

Oriard, M. (1991). *Sporting with the gods: The rhetoric of play and game in American culture.* New York: Cambridge University Press.

Sartre, J.-P. (1981). *The family idiot: Gustave Flaubert,* 1821–1857, Vol. 1. Chicago: University of Chicago Press.

Seymour, G. (1996). "Give Jordan whatever he deserves," *Champaign-Urbana News Gazette*, May 21, B-3.

Strom, S. (1996). "From sweetheart to scapegoat," *New York Times,* June 27, C-1, C-6.

Taylor, P. (1999). "Michael's miracle," *Sports Illustrated,* January 20, 112–118. (Special Collector's Edition: Michael Jordan: A Tribute).

Vancil, M. (Ed.). (1993). *Rare air: Michael on Michael.* Text by Michael Jordan, Photographs by Walter Iooss, Jr. San Francisco: Collins.

———. (Ed.). (1995). *More rare air: I'm back.* Text by Michael Jordan, Photographs by Walter Iooss Jr. San Francisco: Collins.

Vecsey, G. (1996). "Who'd win best-of-nine playoffs?" *New York Times,* June 17, B-15.

Urschel, J., and M. Hiestand. (1996). "Huge salaries 'unfathomable' to many people," *USA Today,* July 16, 1A.

Wise, M. (1999). "Jordan exits gracefully, and at the top," *New York Times,* January 14, C21–C22.

# 2

# Michael Jordan and His Uniform Number

## Edward G. Armstrong

The postmodern era marks the beginning of something different in world history—a "hyperconsumerism" resulting from the fixation of image and style (Jarvis 1998). Michael Jordan (henceforth, MJ) exemplifies this new information age (LaFeber 1999). MJ expresses the postmodern celebrity economy and becomes an aspect of this cultural characterization. Examining the commodification of MJ's uniform number (henceforth, un) results in a discussion of the way MJ transformed himself into a saleable commodity. But before the argument can be carried any further, a basic exposition of un's and MJ is needed.

Athletes throughout the world are assigned un's to facilitate their identification by fans. According to the aphorism: players are known "by the numbers." In postmodern sports, this relationship is sometimes reversed—un's are identified with certain athletes. Un's develop teleologically, emerge in the form of a general design, and embody hierarchy (Armstrong 1986). MJ's un's, in particular, demonstrate the prevalence of postmodern cultural productions and the semiotic extension of discursive boundaries (Armstrong 1996). The way un's become charged with unique meanings and unfold on multiple levels transcends their original purpose.

MJ is a "world icon" (LaFeber 1999, 17) studied by "Jordanologists" (Halberstam 1999, 393). It is impossible to underestimate MJ's global significance and the attendant global presence of his un 23. MJ is the most recognized person in the world (*Advertising Age,* January 18, 1999; *People,* March 15, 1999). *Sports Illustrated* has pictured him on its covers more than anyone else. In 1999, his record total reached forty-eight (cnnsi.com, December 10,

This chapter is adapted, by permission, from E. Armstrong, 1996, "The commodified 23, or, Michael Jordan as Text," *Sociology of Sport Journal,* 13(4):325–343.

1999). According to the *Wall Street Journal,* the typical Chinese youth reveres MJ (November 12, 1997). One observer estimates that in Hong Kong a million children dress in MJ's un 23 (*Saint Paul Pioneer Press,* November 28, 1993). Travelers find tattered replicas of MJ's jersey in rural parts of Asia and Africa (Halberstam 1999). Cleveland Cavaliers President Wayne Embry is certain that "[t]here are more No. 23s out in the world than any other number" (*Chicago Tribune* [henceforth, *CT*], January 14, 1999, section 4, 5). As U.S. Secretary of Commerce William Daley reports: "There's been no place I've been, in 35 countries, honestly, that I haven't seen a [Chicago] Bulls 23 jersey" ("Inside Politics," CNN, January 13, 1999).

## From 23 To 45: Immanence Illustrated

In senior high school and while playing college ball for the North Carolina Tar Heels, MJ wore un 23. Likewise, MJ had un 23 while a member of the Bulls from 1984 to 1993. MJ un-retired on March 19, 1995, and re-retired on January 13, 1999. With the exception of his first twenty-two games in 1995, MJ again donned un 23. For those first few games after his return to the Bulls, he picked a new un, 45. "Old Jordan, No. 23. New Jordan, No. 45" (*Milwaukee Journal Sentinel,* May 12, 1995, 9C). MJ's movement from 23 to 45 and back again articulates the postmodern motif of immanence.

In traditional societies, sports attached themselves to the realm of the transcendent. Athletic contests pleased the Gods; athletic festivals became forms of worship. But the process of secularization affected modern sports, which were played for their own sake or for some other secular end. Secularization is the negation of value systems grounded on supernatural and sacred legitimations (Berger 1969). Alternatively, postmodern sports engage a redefined notion of immanence, one that avoids any religious implications. Instead, immanence is the ever-expanding nature of human consciousness to characterize itself symbolically (Hassan 1992). In traditional societies, nature is a reflection of the sacred. The postmodern project finds that nature is a social construction and sees the genealogy of nature as discursively shaped into an immanent system of cultural creations.

Postmodernism rejects the supernatural foundation of athletics. But postmodern athletes develop and represent a new kind of mystic reality. MJ did not perform to honor god; his performances were evidence in themselves that he is god. In the words of *Seattle Times* sportswriter Steve Kelley: "[MJ] never got old. He was transcendent" (*CT,* January 13, 1999, section 4, 4). After MJ scored a playoff-record sixty-three points, Boston Celtics great Larry Bird commented: "I thought it was God, disguised as [MJ]" (*USA Today,* April 20, 1999, 3C). A *CT* commemorative section (March 24, 1995, section 10) called MJ's first postretirement appearance a "Game of Biblical Proportions" (5). Within this section, one writer referred to MJ's return to the NBA as the "second coming" (13). With "no irony," MJ was known by his peers as "Black Jesus" (Wiley 1999, 11). MJ even had the power to heal the sick. After MJ visited a fan who was confined to a wheelchair, she began walking again (*CT,* July 18, 1995). People kneel and pray before "The Spirit," a 2,000-pound bronze statue of MJ placed outside the United Center (*New York Times Magazine,* April 21, 1996). While MJ practiced free throws before a game in Los Angeles, a fan ran out on the court. Jason Caffey of the Bulls provides this eyewitness account. "[The fan] dived at his feet and started kissing them. The security had to come and pull him off of Michael's feet—he wouldn't let them go. I'd never seen anyone worshiped like that" (*New York Times Magazine,* April 21, 1996). According to political commentator Ze'ev Chafets, fans in Israel call MJ "God." "The ones who are blasphemers don't call Michael that. But anyone who is truly religious and spiritual knows we are watching God" (*CT,* June 17, 1996, section 3, 6). When the Bulls participated in a tournament in Paris, a newspaper, *France-Soir,* acknowledged MJ's arrival with the words, "It's God in person" (*Sporting News,* December 22, 1997, 14). Because both black and white children wear un 23 and see 23 as a sign of success and achievement, the Rev. Jesse Jackson called MJ "the light" (*CT,* November 1, 1994, section 4, 11). University of Utah basketball coach Rick Majerus labeled MJ "a prophet in his own land" (*CT,* January 13, 1999, section 4, 3). As a high school sophomore, MJ is thought to have spent the winter "willing himself to grow from 5-9 to 6-4" (*USA Today,* June 3, 1998, 15A).

Contrary to the popular notion that "MJ is God," *Sports Illustrated* (January 25, 1999) asked: "What if there's a real God . . . and He is serious about that whole graven image thing?" Further, journalists have called upon MJ to respond to his deification. MJ's statement: "It's certainly an embarrassing situation for me. I play the game of basketball . . . I try to entertain for two hours and then let people go home to their lives . . . I could never consider myself a god" (*Sports Illustrated,* October 27, 1997). But an example from traditional societies calls into question MJ's desire to relate to others as fellow mortals.

Traditional sports are linked to supernatural domains. They provide ways to honor families and to answer questions concerning mortality. The Mayan-Aztec ball-court game exemplifies traditional sports (Guttmann 1978). The game is framed by a myth in which two brothers lost a contest against the gods and paid the price for defeat—death. But children of one of the dead brothers beat the gods in another match. As a result, the brothers' heads rose to the heavens and became the sun and the moon. This myth has children resurrecting deceased progenitors.

In the modern (secular) social order, sports have become the most universal and pervasive form of popular culture and as such, sports are far removed from concerns about the supernatural, one's family, and one's mortality. Both family and matters of life and death fill MJ's postmodern world. But MJ distills these concerns quite differently than they were when traditional societies encountered the supernatural. MJ's first retirement (October 6, 1993) was motivated by an awareness of the fragility of life and the certainty of death:

> [W]hen you've been given a gift to see something, you should cherish it while you still have the opportunity, because that's not always going to be there . . . . This is my time to leave because I'm not always going to be there. (*CT*, November 1, 1994, section 4, 7)

He also wanted to fulfill his lifelong ambition to pursue a baseball career. During his second farewell oration, family replaced fear of death as the central retirement rationale: "Being a parent . . . [is] the challenge that I have in front of me and I look forward to it" (*CT*, January 14, 1999, section 4, 4). In fact, MJ claimed that decisions about his basketball career were based on factors outside the sport world—primarily his family (*CT*, October 31, 1995, section 4, 8). Family concerns circumscribed MJ's un 23 and un 45.

Larry Jordan, MJ's older brother, wore un 46 when MJ began playing organized athletics. At the first opportunity, MJ chose un 23—one-half of Larry's un (*CT*, September 1, 1992). Anticipating MJ's stardom on the Laney High School basketball varsity, Coach Clifton "Pop" Herring gave him a choice between the un's formerly assigned to all-conference seniors James Beatty (23) and Dave McGhee (33) (*CT*, January 11, 1998). MJ selected 23 because it was "roughly half the [Laney H.S.] 45 that Larry wore" (Naughton 1992, 44). Larry reciprocated when he joined the Chicago Express—he picked MJ's un 23. Larry, however, changed to un 4 after fielding too many questions about his brother (*CT*, June 24, 1988). After MJ decided to end his retirement and to return to the Bulls, he had only one request: "Just One Demand: No. 45" (*USA Today*, March 20, 1995, 2C). As MJ dramatically announced: "Twenty-three was the number my father last saw me in, and I wanted to keep it that way for him" (*New York Times*, March 20, 1995, B10). On July 23, 1993, two eighteen-year-old men murdered James Jordan, MJ's father. A month and a half later, MJ retired (*CT*, March 26, 1995). The robbers shot Mr. Jordan to death in his Lexus, which had the license inscription

UNC 0023 representing MJ's college and un (*USA Today,* August 18, 1993). (MJ's cars once had plate numbers JUMP 23 and UNC 23 [*Sporting News,* December 8, 1986].)

At first, fans felt that MJ's rejection of un 23 to honor his father signified love and loss (*CT,* March 24, 1995). But after only twenty-two games in un 45, MJ returned to un 23. His un ceased serving as a "father-and-son bonding episode" (McDonald 1996, 356). MJ dropped the 45 adorned for patricentric purposes without a second thought, thereby exemplifying a postmodern vision of immanence.

## From 45 to 23: A Decanonization Demonstration

Modern games are played within a strict set of rules. The NBA's bureaucracy exists to ensure all teams and players follow the league's rules. The postmodern project is a challenge to all conventions of authority (Hassan 1992), such as the NBA's bureaucratic hierarchy. Postmodernism displays a thematic concern with subversive resistence to modern mechanisms of social and personal control (Jarvis 1998). The postmodern enterprise is an articulation of oppositional meanings and a rejection of privileged canonical beliefs (MacDonald 1990). Now to the saga known as "Jerseygate" (*Sporting News,* May 22, 1995, 43).

NBA bureaucrats responded swiftly to MJ's decision to switch jersey un's. Deputy Commissioner Russ Granik issued a statement demanding that the Bulls prohibit MJ from wearing any un except 45 (*CT,* May 12, 1995). For ignoring the league's command, the NBA fined the Bulls $25,000 for each game MJ did not dress in un 45 (*CT,* June 22, 1995). MJ initially responded, correctly, it turns out, by stating that "[t]here's no [NBA] rule saying I couldn't change my jersey number" (*CT,* June 22, 1995, section 4, 4). Granik, in turn, answered MJ by invoking an unwritten NBA policy. Simply stated: "You have to apply to the league when you want to change your number and that applies equally to every player in the league" (*CT,* June 22, 1995, section. 4, 4).

According to NBA spokesperson Jan Hubbard, this was the first time in NBA history that a player simply changed un's (*CT,* May 11, 1995). Further, as Commissioner David Stern recognized, no NBA player has worn one un for a long time, retired, switched un's and then wanted to go back to his original un. Consequently, Stern remarked, "any interpretation is possible" (*CT,* May 17, 1995, section 4, 5). But the interpretation that appears self-evident involves the principle of universality. A primary function of bureaucracies is to enforce universally an organization's rules and regulations.

Modern sports are premised upon the universality principle—that the rules are the same for everyone. This was one of the points made by the NBA's Russ Granik when he detailed the dimensions of the league's unwritten un norms. On the one hand, "human quirks" are supposedly eliminated (Guttmann 1978, 66). But on the other hand, spontaneity and passion are necessarily diminished (Rojek 1995). Institutionally based constraints is one of the key characteristics of the modern self. But the postmodern self is polysemic, articulated by a diverse system of signs (Rojek 1995). By diversity is meant that no one is anchored in a singular system of meaning (Gerholm 1988). Opposed to the modern idea of the self, the postmodern version embodies impulsiveness (Wood and Zurcher 1988) and an inclination for constant self-creation (Wolin 1990). Here each "reality of self gives way to . . . the playful probing of yet another reality" (Gergen 1991, 7). In fact, when queried about his self-identity, MJ stated that he planned on becoming even "more outgoing and playful" (*Newsweek,* September 22, 1997).

MJ's disregard for the NBA's unwritten un norms was marked by Shaquille O'Neal's adherence to the rules. When Terry Catledge left the Magic, O'Neal's Louisiana State Tigers un 33 became available. But the NBA denied Shaq's request to switch from 32 to 33 (*CT,* May 12, 1995). Shaq complied with the NBA's wishes. (O'Neal signed with the Los Angeles Lakers at the start of the 1996–1997 season. Because the Lakers had retired both un 32 [for Magic Johnson] and un 33 [for Kareem Abdul-Jabbar], he took un 34. As O'Neal explained: "I chose 34 because that's what my father wore when he played ball in the Army" [*Milwaukee Journal Sentinel,* July 19, 1996, 2C].)

The NBA could have easily forced MJ to wear 45 or to sit out the playoff games. But the league simply fined the Bulls. It appears that the NBA's modern principle of universality is taking a postmodern turn, because there are three other instances in which the league manifested the idea of diversity. Although the NBA's written rules prohibit two-digit un's that start with either 6, 7, 8, or 9, in 1993, the league allowed two players to wear un's in the seventies because of their heights: Shawn Bradley, Philadelphia 76ers, height: 7-feet, six-inches, un 76; and Gheorghe Muresan, Washington Bullets, height: 7-feet, 7-inches, un 77. (After the start of the 1997–1998 season, Bradley was assigned Dallas Mavericks un 44. During March 1999, Muresan joined a new team, the New Jersey Nets, but retained his un 77.) The NBA also permitted Dennis Rodman to appear in Bulls un 91. (The Bulls retired Rodman's usual un 10 to honor Bob Love. Rodman reasoned: 9 + 1 = 10 [*CT,* October 6, 1995].) The NBA also allowed Rodman to wear un 73 with the Los Angeles Lakers. (He wore 73 to commemorate his seven consecutive rebounding titles and three straight championships. In addition, 73 was the reverse of his age [nba.com, February 26, 1999]. Another possibility: 7 + 3 = 10.) By allowing Rodman to diverge from the un norms, the NBA actively contributed to Rodman's reputation as "the most bizarre of sports entertainers" (*CT,* December 12, 1999).

### From 45 to 23: Questioning Postmodern Intensities

Sports in traditional societies were a way to seek supernatural favors through ritual performances. Modern sports are built upon rational canons (Guttmann 1978). Along this rational-irrational line, postmodern sports are more similar to those found in traditional societies than the modern alternatives. In both traditional and postmodern societies, material objects come before the subjects with heightened intensity (Jameson 1991). But postmodern intensities are a substantially different kind of emotional expression. These intensities are "free-floating" and can take euphoric or disruptive forms (Ritzer 1996, 157). Post-modern feelings differ from the emotional displays in traditional societies where actions attempted to appease or to gain favors from a supernatural realm. Postmodern theorists find that traditional superstitions were directed toward an object that was a mere "mirage of signification" (Jameson 1991, 26).

The question is: Why did MJ change un's before the second game against the Magic? At least three different answers are available. Unlike the modern notions of a unique truth and an objective world, postmodernism disrupts the hegemony of science by finding conflicting worlds in the making (Hassan 1992). The idea of constantly changing social constructions replaces the belief in a stable realm of objective facts (Denzin 1991).

First, MJ saw 23 as a lucky number. To begin, MJ believed that un 45 was "bad luck" (*CT,* October 13, 1995, section 4, 4). Alternatively, he considered 23 a lucky number. The view that some un's are lucky while others are unlucky pervades the world of sport. Survey researchers found that most (69 percent) athletes had un-generated superstitions (Eitzen and Sage 1993). From an anthropological perspective, certain un's become taboo. Players refuse to wear particular un's and ask to change their un's during periods of poor performances (Gmelch 1981).

In the first 1995 playoff game against the Magic, Nick Anderson guarded and outplayed MJ. Anderson stole the ball from MJ at the end of the contest, a turnover that cost the Bulls the game and perhaps the series (*CT,* May 21, 1995). After the game, Anderson explained his success by noting that "No. 45 doesn't explode like No. 23" and that "[No. 45 is] not the same as No. 23"

(*CT,* May 11, 1995, section. 4, 12; May 9,1995, section 4, 8). Before the next game, MJ un-retired un 23, played great and led his team to victory. Reporters offered obvious explanations. First, MJ was indeed superstitious (*CT,* May 11, 1995; *USA Today,* May 12, 1995). Second, un 23 served as MJ's "good-luck charm" (*CT,* May 14, 1995, section 3, 14).

For James DiFillipo, following MJ's numerical switch turned out salubrious. While hospitalized awaiting a heart transplant donor, DiFillipo replaced the 45 taped to his Heartmate ventricular assist device with number 23. In DiFillipo's words:"The number 45 hasn't been very lucky for either of us" (*Sports Illustrated,* May 22, 1995, 16). Shortly thereafter, the hospital found a donor and doctors completed a successful transplant operation. Unfortunately for MJ, the rest of the playoffs did not go as well as Mr. DiFillipo's operation. His performances resembled Game 1 not Game 2. MJ was so bad that Sam Smith, the *CT*'s primary basketball writer, played on MJ's "Air Jordan" nickname, calling him "Err" Jordan instead (May 20, 1995, section 2, 1).

Next, MJ used un 23 as a motivational tool. Sport activities demand "emotional work [or] getting psyched to play" (Snyder and Ammons 1993). Before Game 2, MJ decided "to psych himself up" by wearing un 23 (*CT,* May 19, 1995, section 4, 5). After Game 2, Anderson admitted in awe: "No. 23, he made some shots" (*CT,* May 11, 1995, section 4, 5). Initially, Magic coach Brian Hill believed that "the number on his [MJ's] shirt doesn't mean anything" (*CT,* May 11, 1995, section 4, 5). But when he realized that MJ changed un's, he changed his mind. In Hill's words:"I looked at his shirt and said, 'Oh (expletive) [*sic*], he's wearing No. 23 tonight'" (*CT,* May 11, 1995, section 4, 5). Pat Williams, Magic general manager, rhetorically suggested that his team should whip un 45 on MJ to slow him down (*CT,* May 13, 1995).

MJ and John Ligmanowski, the Bulls equipment manager, rejected any suggestion that Anderson's comments motivated the un-retirement of un 23. Instead, MJ simply decided that he felt more comfortable and more confident in 23 (*CT,* May 17, 1995). Amazingly, MJ said that he didn't view Anderson's comments in a harsh way (*New York Times,* May 17, 1995). In fact, Ligmanowski takes full credit (or blame) for the un switch. According to Ligmanowski, it was his idea that MJ switch back to un 23. Of course, as Ligmanowski attests, "[Anderson's comments] had absolutely nothing to do with it" (*CT,* May 13, 1995, section 2, 4). Reporters, however, doubted both MJ and Ligmanowski. The common consensus: Anderson caused MJ to change un's from 45 to 23 (*CT,* June 10, 1995; *USA Today,* May 23, 1995).

Finally, for MJ, un 23 represented the "real" MJ. After the Game 2 victory, Bulls coach Phil Jackson praised MJ as follows: "His official statement was the jersey. It said how he was going to play tonight" (*CT,* May 11, 1995, section 4, 1). By dropping 45 in favor of 23, MJ announced that the old MJ has returned (*USA Today,* May 11, 1995). MJ reduced himself to a un. The experience of a material signifier, his old un 23, became the real MJ. By implication, therefore, the MJ bedecked in Bulls un 45 was counterfeit. As ESPN reported: "[MJ] is really back—the one that wears number 23" ("SportsCenter," May 11, 1995). The nature of intensities as free-floating forms of feeling is demonstrated by MJ's un switch. His act was an emotionally-based whim-of-the-moment and a knee-jerk, narcissistic invocation. Only when yielding to inner desires does the postmodern impulsive self feel most "real" (Schmitt and Leonard 1986).

## The Retirement Spectacle

Once the qualitative categorizations that embody traditional societies fade, modern society turns toward the creation of ever-expanding quantitative, often minute, distinctions. Instead of appeasing gods, athletes can break records. But this modern form of immortality is potentially short-lived. Subsequent athletes can produce even better performance statistics and establish new records. Un retirement is a way to make athletes permanently immortal by forever preserving them in the fans' collective memory (Joseph 1986; Schmidt and Leonard 1986). A defining principle behind un retirement is that whoever wore that un performed so singularly that no one in the future could possibly equal his or her accomplishments (*CT,* December 20, 1987).

The first time the Bulls retired MJ's un 23, the team raised more than $2 million through ticket sales to go to the construction of a Boys and Girls Club named after MJ's father (*CT,* November 1, 1994; July 26, 1995). On the day of the ceremony, the *CT* invited its readers to wear a color-copy of MJ's jersey that was included within its daily edition (November 1, 1994). A photograph of MJ raising un 23 to the United Center rafters adorned the cover of the *Chicago Tribune Magazine*'s "The Year: Words and Pictures" issue (January 1, 1995). Bulls coach Phil Jackson was well aware that un retirement confers symbolic immortality when he spoke as follows: "We buried Michael Jordan, number 23 of the Chicago Bulls' three-peat championship team" (*CT,* October 31, 1994, section 3, 3).

Ceremonies are supposed to accomplish something important with finality—once and for all (Goffman 1974). But MJ returned to play for the

Bulls. Retrospectively interpreted, therefore, MJ's retirement ceremony obviously lacked finality. The once in a lifetime "Salute to Michael Jordan" ceremony became a postmodern spectacle, a slide into a sphere of simulation and fascination with nostalgia (Baudrillard 1983). Postmodern spectacles create a hyperreality that is more real that the reality it is designed to represent (Denzin 1986). Because MJ resumed his playing career, fans were left with memories of the ceremony and not with idealized recollections of what the ceremony was supposed to commemorate.

Sport is a major field of the spectacle (Kellner 1996). TNT, a cable network, broadcast the ceremony throughout the nation. Prior to MJ's un retirement, the media assumed that fans were only interested in the honors given to their home team players. Such a nationwide broadcast was unprecedented. Postmodern media create an illusion of viewer participation in the events they highlight. Fans throughout the country passively observed this spectacle "from within the privacy of their homes" (Kellner 1996, 459). Its Nielsen cable rating almost doubled what TNT got for regular-season NBA games (*USA Today*, November 3, 1994).

Television producers designed MJ's un retirement spectacle and fans consumed the spectacle that they fabricated (Best 1989). Unquestionably, it was a "made for TV event" ("SportsCenter," ESPN, March 18, 1995) One reviewer labeled the ceremony "not Jordanesque" because the appearances of "Hollywood stars as talking heads" far outnumbered the basketball tributes (*USA Today,* November 3, 1994, 3C). Supposedly, the "TV glitz" ruined MJ's farewell ceremony (*CT,* November 2, 1994, section 4, 1). Bulls vice president of marketing Steve Schanwald apologized that the basketball event became an entertainment show and blamed the television producers for reversing what he thought were the self-evident priorities (*CT,* November 4, 1994). MJ, however, defended the producers and even challenged the sport-entertainment dichotomy. In his words: "[After all it's] all about entertainment" (*CT,* November 2, 1994, section 4, 5).

In a way not originally intended, MJ's unretirement ceremony demonstrates and substantiates the postmodern vision of the nonfixity of everything existing in society. After all, MJ un-retired his un 23. Because MJ ignored the eventfulness of the past, he dissolved the narrative of history in favor of a crisis of historicity (Jameson 1991). Acquiescing to MJ's wishes, the Bulls removed MJ's 23 banner from the United Center rafters. As MJ made clear: "I asked them to take the number down because I'm still playing. I'm not retired" (*CT,* October 18, 1995, section 4, 2). During MJ's second retirement news conference, the Bulls unveiled the same un 23 banner with the now inaccurate playing dates, 1984–1993 (*CT,* January 14, 1999).

## The Fragmented MJ

In traditional societies, athletes often wore emblems that symbolized supernatural realms. But in modern society, athletes, among others, are often reduced to serial numbers (Guttmann 1978). Besides allowing fans to identify players, serial numbers, or synonymously, un's, promote the quantification and evaluation of athletic performances. Un's simplify observations of performances, making it easier for management to judge relative abilities. But differentiations based on allegedly objective, quantifiable indicators are further evidence for a fragmented cultural universe of postmodernity (Gerholm 1988).

In modern sports, un's listed on a program identify the names of the players on the field. Although the modern self is considered authentic, enumeration by un's is seen as an alienating force. This relationship is reversed in postmodern sports. Here certain un's are identified with certain luminary players. In postmodern context, "self" is a staged signifier (Vester 1989). It is a discursive horizon of identity, composed and constituted by speech (Voss and Schutz 1989). Narratives about MJ's 23 versus MJ's 45 serve to convey and constitute the fluidity of MJ's self. Consider the following headline: "No. 45 May Be No. 23 Next Week" (*CT,* March 11, 1995, section 2, 1). The athlete-un link was not mentioned in the article that followed. Of course, it was assumed that everyone reading the article would recognized the un's. They would identify MJ by his un 23 and they would identify un 23 with MJ. Un 45 was MJ's former Chicago White Sox (spring training) baseball un. At the time of the headline, however, neither un had an actual, real-life referent. Un 23 was retired by the Bulls. Un 45 no longer belonged to MJ on the baseball diamond because he had retired from the sport.

As MJ alleged: "No matter what happens, you're always going to be the number they see you in" (*CT,* December 12, 1995, section 4, 3). Identifying anyone in this manner reduces them to a numerical fragment (Jameson 1991). For example, Chicago's SportsChannel telecast a 23-hour special program about MJ entitled "Arrival of Flight 2345" (*CT,* November 6, 1995). Further, a spokesperson for the Illinois Lottery noted that players disproportionately pick 2-3-4-5 in the Lottery's Pick Four drawing. It was estimated that these numbers were selected nearly six times as often as other possible combinations (*CT,* November 7, 1995; *USA Today,* November 7, 1995).

When one identifies oneself numerically, one actively reduces oneself to a numerical fragment. Earlier in his career, MJ's goal was to have annual salary matching his un: $23 million (espn.sportszone.com, November 20, 1997). Shortly after reactivating un 23, MJ stated: "No. 23 is me" (CT, May 17, 1995, section 4, 4). By accepting un 23 as a personal identity tag, other un's are automatically rejected. Before a February 14, 1990, game in Orlando, someone stole MJ's uniform. MJ had to wear the Bulls spare jersey bearing un 12. Quite disturbed by the heist and the consequent temporary un, MJ refused to sign any autographs in Orlando (Star Tribune [Minneapolis], February 18, 1990). USA Basketball, the organization that serves as America's governing body for the sport, randomly assigns un's to members of the Olympic and World Championship teams (CT, September 1, 1992). Because of international restrictions, only un's 4 to 15 are available. As a member of the 1992 Olympic Gold Medal squad (the original Dream Team), MJ was assigned un 9. Oddly enough, when MJ arrived the 1994 White Sox spring training camp, he never even requested un 23. In MJ's words: "I wanted '00' and they gave me '45'" (USA Today, February 18, 1994, 3C). At the time, Sox un 23 belonged to third baseman Robin Ventura who neither volunteered nor was asked to give up his un. And for at least one appearance as a member of the Scottsdale Scorpions of the Arizona Fall League, MJ wore un 35 (Saint Paul Pioneer Press, October 8, 1994).

For one NBA contest, therefore, MJ could have said, "12 is me." During the Olympic games, he could have stated, "9 is me." During two minor league baseball seasons, he could have acclaimed, "45 is me" and "35 is me." But only one fragment, the signifier 23, was given primacy. The fragment, 23, came first; his name, MJ, came second. When MJ contemplated leaving the Bulls, he made the "ultimate postmodern move into self-referentiality" (Epstein and Lichty 1997, 324). MJ shared these inner thoughts with the press: "To see the No. 23 and Michael Jordan's name associated with another city doesn't really sound right" (Sporting News, January 6, 1997, 30). Note that MJ mentioned his un first and his name second. Unquestionably, in the postmodern context, the interpreters themselves establish the principles of interpretation (Donato 1972).

## The Commodified 23

Spectating and playing roles are rigidly distinguished in modern sports. Typically, the former pay to watch while the latter are paid to perform. In the transformation from modern to postmodern society, business imperatives increasingly affect the sports themselves and their participants. Postmodern society is primarily characterized by the process of commodification (Denzin 1986). In the postmodern world, "the commodity is immediately produced as sign, as sign value, and . . . signs (culture) are produced as commodities" (Baudrillard 1981, 147). Commodification makes the spectator-player distinction problematic because after the purchase of authentic jerseys, it is difficult to tell the difference between the play-actor and the team-player. By interpreting identical appearances, the former is seen as costumed while the latter is considered uniformed (Stone 1970).

The most frequently considered mythic function of American athletics is the creation of the sports hero (Real 1982). Clothing is "one of the easiest ways of identifying oneself with a particular basketball idol" (Andrews, Carrington, Jackson, and Mazur 1996, 445). Players and fans wear un 23 because MJ is their role model. Throughout his playing career, Derek Anderson, un 23 on the Cleveland Cavaliers, patterned himself after MJ (*CT,* November 12, 1997). Twin sisters, Coco and Kelly Miller, both wanted to wear MJ's 23. Their compromise: Kelly had 23 on the Rochester (Minnesota) Mayo H.S. Spartans while Coco took the un in summer league play (*Saint Paul Pioneer Press,* April 16, 1995; *Star Tribune* [Minneapolis], March 13, 1996). On the 1999–2000 Georgia Lady Bulldogs, however, Kelly, the firstborn, had un 23 while Coco wore 35 (georgiadogs.com, December 18, 1999). Children are also drawn to un 23. Eighth-grade superstar Cory Little, the subject of an ESPN (June 2, 1993) special, picked 23. Jeff Hornacek, formerly of the Utah Jazz, has two sons, aged 6 and 8, who wore MJ's un 23 jerseys at home. "They go upstairs on their (toy) baskets and they're not pretending they're me dunking the ball. They're pretending they're Michael" (*New York Post,* June 5, 1997, 84).

Perceived attachments to MJ apparently embarrass some players. Harold Miner, un 23 on the Southern California Trojans, was nicknamed "Baby Jordan." Besides sharing un 23, MJ and Miner had shaved heads and stuck out their tongues while shooting (*CT,* February 26, 1992). Yet Miner swore that he was not trying to copy (*CT,* March 7, 1990). Terrance Simmons, un 23 on the Minnesota Gophers, had MJ memorabilia covering every inch of space in his bedroom. Still Simmons said that wearing 23 was a mere coincidence, that he tried in vain to have the un changed (*Saint Paul Pioneer Press,* December 11, 1999).

Alternatively, Michael Hakim Jordan, un 23 on the Penn Quakers of the Ivy League, obviously "cultivated a good sense of humor about his nominal coincidence" (*Sports Illustrated,* February 3, 1997, 65). Peer pressure motivated his un selection. In this Michael Jordan's words:

> I wore 13 until my sophomore year in high school. We had an older guy who wore No. 23, but he quit that season. So my older teammates convinced me to take that uniform. I had my two best games after I changed, so I decided to keep it. (*CT,* January 24, 1999, section 19, 31)

Based on actual observations of Chicago high school athletes' un selections, the best players on the court select un 23 (*CT,* November 20, 1989). Jamie Brandon, high-profile star of the 1989 edition of the King H.S. Jaguars, had un 23. But coach Landon (Sonny) Cox saw that Brandon was emulating MJ and not trying to be himself. To make his point, when the first practice began, Coach Cox gave Brandon a jersey with un 25 instead of his usually un 23. Apparently Brandon learned his lesson. When the regular season began, Coach Cox gave Brandon his usual un 23 (*CT,* November 20, 1989).

President Clinton also associated un 23 and greatness. At a White House ceremony honoring the Tennessee Lady Vols, the 1998 National Champions, the President noted the presence of Chamique Holdsclaw, basketball's player of the year. The President stated: "Incidentally, she was wearing No. 23. Like [MJ], she dominated every game of the season" (*New York Times,* November 14, 1998). Holdsclaw commented on the common conclusions about her un:

> It is an honor to be considered in the same breath, but I'm not [MJ]. I'm the first Chamique Holdsclaw. And I think that's where the women's game has to get to, when women are recognized on their own. (*USA Today,* May 5, 1999, 14C)

Holdsclaw selected un 23 "in honor of the 23rd Psalm (The Lord is my shepherd . . . )" (*Sporting News,* March 16, 1998, 13).

Nonplaying devotees of MJ buy his replica jerseys as acts of obeisance. Before and after MJ's temporary retirement, his un 23 jersey sold more than any other sport apparel (*CT,* March 24, 1995; January 1, 1997). During the 1990s, MJ jerseys accounted for one-quarter of all NBA merchandise sales (*Fortune,* June 22, 1998). Frequently, MJ's name and un are featured; the Bulls name and logo are missing. Examples include "Jordan" jerseys (*USA Today,* March 31, 1995) and MJ's line of athletic apparel, "Flight 23 by Jordan." Nike imprinted a stylized "23," "like a light-emitting diode display, but very stretched," on its Air Jordan 11 shoes (sneakers.pair.com, November 28, 1997). Air Jordan 13 has a circular hologram near the back of the shoe that shows the number "23" in an outlined block font. An advertisement for Nike's real-life "Jordan" brand portrays MJ as the head of a fictitious corporation, "23 Jordan Inc." (*Advertising Age,* October 27, 1997). MJ personally examines each product and leaves a note reading, "Inspected by 23." Another product, Bijan Fragrances' "Michael Jordan" cologne, comes in a 1.7 ounce bottle that retails for $23 (*Time,* June 9, 1997). MJ's eponymous restaurants use 23 in many ways. Before MJ's Chicago eatery closed, a giant 23 marked its location (*CT,* September 27, 1999).There the average dinner price was $23 (CuisineNet.com, December 10, 1999). Special deals occasionally appeared on the menu.The so-called "MJ's Pregame Meal," a New York strip steak, was priced at $23 and a 12-ounce glass of Budweiser beer sold for $.23 (*CT,* January 18, 1999, section 3, 3; November 16, 1998, section 3, 3).The planned date for the opening of MJ's New York restaurant was March 23, 1998. Future diners could anticipate speciality dishes prepared with 23 herbs and spices (*New York Post,* February 18, 1998). The address and phone number? Try 23 Vanderbilt Avenue and 212-271-2323 (CuisineNet.com, December 10, 1999). Even rival businesses attempt to trade on the fame of un 23. Chicago's Harry Carey's Restaurant honored MJ after his latest retirement by offering a 23-ounce steak for $23, which was 23 percent off its normal $29.95 price. Plus anyone seated at table 23 received free Bulls tickets (*CT,* Janaury 14, 1999, section 4, 6). Indeed un 23 is a central part of MJ's "trademark image" (Kellner 1996, 461).

Perhaps avoiding hyperbole, *Time* (June 9, 1997, 47) calls MJ "an all-world endorser." Other evidence suggests the globalization of the MJ market (LaFeber 1999). Observers have noted that protestors tearing down the Berlin Wall wore Air Jordans (*CT,* November 1, 1994). In Russia, street vendors sold nesting *matroshka* dolls that began with MJ. Figures of four teammates and the Bulls' mascot rested inside the MJ figure (*USA Today,* August 1, 1994). Finally, recall the previously mentioned observation that travelers find tattered replicas of MJ's jersey in rural parts of Asia and Africa (Halberstam 1999). It is not surprising, therefore, that a Turner Sports spokesperson described the worldwide televising of MJ's return to basketball as follows: "We're experiencing Jorgasm" (*Milwaukee Journal Sentinel,* April 2, 1995, 2C).

Reports predicting MJ's return to the NBA caused a huge demand for his replica jerseys. For example, the 23 jerseys immediately sold out at a Chicago Sportmart outlet (*CT,* March 15, 1995). Even after MJ switched to un 45, many shoppers still sought 23 jerseys because they became collector's items (*USA Today,* March 21, 1995). Most buyers, however, wanted the "latest Jordanwear" (*Philadelphia Inquirer,* March 21, 1995, A1). His un 45 jerseys sold faster than any other sports apparel (*CT,* November 24, 1995). In the words of an official of Champion Products, the only company licensed to sell NBA uniforms to the public, the "demand is unbelievable" (*New York Times,* March 21, 1995, B14). Another official complained that Champion was running out of red cloth for the jerseys (*Sporting News,* April 3, 1995). MJ's new un 45 created a lucrative sport marketing niche because fans who already owned un 23 jerseys would, in all likelihood, go out a buy the new un 45 jerseys (*USA Today,* March 23, 1995). On the night of MJ's homecoming, his first game in Chicago wearing un 45:"The night's selling mantra was the number 45. 45. 45. 45. If it had 45 on it, it sold" (*CT,* March 25, 1995, section 2, 1). The identical situation occurred in New York prior to MJ's first return appearance (*CT,* March 28, 1995). But similar to the change in Coca-Cola, "New Mike" didn't do as well as "Mike Classic" (*Leader-Telegram* [Eau Claire, WI], May 11, 1995, 1D). MJ in un 45 didn't do as well as MJ in 23 so MJ dropped the former un. In the words of a sports merchandiser: "Now we're going to have a 45 industry and a 23 industry" (*Milwaukee Journal Sentinel,* May 12, 1995, 9C).

## Conclusion

In postmodern society, everything becomes a saleable commodity (Featherstone 1991; Jameson 1991). As self-referential tokens of consumption (Manning 1991), MJ's jerseys are given greater salience than MJ himself. The perpetual euphoria of commodification is illuminated by the way MJ and un 23 emerge as postmodern images. But this process of illumination had its critics.

Labeled "No. 23-45-23," the *Sporting News* criticized MJ for creating "the I-am-a-god-and-you're-right-to-adore-me strut" (June 12, 1995, 7). His alleged violation of NBA un rules was seen as another example of the application of the self-serving "Jordan Rules" (*New York Times,* May 15, 1995, B6, B7). Even Phil Jackson, then MJ's coach, interpreted MJ's un switch as a rejection of the idea of equality inherent in the principle of universality. This separated MJ even further from his Bulls teammates (*CT Magazine,* October 8, 1995). MJ's disposal of un 45 after a particularly poor performance was called "numerical whimsy" (*CT,* May 21, 1995, section 4, 1). By un-retiring un 23 and by having the 23 banner removed from the United Center rafters, MJ forced the public into admitting the meaninglessness of his retirement ceremony. Consequently, MJ inadvertently added to a postmodern societal characteristic—public skepticism (*CT,* November 1, 1995). A *Sporting News* writer attacked MJ's overt identification with numerical fragments. In a "Caught on the Fly" column, MJ was referred to in the following manner: "Forty-five . . . 23 . . . hey, Fly's got yer [*sic*] number" (May 22, 1995, 4).

The creation of "Michael the Marketed" is the final issue (*CT,* March 24, 1995, section 10, 3). George Vecsey of the *New York Times* suggested that a capitalist conspiracy was behind MJ's return to the NBA with a new un. After all, "these companies [and by implication, MJ] aren't stupid" (March 20, 1995, B10). Other commentators agreed. A new un means a lot more jerseys to sell and a lot more money for MJ ("UpClose," ESPN, March 28, 1995). Further, MJ's selection of a new un was called "the greatest marketing ploy in the history of sport" ("Sports Reporters," ESPN, March 19, 1995). When MJ switched back to un 23, angry parents wanted sports stores to exchange their childrens' un 45 jerseys for those with un 23 (*CT,* May 12, 1995). Consumers phoned the Bulls and the NBA offices complaining that they were duped into buying un 45 jerseys (*New York Times,* May 15, 1995; *CT Magazine,* October 8, 1995). Bulls General Manager Jerry Krause naively responded by alleging that MJ never told anyone to buy his jersey (*CT,* May 12, 1995). Alternatively, and more in tune with capitalist reality, Scottie Pippen, MJ's teammate, offered consumers this advice: "Tell them to dig deep for 23" (*New York Times,* May 15, 1995, B6).

But the problems of consumers pale in comparison to the plight of exploited and abused Asian laborers working for MJ-endorsed companies. As LaFeber (1999, 130) asks: Should we consider MJ the "greatest endorser of the twentieth century" or "an insidious form of imperialism?" Confronted by this question, "[w]hat are people who love [MJ] but hate global capitalism, to do?" (Williamson 1999, 42). Admittedly, all our gods have become commodities. The one consolation we have is that at least MJ went for a hefty sum (Guterson 1994).

# References

Andrews, D. L., B. Carrington, Z. Mazur, and S. J. Jackson. (1996). "Jordanscapes: A preliminary analysis of the global popular," *Sociology of Sport Journal* 13(4):428–457.

Armstrong, E. G. (1986). "Uniform numbers," *American Journal of Semiotics* 6(1–2): 99–127.

———. (1996). "The commodified 23, or, Michael Jordan as text," *Sociology of Sport Journal* 13(4): 325–343.

Baudrillard, J. (1981). *For a critique of the political economy of the sign.* St. Louis: Telos.

———. (1983). *Simulations.* New York: Semiotext(e)/Columbia University.

Berger, P. L. (1969). *The sacred canopy.* Garden City, NY: Anchor.

Best, S. (1989). "The commodification of reality and the reality of commodification." In *Current perspectives in social theory* (Vol. 9), ed. J. Wilson, 23–51. Greenwich, CT: JAI.

Denzin, N. K. (1986). "Postmodern social theory," *Sociological Theory* 4:194–204.

————. (1991). "Empiricist cultural studies in America." In *Current perspectives in social theory* (Vol. 11), ed. B. Agger, 17–39. Greenwich, CT:JAI.

Donato, E. (1972). "The two languages of criticism." In *The structuralist controversy*, ed. R. Macksey and E. Donato, 89–97. Baltimore: Johns Hopkins University.

Eitzen, D. S., and G. H. Sage. (1993). *Sociology of North American sport*. Fifth edition. Dubuque:Brown and Benchmark.

Epstein, J. S., and P. Lichty. (1997). "Machine: Mapping the multimedia terrain of postmodern society," *Sociological Spectrum* 17:323–339.

Featherstone, M. (1991). *Consumer culture and postmodernism*. London:Sage.

Gergen, K. J. (1991). *The saturated self*. New York: Basic.

Gerholm, T. (1988). "On ritual: A postmodernist view," *Ethnos* 53:190–203.

Gmelch, G. (1981). "Baseball magic." In *The Social World*, ed. I. Robertson, 286–289. New York:Worth.

Goffman, E. (1974). *Frame analysis*. New York:Harper and Row.

Guterson, D. (1994). "Moneyball!" *Harper's Magazine* (September), 37–46.

Guttmann, A. (1978). *From ritual to record*. New York: Columbia University.

————. (1988). *A whole new ball game*. Chapel Hill: University of North Carolina.

Halberstam, D. (1999). *Playing for keeps: Michael Jordan and the world he made*. New York: Random House.

Hassan, I. (1992). "Pluralism in postmodern perspective." In *The Post-Modern Reader*, ed. C. Jencks, 196–207. New York: St. Martin's.

Jameson, F. (1991). *Postmodernism, or, the cultural logic of late capitalism*. Durham: Duke University Press.

Jarvis, D. S. (1998). "Postmodernism: A critical typology," *Politics and Society* 26(1):95–142.

Joseph, N. (1986). *Uniforms and nonuniforms*. New York: Greenwood.

Kellner, D. (1996). "Sports, media, culture, and race—Some reflections on Michael Jordan," *Sociology of Sport Journal* 13(4):458–467.

LaFeber, W. (1999). *Michael Jordan and the new global capitalism*. New York: W. W. Norton and Company.

MacDonald, H. (1990). "Postmodernism and its discontented," *Partisan Review* 57:554–558.

Manning, P. K. (1991). "Semiotic ethnographic research," *American Journal of Semiotics* 8:27–45.

McDonald, M. G. (1996). "Michael Jordan's family values," *Sociology of Sport Journal* 13(4):344–365.

Naughton, J. (1992). *Taking to the air: The rise of Michael Jordan*. New York:Warner.

Real, M. R. (1982). "The Super Bowl: Mythic spectacle." In *Television: A Critical View*, ed. H. Newcomb, 206–239. New York: Oxford.

Ritzer, G. (1996). *The McDonaldization of society*. (Revised edition). Thousand Oaks, CA: Pine Forge.

Rojek, C. (1995). *Decentering leisure*. London: Sage.

Schmitt, R. L., and W. M. Leonard II. (1986). "Immortalizing the self through sport," *American Journal of Sociology* 91:1088–1111.

Snyder, E. E., and R. Ammons. (1993). "Baseball's emotion work: Getting psyched to play," *Qualitative Sociology* 16:111–132.

Stone, G. P. (1970). "Appearance and the self." In *Social psychology through symbolic interaction*, ed. G. Stone and H. A. Farberman, 394–411. Waltham, MA: Ginn-Blaisdell.

Vester, H-G. (1989). "Erving Goffman's sociology as a semiotic of postmodern culture," *Semiotica* 76:191–203.

Voss, D., and J. C. Schutz. (1989). "Postmodernism in context," *New German Critique* 47:119–142.

Wiley, R. (1999). "The mind of Michael Jordan," *Crisis* 106(2):11–12.

Williamson, T. (1999). "Full court press," *Dollars and Sense* 226:42.

Wolin, S. S. (1990). "Democracy in the discourse of postmodernism," *Social Research* 57:5–30.

Wood, M. R., and L. A. Zurcher. (1988). *The development of a postmodern self*. Westport, CT: Greenwood.

**part II**

# J O R D A N

# and Corporate Culture

# 3

# The Sports Spectacle, Michael Jordan, and Nike: Unholy Alliance?

## Douglas Kellner

Michael Jordan is widely acclaimed as the greatest athlete who ever lived. The announcement of his retirement in January 1999 unleashed an unparalleled hyperbole of adjectives describing his superlative athletic accomplishments. Yet his continuing media presence and adulation after his retirement confirmed that Jordan is one of the most popular and widely known sports icons throughout the world. In China, the Beijing *Morning Post* ran a front page article titled "Flying Man Jordan is Coming Back to Earth," and in Bosnia Jordan's statement about his retirement was the lead story on the evening television news, pushing aside the war in Kosovo.[1] An icon of the global popular, Jordan is "a kind of new world prince," in the words of Pulitzer Prize–winning author David Halberstam (1999), who recently published a biography of the basketball legend: "You hear time and again about people being in Borneo or somewhere and coming across a kid in a tattered Michael Jordan T-shirt. He's the most famous American in the world."[2]

Jordan's acclaim and popularity result in part because he is a perfect embodiment of the sports spectacle in which media culture uses high tech wizardry to magically transform sports into a media extravaganza of the highest order. Images of Jordan's windmill dunking, blazing baseline heroics, and flying through the air to net a key shot thrilled sports spectators throughout the world, as did his controlled fadeaway jump shooting and uncanny ability to always bag the decisive shot. Moreover, Jordan provided the spectacle of intense competition and the thrill of winning, perhaps *the* American passion play, having led the Chicago Bulls to NBA championships during six of eight seasons in the 1990s (the two seasons the Bulls failed to win were during Jordan's quixotic retirement to try to become a baseball star in 1993–1995).

In addition to being perhaps the greatest basketball player of all time, Jordan is one of the most successfully managed idols and icons of media culture. Parlaying his athletic triumphs into commercial product endorsements, Jordan became the highest paid celebrity advertising figure ever, endorsing a multitude of products for multimillion dollar fees, promoting his own line of athletic shoes and cologne, and starring with Bugs Bunny in a popular movie *Space Jam* (1996) . Michael Jordan is thus a perfect icon for the end-of-millennium American and global culture, combining extraordinary athletic prowess, an unrivalled record of success and winning, high entertainment value, and an ability to exploit his image into impressive business success.

In a commercial culture that blends celebrity, product, and image, it is only natural that a sports shoe corporation like Nike—as well as many other corporations—would purchase Jordan's star power to promote its products. Accordingly, I wish to argue that the Michael Jordan/Nike connection calls attention to the extent to which media is transforming sports into a spectacle that sells the values, products, celebrities, and institutions of the media and consumer society. The Jordan/Nike nexus calls attention to the *sports entertainment colossus* that became a major feature of media culture at the end of the millennium. The Nike/Jordan alliance discloses the extent to which contemporary society is constituted by image and spectacle and mediated by the institutions of consumer culture. We are thus undergoing an increasing commercialization and spectacle-ization of the world of which Michael Jordan and Nike are a significant and highly revealing part. The following study will thus use the Nike/Jordan nexus to uncover the central dynamics of contemporary media and consumer culture and the implosion between sports, entertainment, celebrity, and commerce in the contemporary era.

## The Sports Spectacle

Professional sports is one of the major spectacles of media culture. "Spectacle" is a multifarious term developed by French Situationist Guy Debord that "unifies and explains a great diversity of apparent phenomena" (Debord 1970, #10).[3] In one sense, it refers to a media and consumer society, organized around the consumption of images, commodities, and spectacles. Spectacles are those phenomena of media culture that embody contemporary society's basic values, serve to enculturate individuals into its way of life, and dramatize its conflicts and modes of conflict resolution. They include media extravaganzas, sports events, political happenings, and those attention-grabbing occurrences that we call news—a phenomenon that itself has been subjected to the logic of spectacle and tabloidization in the era of the O. J. Simpson trials (1994–1996), the death of Princess Diana, a spate of murder trials, the Bill Clinton sex scandals and impeachment (1998–1999), and the battle for the White House in Election 2000. In this chapter, I argue that sports is a largely untheorized and underrated aspect of the society of the spectacle that celebrates its dominant values, products, and corporations in an unholy alliance between sports celebrity, commercialism, and media spectacle.

As we enter a new millennium, the media are becoming ever more technologically dazzling and are playing an increasingly central role in everyday life. Under the influence of a postmodern image culture, seductive spectacles fascinate the denizens of the media and consumer society and involve them in the semiotics of a new world of entertainment, information, and drama, which deeply influence thought and action. In Debord's words:

> When the real world changes into simple images, simple images become real beings and effective motivations of a hypnotic behavior. The spectacle as a tendency *to make one see the world* by means of various specialized mediations (it can no longer be grasped directly), naturally finds vision to be the privileged human sense which the sense of touch was for other epochs; the most abstract, the most mystifiable sense corresponds to the generalized abstraction of present day society. (Debord 1970, #18)

Experience and everyday life are thus mediated by the spectacles of media culture that dramatize social conflicts, celebrate dominant values, and project our deepest hopes and fears. For Debord, the spectacle is a tool of pacification and depoliticization; it is a "permanent opium war" (Debord 1970, #44), which stupefies social subjects and distracts them from the most urgent task of real life—recovering the full range of their human powers through creative praxis. The concept of the spectacle is integrally connected to the concept of separation and passivity, for in passively consuming spectacles, one is separated from actively producing one's life. Capitalist society separates workers from the products of their labor, art from life, and consumption from human needs and self-directing activity, as individuals passively observe the spectacles of social life from within the privacy of their homes (Debord 1970, #25 and #26). The situationist project, by contrast, involved an overcoming of all forms of separation, in which individuals would directly produce their own life and modes of self-activity and collective practice.

The correlative to the spectacle is thus the spectator, the passive viewer and consumer of a social system predicated on submission, conformity, and the cultivation of marketable difference. The concept of the spectacle therefore involves a distinction between passivity and activity and consumption and production, condemning passive consumption of spectacle as an alienation from human potentiality for creativity and imagination. The spectacular society spreads its narcotics mainly through the cultural mechanisms of leisure and consumption, services and entertainment, ruled by the dictates of advertising and a commercialized media culture. This structural shift to a society of the spectacle involves a commodification of previously noncolonized sectors of social life and the extension of bureaucratic control to the realms of leisure, desire, and everyday life. Parallel to the Frankfurt School conception of a "totally administered" or "one-dimensional" society (Horkheimer and Adorno 1972; Marcuse 1964), Debord states that "The spectacle is the moment when the commodity has attained the total occupation of social life" (Debord 1970, #42). Here exploitation is raised to a psychological level; basic physical privation is augmented by "enriched privation" of pseudo-needs; alienation is generalized, made comfortable, and alienated consumption becomes "a duty supplementary to alienated production" (Debord 1970, #42).

In contemporary media culture, sports is a major field of the spectacle. Whereas the activity of participating in sports involves an active engagement in creative practice, spectator sports involves passive consumption of images of the sports spectacle. One of the distinguishing features of contemporary postindustrial societies is the extent to which sports have become commercialized and transformed into a spectacle. During the industrial era, actually playing sports was an adjunct to labor that created strong and skillful bodies for industrial labor and taught individuals both how to play as part of a collective, to fit into a team, and to display initiative and distinguish themselves, thus training workers for productive industrial labor. Modern sports was organized around principles of the division of labor and professionalism, celebrating modern values of competition and winning. Sports in the modern era replicated the structure of the workplace where both individual initiative and teamwork were necessary and sports celebrated at once both competing values. Sports was part of an autonomous realm with its own professional ethic, carefully regulated rules, and highly organized corporate structure. During the postindustrial era, by contrast, spectator sports is the correlative to a society that is replacing manual labor with automation and machines, and requires consumption and passive appropriation of spectacles to reproduce the consumer society. The contemporary era also sees the expansion of the service sector and highly differentiated entertainment industry, of which sports is a key part. Thus, significant resources are currently devoted to the expansion and promotion of the sports spectacle, and athletes such as Michael Jordan are accordingly recipients of the potential to amass high salaries from the profits being generated by the sports/entertainment colossus.

There are many ways in which contemporary sports is subject to the laws of the spectacle and is becoming totally commercialized, serving to help reproduce the consumer society. For starters, sports is ever more subject to market logic and commodification, with professional athletes making millions of dollars from playing and endorsement contracts; further, televisual sports events such as basketball games are hypercommodified through the influence of corporate monies, responsible for such phenomena as the "Bud player of the game," "Miller Lite genuine moments," the "Reebok halftime report," the "AT&T Time Out," and "Dutch Boy in the Paint" statistics. TV networks bid astronomical sums for the rights to broadcast live professional sports events, and superevents such as the Superbowl and NBA championship games command some of the highest advertising rates in television.

It appears that professional sports, a paradigm of the spectacle, can no longer be played without the accompaniment of cheerleaders, giant mascots who clown with players and spectators, and raffles, promotions, and contests that hawk the products of various sponsors. Instant replays turn the action into high-tech spectacles and stadiums themselves contain electronic reproduction of the action, as well as giant advertisements for various products that rotate for maximum saturation—previewing forthcoming environmental advertising in which entire urban sites will become scenes to promote commodity spectacles. Corporations are now franchising sports arenas to be named after their products: following Great Western Bank's payment to have the Lakers' stadium named the Great Western Forum, the franchising of United Center in Chicago by United Airlines, and the America West Arena in Phoenix by America West, Pacific Telesis paid $50 million to name the San Francisco Giants' new stadium Pacific Bell Park and Philip Morris' Miller Brewing unit has paid $40 million to have its name atop the Milwaukee Brewers' new ballpark (*New York Times,* August 23, 1996, C4). The Texas Rangers stadium in Arlington, Texas, supplements its sports arena with a shopping mall and commercial area, with office buildings, stores, and a restaurant in which for a hefty price one gets a view of the athletic events, as one consumes food and drink.

It probably will not be too long before the uniforms of professional sports players are as littered with advertisements as racing cars. In the globally popular sport of soccer, companies such as Canon, Sharp, and Carlsberg sponsor teams and have their names emblazoned on their shirts, making the players epiphenomena of transnational capital. In auto racing events such as Le

Mans 24 Hours or Indianapolis 500, entire teams are sponsored by major corporations whose logos adorn their clothes and cars. And throughout the world,
but especially in the United States, the capital of the commodity spectacle,
superstars such as Michael Jordan commodify themselves from head to foot,
selling their various body parts and images to the highest corporate bidders,
imploding their sports images into the spectacles of advertising. In this fashion, the top athletes augment their salaries, sometimes spectacularly, by endorsing products, thus imploding sports, commerce, and advertising into dazzling
spectacles that celebrate the products and values of corporate America. Recent
years have thus exhibited a dramatic implosion of the sports spectacle, commerce, and entertainment with massive salaries and marketing contracts for
the superstar players /celebrities. The major media conglomerates are becoming increasingly interested in sports channels and franchises and the most
marketable athletes not only earn enormous multimillion dollar salaries, but
are able to secure even more lucrative marketing deals to endorse products,
star in film or TV programs, and even in the case of Michael Jordan to promote their own product lines.

    Although the NBA was once the ne'er-do-well stepchild of the more
successful professional baseball and football franchises, in recent years it has
become one of the most popular of the U.S. sports industries on the global
scale (Andrews 1997). While the NBA fed only thirty-five weekly telecasts to
foreign companies in the mid-1980s during the beginning of Jordan's basketball career, by 1996 the roster had swelled to 175 foreign broadcasts in
forty languages to 600 million households. In this process, David Halberstam
describes Jordan as "the first great athlete of the wired world" (in Coplon
1996, 35).

    The dramatic evolution of the sports spectacle thus has a global dimen-
sion with the major players now becoming international figures, marketed in
global advertising campaigns, films, music, and other venues of media culture.
As Michael Jordan's superstar agent David Falk puts it: "Michael has transcended sport. He's an international icon" (in Hirschberg 1996, 46). Indeed,
in 1996–1997, Falk put together deals that netted Jordan a record-breaking
$30 million contract for the next season; continuing lucrative deals with Nike
and other corporations to promote their products to the estimated tune of
$40 million; the inauguration of his own cologne line, Eau de Michael Jordan;
and a high tech film, Space Jam, pairing Jordan with other NBA superstars,
Bugs Bunny, and other cartoon characters, with accompanying product line
and estimates that Jordan would earn $20 million from the latter two projects
(USA Today, October 14, 1996, 6B). During the same era, Los Angeles Lakers

star Shaquille O'Neal signed a seven-year, $120 million deal, leading his agent to comment: "Shaq represents the convergence of sports and entertainment" (*New York Times,* August 23, 1996, C4).

Competing with baseball and football as the American sport of choice of the contemporary era, professional basketball has emerged during the Jordan era as the game that best symbolizes the contemporary sports/entertainment colossus. To some extent, the three major U.S. sports encapsulate three periods of socioeconomic development. Baseball represents the challenge of a highly individualist country to merge together individual aspirations and talents with teamwork and spirit. Emerging in the nineteenth century, baseball disciplined individuals to fit into teams but still rewarded individual accomplishments during a highly entrepreneurial era of capitalist development.

Football is organized on a mass production industrial model that was appropriate to the era of mass production that reached its highest stage of development in the first half of the twentieth century. Football is a team sport that exemplifies arduous collective physical labor mated with individual achievement. Although the star running backs, quarterbacks, and touchdown scorers often get the credit and headlines, it is disciplined collective labor that provides the infrastructure for football accomplishments and victory. Without a strong defense and well-coordinated offense even the most spectacular players cannot adequately function and their team will rarely win. Moreover, brute strength, valorized in the hard toil of the earlier factory era, was also important in football, a distinctly combat sport, in addition to skill and finesse.

NBA basketball, by contrast, has increasingly featured superstar feats of individual brilliance, especially in the era of Jordan. Professional basketball is also the perfect television sport, fast-paced, full of action, and resplendent with spectacle. Hard-charging, full-court action, balletic shots, and ubiquitous instant replays make basketball the perfect sport for the era of MTV. Perfectly embodying the fragmentary postmodern aesthetics, razzle-dazzle technical effects, and fast pace of today's television, basketball has emerged as the sport of the spectacle, the perfect game for the sports/entertainment society. Once a primarily American game, by the 1990s it had become popular globally.

Moreover, the sports spectacle is at the center of an almost religious fetishism in which sport becomes surrogate religion and its stars demigods. For many, sports is the object of ultimate concern (Paul Tillich's definition of religion). It provides transcendence from the banality and suffering of everyday life. Sports stars constitute its saints and deities, while sports events often have a religious aura of ritual. Sports fans are like a congregation and their cheers and boos are a form of liturgy. In sports events, fans become part of something greater than themselves, the participation provides meaning and significance and a higher communal self, fused with the multitudes of believers and the spirit of joy in triumph and suffering in tribulation. Sports are a break from average everydayness, providing participation in ritual, mystery, and spiritual aura (although, as our discussion is suggesting, sports also celebrates dominant social values such as individuality, winning, teamwork, and, increasingly, commercialism). In the pantheon of sports deity, Michael Jordan is one of the reigning gods, and in the next section I will accordingly engage his iconography and celebrity.

## The Spectacle of Michael Jordan

Among the spectacles of media culture, Michael Jordan is a preeminent figure. As an NBA superstar, Jordan was the very picture of grace, coordination, virtuosity, and all-around skill—adeptly marketed to earn a record salary and endorsements. Jordan received $30 million to play for the Chicago Bulls in 1997 (*Time,* July 29, 1996, 61) and $33 million in 1998; he earned more than $40 million in endorsements and promotions in 1995, making him the highest paid athlete in the world (*The Guardian,* June 11, 1996, 6). Moreover, he reaped more than $45 million in endorsements in 1996, continuing his position as the world's highest paid athlete. In June 1998, *Fortune* magazine estimated that Jordan had generated more than $10 billion during his spectacular professional career in terms of an increase in tickets sold, television advertising revenue, increased profits of products Jordan endorsed, basketball merchandising exploiting Jordan's figure, and his own films, businesses, and product lines (see Johnson 1998). Jordan *is* big business and has accelerated the trends toward the implosion of business, entertainment, and sports.

His Airness, a popular nickname for "the man that flies," thus epitomizes the postmodern sports spectacle both on the playing field and in advertisements and media spectacles. The Michael Jordan spectacle implodes athletic achievement with commercialization, merging his sports image with corporate products, and making Jordan one of the highest paid and most fecund generators of social meaning and capital in the history of media culture. He is the iconic exemplar of the media/sports spectacle, the obsession with winning and success, and the quest for unimaginable wealth that were defining cultural features of the last two decades of the twentieth century.

Jordan first appeared as a rookie with the Chicago Bulls in 1984 and although he was not yet a full-fledged superstar, his agent signed him to what turned out to be an incredibly influential and lucrative contract with Nike. With Jordan and a new marketing agency, Wieden and Kennedy, the Air Jordan product line and Nike's Swoosh symbol became icons of American and then global culture. At the same time, Michael Jordan became an authentic American superstar, generally acknowledged as one of the greatest basketball players of all time, one of the most popular and well-known celebrities of media culture, and since 1988, the sports celebrity most desired to market corporate products. During the era of Nike/Jordan's ascendancy, cable and satellite television and the aggressive promotion of the NBA by its commissioner David Stern increased tremendously the visibility and popularity of professional basketball. The Jordan/Nike era had arrived.

There seemed to be nothing that Jordan could not do on the basketball court. His slam dunk was legendary and he seemed to defy gravity as he flew through the air toward the holy grail of the basket. His "hang-time" was fabled and as C.L. Cole points out (1996), designations such as "Rare Air" "render him extraordinary . . . and even godlike," a figure of transcendence. Nike developed a product line of "Air Jordan" sports shoes around the flying mythology and a 1990 NBA Entertainment documentary titled "Michael Jordan, Come Fly With Me" described the player as "the man who was truly destined to fly," and celebrated him as the very embodiment of professional excellence, morality, and American values. The collection of photographs of Michael Jordan as sports icon, media celebrity, and downhome good guy is titled *Rare Air* and highlights the efficacy of the Michael Jordan publicity machine in fine-tuning his image as a transcendent figure, a god of media culture.

Sports writers too participated in the canonization of Michael Jordan, regularly describing him as "the best player ever," "the greatest basketball player who has ever lived," and even the "greatest athlete of all time." The phrase "there is nothing he cannot do" was frequently used to inscribe Jordan's sign-value as superstar sports deity, and in Nike ads that star Jordan, the corporate logo "just do it," signifies that you too can be like Michael and do what you want to do. The Gatorade "Be Like Mike" commercial also highlights Jordan's status as a role model and embodiment of iconic values and high aspiration.

After dropping out of professional basketball to pursue a professional baseball career,[4] Jordan returned to the Chicago Bulls in 1995 and led the team to three straight NBA championships. In the process, he reinvented himself as a superstar player, moving from his patented flying air shots to become one of the great distance and jump shot scorers of all time. In the words of one analyst:

At 33, Jordan is a half-step slower than he once was. He is more behold-
en to gravity, less nuclear in his liftoff. He can still take wing and be Air
when he needs to, still shift into turbo and batter the rim, but he chooses
his spots now, waits for clear paths. He no longer hurls himself into walls
of elbows and forearms, giving other side's behemoths free shots at his
kidneys. He has traded risk for feel, nerve for guile, spectacle for efficiency . . . and because he is Jordan, even his efficiency can seem spectacular.
(Coplon 1996, 37)

During the 1996–1998 seasons, the Bulls emerged as a popular culture
phenomenon, setting records for attendance, winning regular season games,
and three straight NBA championships. With Jordan, bad-guy extraordinaire
Dennis Rodman, all-around star Scottie Pippen, and Zen-inspired coach Phil
Jackson, the Bulls earned unparalleled media attention and adulation. The
Jordan spectacle helped make NBA basketball globally popular and Michael
Jordan a superstar of extraordinary resonance. Jordan henceforth was identified with ardent competition and winning, embodying the values of hard
drive, success, and coming out on top; his shots regularly won key games and
he became fabled for the magnitude of his competitiveness and drive to win.

Thus, Michael Jordan was both a great player and continues to be a
highly successful marketing phenomenon, which calls attention to the construction of the media/sports spectacle by corporations, public relations, and
the techniques of advertising. Just as Jordan marketed Nike, Wheaties, and
other products, so did these corporations help produce the Jordan image and
spectacle. Likewise, Jordan was used to market the NBA, and in turn its publicity machine and success helped market Jordan (Andrews 1997). A vast marketing apparatus of television, radio, magazines, and other publications help
promote and manufacture the stars of sports and entertainment, attesting to
an implosion between media and sports culture, and thus sports and commerce. Indeed, Jordan became an entire sports franchise with special pitches
geared toward kids (i.e., an 800 number to order Nikes that Jordan gives them
"permission" to call), toward urban teens, and targeting young adults with his
fragrance products. And as Cole has documented (1996), Jordan is part of a
Nike P.L.A.Y. program designed to present a positive corporate image and
promote its products to a youth audience.

Michael Jordan was thus a dazzling sports spectacle who promoted both
commercial sports and the products of the corporations that market products
to sports audiences. His distinctive image is often noted and Jordan's look and
style are truly striking. His shaved head, extremely long shorts, and short socks
were frequently cited defining features that were highlighted in a Spike Lee
Nike ad that in a brilliant effort to get the Nike message across repeatedly

insisted, "It's gotta be the shoes!" (i.e., that made Jordan the greatest). In addition, his wrist band, jersey number 23, and tongue wagging and hanging as he concentrated on a play were distinctive signs of the Jordan trademark image.

In fact, Jordan is so handsome that he has often been employed as a model and his good looks and superstar status have won him countless advertising endorsements for products such as McDonald's, Gatorade, Coca-Cola, Wheaties, Haines shorts, and numerous others. A Gatorade ad tells the audience to "be like Mike," establishing Jordan as a role model, as the very icon of excellence and aspiration. In antidrug ads, Jordan tells the nation to just say no, to avoid drugs, to do the right thing, and to be all you can be, mobilizing the very stereotypes of conservative postindustrial America in one figure. As Andrews points out (1996), Michael Jordan is a paradigmatic figure of the "hard body" (Susan Jeffords) that was the ideal male image of the Reaganite 1980s, a model of the powerful bodies needed to resurrect American power after the flabbiness of the 1960s and 1970s. Jordan is also a fashion spectacle, nattily dressed in expensive clothes, drenched in his own cologne, and exhibiting the trademark shiny bald head. As such, he was the perfect sports icon to market Nike shoes, combining tremendous athletic ability with a well-honed fashion image.

## Jordan, Nike, and the Race Spectacle

Initially, Jordan was perceived as a distinctively *black spectacle,* though many claimed that eventually he transcended race and attained an almost godlike transracial status. It is generally acknowledged that he was the first black athlete to break advertising's color barrier, paving the way for lucrative contracts for the next generation of black athletes. During his difficult transitional year of 1993, when Jordan was under intense critical scrutiny by the media and NBA because of his alleged gambling problems and the unsolved murder of his father, whose death many speculated was related to gambling debts, he became for the first and only time a recipient of the sort of negative press visited upon such African American sports luminaries as Muhammad Ali, Mike Tyson, and then–Chicago Bulls teammate Dennis Rodman.

The Jordan publicity machine has regularly taken the line that Jordan "transcends race" and commentators have claimed that Jordan is "transracial."[5] Jordan himself usually plays it both ways in interviews, admitting that he recognizes he is black but calling upon people to see him as a human being (see, for example, the interview with Larry King on CNN, 1996). Yet, as a cultural signifier, as the "universal singular" who represents more general social significance (Denzin 1996, using Sartre's term), Jordan is a highly polysemic signifier who encodes conflicting meanings and values. Michael Jordan is both an example of what Berlant (1994) calls the "national symbolic" (see the discussion in Cole 1996) and the "global popular" (see the discussion in Kellner 1995 and Andrews, Carrington, Jackson, and Mazur 1996). Jordan embodies national values of hard work, competitiveness, ambition, and success. As a black superstar, he presents the fantasy that anyone can make it in the society of competition and status, that one can climb the class ladder and overcome the limitations of race and class. As a national and global superstar, he represents different things to different people in different countries (see the studies by Andrews, Carrington, Jackson, and Mazur 1996). Indeed, as Wilson and Sparks (1996) remind us, different individuals and audiences are going to receive and appropriate the text of Michael Jordan in different ways according to their own race, gender, class, region, and other subject positions.

As a polysemic signifier, Jordan thus presents a figure that mobilizes many fantasies (i.e., athletic greatness, wealth, success, and upward mobility) for the national and global imaginary, providing a spectacle who embodies many desirable national and global features and aspirations. Yet Jordan is extremely black and his race is a definite signifier of his spectacle, though his blackness too has conflicting connotations. On one hand, as noted, he is a privileged role model for black youth ("Be like Mike"), he reportedly helps mentor young athletes, and he is a symbol of the African American who has transcended race and who is integrated in American society, representing the dream of assimilation, wealth, and success. But as Andrews has demonstrated (1996), Jordan's blackness is overdetermined and has also served to signify black transgressions, as when his gambling behavior became a subject of negative media presentation and his father's murder led to speculation on connections with organized crime. In these images, Jordan is presented as the threatening black figure, as the negative fantasy figure of black deviance from white normality. Jordan's physique, power, and dominance might also feed into the fear of black bodies as Giroux suggests in his analysis of how contemporary media culture is characterized by a simultaneous fascination with the accomplishments of the black male body while also fearing the threat it poses (1994).

Yet Jordan also has done antidrug ads, represents constructive ideals of hard work and discipline, and is frequently presented as a positive role model. Jordan's "just say no" conflicts with his "just do it," creating an ambiguous figure, who at once represents restraint and control, and transgression and excess. However, on the whole, after the negative media representations during 1993 (bad press that perhaps led Jordan to prematurely retire from the NBA), his return to the NBA and succeeding superstar exploits generated unparalleled positive representations. Thus, Jordan overall became positioned in media culture as the "good black," especially against the aggressiveness and visual transgressions of teammate Dennis Rodman who with his bleached and undisciplined hair, earring, fancy clothes, and regularly rebellious behavior represented the "bad" black figure. Jordan is the corporate black, renowned for his business acumen as well as his athletic skill. He is the role model who incarnates basic American values and who fashioned his image into a highly beloved celebrity, deemed the most popular person alive between 1987 and 1993, tying with God in an Associated Press survey as the person black children most admired, and in a poll of Chinese students, he ran neck and neck with Zhou Enlai (Coplon 1996, 37).

Thus, so far and on the whole the Michael Jordan spectacle serves as an icon of positive representations of African Americans. Jordan's concentration was often remarked on and his awesome skills were obviously mediated by intelligence. His "airdriven bullets" seemed to be guided by a highly effective mental radar system and his trademarked "aerial ballets" represented grace and spiritual transcendence as well as brute force. Todd Boyd sees Jordan's talents as exemplary of a black aesthetic and compares him to great black musical performers:

> You can't watch Michael Jordan and not be moved in the way one has been moved, at an earlier time, listening to a John Coltrane solo. When I think about the way the game is played and the influence African Americans have had defining the game and the style of play—they constitute a black aesthetic. It's a style that emanated from the playgrounds, in the hood, and you can follow the lineage from Elgin Baylor to Connie Hawkins to Julius Erving to Michael Jordan to Grant Hill to Allen Iverson. Or, Bill Russell to Wes Unseld to Moses Malone to Patrick Ewing to Dikembe Mutumbo to Alonzo Mourning. These are styles that are very much like, say, the difference between trumpet players, saxophone players and piano players. (Boyd 1997b, 49; for fuller development of his concept of a black aesthetic, see Boyd 1997a)

Jordan combined grace and cool, style and skill, drive and polish, energy and aptitude. Moreover, as remarked earlier, Jordan seemed to embody central American values and to serve as a role model for American youth and as the white fantasy of the good African American. Thus, while it seems wrong to claim, as is often done, that Michael Jordan transcends race, he seems to produce unusually positive representations of African Americans, thus undercutting racist stereotypes and denigration.

The extent to which the spectacles of sports have promoted the interests of African Americans and people of color has not yet been adequately theorized. The African American breakthrough in professional sports perhaps occurred first in boxing, with boxers of color such as Jack Johnson, Henry Armstrong, and Joe Louis becoming renowned champions. But as recently as the 1940s, professional baseball was segregated and athletes of color were forced to toil in "colored" leagues, condemned in effect to the minor leagues. With the breaking of the color line in professional baseball in the 1940s by Jackie Robinson, African American athletes became part of professional baseball and eventually icons of the sports spectacle. Indeed, during the 1950s and 1960s prominent African American baseball players such as Willie Mays and Hank Aaron were acknowledged as superstars of the spectacle.

Black and brown athletes succeeded in equally spectacular ways in professional football, boxing, and basketball. Sports thus became an important route for people of color to grab their share of the American dream and cut of the great spectacle of "professional" (read commercial) sports. On the positive side, the American fascination with sports promoted racial equality, acceptance of difference, and multiculturalism. With the incorporation of black athletes into professional sports they entered mainstream media culture as icons of the spectacle, as role models for youth, and as promoters (often unaware) of racial equality and integration.

In fact, I would argue that the prowess of black sports heros and the rhythms of rock music have done much to promote racial equality and the rights of African Americans and people of color.[6] Postindustrial America became more and more of a media culture and professional sports and entertainment became key features of media culture. Once African Americans were allowed to sparkle and shine in media culture they were able to enter the mainstream—or at least major figures of the spectacle such as O. J. Simpson, Hank Aaron, and Michael Jordan were. In Spike Lee's *Do the Right Thing* (1989), Mookie, a pizza delivery man played by Spike Lee, confronts Pino, the racist Italian son of the owner of the pizzeria about his racist but contradictory attitudes toward African Americans:

| | |
|---|---|
| Mookie: | Pino, who's your favorite basketball player? |
| Pino: | Magic Johnson. |
| Mookie: | Who's your favorite movie star? |
| Pino: | Eddie Murphy. |
| Mookie: | Who's your favorite rock star? Prince, you're a Prince fan. |
| Pino: | Bruce! |
| Mookie: | Prince! |
| Pino: | Bruce! |
| Mookie: | Pino, all you ever talk about is "nigger this" and "nigger that," and all your favorite people are so called "niggers." |

Pino:       It's different. Magic, Eddie, Prince, are not niggers. I mean
            they're not black. I mean. Let me explain myself. They're not
            really black, I mean, they're black but they're not really
            black, they're more than black. It's different.
Mookie:     It's different?
Pino:       Yeah, to me its different.

Nike too has presented African American athletes as "different" in their
ads—as part and parcel of the American dream—thus helping promote them
to superstar celebrity status. Nike also helped promote the NBA and professional basketball to global iconic status, enabling black athletes such as
Michael Jordan to attain world-class superstar status and thus helped present
a positive image of black America. Yet one could argue that these appropria-
tions of the black sports spectacle were geared to sell shoes and other commercial products, that the transformation offered the consumer with the Nike
shoe is a false transcendence, that it does not produce a new superself, but
simply exploits its customer's pocketbook, forcing the unwary purchaser to
buy a product much more expensive than many competing products, simply
because of its sign value and prestige. And while one can affirm Nike's
emphasis on activity and exercise over passivity and apathy, it is not clear that
the sort of activity that Nike is promoting is really going to promote the
interests of minority youth. Gangs versus sports is not the only dichotomy of
contemporary urban life, and one might argue that education, technical skills,
and career choice and motivation are more important for contemporary
youth than running and shooting hoops.

Moreover, the elevation to cultural icons of black athletes such as
Michael Jordan is itself a double-edged sword. On one hand, Jordan is a spectacle of color who elevates difference to sublimity and who raises blackness
to dignity and respect. An icon of the sports spectacle, Michael Jordan is the
black superstar and his prominence in sports has made him a figure that corporate America can use to sell its products and its values. Yet such are the negative representations and connotations of blackness in American culture, and
such is the power of the media to define and redefine images, that even the
greatest black icons and spectacles can be denigrated to embody negative
connotations. As Michael Jackson, O. J. Simpson, and Mike Tyson have discovered, those who live by the media can die by the media, and overnight
their positive representations and signification can become negative. Media
culture is only too happy to use black figures to represent transgressive behavior and to project society's sins onto black figures. Indeed, despite the endemic problem of sexual harassment, Clarence Thomas is the representative figure

for this transgression; despite the troubling problem of child molestation cutting across every race and class, Michael Jackson is the media figure who represents this iniquity; despite an epidemic of violence against woman, O. J. Simpson is the ultimate wife abuser; and although date rape is a deplorable frequent and well-documented phenomena, it was Mike Tyson who became "poster boy" for this offense and then in 1997–1998 for all of the ills of professional boxing after his behavior in a title fight, his violence against seniors in a driving accident, for which he was sentenced to a year in jail, and his generally aberrant behavior (see Dyson 1994 and Hutchinson 1996 on the demonization of black figures).

Hence, such is the racism of American culture that African Americans are the figures of choice to represent social transgressions and tabooed behavior. Michael Jordan has had his bouts with negative media representations, though on the whole his representations have been largely positive and his figure has been used to represent an ideal of blackness that American society as a whole can live with. Indeed, he even presents an image of the transcendence of race that many celebrate as a positive ideal. Yet despite his adulation, it would be a mistake to make Michael Jordan the role model for African Americans or the youth of the world. Comparing Jordan with baseball star Jackie Robinson, who broke the major league color barrier in 1947, Jack White describes Robinson's speaking out against racial injustice, his actions with Martin Luther King, and his constant standing by political principles:

> You can hardly imagine contemporary black sports superstars taking an equally brave stand on a divisive moral issue. Most are far too concerned with raking in endorsement dollars to risk any controversy. In 1990 Michael Jordan, who occupies the psychological spot that Robinson pioneered as the dominant black athlete of his time, declined to endorse his fellow black North Carolinian Harvey Gant over troglodyte racist Jesse Helms in a close contest for the U.S. Senate on the grounds that "Republicans buy shoes too." More recently, Jordan brushed off questions about whether Nike, which pays him $20 million a year in endorsement fees, was violating standards of decency by paying Indonesian workers only 30 cents per day. His curt comment: "My job with Nike is to endorse the product. Their job is to be up on that." On the baseball field or off it, when Robinson came up to the plate, he took his best shot and knocked it out of the park. The superstar athletes who have taken his place, sadly, often strike out. (1997, 90)

When asked what he thought about the L.A. uprisings after the police who beat Rodney King were declared not guilty in May 1992, Jordan replied, in Todd Boyd's paraphrase: "I'm more concerned with my jump shot." Boyd comments: "Nobody's asking you to be Malcolm X, but when an opportunity arises, don't run from it" (1997b, 49). But Michael Jordan, like many athletes corrupted by the sports spectacle and commercial culture, has abrogated his basic political and social responsibilities in favor of expensive clothes, commodities, and a mega-stock portfolio. Nike has played a key role in promoting these values and is thus a major cultural force, a socializer and arbitrator of cultural and social values, as well as a shoe company. There, the Nike/Jordan nexus is worthy of critical reflection as the contradictions of Michael Jordan's persona come to the fore in a striking way in his intimate connection with the Nike corporation.

## Michael Jordan and the Nike Spectacle

Media culture is notorious for destroying precisely the icons it has built up, especially if they are black. Jordan has already received his share of bad as well as adulatory press and during 1996, as Nike was sharply attacked in the media for their labor policies, Jordan was put on the defensive, frequently being asked to comment on Nike's labor practices. In a carefully prepared public relations response, Jordan countered that it was up to Nike "to do what they can to make sure everything is correctly done. I don't know the complete situation. Why should I? I'm trying to do my job. Hopefully, Nike will do the right thing" (cited in Herbert 1996, 19A). Yet the media continued to pester him and he was often portrayed in images during the summer of 1996 turning away from interviewers with a curt "No comment," when asked what he thought of Nike's exploitation of Third World workers, especially women, at extremely low wages.

Nike and Michael Jordan are thus intricately connected. As noted, Nike signed the relatively untested young basketball player to a contract in 1984 and evolved one of the most successful marketing campaigns in history. There have been annual editions of Nike's Air Jordan shoes and Jordan has helped make Nike's corporate logo and Swoosh sign one of the most familiar icons of corporate culture, as well known as McDonald's Golden Arches and the Coca-Cola bottle. From the beginning, Nike deployed the spectacle of Michael Jordan and itself produced ads that celebrated its products in a commodity spectacle. With the return to the Wieden and Kennedy advertising agency in 1987, Nike devised some of the most spectacular advertising campaigns in history, with many featuring Michael Jordan (see the analysis by Goldman and Papson 1998).

One of the distinctive features of the Nike campaigns was the implosion between advertising and entertainment in its ads. Nike hired Spike Lee, who deployed the Mars Blackmon character, played by himself, featured in his first commercial film *She's Gotta Have It* (1986). Nike ad writer Jim Riswold and producer Bill Davenport first thought of using the Spike Lee character "when they noticed that Mars didn't take off his Jordans even to do the nasty. Light bulbs went off in their heads. Was it tough to sell Spike on doing an ad with Jordan? 'I think he would've done the commercial free, just to meet Michael,' says Riswold" (Reilly 1991, 77). Lee accordingly produced the first Michael Jordan Nike ad "Hang Time," using the black and white photography of his debut commercial film to show Mars hanging on a basketball rim while Michael dunks him. Lee used the character shticks from the film, having Mars calling out to Jordan, "Money! Why you wanna leave me hangin'?" and in an ad shot in Mars's, bedroom, shouting: "Shuddup down there! We're trying to make a commercial!" Thus, the ads blended humor and entertainment with the advertising pitch and helped circulate the star/celebrity image of both Lee and Jordan, just as O. J. Simpson's Hertz ads had made him a familiar icon of media culture.

In another ad drawing on *She's Gotta Have It,* Jordan is standing with his arm around the film's star Nola Darling as Mars tries to find out why she prefers Jordan to him, finally concluding "Its gotta be the shoes, *the shoes!"* Lee tired of the Mars persona and in an innovative series of ads in the mid-1990s, Nike disposed of the commodity altogether, drawing on familiarity with the corporate logo and swoosh sign, as well as celebrities such as Jordan, to market their product. In one set of Nike ads, urban blacks discuss the pleasure of playing basketball, while the 1994 P.L.A.Y. campaign featured urban youth in crisis, facing alternatives between bored passivity and (Nike-powered) activity, and sports and gangs (for analysis of these ads see Goldman and Papson 1998, and for analysis of P.L.A.Y., see Cole 1996).

Behind the Nike spectacle, there is, of course, the unedifying reality of underpaid workers, toiling at sub-subsistence wages and under terrible working conditions to produce highly overpriced shoes for youth, many of whom cannot afford and do not need such luxury items. Nike was one of the first major U.S. corporations to shift to a mode of production labeled "post-Fordism" and "flexible accumulation" (Harvey 1989). Shifting production of its shoes from the U.S. to Asia in the early 1980s, Nike first set up factories in Taiwan and South Korea. Both countries had at the time military dictatorships, low wages, and disciplined work forces. They frequently subcontracted work to local companies that would then be responsible for such things as wages, working conditions, and safety. While there were no established unions, the largely women workers in South Korea began organizing in response to poor working conditions, humiliating treatment by bosses, and low wages. At the same time, a democracy movement began in South Korea and at the first sign of labor unrest

> factory managers called in government riot police to break up employees' meetings. Troops sexually assaulted women workers, stripping, fondling, and raping them "as a control mechanism for suppressing women's engagement in the labor movement," reported Jeong-Lim Nam of Hyosung Women's University in Taegu. It didn't work. It didn't work because the feminist activists in groups like the Korean Women Workers Association (KWWA) helped women understand and deal with the assaults. The KWWA held consciousness-raising sessions in which notions of feminine duty and respectability were tackled along with wages and benefits. They organized independently of the male-led labor unions to ensure that their issues would be taken seriously, in labor negotiations and in the pro-democracy movement as a whole. (Enloe 1995, 12)

Conditions and wages improved for Korean women workers, but Nike was in the process of moving production to countries with lower wages and more control of labor, such as China and Indonesia. During the 1990s, Nike's shoes have thus been produced mostly in Asia where the average wage paid to their workers is often below the subsistence level. There was much publicity over Nike's Indonesian sweatshops, where women would be paid approximately $1.20 per day to produce shoes in the early 1990s. In 1992, 6,500 workers in the Sung Hwa Dunia factory in Serang, Indonesia, went on strike and wages were raised to $1.80 a day and eventually to $2.20 a day (Kirshenbaum 1996, 23). Under intense pressure from the Clinton administration to improve working conditions and labor rights, in order not to lose privileged trading status, the Indonesian government raised the minimum wage to (a still pitiful) $1.80 an hour and promised that the military would no longer harass and brutalize workers. But, as Greider reports, the concessions were largely a charade because "despite the official decrees, the military kept on intervening in labor disputes, showing up at the plant gates and arresting strike activists, herding the women back into the factories. This occurred twenty-two times within the first month following the supposed reform" (1994, 43).

In addition, the companies often refused to pay the workers even the legal minimum wage. The response of the Indonesian workers were a series of wildcat strikes, international campaigns to publicize their plight, and continued efforts to organize workers. Accordingly, Nike sought other sites of production, increasing production in China and then moving to Vietnam where the minimum wage is $30 per month and they can return to the one dollar plus change a day wages of an earlier era. Basing his figures on an analysis by Thuyen Nguyen, an American businessman who studied the conditions of Nike workers in Vietnam, Bob Herbert wrote in a *New York Times* op ed piece on "Nike's Boot Camps," noting that Nike workers in Vietnam are paid $1.60 a day while three meager meals cost $2.10 a day. Room rent costs $6 a month, so that Nike's workers are paid subsistence wages and work in conditions described as "military boot camps" with widespread corporal punishment, molestation of women workers, and deteriorating health of the workers (March 31, 1997, A16). There was so much negative publicity concerning working conditions in sweatshops producing Nike gear that the corporation hired Andrew Young to review its labor practices and working conditions (*New York Times,* March 25, 1997). When Young returned some weeks later with a report that whitewashed Nike, they took out full-page ads to trumpet the results, though generally there was skepticism concerning Young's report and his inadequate inspection of the Asian worker's plight.[7]

Consequently, Nike has moved production from country to country to gain ever lower production costs. NAFTA and GATT treaties have made it even easier for Nike and other global corporations to move production across the U.S. border and Nike is thus able to move around its production at will, searching for the lowest labor costs and most easily exploitable working conditions. Meanwhile, its CEO Philip Knight earns millions per year, his stock is worth an incredible $4. 5 *billion,* and Jordan, Andre Agassi, and Spike Lee are paid staggering sums for their endorsements and advertisements (see Herbert 1996). Their profit margins are enormous: Enloe (1995, 13) estimated that for a $70 pair of Nike Pegasus shoes, $1.66 goes for labor; $1.19 to the subcontractor; $9.18 goes for materials; $2.82 for administration and overhead; and Nike thus pockets $22.95 while their retailer takes in $32.20.

With the Asian financial crisis, the situation of Nike workers is even more dire. The *Village Voice* reports that Jeff Ballinger, director of the workers' rights group Press for Change "would like to see Jordan make good on his pledge to visit factories in Southeast Asia where Michael-endorsed products are manufactured. In a cover story for *ESPN: The Magazine* Jordan said, 'I want to go to Southeast Asia to see the Nike plants for myself . . . when basketball is done'" (*Jockbeat,* January 20–26, 1999). Ballinger says that a Jordan visit would highlight the plight of Nike workers in countries such as Vietnam and Indonesia that have been hit by the Asian financial crisis, estimating that "Nike factory wages in Indonesia have dropped to the equivalent of about $1 a day since the currency crash—while the plummeting value of the rupea has translated into about $40 million in labor-cost savings for Nike" (ibid).

Indeed, Nike engages in superexploitation of both its Third World workers and global consumers. Its products are not more intrinsically valuable than other shoes, but have a certain distinctive sign value that gives them prestige value,[8] that provides its wearers with a mark of social status, and so it can charge $130–140 per pair of shoes, thus earning tremendous profit margins. Nike provides a spectacle of social differentiation that establishes its wearer as cool, as with it, as part of the Nike/superstar spectacle nexus. Nike promises transcendence, a new self, to be like Mike, to fly, to gain respect. It enables the customer to participate in the Nike/Jordan magic, to Be Like Mike, by purchasing the shoes he sells. As the Spike Lee/Michael Jordan ad insists, "it's the shoes!" and those who buy the shoes buy into a lifestyle, an image, a commodity-spectacle. But a *New York Times* writer raised the question: "Does being Mike entail any responsibilities beyond doing your best on the court?" And answered:

> Let's ask Inge Hanson, who runs Harlem RBI, a youth baseball and mentoring program. She was mugged earlier this year by a 14-year-old and his 10-year-old henchboys. After they knocked her down and took about $60, a mugger kicked her in the face. The next day, the bruise that had welled up on her left cheek bore the imprint of a Nike swoosh. It lasted for three weeks and she felt sad thinking she was probably robbed to finance a fancier pair of Nikes.

> "But I can't honestly answer your question," she said. "How could Michael Jordan possibly know that by endorsing sneakers—sneakers!—he was involved in a crime? And yet, one does wonder if he has any responsibility to his audience beyond just saying, 'Just Do It!'" (Cited in Lipsyte 1996)

While Michael Jordan tries to present himself as the embodiment of all good and wholesome values, he is clearly tainted by his corporate involvements with Nike in the unholy alliance of commerce, sports spectacle, and celebrity. His symbiosis with Nike is so tight, they are so intertwined with each other, that if Nike is tarnished so too is Jordan (and vice versa—which is one of the reasons that Hertz moved so quickly to sever its ties with O. J. Simpson after the discovery of the murder of his former wife Nicole and her friend Ron Goldman). The fate of Nike and Michael Jordan is inextricably intertwined—with Nike taking on Jordan to endorse their products early in his career, helping make him a superstar known to everyone, while the Air Jordan product-line helped reverse declining sales and helped make Nike an icon of corporate America with a global reach that made Nike products part of the global popular (Andrews 1996). Thus, whereas Jordan was no doubt embarrassed by all the bad publicity that Nike received in 1996, his involvement with the corporation was obviously too deep to "just say no" and sever himself from this symbol of corporate greed and exploitation.

### Concluding Remarks

The media figure of Michael Jordan thus has contradictory effects. While he is a symbol of making it in corporate America, he also is tarnished by the scandals and negative qualities with which the corporations to whom he sells himself are tainted, as well as embodying negative aspects of excessive greed, competitiveness, and other capitalist values. Moreover, although it is positive for members of the underclass to have role models and aspirations to better themselves, it is not clear that sports can provide a means to success for any but a few. The 1995 documentary *Hoop Dreams* brilliantly documented the failed hopes and illusory dreams of ghetto youth making it in college basketball and the NBA. For most would-be stars, it is a false hope to dream of fame and athletic glory, thus it is not clear that Jordan's "Be like Mike" is going to be of much real use to youth. Moreover, the widespread limitation of figures of the black spectacle to sports and entertainment might also contribute to the stereotype, as Mercer suggests (1994), that blacks are all brawn and no brain, or mere spectacular bodies and not substantive persons. Yet, some criticism of Jordan as a basketball player has also circulated. Amidst the accolades after his announced retirement, some criticisms emerged of his style and influence on the game. Stating baldly that "I hate Michael Jordan," Jonathan Chait wrote:

> Whenever I declare this in public, I am met with stammering disbelief, as if I had expressed my desire to rape nuns. But I have my reasons. First, he has helped to change the culture of sports from one emphasizing teamwork to one emphasizing individualism. The NBA has contributed to this by promoting superstars ("Come see Charles Barkley take on Hakeem Olajuwon!"), but Jordan buys into it, too. Once he referred to his teammates as his "supporting cast," and in last year's finals he yelled at a teammate for taking a shot in the clutch moments that he, Jordan, should have taken—after his teammate made the shot. The result is a generation of basketball players who don't know or care how to play as a team. (*Slate* evening delivery: Tues., Jan. 19, 1999)

Chait also complained that Jordan was "the beneficiary of extremely favorable officiating," that "Jordan has been so spoiled and pampered by his special treatment that he expects a trip to the foul line every time an opponent gets near him, and he whines if he doesn't get it . . . . The prevailing ethic in American sports used to be teamwork, fair play, and rooting for the underdog. Michael Jordan has inverted this ethic" (ibid.). Others noted that Jordan was so competitive and obsessed with winning that he was downright "predatory," as teammate Luc Longley put it: "Opposing player Danny Ainge described Jordan as destroying one opponent like 'an assassin who comes to kill you and then cut your heart out. Jordan, skilled at verbal blood sport,' is hard on teammates and harder still, even merciless, in baiting and belittling his nemesis, [Chicago Bulls general manager] Jerry Krause" (Novak 1999, X3).

Furthermore, his obsession with wealth, highlighted in Spike Lee's nickname for Jordan—"Money"—circulates capitalist values and ideals, promoting the commercialization of sports and greed, which many claim has despoiled the noble terrain of sports. Jordan is the prototypical over-achiever, pushing to win at all costs with his eyes on the prize of the rewards of success and winning. Moreover, as noted, so far, Jordan has not assumed the political responsibilities taken on by other athletic idols of his race such as Jessie Owens, Joe Louis, Jackie Robinson, or Muhammad Ali. As Toure put it:

> Any cause he might have championed—from something as morally sim-
> ple as supporting the candidacy of fellow North Carolinian Harvey Gant,
> who lost two close Senate races against Satan's cousin, Jesse Helms, to any
> stand against any sort of American injustice—would have been taken seri-
> ously because it was endorsed by Jordan. Yet as careful as he has been at
> vacuuming every possible penny into his pocket . . . he has been equally
> diligent about leaving every bit of political potential on the table. Couldn't
> the world's greatest endorser have sold us something besides shoes? (*Village
> Voice,* January 27–February 5, 1999)

Jordan has generally symbolized the decline of politics and replacement of all social values by monetary ones that has characterized the past decades. Such issues are relevant in assessing the Jordan-effect because superstar celebrities such as Michael Jordan mobilize desire into specific role models, ideals of behavior, and values. They produce an active fantasy life whereby individuals dream that they can "be like Mike," to cite the mantra of the Gatorade commercial, and emulate their idol's behavior and values. Thus, part of the "Jordan-effect" is the creation of role models, cultural ideals, values, and modes of behavior, and thus scrutiny of what sort of values and behavior the Jordan spectacle promotes is relevant to assessing the cultural significance of the phenomenon.

Because the figures and spectacles of media culture play such an impor-tant role in the culture, it is important to develop critical insight into how media culture is constructed and functions. In this chapter, I have attempted to theorize the role of the sports spectacle and in particular the significance of the Jordan/Nike nexus in postindustrial America and to articulate the importance for media culture of sports and the representations of a black superstar. I have tried to provide critical insights into the contradictory mean-ings and effects of the sports spectacle, the ways that sports provides figures and ideologies to reproduce existing values, and the complex meanings and effects of a superstar such as Michael Jordan.

Insight into how media culture works and generates social meanings and ideologies requires a critical media literacy that empowers individuals and undermines the mesmerizing and manipulative aspects of the media spectacle (Kellner 1995 and 1998). Critical cultural studies is thus necessary to help demystify media culture and produce insights into contemporary society and culture. Reflection on the Nike/Jordan nexus reminds us that media culture is one of the sites of construction of the sports/entertainment colossus and of the icons of contemporary society. Media culture is also the stage on which our social conflicts are worked out and our social reality is constructed, so the ways that the dynamics of gender, race, class, and dominant values are played out is crucial for the construction of individual and society in contemporary culture. Since Michael Jordan embodies crucial dynamics of media culture, it is important to understand how the Jordan image functions, its manifold and contradictory effects, and the ways that the Jordan sports/entertainment spectacle embodies social meanings. Since the Jordan adventure is not yet over, his figure remains a source of fascination that should evoke evaluative scrutiny by critical cultural studies and social theory.

# Notes

My comments on the sports spectacle and use of Debord draws on work with Steve Best in our book *The Postmodern Turn* (Guilford 1997). Thanks to David Andrews for providing material and comments that have helped with the production of this study.

1. On the China and Bosnia references, see McGraw and Tharp (1999). Summing up Jordan's achievements, Jerry Crowe (1999, D1) writes: "His resume includes five most-valuable-player awards, twelve All-Star appearances, two Olympic gold medals and a worldwide popularity that filled arenas and boosted the stock of the companies with which he was affiliated" (*Los Angeles Times,* January 13, 1999, D1) . In addition, he garnered six NBA championship rings, ten NBA scoring titles (a record); a 31.5 regular-season scoring average (best of all times), a record sixty-three points in a playoff game, 5,987 career playoff points (best all time), and made the game-winning shot a record twenty-six times during his NBA career. Tributes included: Indiana coach Bob Knight, who mentored the budding superstar in the 1984 Los Angeles Olympics, called Jordan "the greatest basketball player ever . . . the best player involved in a team sport of any kind"; Coach Pat Riley of the Miami Heat called him "the greatest influence that sports has ever had"; Jerry West, former NBA superstar and executive vice president of the Los Angeles Lakers, called him "the modern day Babe Ruth"; Jason Williams of the New Jersey Nets sanctified him as "Jesus in tennis shoes" (all quotes from Crowe, 199), adding to the Jordan religious iconography coined by Boston Celtics great Larry Bird who

marvelled God disguised as Michael Jordan after Jordan scored sixty-three points against the Celtics in a 1986 playoff game.

2. Halberstam, quoted in *People,* January 25, 1999, 56. In its front page story on Jordan's retirement, *USA Today* "employed three 'greats,' five 'greatests,' one 'greatness,' two 'marveouses,' three 'extraordinarys,' one 'unbelievable,' one 'unmatched,' two 'awe-inspirings,' two 'staggerings,' one 'superstar'" and a superhybolic "great superstar" *(Sports Illustrated,* January 25, 1999, 32). Television talking heads commenting on Jordan's retirement speculated if he would run for President or "compete with Bill Gates in the business arena" (ibid), while in a completely earnest front-page story the *Chicago Tribune* suggests that Jordan could be an astronaut (cited in *Time,* January 25, 1999, 68) . But the winner in the Michael Jordan Retirement Hyperbole Contest is Bill Plaschke: "Hearing that you'll never see Michael Jordan play competitive basketball again is hearing that sunsets have been canceled. That star-filled skies have been revoked. That babies are no longer allowed to smile" *(Los Angeles Times,* January 12, 1999, D1).

3. Debord's *Society of the Spectacle* (1967) was published in translation in a pirate edition by Black and Red (Detroit) in 1970 and reprinted many times; another edition appeared in 1983 and a new translation in 1994, thus, in the following discussion, I cite references to the numbered paragraphs of Debord's text to make it easier for those with different editions to follow my reading. The key texts of the Situationists and many interesting commentaries are found on various Web sites, producing a curious afterlife for Situationist ideas and practices. For further discussion of the Situationists, see Best and Kellner 1997, chapter 3.

4. For the complex events that led Jordan to this seemingly bizarre decision, see Smith 1995 and Halberstam 1999. During 1993, Jordan's gambling habits were criticized and increasingly the subject of scrutiny, and when his father was mysteriously murdered there were speculations that the murder was related to gambling debts. The NBA intensified its scrutiny of Jordan, and he abruptly quit basketball to pursue a quixotic and failed minor league baseball career, returning to professional basketball eighteen months later to achieve his greatest athletic triumphs.

5. This line frequently appeared in interviews upon Jordan's retirement by Mark Vancil who edited the *Rare Air* Jordan photography books and has been regularly cited by commentators since the mid-1990s. Frank Deford argued in the *Sports Illustrated* collector's issue published after Jordan's retirement that Jordan is not "a creature of color" and transcends the racial divisions that have so sundered U.S. society. Matthew DeBord has recently written that Jordan is "trans-racial, the first African American cultural hero to massively evade blaxploitation by rising above it, elevating to a zone of rarefied commerce where the only pigment that anyone worries about is green" (1999). At times in Jordan's reception, this transcendence of race appears to be taking place, but such claims ignore the negative press of 1993 and the fact that African American celebrities can easily become whipping boys as well as poster boys. For a more nuanced analysis of the stages of Jordan's racial signification, see Andrews in this volume. For a critique of the oft-cited claim that Jordan transcends race, see the article by Leon E. Wynter (1999).

6. Of course, Malcolm X, Martin Luther King, and the civil rights movement did more to dramatize the plight of African Americans, but I would argue that sports and entertainment helped promote the interests of blacks and that the tremendous achievements of black athletes, music performers, and entertainers were essential in getting

mainstream America to accept and respect blacks and to allow them into the mainstream—in however limited and problematic a fashion.

7. For a detailed critique of Young's report, see the study by Glass 1997.

8. On the concept of sign value, see Baudrillard 1981; Goldman 1992; and
Goldman and Papson 1996.

# References

Andrews, D. L. (1996). "The fact(s) of Michael Jordan's blackness: Excavating a floating
racial signifier," *Sociology of Sport Journal.* 13(2):125–158.

———. (1997). "The (Trans)National Basketball Association: America's commodity sign
culture and global localization." In *Articulating the global and the local. Globalization
and cultural studies,* ed. A. Cvetovitch and D. Kellner, 72–101. Boulder: Westview
Press.

Andrews, D. L., B. Carrington, S. Jackson, and Z. Mazur. (1996). "Jordanscapes: A preliminary analysis of the global popular," *Sociology of Sport Journal,* 13(4):428–457.

Baudrillard, J. (1981). *For a critique of the political economy of the sign.* St. Louis: Telos Press.

Best, S., and D. Kellner. (1997). *The postmodern turn.* New York: The Guilford Press.

Berlant, L. (1994). *The anatomy of national fantasy.* Chicago: University of Chicago Press.

Boyd, T. (1997a). *Am I black enough for you? Popular culture from the 'hood and beyond.*
Bloomington: Indiana University Press.

———. (1997b). "Hoopology 101. Professor Todd Boyd deconstructs the game," *LA
Weekly.* May 23–29, 49.

Cole, C.L. (1996). "American Jordan: P.L.A.Y., consensus, and punishment," *Sociology of
Sport Journal* 13(4):366–397.

Coplon, J. (1996). "The Best. Ever. Anywhere," *The New York Times Magazine,* April 21,
32–37, 44, 54.

Crowe, J. (1999). "He's hanging it up." *Los Angeles Times,* January 13, D1.

Debord, G. (1967). *Society of the spectacle.* Detroit: Black and Red.

DeBord, M. (1999). "Children of the Jordan age," *Feed,* January 29 (www.feedmag.
com/essay/esl67.shtml).

Denzin, N. K. (1996). "More rare air: Michael Jordan on Michael Jordan," *Sociology of
Sport Journal,* 13(4), 319–324.

Dyson, M. (1993). *Reflecting black.* Minneapolis: University of Minnesota Press.

Enloe, C. (1995). "The globetrotting sneaker," *Ms.* March/April, 10–15.

Giroux, H. (1994). *Disturbing pleasures.* New York: Routledge.

Glass, S. (1997). "The young and the feckless," *New Republic,* September 8–September
15, 20.

Goldman, R. (1992). *Readings ads critically.* London and New York: Routledge.

Goldman, R., and S. Papson. (1996). *Sign wars*. New York: Guilford Press.

———. (1998). *Nike culture*. London: Sage.

Greider, W. (1994). "The global sweatshop," *Rolling Stone*, June 30, 43–44.

Halberstam, D. (1999). *Playing for keeps: Michael Jordan and the world he made*. New York: Random House.

Harvey, D. (1989). *The condition of postmodernity: An enquiry into the origins of cultural change*. Oxford: Blackwell.

Herbert, B. (1996). "Nike's pyramid scheme," *The New York Times*, June 10, pp A19.

Hirschberg, L. (1996). "The big man can deal," *The New York Times Magazine*, November 17, 46–51, 62–65, 77–78, 82, 88.

Hutchinson, E. O. (1996). *Beyond O. J.: Race, sex, and class lessons for America*. Los Angeles: Middle Passages Press.

Horkheimer, M., and T. W. Adorno. (1972). *Dialectic of enlightenment*. New York: Continuum.

Johnson, R. S. (1998). "The Jordan effect: The world's greatest basketball player is also one of its great brands. What is his impact on the economy?" *Fortune*, June 22, 124–126, 130–132, 134, 138.

Kellner, D. (1995). *Media culture*. London and New York: Routledge.

Kirshenbaum, G. (1996). "Nike's nemesis," *Ms.*, (November/December), 23.

Lipsyte, R. (1996). "Pay for play: Jordan vs. old-timers," *The New York Times*, July 14, B2.

McGraw, D., and M. Tharp (1999). "Going out on top," *U.S. News and World Report*, January 25, 55

Marcuse, H. (1964). *One-dimensional man*. Boston: Beacon Press.

Mercer, K. (1994). *Welcome to the jungle: New positions in black cultural studies*. New York: Routledge.

Novak, R. (1999). "Riding the air," *Washington Post*, January 31, X3.

Reilly, R. (1991). "He's gotta pitch it," *Sports Illustrated*, May 27, 74–86.

Smith, S. (1995). *Second coming: The strange odyssey of Michael Jordan—from courtside to home plate and back again*. New York: HarperCollins.

White, J. E. (1997). "Stepping up to the plate," *Time*, March 31, 90.

Wilson, B., and R. Sparks. (1996). "'It's gotta be the shoes': Youth, race, and sneaker commercials," *Sociology of Sport Journal* 13(4): 398–427.

Wynter, L. E. (1999). "The Jordan effect: What's race got to do with it?" *Salon*, January 29 (www.salon.com/money/feature/1999/01/29feature.html).

# 4

# Nike's America/America's Michael Jordan

## C. L. Cole

The family is the most human, the most powerful, and by far *the most economical system for making and keeping human beings human* . . . . Throughout modern industrial societies and across diverse cultures, the dominant and most successful family form has been the two-parent family . . . . Indeed, anthropologists long have recognized the two-parent home . . . as a common foundation of human societies. (*Families First, Report of the National Commission on America's Urban Families*, 1993, emphasis added)

### Sport vs. Gangs: Another Human Interest Story

During 1987, described by Mike Davis (1990) as the year the "crack blizzard hit Southcentral in full" and gang murders became a "headline atrocity," the *Los Angeles Times* published a lengthy, three-part series entitled "Sport vs. Gangs." The articles in the series appear under three different, but telling headlines: "The Killing Fields," "Drug Money—Selling Out of a Generation," and "Coaches Fight Recruiting War of a Different Nature." In this series, "real life in urban America" appears from the point of view of members of the Los Angeles Police Department (LAPD), the Los Angeles District Attorney's Office, and school officials (including coaches who serve as parental figures).[1] The narrative's "human interest" angle is motivated by the presumed struggles around character and moral worth faced by black youth and the consequences of those struggles and conflicts for the broader inner city community and "America." Those struggles and conflicts are rendered intelligible through sports and gangs, represented as *the* two practices vying for the agency and souls of African American male youths in urban

This chapter was originally published as "American Jordan: P.L.A.Y., consensus, and punishment," by C. L. Cole. *Sociology of Sport Journal* 13(4):366–397. It is reprinted by permission of Human Kinetics Publishers.

America. Through the testimony and personal dramas of those authorized to police and punish, the series depicts the declining participation in sport programs in Los Angeles County schools and the escalating influence of African American youth gangs as related problems.

In "Sport vs. Gangs," sport appears as the site of conventional values that fosters hopes and possibilities for both the individual and community. Sport is depicted simultaneously: as a practice that leads to a healthy and productive life; as that which distinguishes a previous and properly disciplined and productive generation of African Americans from today's inner city youths; and as the inner city's means for realizing America's utopic promises. The generational-sport logic is confirmed by representatives of the previous generation of "decent" black youth, popular figures of discipline, who "re-member" the relations among urban priorities, communities, and political order. For example, Los Angeles Laker basketball player Byron Scott, who grew up in Inglewood, is quoted as saying:

> I think they're [the current generation of black urban youth] discouraged. In '79 we looked at sports as a way out of the ghetto. You know, to make it, to buy your mother and father things they've always wanted. I think kids today look at it pretty much the same way, but they don't want to work at it. They want to find the quick money and sell drugs. (quoted in Teaford and Yount 1987, III-12)

Gangs and the relations, behaviors, styles, and desires they promote are depicted as the preferred choice of today's generation of black youth. Moreover, gangs are identified as solely responsible for subverting sport—its values and the possibilities it establishes—and for destroying athletes (the series begins with a coach's description of a gang murder of one of *his* athletes). The seriousness of gang-related threat is emphasized and rendered visible through gang activities that are no longer contained within traditional settings (gang turf) or directed at predictable targets (enemy gangs). Evidence of such spatial transgression is repeatedly depicted through gang violations of, and eruptions of gang violence in, various spaces associated with sport. In this narrative, gang violence appears "epidemic," as an out-of-control violence in need of regulation, through these sport-related violations. Gangs are not only identified as what/who are responsible for the decline in sport participation, but, and by extension, as what/who are responsible for the breakdown, disorder, and impoverishment of the inner city. Overall, the rise of violent African American gangs is attributed to pathological psyches, insatiable consumer desires, inexplicable quests for status, and the rewards of participation in the illicit drug economy: "The arrival of cocaine and crack, its derivative, as economic elements in the inner city has realigned values, according to administrators and coaches. From this has sprouted a new materialism . . . And it transcends the discipline and dedication needed to pursue athletics. Money is the idol." (Yount and Teaford 1987a, III-1).

The decline of sport and the inner city community, assessed through the escalation of African American gang activity, completes its final turn as global forces are imagined through the local signs of the "international drug economy": drugs, firearms, insatiable consumption, willful destruction, and racialized monstrosity. Black gangs, not only working with but apparently supported by international suppliers of mass-market crack, are now armed with Uzis, Mac-10 machine guns, sawed-off shotguns, and semi-automatic rifles. Youth gang greed, represented as astonishing and extraordinary, is identified as the source of an incomprehensible brutality. Racially coded violence and greed, embodied in the figure of the African American gang member, are the apparent and decisive factors in the decimation of the local community. Destructive gang activity and the decline of sport are used to build a case that identifies African American gang members as the cause of the poor quality of life experienced by inner city residents. Tougher, more effective policing is identified as the obvious—and only—solution. LAPD interests, advanced in the name of African American community interests and protection, are expressed in terms of the need for high powered weapons since they, like the local community, are outgunned by gangs. The call to upgrade their weapons (to secure more powerful and destructive equipment) is taken up through a proclaimed state of emergency advanced through the rhetoric and declaration of war. The rhetoric itself suggests that the situation exceeds the call for punishment.[2]

The *LA Times* series, "Sport vs. Gangs," encompasses an array of issues that have become immediately recognizable as "urban problems"—family breakdown, gangs, drugs, incomprehensible violence, the decline of sport, and inadequate policing and police resources. Indeed, this predominant, nationwide understanding of "urban problems" is confirmed by the excessive and wide variety of attention that inner city youth violence and police receive in both the scientific and popular realms. America's anxieties around crime, drugs, family breakdown, and violence, encouraged and shaped by the mainstream media, are demonstrated by financial, political, and affective investments associated with the frequent and unending demands for "improving" and strengthening the criminal justice system. Those demands, expressions of fear and the desire for punishment, are manifest in calls for "more control"—more arrests, more police, more prisons, more crime bills, more prisoners. Scientific and government reports and media coverage generally have led Americans to believe that their vulnerability to random violent crimes has significantly increased. The images of violence and crime animating such fears are routinely constituted through intertwined images of race, drugs, and sport.

Since 1968, six major federal crime bills have been signed into law in the United States. Anticrime legislation passed in 1984, 1986, and 1988 targeted and increased sentences related to illicit drug use and sales. Narrations of race, drugs, and sport organize the American imagination through national atrocity tales such as the mainstream media's coverage of University of Maryland African American basketball star Len Bias's death from cocaine intoxication (Donzinger 1996; Miller 1996; Reeves and Campbell 1994). The images of threat to law and order, spun through such atrocity tales, were instrumental in justifying Reagan's declaration of war on drugs (a war first declared by Nixon in 1970) and the 1986 passage of a sentence for crack possession (primarily used by poorer minorities) that was one-hundred times greater than that for powder cocaine (primarily used by upper- and middle-class whites). The news coverage of the debates around the 1994 anti-crime legislation—the most expensive crime bill in national history—highlighted Republican efforts to discredit crime prevention programs through their ridicule of Midnight Basketball as coddling criminals (whose "truth of being" suggests that they are beyond rehabilitation). The bill provided an additional $23 billion for law enforcement (including $9.7 for prisons), tied state eligibility of federal funds to "truth-in-sentencing," and added the death penalty to over a dozen sentences.[3]

The provisions established by these crime bills have yielded substantial expansion in prison construction as well as prison populations. Since 1980, six hundred new prisons have been built to house an incarcerated population that has increased from 500,000 to 1.5 million (Donzinger 1996). As a result of the highly racialized patterns of arrest, conviction, and sentencing associated with the drug war, at least one-third of African American males between the age of eighteen and thirty-four who live in a major urban area are under some form of control by the criminal justice system (U.S. Department of Justice 1995). The overall incarceration rate of young African Americans (ages eighteen to thirty-four) is an astounding six times that of whites. While what "calls for punishment" seems self-evident and apparently justifies the growth of America's prison–industrial complex, it is more likely that the murder rate and that of other serious crimes have actually and steadily declined.[4] Moreover, the declaration of war by L.A. officials on African American youth, the obvious criminalization of African American urban males, and the increasing demand for harsher punishment directed at younger offenders, suggests that what calls for punishment may be more complex than it appears.

I elected to begin this chapter with the *LA Times* series because it effectively demonstrates the means by which a racially and economically specific articulation of sport and crime accrued power in the American imagination during the 1980s. That is, the series encodes and enacts a number of narrative strategies that have positioned sport and gangs as the most important influences in the lives of urban adolescent black males. In the national imagination, sport and gangs constitute the commonsense administration of the corporeal capacities of black youth; they split black youth into forces of good and evil; and they ground racially coded national utopic and dystopic fantasies.[5] Moreover, the narrative strategies enacted in the *LA Times* series can be used to demonstrate that the identity categories of the African American urban athlete and the African American gang member that govern the late modern American imagination are, despite their apparent self-evident status, historically contingent, relational, and performative. While the series addresses what it represents as a problem endemic to the contemporary urban environment, the *gang problem is made to matter* (that is, the meaning and form of the gang problem materialize) through the presumed distinction and inverse relationship between gangs and sport and the exclusions on which that relationship depends, encodes, and enacts. The presumed distinction, inverse relationship, and requisite exclusions ground familiar knowledges of urban conditions and popular understandings of the utopic and dystopic possibilities of American inner cities.

The investment in, and plausibility of, the privileged position of sport and gangs and their relationship is, to a great extent, derived from an even more familiar and fundamental conceptualization of inner city poverty and dependency: racially coded family breakdown. Sport and gangs are represented not only as channels for what are understood to be the corporeal predispositions of African American youth but as the available substitutes for the "failed black family," a "failure" routinely encoded and enacted through the racially coded identities of the welfare mother and absent patriarchal figure. In the absence of the modern family unit, sport is positioned as *"the most powerful, and by far the most economical system for keeping human beings human."* Sport is narrated as indispensable to community production and well-being as the figure of the coach is made to represent the sanctioned nurturing father-child relationship depicted as unavailable in the African American community. The "breakdown of the black family" and its pathologization through the figures of the matriarch and the absent inseminating black male are historical mechanisms for displacing the social, economic, and political forces that shape the lives of the urban poor.[6] "Modern logic" (including presumptions about the nuclear family and the normal/deviant) and the more specific context of late

modern America combine to formulate, couple, and bind the figures of the
athlete and criminal through the overarching constructs of urban space, race,
and the family.

Although presented as distinct and self-referential, the categories of
inner city athlete and gang member are not meaningful in and of themselves
but gain their meaning through reference to the other. That is, the gang
member, whose deviance is expressed through the breach of the work ethic,
failed discipline, pathological greed, compulsion, and violence, produces
what/who are normal and acceptable: the urban African American athlete.
Additionally, the categories are embedded in a containment logic: the loss of
and threat to the healthy and productive body is narrated through the non-
productive and violent body of excess (in terms of both violence and consumption) in need of regulation. This dyadic relation governs the prominent
representations and, thus, "our" knowledge, of African American youth,
including the popular racially and economically coded knowledges of criminalized masculinity. Moreover, the sport/gang dyad locates betrayal and
destructive processes within the inner city community and thereby stabilizes
a series of identities and values that are implicated in, but appear to exist apart
from, the conditions and problems of urban America. While the desires and
acts of youth gangs threaten to make visible the material forces responsible
for the conditions of America's inner cities, those acts and desires are imagined apart from material conditions as well as the seductions of late consumer
capitalism. In other words, the material conditions that shape the lives of
urban youth and African American inner city communities (the effects of
transnationalization, joblessness, and the defunding of social programs) are
reterritorialized through *somatic identities* classified, visualized, and essentialized (though always relational, contingent, and performative) through the
practices of sport and gangs. Somatic reterritorialization establishes the plausibility of an explanation that reduces participation in sports or gangs to an
expression of a truth-of-being and individual *choice*. The reduction of desires
and the conditions of late modern America's inner city to individual choice,
works to stabilize America's foundational categories (those categories and values that ground American identity but whose stability would be challenged
if the material conditions and forces that shape the inner city were seriously
examined). Moreover, the sport/gang dyad, its corresponding somatic reter-
ritorializations, and its exclusions not only inscribe racialized criminal and
threatening masculinity and stabilize fundamental categories embedded in
"America," but *produce* desires for policing, punishment, and revenge directed
at African American inner city youth.

African American sport celebrities, in this case Michael Jordan, appear to give credibility to such narratives while obscuring their contingency. Despite the apparent credibility Jordan brings, his implication in the sport/ gang narrative is not immediately evident because of an illusory distance produced through his hyper-human status. It is precisely Jordan's hyper-humanness, a celebrity status that seems to circumvent the representational parameters of African American men, that is symptomatic of the need to take Jordan's location and function in this historical dynamic seriously. Indeed, it was during the 1980s, in the midst of America's panic around urban crime, drugs, violence, and heightened racism that Michael Jordan came of age as American Jordan.[7] I use the term *American Jordan* to refer to Jordan's position as a "representative character" of America's political culture (see Bellah et al., 1985) and as an affective figure in the national symbolic (see Berlant 1991). As a figure in the national symbolic, American Jordan reproduces national fantasy—by which I mean the nation's imagined origins, organization, and character.[8] As Lauren Berlant (1991) explains: While citizenship is perhaps most conspicuously governed by laws that decide rights and regulations, the national symbolic is fabricated through a network of law, territory, language, and experience, which binds regulation and desire (4–5). American Jordan is both a product of and exists at the intersection of political life and affect, the site at which national fantasy is generated and affirmed.

To the extent that we fail to consider how American Jordan is implicated in the racially coded sport/gang dyad governing the late modern American imagination, we perpetuate his illusory abstraction from the conditions of his possibility while obscuring his (and our) position in their reproduction. Taking seriously the historical and invisible forces through which Jordan was made, popularized, and commodified has the potential to make a difference in how we imagine the late modern American identities and desires solicited and stabilized through American Jordan. Understanding Jordan's position in national culture, and the implication of his embodiment in national fantasies and anxieties that dominated 1980s and 1990s America, requires that we consider what it means that America, a political body, and Nike, a meta- or transnational body, are given *form* through an affective figure like Jordan. This includes examining how the multiple desires and pleasures mobilized through identification with Michael Jordan are deeply implicated in racially coded deviance and its affective solicitations, especially the "revenge" underlying the contemporary "will to punish."

## National Consumption: Nike, Michael Jordan, and Basketball

The massive growth of Nike, Inc. during the 1980s, indicated by the in-
escapable presence of its emblems, its permeation of diverse spaces, and its fiscal success, cannot be separated from its most famous and pervasive
embodiment, Michael Jordan. Indeed, the place that Nike, Michael Jordan,
and basketball hold in the contemporary American imagination is clearly
indicated by the patterns of national consumption through which American
consumers exhibit their persistent fascination with and loyalties to the
"brand," "person," and "sport." Moreover, America's preoccupation with
Michael Jordan is evidenced by his excessive commodification. His innumerable commodified forms are fueled by popular sentiments of excellence,
authenticity, sincerity, generosity, and responsibility and a rhetoric that inter-
twines community, nation, tradition, development, and good times. Both
Jordan's rise to stardom and Nike's celebrity status are implicated in "optimistic" representations of America, America's youth, and America's future. Of
course, what counts as optimistic relies on presupposed values, beliefs, and
desires and thus suggests the "address" of these promotional discourses.

Typically (but with routine and telling interruptions), Jordan and Nike
are visualized as "embodiments" of exceptional character. Both seek to be
defined by their apparent willingness to inaugurate, participate in, and sustain
"programs" that address what are articulated and recognized as America's
social problems. In the context of contemporary America, Nike represents
itself as the quintessential postmodern corporation: not only does Nike
appear technologically hip, innovative, and worldly (the American global citizen), but it promotes itself as a corporation that prioritizes public issues and
cares about public well-being. Moreover, both are continuously symbolically
engineered as "brand" and "individual" in ways that align them with modern
ideals of progress and prosperity. Public opinions of the Jordan/Nike hybrid
(American Jordan) are routinely shaped and enhanced through promotional
discourses that repeatedly credit both with "giving something back" to
American communities and even participating in that which "America" sees
as its most noble project, the globalization of democracy.[9]

In the context of "America," Michael Jordan is not only Nike's most
pervasive commodified protagonist, he is a national symbol—America's most
prominent embodiment of agency and transformative possibility and an
affective sign of unity and utopic possibilities. While Jordan's celebrity
potentially signifies the end of the historical pathologization and stigmatiza-
tion of African American men, at least in the realm of the popular, his image

contrasts starkly with the graphic representations of criminalized African American men regularly circulated and consumed. Although Jordan exemplifies late modern America's "self-made man," he was "made in America" (by which I mean to designate themes in which he is implicated) alongside and within an explosion of popular depictions of African American men, especially black urban youth, as threatening and in need of policing. These apparently discrete corporeal identities (superstar/hero and criminal) take on different meaning in the context of African American novelist James Baldwin's (1985) claim that "[t]he country's image of the Negro which hasn't very much to do with Negro, has never failed to reflect with a kind a frightening accuracy *the state of mind of the country*" (cited in Riggs 1991, emphasis added). For my purposes, Baldwin's declaration is a powerful and necessary point of departure because it interrupts the modern separation between subject and object as it challenges the common sense (and scientific) epistemology of representation. By suggesting that images of blackness (in this case, two extremely different representations of African American men) are indicative of *the nation's state of mind* rather than an expression of an object's ontological status, Baldwin draws attention to the complicated links among the territorialization of space, political and moral orders, sight, and corporeal identity. The visual domain then is more complex than it seems: processes of objectivity and subjectivity are intertwined and bound within the history of "nation."[10] In order to understand the American mind, we need to seek to understand the two, apparently opposed and unrelated, representations of African American urban youth.

Michael Jordan, Nike, and basketball became national referents (prominent signs in dominant modes of representation) during a period in which "America's state of mind" was bound to the transnational dynamics (what Connolly [1995] calls "the globalization of contingency") governing late modern America. I think of the combined effects of these dynamics in terms of the *aftershocks* of post-Fordism and Reaganism and *afterimages* of modern America. I use the term *aftershocks* to draw attention to the ongoing dispersions of the initial extreme and intense transformations of communication technologies and the capitalist economy characteristic of transnationalization. These massive restructurings are expressed within America's borders through uneven and exponential growths in un(der)employment, poverty, and homelessness, particularly in urban areas caught between a declining manufacturing base, corporate downsizing, and the rise of service industries, urban renewal, and gentrification (Denzin 1991). Part of this dispersion dynamic (and under the guise of addressing the problems created by the liberal welfare

state) includes the government's systematic defunding of social welfare programs. While welfare and social benefits were cut, including Aid to Families
with Dependent Children (AFDC) and urban recreation programs (federal
monies were completely withdrawn between 1985 and 1990), monies were
expressly redirected to policing through multiple federal crime bills. During
the last twenty years and in the context of postindustrial urban renewal, the
NBA, Nike, Michael Jordan, and America's "prison-industrial complex" all
flourished economically and as sites of knowledge production.

I use the term *afterimages* of modern America to draw attention to the
complex relations among knowledges, vision, and corporeal identities implied
in Baldwin's comment. Despite our location in late modernity, I understand
those relations to be inextricably bound to (enabled and limited by) authority structures of identity generated through modern mechanisms of power.
Although identity seems self-referential and somatically bound, Foucault
(among others) has demonstrated how identity is contingent and dependent
on what it excludes. Drawing on insights into the formation of modern identity elaborated by Foucault's concept of normalization, I understand the modern regime to be organized around a division between and interdependence
of the normal and abnormal. The normal (self) cannot know itself by reference to itself but is produced and stabilized through the location, containment, and visualization of the deviant, the criminal, and the pathological (as
corporeal identities). Modern strategies of power function by imagining acts
through the received categories of corporeal identities—thus, the designation
of "what/who" throughout this text. In other words, the invisible operations
and strategies of modern power are rendered visible in their effects as they
enable and constrain what/who we see as deviant. The momentum and force
accrued by corporeal identities are always embedded in conjuncturally specific conditions.

Foucault's work provides insight into the "ways of thinking" about social
problems and the effects of transnationalization and neoconservative antiwel-
farism and how the categories and logics governing ways of thinking make it
difficult for us to see and think otherwise. The intense changes and social problems facilitated by those forces are enacted and encoded within American
boundaries through already vulnerable and stigmatized populations, especially
those identified with urban space. In other words, the logic of corporeal
deviance works to visualize the devastating effects of late capitalism through
epidemics of welfare dependency, teenage pregnancy, family breakdown, and
excessive crime and violence. Aftershocks and afterimages converge in the
administration of various deviant bodies identified as unproductive, dependent, morally depraved, compulsive, violent, and threatening. Those already

vulnerable bodies whose circumstances of daily life threaten to dissolve the markers of certainty said to govern all Americans ("the practices of fairness, neutrality, impartiality, and responsibility" [Connolly 1995]) are made even more vulnerable as they are used to shore up boundaries of the body politic.

Despite the common sense and perhaps now even tired and stereotypical categories of the athlete and gang member, the sport/gang dyad is part of the dynamic described above and continues to govern ways of thinking about urban youth, middle-class consumers, and the relations between America's middle-class and urban youth. The dyad has served as a relatively uncontested frame of reference in public service announcements (PSAs) and public policy concerned with urban youth, crime, and violence. As suggested earlier, basketball star Len Bias's death from cocaine intoxication was made into a pivotal event in Reagan's war on drugs through the sport/gang dyad (see Reeves and Campbell 1994, 136–144). The predominant advertising campaigns of the 1980s, Nike's *Just Do It* and Reagan's *Just Say No*/war on drugs, were grounded in the sport/gang dyad. During the 1990s, those campaign slogans merged in Operation PUSH's boycott slogan "say no to Nike" and Partnership for a Drug Free America's inner city campaign designed by a former Wieden and Kennedy (Nike's ad agency) employee.[11] Moreover, the dyad manages the contradictions and anxieties created through America's self-representation as a caring and compassionate nation and the increasing calls for harsher criminal punishment directed at youth.

In this chapter, I use Nike's P.L.A.Y. campaign to examine the knowledges advanced and the desires mobilized through the corporeal identity "Michael Jordan." I begin the next section by briefly introducing three controversies surrounding Nike's social responsibility (as it is popularly imagined) in an effort to demonstrate how the complexities of marketing and managing African American men and popular sentiments about corporate responsibility reproduce particular knowledges and configurations of power. Following this work, I present the P.L.A.Y. campaign (Nike/Jordan) as it (they) is (are) typically presented in and to the public. That is, my general aim is to provide a basic and commonsense portrayal of P.L.A.Y. Next, I advance a critical interpretation of P.L.A.Y. based on a series a questions: How do we make sense of Nike's corporate call to activism? How is it possible that Nike has not been criticized for marginalizing, even trivializing, more serious and complex issues, especially as those issues have taken shape in post-Rodney King America? How is it possible that Nike advances a call to activism based on sport and fitness activities while America's urban areas are plagued by problems ranging from malnutrition, AIDS, drug use, gangs, murders, to teenage pregnancy, inadequate health care, unemployment, homelessness, and police brutality? In order to respond to such questions I draw attention to what/who are made visible through P.L.A.Y. and the radical troping of transcendence, violence, and criminality that shapes American consciousness and motivates calls for increased policing and punishment. I seek to examine how the political economy of intelligibility that sites/sights "American Jordan" is implicated in and contributes to those knowledges that govern the contemporary American imagination in ways that criminalize African American youth and racialize punishment, while displacing and concealing the violence of the integrated circuits of transnational capitalism. Stated differently, this chapter seeks to understand how particular configurations of power are reproduced despite proposals and intentions to do otherwise.

## Nike, Responsibility, and the American Imagination

> The criminal, who is aware of all the circumstances attending his case, fails to find his deed as extraordinary and incomprehensible as his judges and censurers do; his punishment, however, is meted out in accordance with precisely the degree of *astonishment* that the latter feel when they regard the incomprehensible nature of his deed.
> —Frederick Nietzsche, *Human, All Too Human*

In this section I briefly consider three public events preceding Nike's launch of P.L.A.Y., because they neatly encapsulate popular debates over Nike, Michael Jordan, social responsibility, and race—in short, they represent the sort of "public relations crises" P.L.A.Y. was developed to manage. The urban sneaker crime wave that surfaced in 1990 as an element in the media-hyped crime wave called into question what/who were responsible for sneaker-related violence. Several months later, Chicago-based civil rights organization Operation PUSH (People United to Serve Humanity), founded in 1971 by Jesse Jackson, sought to develop a national boycott to challenge Nike's failure to invest in the black community. In the midst of the L.A. rebellions, Nike aired a series of ads directed by Spike Lee, which became the object of criticism. The ads were designed to address racial tensions, thereby presenting Nike as socially conscious, and to promote Nike's "Air Raid" line.

Occasional media reports of sneaker crimes began the same year that Air Jordans became a consumer reality. Five years later sneaker crimes became news when two print-media articles drew national attention, becoming the point of departure for innumerable televised, print, and radio news reports: Rick Telander's (1990) "Senseless" and Phil Mushnick's (1990) "Your Shoes or Your Life" (which gained national attention through Spike Lee's public response). Although the Telander and (to a lesser extent) Mushnick articles influenced mainstream media's coverage of sneaker crimes, the narrative of sneaker violence gained its force and momentum from the sport/gang dyad and media-hyped crime wave already in place.

The media's preoccupation with "sneaker crimes" can be attributed, to a great extent, to the complex semiotic space occupied by sneakers and urban African American athletes and a crime wave narrative whose favorite recruit was the seemingly senseless, incomprehensible, and shocking crime. The sneaker crime, which violated the line dividing America's racially coded utopic and dystopic figures, elicited responses of moral outrage. That outrage followed multiple lines: Outrage was directed at the "three figure sneakers"; high profile African American celebrity endorsers charged with inciting those crimes; and a generation of inner city youth whose values were designated incomprehensible. Despite the variety of sport-related commodities identified as objects of crime (including high profile Starter jackets and the Reebok Pump), Nike's Air Jordan sneaker was recruited to and remained the central and prominent sign of the racially coded sneaker crime.[12]

In general, the narrative functioned to "assess" what/who were greedy, criminal, and monstrous. Although sneaker companies were immediately accused of inspiring criminal activity among poor inner city youth by creating high status consumer goods or by magically injecting high status into the shoes, the contradictory logic eventually was settled through the stabilization of the sport/gang dyad. In part, that binary was stabilized through the figure of Jordan, whose image crisis was circumvented (wittingly or not) by Telander's narrative in which the sneaker crimes were framed in terms of a personal tragedy for Jordan.[13] Jordan's heroic position is established in "Senseless," and is managed throughout the narrative through the representation of his visible disturbance and concern over the killing of a Baltimore youth over a pair of Air Jordans. Repetitions of Jordan's inability to have foreseen this consequence of his celebrity endorsements serves as evidence of his distance from threatening urban youth. In Jordan's words, repeated by media across the country: "I thought I'd be helping out others and everything would be positive. I thought people would try to emulate the good things I do. They'd try to achieve to be better. Nothing bad." Media consumers were narratively aligned with Jordan through a strategy that equated Jordan's problem and *our* problem: the crimes were depicted as forcing Jordan and us to ask some hard questions. Jordan and the force of the logic governing the representation of African American youth work to return the cause of sneaker violence to urban African American youth.

The category of "use," invoked through sport (cast as pure utilitarian) and fashion (cast as the pollution of the symbolic) also reestablishes the distance between utopic and dystopic figures. Fashion, articulated with the nonathlete/gang member who uses the shoes for street status, serves as a means to call into question the values and priorities of a generation of youth who have appropriated sporting apparel as "a sort of uniform for the forces of darkness" (Marsh 1990). Nike, Jordan, and "we" are distanced from racially coded criminality as the strategies deployed to resettle the binary work to displace concerns about the conditions of existence in urban America.[14]

Later the same year, Operation PUSH called for a boycott of Nike.[15] The boycott was not directed at Nike's advertising practices as criticized in the sneaker crime narrative. Instead, PUSH sought to intervene in Nike's failure to invest in black-owned businesses, especially black-owned banks, media, and advertising agencies. More specifically, PUSH argued that given Nike's profits from the African American community, Nike should return the business (Hume 1990; Raspberry 1990; L. Wynter 1990). In this case, Nike explained away its absence from black media by appealing to the earlier criticisms directed at Nike for marketing expensive shoes to black youths. Moreover, Nike challenged the accusations made by PUSH by citing its contributions (in 1989, three-quarters of the $10 million spent on philanthropic causes was directed to inner city neighborhoods), its affirmative action hiring practices, its use of black celebrities such as Michael Jordan, and its intention to do more (Raspberry 1990).

The changes that Nike made were less the response to an affective boycott (the boycott actually received minimal media and youth support), than they were to the potential so-called public relations concerns that PUSH had identified. Nike did not hire a black-owned but a multiethnic advertising agency, Muse Cordero Chen, Los Angeles, as strategic advisor for it proeducation and antidrug campaign (Nike's primary response to the sneaker crime panic). Additionally, Nike bought time on Black Entertainment Television during sports events and, with the advice of Muse Cordero Chen, sought to invest $2–3 million on highly specialized ethnic media (Magiera 1990). Additionally, Nike added its first African American to its board and reevaluated its "multiethnic" hiring practices.

In 1992, Nike received substantial criticism for a series of advertisements, shot on location in South Central Los Angeles by director Spike Lee, which aired just after the L. A. rebellions. The ads took "racial tolerance" as their rallying point. In this case, the promotion of racial tolerance was made through the dramatization of racial division and conflict. For example, one ad, "Black & White," focused on racial tensions between basketball players who refused to play together. Although popular criticisms were most explicitly directed to Nike's use of the Los Angeles crisis to launch a new product (Nike's "Air Raid" sneaker) and Spike Lee's self-promotion, the ads acknowledged racial tensions that are typically denied.

These controversies and the issues they raise provide insights into the address and reception of P.L.A.Y. Such criticisms, which stand in contrast to the enthusiastic approval surrounding P.L.A.Y., highlight the categories, principles, values, and even aesthetics by which Nike solicits identification and consumption. As we can see in P.L.A.Y., Nike displaces racial differences with America's "shared identity" in order to promote itself as socially responsible.

## P.L.A.Y.'s Portrait of America

> I ask you to remember that even as we say no to crime, we must give people, especially our young people, something to say yes to.
> —Bill Clinton, State of the Union Address, January 1994

P.L.A.Y., an acronym for Participate in the Lives of America's Youth, is a $10 million dollar a year Nike-sponsored initiative that aims to provide safe, clean, accessible facilities and recreational opportunities "to kids." As Nike CEO Phil Knight explains, Nike initiated P.L.A.Y. as an expression of its concern and its felt need to take action around the conditions limiting children's play. Knight identifies increased violence and decreased funding as the causes of America's crisis, which he defines in terms of diminishing kids' access to fitness activities and sport. In a statement that consolidates the rhetoric of minority rights and nationalist principles, Knight explained how Nike seeks to do the right thing by protecting the rights of all children to participate in sport:

> There's a crisis in America right now. Kids' sports and fitness programs are being axed from schools and the country's playgrounds aren't safe anymore. Access to play should be a kid's inalienable right. Nike wants to lead the charge to guarantee that these rights to America's children are preserved . . . . The time has come to take action on this issue, simply because it's the right thing to do.

Through P.L.A.Y., Nike mobilizes and builds alliances with celebrities, consumers, corporations, and already established community-oriented service programs that aspire to attend to and treat inner city problems and the disadvantaged youth affected by those problems. Under the sign of P.L.A.Y., Nike helps to create and sustain a national "mood" or sensibility founded on what is represented as real possibility, control, and comfort; a mood or sensibility forged over and against despair, disillusion, suffering, fear, and turbulence. This mood is advanced through Michael Jordan and Jackie Joyner-Kersee, the national co-chairs of P.L.A.Y. Other Nike athletes have committed thousands of hours to the project. Additionally, a Nike-established Athlete Leadership Council spearheads the effort along with a Kids' Advisory Board made up of television stars and five Boys and Girls Club "youth of the year" winners. The P.L.A.Y. confederation also includes the Boys and Girls Clubs of America (Nike's official three-year partner in P.L.A.Y.), the Corporation for National Service, Ameri-Corps (referred to by Bill Clinton as America's "domestic peace corps"), and Gifts in Kind America Teamwork, which provides new sports apparel, equipment, and accessories to charities who work with "at-risk" youth. The countless projects spawned, inducted, and nurtured under or alongside P.L.A.Y.'s signature range from Reuse-a-Shoe, Inner City Games, Midnight Basketball (which gained national attention during the debates over Clinton's Crime Bill during August of 1994), City Block Soccer, Nike NHL Street Hockey, Nike PLAY Tennis This Summer, and the USA Track and Field Junior Olympics. Additionally, Nike works in tandem with already established community service-oriented projects such Oakland's Project Playground, The Atlanta Project, and STAYFIT KIDS.

Nike delayed the launch of P.L.A.Y., originally scheduled for the 1994 Super Bowl, because, according to one spokesperson, the advertisements were not splashy enough for the event (DeSalvo 1994). However, the delay positioned the campaign in the zone of attention directed at public funding of urban recreation programs. The ad, entitled "What If. . . . There Were No Sports," premiered during Men's and Women's National Collegiate Athletic Association's Basketball Championships. Not only did this immediately locate the ad in relation to "America's urban sport," but the postponement allowed Nike to ground P.L.A.Y., ostensibly about children's right to play, firmly within in a context in which public attention was drawn to the federal crime bill and federal policies regarding urban recreation programs and crime prevention. Federal funds for Midnight Basketball Leagues were approved on March 31 during the debates related to "Goals 2000: Educate America Act." Moreover, the delay positioned Nike's P.L.A.Y. alongside two PSAs that addressed urban youth, violence, and playground safety sponsored by the National Crime Prevention Council, The Advertising Council, and the Bureau of Justice Assistance, Office of Justice Programs, U.S. Department of Justice.[16] In other words, P.L.A.Y. was not simply brought into public view through two sixty-second ads created by Wieden and Kennedy but through an immediate context in which a state-legitimated racially coded discourse on urban recreation and crime had been established. Moreover, the campaign's link to racially coded inner city problems gained force and momentum from its association with basketball, Jordan, and other African American athletes.

Although athletes such as Ken Griffey Junior, formerly of the Seattle Mariners, Steve Young of the San Francisco 49ers, and Mia Hamm of the U.S. Women's National Soccer team, appear in the ads, Michael Jordan and Jackie Joyner-Kersee remain the featured athletes, narrators, and representatives. Both advertisements begin with a hypothetical question "What if . . . there were no sports?" The question animates reflections on America and America's future in order to lay out the main points of the initiative: without sports, and adult volunteers, kids will be alienated and will turn to the streets to fill time and where gangs provide their values. The ads conclude with a toll-free phone number, 1–800–929-PLAY, that can be called for more information. Below the number is Nike's now familiar swoosh. The P.L.A.Y. hotline is answered by a recorded message from Jordan and Joyner-Kersee who identify themselves as national ambassadors for P.L.A.Y. and encourage callers to get involved and make a difference. The recorded message provides the phone number of local Boys' and Girls' Clubs, extends information about Street Hockey, and offers callers a Nike P.L.A.Y. brochure. Within three months, Nike had received 200,000 phone calls and by 1996 more than 500,000 calls.

The P.L.A.Y. pamphlet is aesthetically appealing and easy to read. The cover includes a grainy closeup photograph of a basketball bound by the hands of African American youth, which fades into an empty background. Nike's now signature P.L.A.Y. logo is positioned center—stamped across the hands embracing the ball.[17] Nike's signature swoosh symbol is positioned bottom-center. The inside cover asks: "No ball. No playground. No place to go. What if there were no sports? What would a twelve year old do after school?" (Although left unanswered, the question is, of course, meant to elicit an unconscious response.) The brochure lays out the ground on which the P.L.A.Y. campaign stands by describing the contemporary conditions that have spawned Nike's response:

> For America's youth . . . going out to play is getting tougher all the time. Budget cuts are forcing schools to scale back or eliminate sports and physical education programs. Communities can't afford the upkeep on public parks and recreation facilities. Safety issues have many parents fearful of letting children out of their sight. [Nike's response]: P.L.A.Y. is Nike's war on complacency, with a multimillion dollar national campaign leading the way—major athletes are using their muscle to issue a call to action for everyone to take part. [Nike partnerships]: Aggressive Partnerships Are Key. [Nike's financial contributions]: A $1 million dollar grant from the Nike Just Do It Fund will help the Clubs [Boys and Girls Clubs of America] develop even more sports . . . . In addition, Nike has committed

more than $650,000 to a national communications campaign to help gen-
erate more support for the Clubs. Another $150,000 goes to local Clubs
in 30 cities across the country, courtesy of Nike Tour golf tournaments.
The Nike Just Do It Fund also supports many non-profit, community-
based sports and fitness programs for kids, ranging from Special Olympics
to Midnight Basketball. Moreover, Nike Sports Marketing Department
contributes more than $2 million annually to sponsor kids' races, camps,
and clinics.

The core of P.L.A.Y. is outlined in a four-page spread (which includes a full-
page photograph of Nike-kids team) of what is called "A Revolutionary
Manifesto: A Kid's Bill of Rights." The principles motivating the Kids'
P.L.A.Y. Movement can be summarized, according to Nike, in terms of "every
child['s] inalienable right to an active life; the joy of sport, and to the pursuit
of fun." As part of its effort to contribute to the goals named in "A Kid's Bill
of Rights" and to dissolve the prohibitive barriers repeatedly identified, Nike
committed to refurbishing ten playgrounds in ten different American cities.[18]
In the brochure, we are told that Nike's Environmental Action Team
(N.E.A.T.) developed a program to collect and recycle old Nike shoes for
indoor and outdoor sports courts, playgrounds, and tracks: larger segments of
youth are provided with space to participate in sports and physical activity
through environmentally sound practices in which used shoes, which would
otherwise contribute to the landfill crisis, are recycled. Although Nike sees
itself as P.L.A.Y.'s coordinator and provides models for community activism,
we are told that the voices we hear are not those of a corporation: "kids" are
the authors of the desires expressed through the "Bill of Rights," the result of
a Nike-sponsored youth fitness summit held in 1993 in Washington, D.C.

In addition to donating playgrounds, Nike sponsors an induction ceremony of sorts. The ceremonies feature Nike celebrities ranging from Spike
Lee, Michael Jordan, and Scottie Pippen to Ken Griffey Jr., Jackie Joyner-
Kersee, and Sheryl Swoopes. The opening ceremonies are events that are
organized around celebrity, community, youth, and dreams. Celebrities typically give inspirational speeches in which they recall their childhood dreams
and their achievements, and link the Nike-donated court with the dreams of
the community. The inspirational speeches point to the need for hard work,
individual responsibility, and self-determination. For example, Ken Griffey Jr.
reiterated a familiar message of hope and possibility: "I had a dream that was
to go out and play major league baseball. That's what this basketball court is
for—your dreams, whatever they are. . . . It's important to do things you
want." For Nike, these community gatherings provide invaluable public relation and photo opportunities. The photographs depict magical moments in

which local youth see their heros and in which Nike is positioned as a community maker.

The popular representation of P.L.A.Y. as a response to the now routine violation of kids' rights to participate in sport and fitness, along with public responses to P.L.A.Y., provides a strong sense of Nike's popular profile. For example, Kathy DeSalvo (1994), advertising critic for *Shoot,* characterizes Nike's P.L.A.Y. advertisement, "The latest Nike offering features Michael Jordan and is sports-related, but that's where the similarity to other spots end ... [it] isn't meant to sell shoes" (12). *Advertising Age's* Jeff Jensen's (1994) evaluation is consistent with DeSalvo's: "The newest Nike TV commercials don't feature Godzilla, Bugs Bunny, or any crazed shoe-sniffing referees. They do star Michael Jordan, but not as his usual basketball superhero self. And while the Nike logo is flashed at the end, the two spots don't plug any products" (3). Both critics contrast P.L.A.Y. to previous ads to suggest that the visual absence of products is an indication of Nike's character and its concern for common good over and above its own interests. Nike's latest promotional campaign is translated into evidence of its good will and its willingness to take real financial risks in order to, in this case, sustain America's dream of society. Nike is exalted for sponsoring P.L.A.Y. "despite" market pressures and declines in its stock (which dropped from $80 to a low of $35), basketball shoe sales, and its European market (because of the recession).[19] In the realm of the public, P.L.A.Y. and other Nike public service–style advertisements serve as expressions of Nike's conscience and its overlapping commitment to and investment in America.

In the next section, I offer a critical reading of the television ad and campaign. My goal is not directed at exposing the limits of a strategy that addresses urban problems through sport and fitness activities, nor is it directed at underscoring the hypocrisy behind Nike's activism and its claim to social responsibility.[20] The parameters established by such issues would obscure what I argue is one of the most compelling aspects of the campaign: Jordan/Nike hybrid's implication in the reproduction of the national imagination. Given this, I want to redefine the questions identified in my introduction in ways that facilitate an examination of "imagined community" (as it is fabricated through racial deviance) as it is made and remade under the sign of social responsibility—Nike style: How does such a public service–style advertisement/campaign make sense to us? What sense does the ad make *of* us? *of* America? *of* Nike? How are we to understand the position of Michael Jordan in this ad? Or, perhaps more usefully, how does Michael Jordan's position in this ad help us understand *his* position and popularity in American culture? How are we to understand the hopes, dreams, and knowledges that are disseminated in the name of sport? How does this ad, and numerous others like it, contribute to articulations of urban problems that make certain solutions seem plausible?

## Representing the New Urban Order:
## America, P.L.A.Y., and Michael Jordan

> *City Attack* is Nike's way of getting underground . . . There are a lot of kids in L.A. and New York, mainly African American and Hispanic, who buy a lot of shoes. These kids don't care about big national celebrities. They don't think of Michael Jordan as a role model; once he's on the magazine stand, he's not cool anymore.
>
> —Imin Pao, *City Attack* art director

Although both Spike Lee's "Air Raid" narrative and P.L.A.Y. appear to be and address signs and conditions of the times, P.L.A.Y. seems quite intentionally distanced from Spike Lee's campaign. P.L.A.Y. does not establish a new product (at least not in any direct or visible way); it does not address a specific incident; and its articulation of racial difference differs. In the Spike Lee ad, racial difference is made visible through performance, style, and expressive practices popularly associated with black urban America. Those differences are further imagined through pan–African colors and the signature style of America's most famous African American director. In P.L.A.Y., Lee's signature closeups and angular shots are replaced by a series of black and white moving stills shot on location in rural and inner city America. The director is not Spike Lee, but Los Angeles–based Melodie McDaniel, known for her still photography and music videos. In P.L.A.Y., the significance of racial difference is denied and translated into sameness through a discourse of rights, agency, nation, unity, and transcendence. That is, what matters is a solidarity around a more primary identity (nation) and the collective values that hold the nation together. Nation (not race), its corresponding sense of territory, imagined community, and democratic culture, is the prominent rallying point of the campaign. Michael Jordan (not Spike Lee) is crucial to P.L.A.Y. and its mobilization of national fantasies and desire.

P.L.A.Y. has provided Nike with extensive and inexpensive promotional space. The front cover of the premiere issue of *HOPE Magazine* features four racially diverse youths, presented against a milky, pastel background, who embody the possibilities and promises of America's multicultural future. Among the hard work and good deeds indicative of America's optimistic future identified on the cover is Nike's P.L.A.Y. Campaign: "Cool Courts for

Kids: Nike's P.L.A.Y. for Change and Other Surprising Signs of Hope." Unlike the responses to sneaker crimes, P.U.S.H., and Spike Lee, *Hope's* article on P.L.A.Y. is inspirational and uplifting: it is about community "makers" rather than "takers," the forces of good, rather than evil. The article, entitled "Nike's P.L.A.Y. for the Neighborhoods," draws attention to the Youth as Resources (YAR)-Playground Project which was designed by three high school age girls in their efforts to provide a playground for the Chicago's Robert Taylor Homes. The Robert Taylor Homes, the nation's largest publicly funded housing project, is populated by 12,320 mostly poor and unemployed African Americans. More than 80 percent of the children who live at Robert Taylor live in poverty. Although the article chronicles the tenacious efforts of the girls, its featured hero is Nike, the project's first (but not only) corporate sponsor. But it is Michael Jordan who is identified as the ultimate force of good because he is credited with soliciting Nike's participation in the project.

Primarily, the story highlights and extends high praise to Nike for its contributions (a new, "environmentally sound" basketball court and an opening ceremony featuring Nike celebrities) and its concern with and compassion for youth. The Nike-donated playground is represented as offering options and choice to the youth that live in the Robert Taylor Homes. Both the playground project and Nike's contribution accrue meaning and value over and against what is described as the South Side's rampant crime.[21] Crack, gangs, violence, murders, and dream-less youth drive the implicit "crime prevention" logic of the narrative. Local youth are quoted as they recite the significance of the playground through familiar terms that reduce the complexities of daily life in Chicago's South Side to gang violence with sport activity as the antidote. The article concludes with a benefit auction to expand the playground project sponsored by Michael Jordan's Restaurant.

Although published two years after Nike's official launch of P.L.A.Y., the article enacts the knowledge/power network motivating P.L.A.Y. and its popular reception. *Hope's* commendations, indicative of the sort of cost-effective promotional spaces that Nike has gained through P.L.A.Y., accrue meaning through knowledges which criminalize black youth. Despite its tone, the advertising narrative enacts the normalizing logic that governs dominant understandings of youth crime and prevention.

### "What if there were no sports?"

The narrator's voice is importantly and unmistakably that of Michael Jordan, one of the nation's most beloved icons. The fact that it is Michael

Jordan asking us to anticipate life without sports, the fact that it is Michael Jordan who has invited the audience to imagine America's sportless future, shapes how viewers look, see, and think about the visual images and experience the narrative. Although it is "Michael Jordan," America's most prominent figure of fantasy and possibility, who serves as the symbolic backdrop for the narrative, and while his question suggests a premonitory tale, the viewer's gaze is met by unexpected documentary footage.

Filmed in the codes of realism and borrowing from a photographic genre associated with America's Depression era, an image is displayed that most obviously evokes the anxieties of loss and more generally shapes the affect elicited by the narrative. The camera closes in on a lone girl imagined through codes that recall a moment of crisis and the emotional landscape and suffering of another time and place—1930s rural America. She is the sign of national history. The image of the girl captures her wounds and her victimhood: she is motionless, the picture of innocence, sadness, and alienation. She is the child-citizen, impoverished and deprived, a casualty who attests to what has been but what is understood to be an aberrant moment in American history. The initial suspicion (elicited by Jordan's voiceover) that the narrative might be autobiographical is deferred, but not denied. The image, the question, and the narrator anchor perceptions of the images that follow.

## "If you couldn't join a team, what would you join?"

How is it that "we" immediately know the answer to a question that asks us to imagine how the need to belong will be satisfied in a nation in which sport-related options are absent? The question is one that not only recalls the need to belong and to be part of a community but one that rapidly shifts to America's immediate context. While the opening image draws attention to a national crisis associated with external conditions and pressures, these codes draw attention to America's contemporary crisis and the troubled urban youth indicative of that crisis. Here we see urban youth, whose facial expressions and body posture connote pain, anger, and danger. The identities invoked are prescribed, overburdened, and saturated with meaning. *We* have to ask: what kind of values will youths learn from *this* community? The image we see appeals to the underside of America, its dominant signs, codes, and spaces in order to bring discipline, desire, and will into question. An overall sense of desolation, emptiness, poverty, and lawlessness are positioned against a landscape of barbed wire and a run-down public housing project. Without the discipline of sport, lawlessness escalates; boredom and resentment are turned into disorder. When sport falls, anger, gangs, drugs, and violence rise.

Although the second image appears to follow easily from the first, the two images stand in complex relation to one another. As we move from the wounds of innocence to idle youth and broken spirits, our vision is widened. The rhetoric of absence renders visible urban America, its conflicts, threats, and the hostilities associated with it. Although the bodies are most familiar as signs of danger, signs of a generation whose violence is inexplicable but continues to escalate, the meaning and the emotional impact of the image is complicated because of its narrative placement. While typically inserted into tales of normalization and moral outrage, in this context it is rendered more a cautionary tale. Still, we wonder if the narrative will continue to move us deeper into urban space and the horrors associated with it. What will the next image bring?

## "If you couldn't dream of touchdowns, what would you dream?"

The question and image do not move us deeper into urban life and, therefore, bring relief. Instead, we are asked, what, if not sport, will motivate America's youth to dream of possibilities, of realizing one's potential? How will and what kind of ambitions will be imagined? What values will shape the dreams of children? The question reinforces the meaning that sport brings to life.

To deny possibilities, to impose boundaries on dreams, is equivalent to undermining freedom. What is at stake is the American Dream itself. Those values are accrued over and against the values and meanings inscribed on black urban youth.

## "What if you did something?"

The question, which presumes the value of sport, our present situation (whose key point of reference remains racially coded violence), and the project that is "America," is direct and to the point: It is a call to action. As Nike's address shifts, the mood alters. Nike's address is now to us, adults who should be troubled by the limits and dangers of such a world, by the images of childhood we see, especially because of what we imagine a proper childhood to be. The hail here is one of solidarity, community, and unity. Nike, Michael Jordan, sport, and "we" are linked in a chain of possibility. We can make a difference. We can participate in America's future, we can help make history.

## "What if you coached a team?"

Nike offers an answer, a realistic possibility. Again, a sense of belonging and community is invoked that links the local and the nation. The images are no longer idle and dystopic but connote life through energy, pulsating movement, and activity.

## "Put up a new rim?"

Here the camera settles on a tattered crate serving as basketball hoop—a trace of unacceptable conditions available for play in urban America. Nike's message is clear. It is a practical challenge to the contemporary conditions that deny kids access to sport activities. We can all share in the effort, even the little things we do will help change lives.

### "What if there were no sports? Would I still be your hero?"

Our identifications and desires are directly addressed. These questions appeal to the stakes in maintaining sport, the transformational power of sport, the ability of sport to shape lives, to sustain common culture, to make heroes for us. The questions simultaneously recall specific images and fears directly related to how African American men are imagined in the realm of the popular. Here, the diverse images, figures, and spaces (specifically decaying rural and urban America) are unified through a monument of human possibility and achievement already central to the production of national intimacy, Michael Jordan.

It is only after the transformative power of sport has been confirmed that Jordan, who figures remarkable performances, is visibly located in the narrative. The loss of sport is equated with the loss of Michael Jordan and all that he embodies: greatness, excellence, transcendence, and grace. America's fantasies are condensed on his body: without sport, we will be denied Nike's pleasures, moods, and products. Although Jordan remains unmarked, that is, Jordan is not located in a specific context, Michael Jordan, sport, and Nike make and mark differences.

Michael Jordan and his life document the truth of the narrative.

The P.L.A.Y. campaign breaks from (or so it seems) the "need for more police" mentality as it represents itself as a socially progressive program based on a call for social and political unity around children. Unlike incitements for expanded punishment or the categories that mobilize our desires for revenge, Nike seems to "offer" something different by addressing social injury. The promotion represents Nike as, in a word, responsible. Despite its apparent distance from policing and punishment scenarios, the P.L.A.Y. campaign depends upon a story relentlessly played out in the minds of Americans.

The public service–type advertisement renders "America" intelligible through a key organizing feature of political culture: childhood. Play and sports are promoted as uniquely valuable elements of childhood to which all youth are entitled and deserve. Given the collective fantasy childhood (homogenized by collapsing geography, economy, and race), and the location of sport in modern culture, restrictions on physical activity are seen as interrupting a natural dimension of childhood; by extension, such restrictions are understood to be un-American. In P.L.A.Y., Nike enacts the logic of "minority-identity" as it recalls the child-centered ideals and the fantasies associated with play and sport in order to imagine victims whose rights it aspires to protect and to mobilize our desires.[22]

P.L.A.Y. is represented from the kids' point of view: a site through which kids have, in their own voice, identified injustices and called on American adults to provide and manage their right to a natural and proper childhood.

Through P.L.A.Y., Nike imputes a self-conscious identity to kids as "American kids" who are aware of the conditions in which they live and their entitlements. Kids, represented as autonomous in their identity and their calls to action, are represented as dependent on adults to protect their civil rights to sports and play. At the same time, Nike positions itself as a democratizing force which fosters the development of an informed and pro-active community. Nike's invocation of the "Bill of Rights" appeals to diverse nationalist sentiments as it mobilizes images of a particular political order, power, individuals, and rights.[23] As Nike invokes the nation and the authority that *is* America, Nike (a transnational corporation that has no boundaries) codifies itself as "American" at a time when, as William Connolly (1995) aptly puts it, "[o]nly democratic citizens remain locked behind the bars of the state . . ." (157). That is, Nike enacts familiar themes constitutive of the national imagination and whose terms limit how we imagine power, responsibility, and violence in late modern America.

Moreover, childhood is deployed to provoke an origin story of adult character. That is, play and sports are represented as components of a proper (natural) childhood that leads to accomplished adulthood. The line drawn from childhood to sport to Michael Jordan narrates "belonging" and the making of the ideal, productive citizen. "Childhood," the precious and sacred moral center of the nation, is articulated with America's past, its present, and its future. A sportless and playless landscape represents the theft of childhood, loss of hope, and absence of democratic culture as we imagine it. In this sense, Nike is part of a national cultural industry that seeks to fulfill the aims of national reproduction.

Nike's invocation of "America" does not stop at explicit calls to nation, but is invoked daily through Michael Jordan. P.L.A.Y. is a particularly useful example of how Michael Jordan is narrated as a national stereotype that binds "American consumers," an imagined community, together. To a great extent, American consumers take pride in Jordan because he is a sign of what it means to be an American and a sign of what is possible for anyone who works hard and plays by the rules. Michael Jordan serves as an especially affective figure through which the interdependence of Nike (transnational body) and America (political body) are given form in ways that conceal the complexity of the terrain that Nike occupies and the conditions that organize daily life in the United States. In the next section, I discuss the relation between the national symbolic, P.L.A.Y., and Michael Jordan. Here, I suggest that this national imagination relies on a racially coded truth of childhood.

## Made in America: The Fabrications of Nike and Michael Jordan

Revolution in America was a different matter. Here, it meant the unfolding of a redemptive plan. It required progress through conformity, the
ordained succession from one generation to the next. What the American
Puritan fathers had begun, their sons were bound to complete—bound by
covenant and precedent.

—Sacvan Bercovich

The revolution is here.
—Nike poster featuring Eddie Jones, Jimmy Jackson,
Jason Kidd, Joe Smith, Kevin Garnett, 1995

Jamie Barrett, copywriter for Wieden and Kennedy, ranks Jordan, "the ultimate sports icon of the generation," as the most meaningful and consequential presence in Nike's P.L.A.Y. campaign. Jordan's grace, physical
attributes, physical feats, and especially his apparent ability to defy gravity
(that is Jordan's "special-effect" hang time) have inspired a sense of awe as
he has captured America's imagination. His athletic abilities have brought
millions to their feet and have been met with thunderous ovations. Jordan
has been named the greatest basketball player to play the game, his talent
unsurpassed by any other player. "The ultimate sports icon of the generation," the title Barrett bestows on Jordan, is mild compared to those that circulate on a daily basis in the United States. Jordan is routinely glorified in
terms that render him extraordinary (thus his designation as "Rare Air")
and even godlike.

We are repeatedly told that America's respect and admiration for Jordan
are not simply responses to his basketball talents but to his character. Jordan
is seen as an uplifting figure, the personification of America's ideals, and a
symbol of America's dedication to excellence. That is, Jordan is seen as an
exemplary figure of America's cultural and political order and the embodiment of the abstract concepts and promises invoked by America (rights, justice, freedom, and community), the America that serves as the condition of
his possibility, achievements, and rewards. In the American imagination,
excellence and morality are intertwined—success and virtue are mutually signifying. Just as Jordan's success is a sign of his grace, the failure of others is a
sign of their depravity.

The most instructive phrases regarding Jordan's place in the national
imagination are related to the continual, varied, and widespread allusions to
his capacities for transcendence. For example, Nike public relations director
Liz Dolan argues that Nike does not think of Jordan in racial terms. In her
words, "We don't think of our athletes as black and white. We think of Mike

Jordan as the best basketball player in the world" (Grimm 1990). Similarly, *Ad Week* columnist Matthew Grimm (1990) writes, "Jordan's celebrity transcends any pigeonhole—race, sports or otherwise." The rhetoric of transcendence is tied to notions of exceptionalism that appear to distance Jordan from the semiotic field that locates and positions other African American men/players. Additionally, the repetition of transcendence masks the power/knowledge grid through which Jordan is made intelligible and through which American identities are constituted. While transcendence distances Jordan from the weight of history and positions him in the realm of the extraordinary, it simultaneously marks a moral designation.

It is under signs of transcendence and morality that apparently unrelated figures and spaces are brought together, coordinated, and unified, and that the broad networks of power that are Nike (transnational corporation) and America (political order) are given a face and a body. Jordan, situated as a national stereotype through the trope of transcendence, functions to mystify social realities in the name of the American project. The contingencies that underlie America's foundational categories are erased through Jordan: despite the historical and local particularities of the meanings he embodies, we imagine those meanings and values as abstract and transhistorical. Foucault's insights regarding modern power suggest that ignoring or underestimating the interdependence of identity categories works to conceal the violence manifest in images of self-unity. Lauren Berlant (1994) emphasizes how the national stereotype exceeds its function as a figure of imagined community because it

> masks this violence in images of self-unity, of the body's natural adequacy to the identity that names it violently . . . . [T]he national stereotype is a hybrid form, a form of feeling, of alienation and of sociality; the stereotype circulates between subjects who have power as a kind of cultural property they control; it circulates among minority subjects as both a site of masochistic identification (the minority/colonial subject as cultural property recognizes itself in the objective circulation of its own form); it is additionally a site of political power, of apparent magical embodiment, and of collective authority . . . . [W]hen the thing the national stereotype represents is a "minority" person, the ambivalences of the culture that circulates the form are brought to the fore, for the national minority stereotype makes exceptional the very person whose marginality, whose individual experience of collective cultural discrimination or difference, is the motive for his/her circulation as a collective icon in the first place. (156)

The interpretations and judgments shaped and authorized through American Jordan are especially pronounced through the *rhetoric of absence* that is deployed in P.L.A.Y.[24] Moreover, the narration of the absent transcendent figure illustrates how morality and excellence and deviance and surveillance are intertwined in the national imagination. That is, the rhetoric of absence provides an opportunity to examine how a national "we" is mobilized over and against those marked as others. In P.L.A.Y.'s closing questions, Jordan asks us to envision what/who he would be if there were no sports. The autobiographical element of the narrative is no longer denied, and, for the first time, we see Jordan. The questions, the response, and the image of Jordan tell us much about the knowledges that inform our understanding of Michael Jordan, the driving force behind P.L.A.Y. If we did not imagine American Jordan in the space of sport, where would we imagine him? What /who would we imagine? The rhetoric of absence is deployed to recall specific images that directly relate to how "nontranscendent" African American men are imagined in the realm of the popular. In this sense, Jordan is never simply an ideal, but an expression of invisible forces and dynamics that have shaped America's vexed relationship with African American men and reshaped the urban order. Michael Jordan embodies competing forms of black masculinity, one of which is produced through a space ordered by sport and over and against the values and identities associated with a sportless world, a distinction marked by a racialized, lawless urban-scape. Jordan's value is expressed through transformation, a transformation accomplished through sport. Here, we have a positive image and call to action: if we do not provide opportunities for kids, the next Michael Jordan may not appear. This racialized containment, expressed through America's imagination of what and who Michael Jordan would be had he strayed from sport, suggests that we need to rethink the national fantasy of childhood as that fantasy is rearticulated in P.L.A.Y.

P.L.A.Y. is most obviously represented as a tale of proper childhood and the transformation through sport from natural childhood to accomplished adulthood. But, in the P.L.A.Y. narrative, not all children are visualized through the trope of innocence. Although announced as a project for all of "America's kids," the concerns declared through P.L.A.Y., most vividly expressed through the crisis phrases "What if there were no sports? Would I still be your hero?" are expressly inscribed on the bodies of black youth. Black youth exist outside the discourse of innocence which is displaced by geography as certain "kids" are marked as sources of danger. Although race is not mentioned explicitly, blackness is invoked through contextual rhetoric. Black youth are rendered visible through a trope of desperation that indexes geographical location (inner city) and the youth who inhabit it (geographical/racial Other) as perpetual sites of deviance and threat. Whereas sport and physical activity are used to shore up America's bourgeois fantasy of childhood fun and play for white middle-class youth, sport and physical activity function to regulate, discipline, and police already deviant bodies in urban areas (deviant-normal transformation). For urban black youth, "childhood" is always already a compromised category. In the context of urban America, sport is not about kids' play and bodily movement, but a moral and normative imperative. Without sport (the socially sanctioned surrogate family), inner city youths are at once at risk from pressures from peers and the sources of danger. Our attention is once again directed to crime, law and order, discipline, and their correlates: gangs, drugs, sport, and Nike.

While P.L.A.Y. appears to break from popular discourses on crime and seemingly shifts the terms of the popular dialogue on inner city youth in the context of the dominant "get tough" and now the three-strikes approach, P.L.A.Y. makes sense and gains force and momentum through its appeal to and reliance on two figures that organize America's imagination. P.L.A.Y. is yet another expression of what /who we understand to be America's urban problems and how race is made to matter and not matter in the national imagination. Nike's call to make over America's cities and American childhood—Nike style—recalls not only Nike's social conscience but recalls *the* nationally imagined Other figured through those bodies of African American youth.

## American Jordan: Rituals of Consensus and Vengeful Desires

Agency belongs to a way of thinking about persons as instrumental actors who confront an external political field. But if we agree that politics and power exist already at the level at which the subject and its agency are articulated and made possible, than agency can be *presumed* only at the cost of refusing to inquire into its construction . . . . In a sense, the epistemological model that offers us a pregiven subject or agent is one that refuses to acknowledge that *agency is always and only a political prerogative.*

—Judith Butler

Michael Jordan's elevation to "national hero" is popularly represented as a sign of racial progress. As one of America's best-beloved icons and a central symbol of cohesion, it would seem that Jordan even holds the potential to stimulate a popular critical examination of the historical images and claims motivating the criminalization of African American men. Yet, the values and beliefs inscribed on and circulated through Jordan are not only incongruent but are intertwined with prominent ways of thinking about and seeing African American men. Lauren Berlant (1994) addresses the cultural work performed by exceptional figures such as Jordan:

In moments of intensified racism, homophobia, misogyny, and phobias about poverty, these "positive" icons of national minority represent both the minimum and the maximum of what the dominating cultures will sanction for circulation, exchange, and consumption. As iconic minority subjects, they prove to the hegemonic public the potentialities of the denigrated marginal mass population; as minority exceptions, they represent heroic autonomy from their very identity; as "impersonations" of minority identity, they embody the very ordinary conditions of subjective distortion that characterize marginality. Thus, there is no "authentic" or correct way to read the national stereotype as false consciousness: insofar as it is a ligament of sociality, its meaning must be indexed according to its particular origins and uses. (156)

P.L.A.Y., a promotional discourse generated by Nike, draws on and enacts codes implicated in America's authorizing categories, America's origin story, and imagined community. Promotional discourses such as P.L.A.Y. are appealing because they offer faith in America, in the American system, and the American way of life. Personal and national identities are both threatened ("What if there were no sports?") and secured in P.L.A.Y. as foundational categories such as responsibility and free will (which are under constant threat) are stabilized. In a period of high cynicism and in which people struggle every day to fulfill the need to be part of something meaningful, projects such as Nike's P.L.A.Y. provide feelings and opportunities that suggest that "we" (members of imagined community) can be, or are, part of something that makes a difference.

P.L.A.Y. is an element in America's ritual of consensus. "American Jordan" mediates America's "imaginary community" and embodies the abstract ideals associated with the American way of life and America's mythic origins. In P.L.A.Y., Americans are invited to look at Jordan to see the American mission, a body politic distinguished by its "chosen status." "American Jordan" is rendered intelligible through those values and principles that limit how we imagine power, agency, responsibility, and violence in late modern America. However, Jordan is not the essential embodiment of American ideals but a figure that has been used to represent and give concrete form to the abstract values and principles that govern America. The articulation of Jordan brings affect, stability, and anxiety to the experience of these categories. Perhaps then it would be more useful to move away from the idea that Michael Jordan has captured the American imagination; and, instead, consider how the American imagination has captured Jordan.

While Nike and Jordan are narrated as caring, compassionate, charitable, and virtuous, and while both are implicated in the liberal humanist themes of "self-made" and "made in America," both are products of transnational capital and its reorganization of America's urban economy and its associated problems. Such problems include urban renewal, loss of manufacturing jobs, defunding of welfare programs, infant mortality, overcrowded and substandard housing, the war on drugs, heightened police brutality, and phenomenal rates of incarceration. But the truths of "urban decay" and "violence" are displaced and located in the breakdown of the family and black urban youth. Indeed, modern power and its logic make it difficult to imagine anything else. While it is not my intention to simply dismiss gang crime and violence, it is my intention to demonstrate that such truths of violence can only be produced through a series of exclusions.

America's origin story, the legacy of destiny, and the rhetoric of the American way of life in which P.L.A.Y. is grounded erases the violences of America's founding. Such violences include U.S. Indian policy and racial slavery. As Connolly (1995) shows, the authority that is America, that is, America's founding categories (freedom, liberty, rights, justice, responsibility, and agency) forge a deceptive unity only through violence. While the meanings of such categories appear certain and while they operate as absolutes in what is presumed to be a universal language of democratic ideals, their contingencies and operations as universals within social and historical specificities can only be masked by "wasting" those who threaten to disturb them. Indeed, the sport/gang narrative animating P.L.A.Y. imagines sovereign agents who make choices about their fate: those who continue to participate in gangs could have just said no by just saying yes to sport. The violences of their conditions (produced through late capitalist dynamics and public policies bound to modern logic driven by the mythic family) are erased, as the incomprehensibility of their "crimes" mobilizes desire for revenge. Of course, the violences produced by transnationals like Nike cannot be contained within "America" but permeate numerous spatial zones and zones of production.

## Notes

1. See Lubiano (1996), for a useful discussion of media consumers' fascination with "real life" in urban America.

2. The desire for policing stands in stark contrast to previous understandings of the LAPD's relations to inner city neighborhoods. Davis (1990) provides an excellent overview of that historical relationship.

3. Truth-in-sentencing requires that 85 percent of the sentence be served.

4. There are two primary methods of collecting crime statistics: the UCR (Uniform Crime Report) and the NCVS (National Crime Victimization Survey). The UCR is compiled by the FBI and is based on the reports of 17,000 police departments. While the UCR is most often cited in the media because its state-by-state breakdown allows media and politicians to generate local stories, its statistics are highly misleading. Increases in crime cannot be separated from enhanced surveillance technology and record keeping and categorical discrepancies. The NCVS is compiled by the Census Bureau through polling techniques and is typically thought to provide a more accurate assessment of crime. For a discussion on the differences see Donzinger 1996.

5. The logic of corporeal capacities and the rhetorical appeals to a violent and destructive generation are implicated in the resurgence of neo-eugenic logic during the 1980s.

6. "The Negro Family: The Case for National Action" (1965), more commonly known as the *Moynihan Report,* initiated the scapegoating of the black family. This theme gained force during the 1980s through antiwelfare rhetoric and continues to be a site of ritual consensus. See Coontz (1992) and Gray (1989) for important examinations of that scapegoating.

7. I use the term *America* to represent the United States because of its historical link to myths of origin, imagined community, and rituals of consensus (as discussed by Bercovich 1993).

8. My understanding of imagined community, as the relations among the territorialization of space, ordered identities, and the moral order, is developed from Benedict Anderson (1983), Lauren Berlant (1991), and Homi Bhaba (1990). Work by Michael Rogin (1987) and Sacvan Bercovich (1993) are crucial to my understanding of the "American" project. Still, a Foucauldian-informed understanding of modern power, identity, and the body and a Derridean understanding of sovereignty and presence remain pivotal to my understanding of how discourse works.

9. Understanding the "American imagination" (its foundational categories of democracy, liberty, freedom, and historical legacies) is requisite to understanding how Americans see themselves in relation to the rest of the world as well as America's perception of a global desire for things American. For example, American mass media typically codify democratic movements in other countries through America's myth of origins: the thirty-foot-high goddess of democracy displayed in Tiananmen Square was represented by the mass media as a copy of the Statue of Liberty. I agree with Linda Zerilli (1995) who contends that the important issue is not whether the statue really was or was not a copy but the configuration of national identity invested in such representations.

10. The complexity of the visual domain is made evident in George Holliday's eightyone-second videotape of Rodney King being brutally beaten by four members of the LAPD and its interpretation by a jury. The video marks a moment in which America was confronted with evidence of the typically obscured policing practices and forms of violence regularly faced by African Americans. While the brutality and punitive excesses rendered visible on the videotape appeared to be unquestionable, the violence directed at the body of an African American man was seen and inverted to represent white vulnerability. For excellent discussions of this inversion, see Judith Butler's (1993) "Endangered/Endangering: Schematic Racism and White Paranoia" and the statement issued by the

Society for Cinema Studies (1992) published in *Jump Cut,* 37, 2. For a classic discussion of the visual order, subjectivity, and race, see Frantz Fanon's (1967) *Black Skin, White Masks.*

11. The ad-image combines a youth in a Jordan-in-flight pose and antidrug slogan inspired by the just-do-it philosophy (Elliot 1993).

12. Although Air Jordan was the nation's hottest athletic shoe since its introduction, its narrative prominence cannot be reduced, at least not in any simple way, to popularity. Although space constraints do not allow me to address this here, I want to point out that appearance of Air Jordan in Spike Lee films and hip-hop culture are important dimensions of their popularity and narration. Of course, the most important element in its recruitment to center stage was Jordan and his position in the American imagination.

13. The distance from "trouble" and criminalized African American youth is crucial to processes of consumer identification. This is discussed in detail in relation to Magic Johnson in Cole 1996 and Cole and Denny 1995; and in relation to Jordan in Andrews, 1996 and Cole and Andrews 1995.

14. Nike responded by initiating its now common practice of using athletes to do some sort of "public service message" (S. W. Coleford 1990). In response to controversies created by sneaker crimes, including associations between Nike and drug monies, Nike initiated a $5 million series of antidrug, stay-in-school ads featuring Michael Jordan and David Robinson. The ads functioned to contain the popular identity of athletes as distinct and distant from dangerous and criminal youth. Moreover, they are located as key components in the solution rather than part of the problem.

15. In 1980, Operation PUSH had mobilized a forty-day boycott of Coca-Cola which resulted in the first black-owned franchise and $30 million directed to black-owned businesses. Over the next decade the organization had a lower profile and concentrated on local issues because of Jackson's concentration on Washington politics.

16. Although presented as a new project, the P.L.A.Y. campaign clearly draws from and builds on a broader series of projects directed at urban youth and recreation. For example, the National Association of Midnight Basketball was founded in 1986 by G. Van Standifer. In 1993, more than 120,000 youths participated in the Inner City Games, founded by Danny Hernandez, in Los Angeles and Atlanta. The Inner City Games gained notoriety when the host community in Los Angeles was left untouched during the L.A. rebellions. Other programs presented as alternatives to gangs and linked to crime prevention include The Judo Challenge, Soccer in the Street, and locally based projects such as Denver's Night Moves, Dayton's R.I.S.K. (Recreation-Intervention Supports Kids), Fayetteville's T.E.A.M. (Teaching-Exercising-Alternatives-Mainstreaming). Additionally, corporations such as the Sporting Goods Manufacturers Association support R.B.I. (Reviving Baseball in the Inner City). The logic that supports sports as crime prevention and as an alternative to gangs was endorsed by Surgeon General Joycelyn Elders who argued for sport as a means to develop "positive gangs." In addition to drawing from and building on the momentum from these programs and the popular logic already in place, P.L.A.Y. repackages advertisements and other contributions already made by Nike and Michael Jordan. For example, Jordan and Nike each contributed $100,000 to the Marcus Palmer Foundation, a foundation that addresses the school funding crisis in Chicago by intervening in cuts that would eliminate afterschool programs for high school students.

17. Although the Nike swoosh still holds the greatest cultural currency, the P.L.A.Y. logo has gained currency and appears regularly as Nike's signature on televised sport events and other programs. Nike appears to be deploying a number of logos to manage its different consumer markets including All Condition Gear, P.L.A.Y., and most recently, variations on the swoosh.

18. Nike entered into a working relationship with Dodge-Regupol, a Pennsylvania-based corporation that specializes in recycling rubber products and producing products from rubber scraps, polymers, and additives, in order to refurbish the playgrounds.

19. The decline in sales was attributed to the increasing popularity of sturdy leather boots and outdoor shoes. Nike's "recovery" has been attributed to a resurgence in basketball shoe sales and the successful development of Nike's outdoor line, All Condition Gear (Trumbull 1995a).

20. For an excellent critique of the limitations of sport and fitness as means to improve quality of life, see Ingham 1985.

21. For a discussion of relation between post-Fordism and the conditions of Chicago's South Side, see Wacquant (1994).

22. See Frederick Dolan (1994), *Allegories in America,* for a discussion of the historical codification of the American body in terms of vibrancy, spontaneity, and life, and the un-American body in terms of death.

23. Here, I am referring to Nike's popular biography, how Nike has forged particular connections to manage its position as "celebrity" in public culture. In brief, Nike imagines itself as "American" and through a story in which its dominance is linked to self-making and social progress. This is especially apparent in its women's campaign and more recently in its "The revolution won't be televised, basketball is the truth" campaign. For a discussion of Nike women's campaign and Nike as celebrity, see Cole and Hribar (1995).

24. Jordan's absence from the NBA (his first retirement) vividly demonstrates his location in knowledges that produce racially codified deviance. Coverage focused on what/who "we" see in a "generation" of players in the absence of the transcendent figure. Not surprisingly the players are narrated through tropes of danger and violence; marked by a historically unprecedented skill deficiency, lack of productivity and discipline; driven by pathological psyches and infantilized consumer habits. In sum, the loss of excellence is equated to loss of moral excellence. Family is deployed rhetorically to explain what/who they are and who they offend. The narration of lost excellence also claims that this generation of NBA players is responsible for interrupting the NBA's continuous popularity and prosperity. Following the lead of several high-profile articles that assessed and classified the NBA as a national sore, popular author and journalist Terry Pluto (1995) published the NBA's version of the most reactionary and popular attacks on multiculturalism and the corresponding crisis it has generated in America, Alan Bloom's (1987) *Closing of the American Mind* and Dinesh D'Souza's (1991) *Illiberal Education.* In *A Fall from Grace,* Terry Pluto raised questions about the NBA's destiny and its ability to sustain its popularity and financial growth. As Pluto's title suggests, and echoing the already familiar demonization and criminalization of NBA players, Pluto predicted the NBA's calamitous future, even its rapid deterioration, as the result of misguided behaviors, egotism, and corrupt souls. Finally, the rhetoric of absence suggested that the NBA's destiny relied on the ability to locate and

recognize another Jordan, another player "touched by grace," another player clearly distinguished from the rank and file NBA players. Again, Jordan's normalizing function was made clear in a question repeatedly asked in his absence "Who will be the next Jordan?" along with its accompanying metaphors of crisis, spirit, soul, and grace. The search was for another player who transcended the gravitational pull to and by which other players were subjected and restricted; another player who displaced historical limits and violences would work as a counterforce to halt the moral decay by distancing the NBA from pariahs of racial deviance. The message was clear: if players are virtuous they will rise—we will know who they are because their success will be a sign of their grace. The narration of the struggle as one between the sacred and profane, in which biblical metaphors were increasingly prominent, is telling given America's origin myth.

This is a short answer to big, but interesting questions. Andrews 1996 and Cole and Andrews 1995 offer preliminary answers to this question. We address what motivates this outrage (over relatively minor infractions) in Cole and Andrews 1996.

# References

Anderson, B. (1983). *Imagined communities: Reflections on the origins and spread of nationalism*. London: Verso.

Andrews, D. L. (1996). "The fact(s) of Michael Jordan's blackness: Excavating a floating racial signifier," *Sociology of Sport Journal*, 16(2), 125–158.

———. (1997). "The (Trans)National Basketball Association: America's commodity sign culture and global localization." In *Articulating the global and the local. Globalization and cultural studies*, ed. A. Cvetkovich and D. Kellner, 72–101. Boulder: Westview Press.

Andrews, D. L., and C.L. Cole. (eds.) *NikeNation: Technology of an American sign*. Manuscript in preparation.

Anners, J. (1995). "Crime and safety: Community voices in the national debate," *Social Policy* 25:22–26.

Baron, K., M. Corcoran, B. Ivry, A. E. Kornblut, R. Regen, T. Sutton, and S. Williams. (1996). "The 30 most powerful twentysomethings in America," *SWING*, January, 34–59.

Bellah, R. N., R. Madsen, W. M. Sullivan, A. Swidler, and S. M. Tipton. (1985). *Habits of the heart: Individualism and commitment in American life*. New York: Harper and Row.

Berlant, L. (1991). *The anatomy of national fantasy: Hawthorne, utopia, and everyday life*. Chicago: University of Chicago Press.

———. (1994). "America, fat, and the fetus," *Boundary 2*, 21(3):145–195.

Bercovich, S. (1993). *The rites of assent: Transformations in the symbolic construction of America*. New York: Routledge.

Bhaba, H. (ed.) (1990). *Nation and narration*. London: Routledge.

Bloom, A. (1987). *The closing of the American mind.* New York: Simon & Schuster.

Brown, W. (1995). *States of injury.* Princeton: Princeton University Press.

Burwell, B. (1994). "Get real, purists: Jordan is baseball seasons' savior," *USA Today,* October 7, C-3.

Butler, J. (1992). "Contingent foundations: Feminism and the question of postmodernism," In *Feminists theorize the political,* ed. J. Butler and J. Scott, 3–21. New York: Routledge.

——. (1993). "Endangered/endangering: Schematic racism and white paranoia." In *Reading Rodney King: Reading urban uprising,* ed. R. Gooding-Williams, 178–195. New York: Routledge.

Campbell, C. P. (1995). *Race, myth, and the news.* Newberry Park, CA: Sage.

Carby, H. (1993). "Encoding white resentment: *Grand Canyon*—A narrative of our time." In *Race identity and representation in education,* ed. C. McCarthy and W. Crichlow, 236–250. New York: Routledge.

Cole, C.L. (1996). "P.L.A.Y., Nike, and Michael Jordan: National fantasy and the racialization of crime and punishment," *Working Papers in Sport and Leisure Commerce* 1(1), University of Memphis.

Cole, C.L., and D. L. Andrews. (1996). *Policing the NBA: The reconfiguration of black masculinity in late modern America.* Paper to be presented at the annual meetings for the North American Society for the Sociology of Sport, Birmingham.

——. (1996). "'Look—It's NBA *ShowTime!*': Visions of race in the popular imaginary," *Cultural Studies: A Research Volume,* 1:141–181.

Cole, C.L., and H. Denny. (1994). "Visualizing deviance in post-Reagan America: Magic Johnson, AIDS, and the promiscuous world of professional sport," *Critical Sociology* 20(3):123–147.

Cole, C.L., and A. Hribar. (1995). "Celebrity feminism: *Nike Style* (Post-Fordism, physical transcendence, and consumer power)," *Sociology of Sport Journal,* 12(4):247–269.

Cole, C.L., and M. Orlie. (1995). "Hybrid athletes, monstrous addicts, and cyborg natures," *Journal of Sport History,* 22(3):229–239.

Coleford, S.W. (1990). "Athlete endorsers fouled by slayings," *Advertising Age,* March 19, 64–65.

Conniff, R. (1996). "Meet the kids in teen lockup," *The Progressive,* February, 27–29.

Connolly, W. E. (1995). *The ethos of pluralization.* Minneapolis: University of Minnesota Press.

Coontz, S. (1992). *The way we never were. American families and the nostalgia trap.* New York: Basic Books.

D'Souza, D. (1991). *Illiberal education: The politics of race and sex on campus.* New York: The Free Press.

Davis, M. (1990). *City of quartz: Excavating the future in Los Angeles.* London: Verso.

Denzin, N. (1991). *Images of postmodern society.* London: Sage.

DeSalvo, K. (1994). "The P.L.A.Y.-ers: Wieden and Kennedy, Palomar Pictures," *Shoot,* April 15, 12.

Dolan, F. (1994). *Allegories of America.* Ithaca: Cornell University Press.

Dooley, M. (1996). "The next level of graffiti," *Print,* May, 82–89.

Donzinger, S.R. (ed.) (1996). *The real war on crime: The report of the National Criminal Justice*

*Commission*. New York: HarperCollins Publishers.

Dumm, T. L. (1993). "The new enclosures: Racism in the normalized community." In *Reading Rodney King: Reading urban uprising*, ed. R. Gooding-Williams, 178–195. New York: Routledge.

Dyson, M. (1993). "Be like Mike: Michael Jordan and the pedagogy of desire," *Cultural Studies*, 7(1): 64–72.

Elden, J. (1995). "Drug sentencing frenzy," *The Progressive*, 59(4):25.

Elliot, S. (1993). "The partnership for a drug-free America accentuates the positive in a new campaign," *New York Times*, October 1, C-16.

Fanon, F. (1967). *Black skin, white masks*. New York: Grove Weidenfeld.

Flannery, P. (1994). "Barkley turns role model; new tv ad targets teen violence," *The Phoenix Gazette*, A-1.

Foucault, M. (1979). *Discipline and punish: The birth of a prison*. trans. A. Sheridan. New York: Vintage Books.

———. (1980a). *The history of sexuality*, Vol., I, Trans. R. Hurley, New York: Vintage Books.

———. (1980b). "Truth and power." In *Power/knowledge: Selected interviews and other writings, 1972–1977*, ed. C. Gordan, 109–133. New York: Pantheon.

———. (1980c). "Two lectures." In *Power/knowledge: Selected interviews and other writings, 1972–1977*, ed. C. Gordan, 78–108. New York: Pantheon.

———. (1989). "What calls for punishment?" In *Foucault live*, ed. S. Lotringer, 280–292. New York: Semiotext(e).

Fraser, N. (1995). "Clintonism, welfare, and the anti-social wage: The emergence of a neo-liberal political imaginary." In *Marxism in the post-modern age: Confronting the new world order*, ed. A. Callari, S.Cullenberg, and C. Biewener, 493–505. New York: The Guilford Press.

Garfield, B. (1992). "Nike scores points with Spike's unity plea," *Advertising Age*, June 8, 50.

Gest, T., and V. Pope. (1996). "Crime time bomb," *US News and World Report*, March 25, 28–36.

Goals 2000: Educate America Act. (1994, March 31). Public Law (20 USC 5801, 103–227).

Gray, H. (1995). *Watching race: Television and the struggle for blackness*. Minneapolis: University of Minnesota Press.

———. (1989). "Television, black Americans, and the American dream." *Critical Studies in Mass Communication*, 6:376–386.

Grimm, M. (1990). "Don't blame sneakers for inner-city crime," *Adweek's Marketing Week*, 31(19): 65.

———. (1994). "Nike reinvests in child's P.L.A.Y.," *Brandweek*, March 28, 9.

Hetter, K. (1996). "A Pittsburgh court battles the tide," *US News and World Report*, March 25, 37–38.

Hudson, G. (1990, May 9). "Getting hooked up with drug dealers," *WWJ-News Radio 95*: Detroit, MI.

Hume, S. (1990). "Boycott of Nike ignored," *Advertising Age*, October 29, 59.

Ingham, A. (1985). "From public issues to personal trouble: Well being and the fiscal crisis of the state," *Sociology of Sport Journal,* 2:43–55.

Jensen, J. (1994). "Nike comes out to PLAY," *Advertising Age,* March 28, 3,42.

Junod, T. (1995). "The savior," *GQ,* April, 170–175, 238–240.

Katz, D. (1994). *Just do it.* New York: Random House.

Lacayo, R. (1994). "Lock 'em up!" *Time,* February 7, 50–53.

Lubiano, W. (1996). "But compared to what?" In *Representing black men,* ed. M. Blount and G. P. Cunningham, 173–204. New York: Routledge.

Magiera, M. (1990). "Nike taps minority shop," *Advertising Age,* November 19, 15.

Males, M., and F. Docuyanan. (1996). "Crackdown on kids: Giving up on the young," *The Progressive,* 60(2): 24–26.

Marsh, J. (1990). *SCMP* (Nike Advertising Oral History and Documentation Project c. 1976–1992, Series 1- Subseries B, Center for Advertising History, National Museum of American History, Smithsonian Institution).

Massing, M. (1995). "Ghetto blasting," *The New Yorker,* January 16, 32–37.

McCarthy, C. (1995). *Reading the American popular: Suburban resentment and the representation of the inner city in contemporary film and t.v.* Paper presented at the Unit for Criticism and Interpretive Theory Colloquium Series, UIUC.

Miller, C. (1992). "Advertisers promote racial harmony; Nike criticized," *Marketing News,* July 6, 1.

Miller, J. (1996). *Search and destroy: African-American males in the criminal justice system.* Cambridge: University of Cambridge Press.

Mushnick, P. (1990). "Your shoes or your life," *New York Post,* March 2.

Nietzsche, F. (1986). *Human, all too human.* trans. R. J. Holingdale, New York: Cambridge University Press.

Orlie, M. (1995). "Forgiving trespasses, promising future." In *Feminist interpretations of Hannah Arendt,* ed. B. Honig, 337-356, University Park: Pennsylvania State University Press.

P.L.A.Y. (1994). [Brochure]. Beaverton, OR: Nike, Inc.

Parenti, C. (1996). "Making prisons pay," *The Nation,* January 26, 11–14.

Parenti, M. (1986). *Inventing reality: The politics of the mass media.* New York: St. Martin's Press.

Pluto, T. (1995). *Falling from grace: Can pro-basketball be saved?* New York: Simon & Schuster.

Raspberry, W. (1990). "When PUSH comes to shove," *Washington Post,* August 26, A-25

Reeves, J. L., R. Campbell and (1994). *Cracked coverage: Television news, the anti-cocaine crusade, and the Reagan legacy.* Durham: Duke University Press.

Reid, R. (1995). "'Death of the family,' or, keeping human beings human," In *Posthuman bodies,* ed. J. Halberstam and I. Livingstone, 177–199. Bloomington: University of Indiana Press.

Riggs, M. (1991). *Color adjustment* [Film]. San Francisco: California Newsreel.

Rogin, M. (1987). *Ronald Reagan: The movie.* Berkeley: University of California Press.

Rose, T. (1994). *Black noise.* Hanover, NH: Wesleyan Press of New England.

———. (1995). "Rap music and the demonization of young black males." In *Black male,* ed. T. Golden, 149–158. New York: Harry N. Abrams.

Smolowe, J. (1994). ". . . and throw away the key," *Time,* February 7, 54–59.

Society for Cinema Studies. (1992). "Statement on the Rodney King verdict," *Jump Cut,* 37, 2.

Stein, B. (1995). "Cops make crack in California," *The Progressive* 59(4): 22–24.

Swift, E. M. (1994). "Why the NHL's hot and the NBA's not," *Sports Illustrated,* June 20, 30–40.

Taylor, P. (1995). "Bad actors," *Sports Illustrated,* January 20, 18–23.

Teaford, E., and R. Yount. (1987). "Drug money—selling out of a generation," *Los Angeles Times,* June 24, III1, III8.

Telander, R. (1990). "Senseless," *Sports Illustrated,* May 14, 36–49.

Terry, J., and J. Urla (1995). *Deviant bodies.* Bloomington: University of Indiana Press.

Trumbull, M. (1995a). "Nike regains its sales footing," *Christian Science Monitor,* January 30, 8.

———. (1995b). "Recycling program turns new shoes into new inner city playground," *Christian Science Monitor,* January 30, 8.

U.S. Department of Justice. (1995, August). *Prisoners in 1994.* (NCJ-151654). Washington, D. C.: U.S. Government Printing Office.

Venkatesh, S. A. (1994, August). *Black gangs and the reconstitution of "community" in an urban ghetto.* Paper presented at the annual meetings of the American Sociological Association, Los Angeles.

Wacquant, L. J. D. (1994). "The new urban color line: The state and fate of the ghetto in postFordist America." In *Social theory and the politics of identity,* ed. C. Calhoun, 231–276. Oxford: Blackwell.

Wynter, L. E. (1990). "Sneaker makers face scrutiny from PUSH," *Wall Street Journal,* July 19, B-1 .

Yount, R., and E. Teaford. (1987a). "The killing fields: In some L.A. County schools, it's a matter of life and death," *Los Angeles Times,* June 23, III1, III4.

———. (1987b). "Coaches fight recruiting war of different nature," *Los Angeles Times,* June 25, III1, III12.

Zerilli, L. (1995). *Sexual difference and the democratic symbolic: Reflections on the Statue of Liberty.* Paper presented at the annual meetings of the American Political Science Association, Chicago.

# part III

# JORDAN

## and Identity Politics

**5**

# The Fact(s) of Michael Jordan's Blackness: Excavating a Floating Racial Signifier

## David L. Andrews

The fact of Michael Jordan's blackness, to paraphrase Frantz Fanon (1967), is arguably one of the most pivotal, yet strangely overlooked, questions posed by contemporary American culture. In spite of the pervasiveness of the crass color-blind credo so gleefully expressed by Jerry Reinsdorf, owner of the Chicago Bulls, "Is Michael Jordan black? . . . Michael has no color" (quoted in Kornbluth 1995, 26), close examination of Michael Jordan's popular signification reveals a complex narrative incorporating many of the historically grounded racial codes that continue to structure the racial formation of the United States. Far from his racial identity being nonexistent, or extraneous to his social and cultural significance, the imaged persona of Michael Jordan represents an important site of mediated popular culture at which particular racial ideologies are publicized and authorized in support of the multiple inclusions and exclusions that delineate the post-Reaganite American imaginary. Jordan's image exemplifies what Reeves and Campbell (1994, 49) identified as "a spectacle of surveillance that is actively engaged in representing authority, visualizing deviance, and publicizing common sense" in a way that has profound implications for the structuring, disciplining, and experiencing of race in contemporary America. For this reason, Michael Eric Dyson was wholly correct in contending that Jordan is "a supremely instructive figure for our times" (1993, 71).

While asserting the central importance of Jordan's racial identity, it is also necessary to underscore that his covert racial signification has displayed a distinct lack of uniformity; a condition of instability that clearly corroborates

This chapter was originally published in the *Sociology of Sport Journal,* 13(2), 1996: 125–158. It is reprinted by permission of Human Kinetics Publishers.

Grossberg's poststructuralist leitmotif that "no element within the cultural field has an identity of its own which is intrinsic to it and thus guaranteed in advance" (1992, 39). As Hall noted, anticipating his notion of a conjunctural "Marxism without Guarantees" (Hall 1983), there are no necessary correspondences, or for that matter noncorrespondences, between meanings and cultural symbols:

> The meaning of a cultural form and its place or position in the cultural field is not fixed once and forever . . . . The meaning of a cultural symbol is given in part by the social field into which it is incorporated, the practices with which it articulates and is made to resonate. (Hall 1981, 235)

As a cultural construct, Jordan's mediated racial identity is neither stable, essential, nor consistent; it is dynamic, complex, and contradictory. Thus, it is perhaps more accurate to refer to the facts of Michael Jordan's blackness, and to assert his status as a floating racial signifier who, in Derridean terms, is constantly under erasure (Derrida 1978).

Borrowing judiciously from cultural studies, poststructural, and postmodern theorizing, this project is prefigured on the understanding of subjectivity as being constantly (re)formed through individual subjects shifting and unpredictable engagements (either corroborative, oppositional, ambivalent, or complex permutations of all three) with the telediscursive texts that infuse everyday lives within America's ocular democracy (see Baudrillard 1988; Clarke 1991; Dery 1993). The dominant vectors of the popular media represent points at which power intersects with discourse in an attempt to normalize, and thereby constitute, particular subject positions and the specific forms of authority associated with them (Giroux 1994; Hall 1994). With this in mind it is of vital importance to delineate the popular discursive economies that, through dialectic engagement, have a necessarily profound effect upon the formation and experience of human subjectivity. Hence, this chapter is designed to contribute toward the project of critical media literacy (Giroux 1992, 1994; Kellner 1991, 1995; and McLaren 1993, 1994), which encourages/implores readers to question, both in a specific and broader sense, their engagement with the popular media and the effects of such engagements on the creation of the subjective understandings of racial selves and others that have such a profound effect upon the structure and experiencing of everyday life (see Cole and Denny 1995). The aim of this chapter is to provide a contextual interpretation of the dominant racial discourses that have fashioned the mediated icon, Michael Jordan, in accordance with the shifting imperatives of the reactionary post-Reaganite cultural agenda. More specifically, this chapter examines how the racial meaning and significance of

Michael Jordan is perpetually being deferred in light of the endless chain of racial signifiers that have been attached to his signified image, through the conjunctural and intertextual machinations of the popular print and electronic media. Consequently, I hope to develop a critical understanding of Michael Jordan that highlights "the elasticity and the emptiness of 'racial' signifiers as well as the ideological work which has to be done in order to turn them into signifiers in the first place" (Gilroy 1991, 39), and thereby disrupts the notion of essential systems of racial differentiation and instead confronts race as a conjuncturally informed, and materially manifest, discursive construct (see Smith 1994). However, before reconstructing the sequential complexities of Michael Jordan's racial articulation, it is first necessary to provide a concise genealogy of the shifting aggregates of popular racial discourse engaged by this process.

## An Abbreviated Genealogy of Popular Racial Signification

As Omi and Winant (1994) persuasively argued, the European *conquest* of America initiated the implementation of a racial formation project that is still informing the everyday lives of contemporary Americans. As a result it is necessary to delve into the recesses of European colonialism in order to exhume the derivations of contemporary racial discourse. Although Williams's hypothesis that "slavery was not born of racism: rather, racism was the consequence of slavery" (1961, 6), provided an insightful, if exaggerated, commentary on the emergence of race-based discrimination, it crucially overlooked the presence of earlier European representations of Africans (Miles 1989). It is perhaps more accurate to contend that these earlier "relatively disorganized" (Omi and Winant 1994, 62) representations of Africanness were subsequently rearticulated within the project of slavery. During the eighteenth century, in order to justify the process of systemic slavery (Blackburn 1988) required of plantation-based colonial capitalism, an overtly racist discourse developed which substantiated the *African* as a distinctive racial Other. The significatory violence (Derrida 1981) of this burgeoning racial biotechnology effectively legitimated the practices of economic exploitation, and corporal brutality, meted out against enslaved populations within North America and the Caribbean.

Justifying the dehumanization of the African Other was particularly necessary in light of the collective celebration of freedom and equality that marked the bourgeois revolutions of the eighteenth century, and ushered in the adolescence of industrial capitalism:

> Capitalism's reliance on slave labour became an anomaly requiring explana-
> tion. It was in this context that the idea blacks were subhuman, and there-
> fore did not demand the equal respect that was increasingly acknowledged
> as the right of human beings, began to take hold. (Callinicos 1993, 28)

The required bipolar distinction between the European American Self and
the African (American) Other was realized through the mobilization of a system of previously identified, if not fully developed, stereotypical differences,
which generated an economy of antithetical racial signifiers. As Gilman eloquently noted:

> Stereotypes are a crude set of mental representations of the world. They
> are palimpsets on which the initial bipolar representations are still vague-
> ly legible. They perpetuate a needed sense of difference between the "self"
> and the "object" which becomes the "Others." Because there is no real
> line between self and the Other, an imaginary line must be drawn; and so
> that the illusion of an absolute difference between self and Other is never
> troubled, this line is as dynamic in its ability to alter itself as is the self.
> (1985, 17–18)

The conflation and subsequent promotion of phenotypical and sociocultural
characteristics, as compelling evidence of the inferior status of the African
(American) Other, was crucial to the establishment of suggestive racial stereotypes. Distinctions between *them* and *us* were thus enforced through the popular representation of the savage, bestial, and uncivilized black African, in *différance*
to the restrained, cerebral, and civilized white European American. In this way
a racial hierarchy was implemented that justified systemic slavery to the popular imagination on both sides of the North Atlantic. As the noted Scottish
Enlightenment philosopher David Hume stated, "I am apt to suspect the
negroes, and in general all the other species of men (for there are four or five
different kinds) to be naturally inferior to the whites" (quoted in Callinicos
1993, 24). In a similar vein, Thomas Jefferson pronounced, "[T]he blacks,
whether originally a different race, or made distinct by time and circumstances,
are inferior to the whites" (quoted in Omi and Winant 1994, 64).

Although modern racist discourse developed in tandem with the institution of slavery, the widespread abolition of slavery during the course of the
nineteenth century did not result in the demise of racist discourse. Indeed, the
forces of scientific hegemony and accelerated Western imperial expansion,
which dominated the post-Enlightenment world, combined to regenerate and
scientize racist ideology in justifying the subjugation of peoples of color
within the various Imperial orders. Through the spurious appropriation of
Darwinian theorizing related to the evolution of species, nineteenth-century
racial science advanced race classifications that announced the "superiority of

the white races over the rest in the process of natural selection" (Callinicos 1993, 17). The spread of such popular scientific racial mythologizing (Fryer 1984) resulted in the phenotypical and sociocultural differences embodied within dominant European representations of the African Other, becoming the focus of scientific investigations intent on identifying inherent, natural, and unalterable biological differences of race (Miles 1989). The scientizing of race, keying on factors such as skin color, hair type, nose shape, and most concertedly cranial dimension and capacity, classified human beings into biologically distinct types, which were strategically grafted to equally distinct psychological and sociocultural characteristics around which the hierarchy of races was formulated. As Giroux noted:

> In this racism, the Other's identity warrants its very annihilation because it is seen as impure, evil, and inferior. Moreover, whiteness represents itself as a universal marker for being civilized and in doing so posits the Other within the language of pathology, fear, madness, and degeneration. (1994, 75)

In other words, "savagery became a fixed condition for the 'Negro' or African 'race', a product of a small brain, and civilization became an attribute of large brained 'white' people" (Stocking 1968, quoted in Miles 1989, 33).

Dominant theories of race, based upon the demeaning conflation of sociocultural and phenotypical differences, were granted further legitimacy with the emergence of genetic science in the late nineteenth and early twentieth centuries. As Dumm surmised, "With the emergence of both evolutionary theory and the science of genetics in the nineteenth century, biological theories of race with their specious logic of genetic inferiority came to the fore and dominated 'scientific' discussions of racial difference" (1993, 181). Vanguarded at least initially by the eugenics movement founded by Darwin's cousin, Francis Galton, geneticists sought to identify precise definitions of race by searching for consistent patterns of genetic constitution, which would subsequently account for the disparate patterns of *natural* evolution experienced by the different races. The teleological nature of early genetic science meant that as well as being greatly informed by them, this burgeoning scientific discourse unwittingly corroborated the residual stereotypes and representations that structured racial hierarchies throughout the Western-influenced world; racial Otherness was now classified in terms of interconnected sociocultural, phenotypical, *and* genotypical differences. As well as being a constituent component of imperialist ideologies, racial genetics found an accommodating audience within the climate and institutions of sanctioned segregation, which marked the postabolitionist American racial formation. As Omi and Winant noted, "In the wake of civil war and emancipation, and with immigration from southern and Eastern Europe as well as East Asia running high, the U.S. was particularly fertile ground for notions such as social Darwinism and eugenics" (1994, 64). The subsequent popularization of hierarchically organized genetic classifications of race provided seemingly rigorous and incontrovertible "scientific" support for the commonsense understandings of racial difference that had invaded popular American consciousness.

Throughout this abbreviated genealogy of racial discourse it should be stressed that, at any given time, the production of (racial) knowledge was not generated by some rational, objective epistemology, rather, it was (and indeed is) contingent upon the conjunctural manifestations and subjective interpretations of power, conflict, and struggle. So it was in the immediate post–World War II era, when the notion of racial classifications as fixed, stable, and hierarchically ordered biological entities became widely discredited within the scientific community. After all, such thinking had provided the philosophical and scientific rationale for the genocidal project of the Third Reich (Mosse 1978). Within this epoch, the notion of biologically distinct races was exploded by the advances made in the field of genetic science, which identified that the genetic variation *within* the so-called races was more significant than the genetic variation *between* these tenuous classifications (Lewontin, Rose, and Kamin 1984; Omi and Winant 1994). Put simply, the maturation of genetic science renounced the notion of objectively verifiable racial groupings as having any basis in biological science. The understanding of race as a biologically constituted classification was superseded by a philosophy predicated on the comprehension of race "not [as] a biologically given but rather [as] a socially constructed way of differentiating human beings" (Omi and Winant 1994, 65).

As within previous historic/scientific ruptures, the demise of dominant ideas of race did not result in the disappearance of racially based conceptualizing. Instead theories of race shifted emphasis and epistemological domains, relocating from the rigid absolutism of the *hard* natural sciences, to the correlational projections of the *soft* social sciences. In Dumm's (1993) view this shift was associated with the widespread repudiation of arguments prefigured upon notions of an essential racial hierarchy. In their place, Dumm identified an alternative investigative logic centered upon the articulation of racial phenotypes to "whatever behavior the racist wishes to attribute to the other, whether it be passivity and laziness or violent hyperactivity" (1993, 181). Dumm's understanding that race became a "marker tied to a series of associated social phenomena" (1993, 181) is partially instructive, however, it downplays the politically charged nature of this moment in the evolution of racial discourse. The social scientists at the forefront of this line of research clearly overlooked the extent to which racial hierarchies had invaded the popular (sub)consciousness—especially their own. This led to a blatant disregard for the influence that the deep rooted and naturalized notions of an inherent racial order had upon the planning, design, implementation, and analysis, of race-based social scientific research projects. Race was uncritically engaged and analyzed as "a normalizing category that uses a shorthand of visible markers to communicate its separations" (Dumm 1993, 182). As a consequence, the seductive scientific "objectivity" of this brand of racially focused social scientific research resulted, not in the destabilizing of an essential racial order, but in its active, if unintended, reinforcement.

The racially oriented social scientific research of the postwar era keyed on investigating the perceived diseased, polluted, and corrupted nature of the racial Other (Gilman 1985). As with any other manifestation of racial pathologizing, this racially corrupt social scientific epistemology fortified the stereotypical markers through which the racial self had come to be defined. This substantial and influential body of work thus reinscribed the pathologizing "line drawn between the 'good' and 'bad'"; the normal and the deviant, the cerebral and the physical, the controlled and the violent, the healthy and the diseased, the white and the black (Gilman 1985, 23). As Gilman (1985, 25) concluded, "In 'seeing' (constructing a representational system for) the Other, we search for anatomical signs of difference such as physiognomy and skin color . . . [which] are always the antithesis of the idealized self," and which became stereotypical signifiers of the pathologized racial Other.

The work of criminologists James Q. Wilson and Richard Herrnstein represents a lucid example of the pathologizing social scientific racism that came to the fore in the 1950s, and which still comfortably resides in many fields of inquiry (most recently expounded in Herrnstein and Murray's [1994] pernicious tome). In 1985 Wilson and Herrnstein published what became a standard work in the field of criminology, and a significant contribution to popular discourse related to criminal behavior. These, and other, conservative architects of the American New Right's punitive law and order agenda focused on racial variations in violent crime rates, and identified people of color as being significantly more likely to commit violent criminal acts than members of the white majority (Dumm 1993). Wilson and Herrnstein's (1985) reactionary thesis pivoted on a predictable relationship between biological characteristics and violent behavior. This borrowed from W. H. Sheldon's classification of somatotypes, which identified the athletic, prominently musculatured, mesomorph as the body type that displayed a greater propensity for aggressive, violent, criminal behavior. This questionable linkage was racialized by Wilson and Herrnstein's heavily implied correlation between the African American male and the mesomorphic somatotype, which stigmatized the African American male as being pathologically aggressive, violent, and criminal:

> Wilson and Herrnstein follow the lead of (or perhaps, they themselves lead) mainstream modern criminology, dividing populations into the normal and the pathological, reinforcing views of the "abnormality" of minorities, and intensifying a general interpretive framework for criminalizing "otherness." (Dumm 1993, 182)

As previously noted, Wilson and Herrnstein's racist criminology significantly informed the instantiation of the racist popular politics of the American New Right, which Denzin (1991, 7) and Giroux (1994, 75) described as the "new cultural racism."

The Reaganite project united the diverse armatures of the New Right through the promotion of cultural rather than overtly political strategies (Grossberg 1992). By locating itself in the formations of popular sentiment, Reaganism evolved into an affectively oriented mediated project that downplayed ideological politicking in order to "inaugurate a new national popular through restructuring our investments in the sites of the popular" (Grossberg 1988, 32). Moreover, the New Right's emotive manifesto became inscribed on Reagan's hyperreal body, which became a simulated embodiment of American popular politics. As the most visible corporeal structure in an "era of bodies" (Jeffords 1994, 25), Reagan came to signify the "hard body" ideology of the hypermasculine assertive, decisive, and aggressive cultural politics to which he gave his name. This political identity was strategically formulated in contrast to the passive, weak, and indecisive "soft body" politics embodied by Jimmy Carter and the Carter regime, which was deemed responsible for plunging America into political, economic, military, and moral decline (Jeffords 1994).

During the 1980s, the domineering and reactionary codes of Reaganite hegemony framed this affective politics through a binary system of embodied identities and differences, which symbolically defined the imaginary and materialization of the New Right agenda:

> In the dialectic of reasoning that constituted the Reagan movement, bodies were deployed in two fundamental categories: the errant body containing sexually transmitted disease, immorality, illegal chemicals, "laziness," and endangered fetuses, which we can call the "soft body"; and the normative body that enveloped strength, labor, determination, loyalty, and courage—the "hard body"—the body that was to come to stand for the emblem of the Reagan philosophies, politics, and economies. *In this system of thought marked by race and gender, the soft body invariably belonged to a*

*female and/or person of color, whereas the hard body was, like Reagan's own, male and white.* (emphasis added, Jeffords 1994, 24–25)

By symbolically nationalizing bodies—equating individual identities and actions with national well-being or decline—Reaganism delineated both the positive and negative signifiers of national popular existence. An emergent cult of hard bodied supermen, epitomized by singleminded, assertive, and successful figures such as Lee Iacocca, Blake Carrington, Donald Trump, Oliver North, John Rambo, and H. Ross Perot (Merrill 1988) distinguished the mattering maps of the New Right coalition; maps that represented suggestive disciplinary models for everyday existence in Reagan's America. On the other side of the New Right's national popular frontier, the new cultural racism conjoined the moral panics surrounding the issues of urban crime, violence, drug abuse, and welfare dependency, under the guise of the irresponsible, indolent, deviant, and promiscuous "soft body" of the essentialized nonwhite urbanite, whose very existence threatened (and in doing so reinforced) the core values of the Reaganite American nation (Denzin 1991). In an ironic twist, the New Right also vilified the African American population through the "right-wing appropriation of the celebrated media achievements of a handful of prominent African American 'individuals'—Bill Cosby, Whoopi Goldberg, Arsenio Hall, Michael Jackson, Michael Jordan, Eddie Murphy, Keenan Ivory Wayans, and Oprah Winfrey" (Reeves and Campbell 1994, 100). The circulation of these high-profile success stories further condemned the struggling African American masses for lacking the personal resolution that, according to Reaganism's doctrine of conservative egalitarianism and color-blind bigotry, was all that was required to achieve in American society (Reeves and Campbell 1994). As a consequence, the bifocal intersections of this racially charged "enemy from within" ideology (Hall 1979; Mercer 1994) meant that "[u]nemployment, poverty, urban decay, school crises, crime, and all their attendant forms of human troubles were spoken of and acted upon as if they were the result of *individual* deviance, immorality, or weakness" (Reinerman and Levine 1989, 127).

As well as shamelessly attacking America's at-risk populations, the New Right also aggressively disparaged the social welfare policies of the 1960s and 1970s, which had actually tried to address the institutionalized racial inequalities that divided American society. Developing upon Moynihan's view of the black family as "a tangled web of pathology" (Department of Labor 1965, 5), influential treatises such as Charles Murray's (1984) *Losing ground: American social policy, 1950–1980* blamed the Great Society reforms for encouraging the purportedly inherent racial pathologies that undermined the work ethic, self-reliance, and moral fortitude of African Americans, and hence inhibited their ability to succeed in American society. According to Murray (1984), misguided social welfare liberalism created a culture of welfare dependency that ruinously contributed to the depletion of America's moral and economic wealth (Denzin 1991). Such antiwelfare antagonism spawned a "new [popular] consensus" related to the perceived needs of the African American community, which did not incorporate "government programs but a good dose of sexual restraint, marital commitment, and parental discipline" (Coontz 1992, 235). This pathologizing disavowal of historically grounded race-based discrimination and differentiation actively disparaged the relevance of racially oriented welfare policies, and justified the slashing of billions of dollars from the welfare budget (see Wacquant 1994, 258–260); without which significant swathes of the African American population became ever more entrenched as permanent members of America's expanding underclass. Rather than apportioning blame for the plight of the African American population at the feet of an increasingly negligent and disinterested state, Reaganism mobilized popular residual racial stereotypes and pathologies that stigmatized and demonized the African American population as a very real threat to themselves, and by inference to American society as a whole. In this way, "People in trouble were reconceptualized as people who make trouble," and as a result, social control inevitably replaced social welfare as the organizing principle of state policy related to urban America (Reinerman and Levine 1989, 127).

This accusatory racial politics reached maturity during the Reagan-Bush administrations, when the hegemony of the New Right fashioned a network of racially focused affective epidemics, which mobilized white fears and insecurities in the face of what became articulated as the increasingly threatening black presence in America. The intrusive reactionary circuits of mediated popular culture circulated this affective orientation for mass consumption through the promotion of stereotypical and divisive, yet commonsense, embodied articulations of race and racial difference. These mass-mediated discourses signified African American culture as being inherently deviant, unproductive, irresponsible, uncivilized, promiscuous, and in contrast to, and thereby threatening toward, the preferred white norm. As Mercer (1994, 176) noted, "[t]he rigid and limited grid of representations through which black male subjects become publicly visible continues to reproduce certain *idées fixes,* ideological fictions and psychic fixations" about the nature of Otherness. The visible markers of race were displayed, and often replayed with accompanying commentary, *ad nauseum.* From the network's nightly news programs, to *Cops,* from *Saturday Night Live* to *Monday Night*

*Football,* popular representations of African American males continued to communicate the separations that the New Right identified as being threats to the American nation. This was ably represented in Giroux's reading of Lawrence Kasdan's (1992) film *Grand Canyon.* As Giroux (1994) noted, within contemporary popular culture racial difference confronts the viewer as being strange, unfamiliar, and ominous. This is most frequently depicted in the portrayal of the American inner city as a zone of difference coded with racial fear, fascination, and threat, and the construction of the black youths who populate the urban environment as signifiers of danger and social decay. Perhaps the most infamous image of a soft bodied African American (Jeffords 1994) was that of convicted Massachusetts murderer William Robert "Willie" Horton. His mug shot, and a distorted interpretation of his criminal record, were used in the notorious television commercials for George Bush's 1988 presidential campaign. In reproaching the crime-fighting record of Bush's opponent, Michael Dukakis (then Massachusetts' governor), these influential texts constructed Horton as "an icon symbolizing the quintessential violent black man," and thus accentuated popular fears and anxieties about black Americans (Feagin and Vera 1995, 119).

The seductive influence of the televisual media, exemplified by the fabrication of Willie Horton, has given racist discourse a residual currency and unwarranted legitimacy that frequently leads to the naturalization of race-based identities and differences within popular consciousness. Mediated racial mobilizations are prominent reference points, reactionary "[s]ocial representations—narratives, symbols, images—that privilege race as a sign of social disorder and civic decay [that] can be thought of as part of a socially constructed 'fear of a black planet'" (Clarke 1991, 38). For this reason, the televisual field has been saturated and schematized by the inverted racial projections of white paranoia, which display an insatiable appetite for images of black men misbehaving (Clarke 1991). Among other things, this obsessive fear/fascination with the body of the racial Other provided Daryl Gates, one-time chief of the Los Angeles Police Department, with justification for the spate of African American deaths at the hands of the police through the supposition that "[w]e may be finding that in some Blacks when [the carotid chokehold] is applied the veins or arteries do not open as fast as they do on normal [*sic*] people" (quoted in Davis 1992, 272), and allowed jurists to view the Rodney King beating as an act of police self-defense against the ever threatening physical presence of the African American male (Butler 1993).

The backlash politics that became emblematic of the Reagan administration (Reeves and Campbell 1994) temporarily assumed a back seat with the election of Bill Clinton and the attendant "post-Bush syndrome" that momentarily afflicted the Republican party (Republican strategist Azliam Crystal, appearing on NPR's *Morning Edition,* November 10, 1994). However, in defeat the Republicans were able to regroup and redefine their political identity in opposition to the initially ambitious, but increasingly defensive and conciliatory, Clinton regime. Through the strategic mobilization of the popular media, the *new* New Right engaged in a concerted attack against Bill Clinton's presidency. This regressive populism targeted Clinton's policies and the "liberal, democratic machine" (Newt Gingrich, Balz 1994, A1) as being representative of, and encouraging, an un-American and inevitably flawed *politically correct* multicultural liberalism, which drew its ideological roots from the Great Society reforms (Lauter 1995). Hence, the new conservative remedy to the threats posed by *Clinton's America* has been a neo-Reaganite allegiance to a vision of a color-blind society. This hyper-reactionary utopia would be realized through the establishment of a color-blind polity (Minzesheimer 1995), that would aggressively repeal any redistributive legislation designed to redress the racial discrimination and practices upon which America was founded.

As in the Reagan manifesto, the *new* New Right's denial of historically grounded and contemporaneously manifest experiences of racial discrimination and differentiation, is designed to legitimate the further slashing of federally funded welfare programs. By dangling the money that would be raised through what is euphemistically called "welfare reform" as the financing for those all-important tax cuts, the *new* New Right currently seems to be in the process of successfully seducing middle America. This regressive racial politics has its most virulent and troubling expression in the debate surrounding affirmative action policies. Whereas Democratic Representative Kweisi Mfume stated, "I am offended at the suggestions that racism is so far past that you don't need remedies anymore. I think people are selling their souls to be the early front-runner in New Hampshire," from the opposite end of the political spectrum Newt Gingrich pronounced, "Affirmative action (laws), if done by some group distinction, are bad, because it is antithetical to the American dream to measure people by the genetic pattern of their grandmothers" (Minzesheimer 1995, 4A). Evidently, such is the control that popular neo-conservatism has assumed over the ideological terrain, that the rigorous debating of black poverty and identity which Cornel West (1993a, 1993b, 1994) identified as the prerequisite for future racial equality has been virtually outlawed from public spaces. The regeneration of Reaganite racial discourse has effectively

> blocked an accurate, historically grounded analysis of the changing politi-
> cal articulation of racial segregation, class inequality, and state abandonment
> in the American city. It has diverted attention away from the institutional
> arrangements in education, housing, welfare, transportation, and health and
> human services that perpetuate the concentration of unemployed and
> underemployed blacks in the urban core. (Wacquant 1994, 265)

Reeves and Campbell's (1994, 261) discerning of an abatement in the
"rugged and ragged individualism" that dominated the Reagan-Bush attitude
toward "black urban America" was hopelessly optimistic. If anything, the
antiblack affect (Entman 1990) of the *new* New Right appears to be a more
strident version of the original model.

As earlier intimated, the popular racial signification of Michael Jordan
represents a fluid narrative that, at differing moments, (dis)engaged various
aspects of the historically accumulated aggregates of popular racial discourse
discussed herein. Hence, by explicating the discursive derivations and demonstrating the evolving manifestations of the facts of Michael Jordan's blackness,
the following section illuminates a series of conjunctural sketches pertaining
to the constitutive inscription of particular racial ideologies onto Jordan's
mediated body.

## Michael Jordan as a Floating Racial Signifier

In Callinicos's terms, the examination of any racial discourse must be engaged
within the contextually specific realms of culture and politics, because "they
[racial discourses] emerge as part of a historically specific relationship of
oppression in order to justify the existence of that relationship" (1993, 18).
Certainly, the racial signification of Michael Jordan can be characterized by
four distinct yet overlapping moments. Each one of these stages in Jordan's
semiotic evolution is contingent upon the climate in racial and cultural politics, and each, in differing ways, represents the conjunctural appropriation
and fleeting curtailment of the endless play of signifiers that have historically
contributed to the violent racial hierarchy (Derrida 1981) of American popular culture in general, and that of the NBA in particular.

### The Natural Athlete: "Born to Dunk"

1982 marked the year in which Michael Jordan first came to the attention of
the nation's sports media. His promising freshman collegiate season was
capped off by shooting the winning basket in North Carolina's defeat of
Georgetown in the NCAA Championship game. Given the frequency with

which this shot has been replayed in the ensuing years, it would be easy to fall into the trap of thinking that Jordan's celebrity status at that time was somewhat similar to its current level. On the contrary, at that time, Jordan was a relatively anonymous figure in the minds of the American viewing public. At this fledgling stage of his career in the national media spotlight, Jordan's identity was primarily influenced by his membership on the North Carolina team, and the championship game became the context for the revealing engagement of contrasting racial signifiers to distinguish the competing teams. The media fabricated the event as an intriguing battle between the methodical strategies devised by Dean Smith (the North Carolina coach), and the hyperactive physical frenzy encouraged by John Thomson (the Georgetown coach): "Carolina was, as Smith put it, 'the hunted,' and Georgetown, quicker, ravaging, downright frightening in its full court press was, 'the hunter'" (Kirkpatrick 1982, 16). Black players on either side, who comprised the dominant racial grouping in the contest, were cast in stereotypical fashion as the contest became an exposition of the mind-body dualism that historically informed racial discourse.

Closely tied to the stereotypical media representation of the pathologically violent and criminal black body, is the popular fascination with the supposed natural athleticism of the African American Other (see Davis 1990). Mercer described this as "that most commonplace of stereotypes, the black man as sports hero, mythologically endowed with a 'naturally' muscular physique and an essential capacity for strength, grace and machinelike perfection" (1994, 178). In his infamous televised remarks, Al Campanis, the one-time Los Angeles Dodgers vice president for player personnel, voiced these stereotypical views, which many Americans probably would not even have questioned, were it not for his subsequent firing:

> They are gifted with great musculature and various other things. They're fleet of foot. And this is why there are a lot of black major league ballplayers. Now as far as having the background to become club presidents, or presidents of a bank, I don't know. (Al Campanis, remarks to Ted Koppel on ABC's *Nightline,* quoted in Omi 1989, 112)

These remarks neatly captured the mind-body dualism that has dominated popular racial discourse related to males of African descent. Similarly, but seemingly less offensively, the popular media's trite celebrations of some inherent African American sporting prowess, also draw from the same reservoir of racial signifiers that characterizes black urban youth as being habitually violent and therefore threatening. The contemporary constructions of both the pathologically criminal and the naturally sporting black body are founded upon a common assumption of the innate physicality of the black body; a racist discourse whose genealogy can be traced back at least to the era of systemic slavery:

> Classical racism involved a logic of dehumanization, in which African peoples were defined as having bodies but not minds: in this way the superexploitation of the black body as a muscle-machine could be justified. Vestiges of this are active today . . . (Mercer 1994, 138)

In this vein, and with specific regard to the 1982 NCAA Championship game, the media alluded to the fact that the white coach, Smith, infused his players with a sense of his superior knowledge of the game, whereas his black counterpart, Thomson, merely assembled a group of players and allowed them to do what came naturally, that is, to rely on their natural physical attributes. It was hardly surprising, therefore, that Dean Smith was lauded more widely for his basketball acumen than either James Worthy, Sam Perkins, or Michael Jordan were celebrated for their input into the victory. When praise was extolled on the North Carolina players, it was usually meted out in recognition of the degree to which they had successfully executed the coach's masterful game plan (Vecsey 1982a, 1982b).

The racial discourse that underscored the media's narration of the 1982 NCAA Championship game clearly displayed aspects of the racial context out of which Michael Jordan, the promotional sign, was initially constructed. Furthermore, throughout the construction of his mediated identity, Michael Jordan's imaged persona has been configured either in congruence with, or in opposition to, the economy of signifiers (as depicted by Lanker [1982]) pertaining to the physical comportment of the African American male. As a collegian the media portrayed him as the latest in a seemingly endless supply of naturally talented and exuberantly physical black bodies. He was, in Cashmore's damning terms, yet another media celebration of "that black magic of nature" (1982, 42). This ubiquitous narrative accompanied Jordan throughout his successful collegiate career, which reached its zenith with his co-captaining the U.S.A. team to a gold medal triumph at the 1984 Los Angeles Olympics, where Jordan was referred to in familiar refrain, "The flashiest men's player was Jordan, the 6ft. 6-in. University of North Carolina senior who has won six awards designating him America's best collegian. *Born to dunk,* he penetrated the zone defenses of opponents to slam at least one goal in each of the eight games" (*emphasis added,* Henry 1984, 50). Having decided to forgo his senior year at the University of North Carolina, Jordan had already been drafted by the Chicago Bulls in the June 1984 NBA draft. This occasion inspired the *Chicago Tribune* sports columnist Bernie Lincicome to sarcastically (due to the rumored interest shown by the Bulls management in making a trade for Jordan) introduce his readership to the Bull's potential "savior" (Logan 1984):

> They [the Bulls] got stuck with Michael Jordan of North Carolina, maybe the greatest natural basketball talent, inch for inch, in this young decade. Nothing they could do. They want you to know that.
>
> They tried to avoid Jordan, tried hard. But nobody wanted to trade with them, swap some big fossil of a center for the third pick in the draft. It was like they were under quarantine or something. So they were forced to do the intelligent thing Tuesday.
>
> They had to take Jordan, even though he is already famous, has had quality coaching, is not a social disgrace and may likely become the next Julius Erving before the old one is in the Hall of Fame. (Lincicome 1984, 1)

Not only did Lincicome identify Jordan's natural ability, his respectable social standing (in contrast to the way many NBA players were perceived at the time), he also provided him with a pertinent professional basketball ancestry. Although Jordan entered into an NBA that had been revitalized by Johnson and Bird's multifaceted rivalry and the marketing strategies that nurtured it (Cole and Andrews 1996), Jordan's already acknowledged televisual presence, "his sinewy combat [which] demanded close-ups and super slo-mo," would generate an identity out of difference to the full court "mark-of-Zorro ricochets" orchestrated by Magic Johnson and Larry Bird (Plagen 1993, 48). Lincicome traced Jordan's basketball lineage, and by inference his racial identity, not to the athletic and indeed racial anomaly represented by the genial Magic Johnson, the Laker's 6ft. 9 inch floor general, but to the natural, uninhibited, free-form grace and artistry of Julius Erving (Plagen 1993). By advancing Jordan as a possible successor to the aging, but revered, Julius Erving, Lincicome engaged the dubious project of basketball social Darwinism. Others subsequently exalted Jordan as the "highest order of basketball's evolutionary chain"; a chain beginning with Elgin Baylor, and comprising Connie Hawkins, Julius Erving, and ending up with the supreme basketball being, Michael Jordan (Ryan 1993, 28).

On entering the league, Jordan took the NBA by storm. He scored twenty-five points in ten of his first fifteen games, including thirty-seven in his third game. Less than a month into Jordan's first NBA campaign, Larry Bird described him as the "best I've ever played against" (quoted in Ryan 1993, 27), and he was compared on national television to Julius Erving, who appeared more than comfortable with the comparison (*ABC Nightly News,* November 4, 1984). However, there was a marked difference in the popular

racial articulation of Jordan and Erving. Although both were primarily racialized by their supposed natural physical attributes, Jordan's image was not
identified in the popular memory for sporting the 1970s black statement,
"bushy Afro," or for being one of the "airborne brothers who defined ABA
ball" (George 1992, 181); overt identifications with black identity that inhibited Erving's popular acceptance, not as a supreme sportsmen but as a national icon. His imaged identity having been fermented within a very different
racial climate, that of the color-blind Reagan Revolution, Jordan necessarily
emerged as a racially understated version of Julius Erving. As such, even more
than Erving, he was always likely to become "the kind of [non-threatening]
figure who goes down easily with most Americans" (Shelby Steele, quoted in
Naughton 1992, 137).

Although Jordan's stellar rookie performances during the 1984–1985
NBA season garnered him considerable national publicity, his initial popular
identity was crystallized through the innovative promotional initiatives
engaged by Nike. In the previous fiscal year Nike had experienced an alarm-
ing decline in sales and sought to redress this by confronting its anonymous
presence in both collegiate and professional basketball. In the spring and summer of 1984, the company surveyed the incoming crop of collegiate players
and set their sights on Jordan. According to Sonny Vaccaro, Nike's intermediary with the collegiate game, Jordan "was brilliant. He was charismatic. He was
the best player Vaccaro had ever seen. He could fly through the air!" (Strasser
and Becklund 1991, 535). Vaccaro's enthusiasm for Jordan went as far as admitting, "I'd pay him whatever it takes to get him" (Strasser and Becklund 1991,
536). On Vaccaro's recommendation, Jordan was pinpointed as the figurehead
who could reassert Nike's position as the sports shoe industry's market leader.
Such confidence in Jordan's playing and marketing potential was confirmed
when the company signed him to a $2.5 million contract. Nike was ridiculed
for taking such a financial risk on an untried player, at a time when it was
experiencing considerable economic troubles. In retrospect such concerns
seem almost laughable, as the Air Jordan phenomenon grossed $130 million in
its first year (Strasser and Becklund 1991, 3); a financial boost that reasserted
Nike as the preeminent sports shoe manufacturer, and elevated the company
to the position of an American corporate icon.

Given the exhilarating telegenicism of Jordan's play, Nike's advertising
company at the time, the Los Angeles based Chiat/Day agency, chose to
develop an innovative campaign for the equally innovative signature Air
Jordan shoes. This involved saturating the electronic media with strategically
coded images of Michael Jordan wearing Air Jordan shoes. Hence, during

early 1985 the first Air Jordan commercial was aired, a slot entitled "Jordan Flight" in which a slow motion Jordan executed a dunk on an urban play-graound to the sound of jet engines accelerating to take off. With this com-mercial, and especially his parting salvo, "Who said a man was not meant to fly?" Michael Jordan's identity was constituted in the minds of the American populace as Air Jordan, "the Nike guy who could fly" (Katz 1994, 7). The locus of Nike's Air Jordan initiative keyed on Jordan's physical prowess, and thus corroborated the taken-for-granted assumptions pertaining to the natu-ralistic element of black corporeality. Jordan's repeatedly valorized sporting body thus became a prominent, if underscored, signifier of racial Otherness; a seemingly material vindication of what popular racist discourse had extolled all along.

## Transcendental Mediation: Reagan's All-American

The early stages of the Air Jordan promotional phenomenon were evidently dominated by the signification of Jordan's *naturally* athletic *black* body. Although racial signifiers pertaining to black physicality have provided a back-drop for the promotional discourse that narrated his stellar career, to a large extent they have been subsumed by a more obtuse relationship to popular racialized codes. In accordance with the prevailing racial politics of the American New Right—founded upon a paranoid defensiveness toward overt expressions of racial difference, and a concomitant dismissive attitude toward the existence of race-based discrimination—Nike's subsequent Air Jordan campaigns inspired the multifarious segments of the American mass culture industry (who subsequently invested in Jordan) into nurturing an intertextu-ally informed identity, which explicitly invested in the affective epidemics that delineated Reagan's America (see Grossberg 1992). Thus, Jordan's carefully scripted televisual adventures on the corporate playground were designed to substantiate an All-American (which in Marable's terms means white) hard bodied identity (Jeffords 1994), which would appeal to the racially sensitive sensibilities of the American mass market. Jordan's phenotypical features could not be overlooked, but his imaged identity could be distanced from the racial signifiers that dominated popular representations of African American males. Corporate image makers recognized that if he was to become "America's play-er" (Sakamoto 1986, 10), they could not afford to explicitly associate him with the threatening expressions of black American existence.

To facilitate this evolution from mall America's flavor of the month to enshrined All-American icon, Jordan's marketing directors realized he had to

be packaged as a Reaganite racial replicant; a black version of a white cultural model who, by his very simulated existence, ensures the submergence and
subversion of racial Otherness (Willis 1991). As David Falk, Jordan's agent at
ProServ surmised, the intention behind the Jordan project was to promote an
"All-American image . . . . Not Norman Rockwell, but a modern American
image. Norman Rockwell values, but a contemporary flair" (quoted in Castle
1991, 30). This process was initiated by Nike's decision to move away from
Air Jordan campaigns that solely displayed his physical talents, to slots that furnished Jordan with an identifiable, if superficial, personality. Thus, Nike's move
from Chiat/Day to the more innovative Wieden and Kennedy agency saw the
introduction of a series of groundbreaking advertising campaigns in which
Jordan interacted with Mars Blackmon, Spike Lee's cinematic alter ego from
the film *She's Gotta Have It.* The apparent willingness of the basketball hero
to spend time with his bicycle messenger fan/friend, demonstrated that for
all his success, fame, and fortune, Jordan was reassuringly just another "down-
to-earth guy" (*New York Times,* February 20, 1989, section D, 7). In true
Reaganite fashion, Jordan's self-evident wholesome humility, inner drive, and
personal responsibility "allows us to believe what we wish to believe: that in
this country, have-nots can still become haves; that the American dream is still
working" (Naughton 1992, 7). In other words, through his comedic inter-
ludes with Mars Blackmon, Jordan was inextricably articulated as a living,
breathing, and dunking vindication of the mythological American meritoc-
racy. Through subsequent creative associations (see Andrews 1998) with
McDonald's, Coca-Cola (latterly Gatorade), Chevrolet, and Wheaties—all
significant All-American corporate icons—Jordan was similarly cast as a
"spectacular talent, midsized, well-spoken, attractive, accessible, old-time values, wholesome, clean, natural, not too Goody Two-shoes, with a bit of dev-
iltry in him" (David Falk, quoted in Kirkpatrick 1987, 93).

Unlike the stereotypical representations of deviant, promiscuous, and
irresponsible black males, which punctuated the ubiquitous populist racist
discourse of the New Right, Jordan was identified as embodying personal
drive, responsibility, integrity, and success. The flight metaphor that dominated the articulation of his imaged persona graphically encapsulated Jordan's
decidedly individualistic and *American* demeanor, "striving for agency, self
determination, differentiation from others and freedom from control"
(Langman 1991, 205). Here was the prototypical simulated Reaganite hard
body (Jeffords 1994), lauded by the popular media for being living proof of
the existence of an "open class structure, racial tolerance, economic mobility,
the sanctity of individualism, and the availability of the American dream for

black Americans" (Gray 1989, 376). This ideology, and indeed the very image of Jordan, cruelly posited that anyone in America could realize the dream regardless of race, color, or creed, the only variable being the individual's desire to take advantage of the opportunities afforded by this *great* country. For, as Herman Gray identified, the repetitious celebration of this color-blind credo within the popular media does little more than reinforce the notion, propagated within more explicit channels of political communication, that the material and economic failure of the African American constituents of the urban underclass is "their own since they [*apparently choose to*] live in an isolated world where contemporary racism is no longer a significant factor in their lives" (1989, 384).

By creating an opposition between Jordan and *them* (the failing and thereby threatening African American throng), the concerted promotion of Jordan as the "embodiment of [Reaganite] American virtue" (Naughton 1992, 154) had the desired effect of downplaying his racial Otherness in a way that mirrored the signification of his equally hard bodied media contemporary, Heathcliff Huxtable (see Jhally and Lewis 1992). According to the novelist John Edgar Wideman, Jordan "escapes gravity" and "makes us rise above our obsession with race" because he leaps the great divide between races and classes by being a down-to-earth, middle-class, and apolitical hero (1990, 140). This notion of Jordan as a figure who transcends race (and indeed sport) was certainly a common theme, voicing as it did the strategic evacuation of race that characterized the Reagan Revolution (Jeffords 1994). As David Falk avariciously conceded, "He's the first modern crossover in team sports. We think he transcends race, transcends basketball" (quoted in Kirkpatrick 1987, 93). An extended article that astutely deconstructed "The Selling of Michael Jordan" (Patton 1986) concentrated on the marketing of Jordan as an individual possessing "uncanny moves on the court and 'a charisma that transcends his sport,'" a personal attribute that turned him into "basketball's most lucrative property" (Patton 1986, 48). Likewise, Donald Dell, the chief executive of ProServ, commented that Jordan was a rare commercial property because he "has a charisma that transcends his sport. He belongs in a category with Arnold Palmer or Arthur Ashe" (quoted in Patton 1986, 50). Clearly, the use of sport in this context (specifically Jordan's sport, basketball) is as a euphemism for race. Jordan is the figure who *transcended* the black identity of professional basketball, and thus garnered a widespread and inclusive simulated appeal that resulted in his becoming America's favorite athlete; a status no black man before him had achieved (Naughton 1992, 137). In doing so, Jordan played a crucial role in making the NBA accessible to the white

American populace who had previously been turned off, and turned away, by the game's overtly black demeanor (see Cady 1979; Cobbs 1980; Cole and Denny 1995; and Cole and Andrews 1996).

Michael Jordan's carefully engineered charismatic appeal (Dyer 1991), which had such an impact on popularizing the NBA to corporate and middle America alike, is not an example of racial transcendence. Rather, it is a case of complicitous racial avoidance, facilitated through the displacement of racial signifiers. Jordan's hyperreal image was charismatic inasmuch as it set him apart from the popular representations of *ordinary* black males, by endowing him with "supernatural, superhuman or at least superficially exceptional qualities" (Weber, quoted in Eisenstadt 1968, 329). The most pertinent of Jordan's "exceptional qualities" related to his understated racial identity, as opposed to his superlative basketball displays. After all, there was nothing about demonstrations of African American physical excellence that the popular imagination would have considered exceptional. Hence, Jordan's image was coveted by the media primarily because of its reassuring affinity with the affective investments associated with America's white-dominated national popular culture. Although the media could not escape the fact that Jordan is of African American descent, his identity has been shrewdly severed from any vestiges of African American culture. Some black superstars, the most prominent being Jordan, have been able to pander to the racial insecurities and paranoia of the white majority primarily because of their ability to shed their black identities in promotional contexts. In doing so, these black mediated icons have achieved a degree of popular approval that superficially would seem to legislate against the presence of race-based discrimination within American society. As Marvin Bressler, the Princeton sociologist, noted, "It has always been possible in the history of race relations in this country to say that some of my best friends are X. Such people are very useful in demonstrating our own benevolence. We must be good people—we love Michael Jordan" (quoted in Swift 1991, 58). Nevertheless, the compulsion for African Americans to disavow their blackness, in order to successfully harness rather than alienate popular opinion, is indicative of the ingrained hegemonic racism within American society. American culture simply does not tolerate individuals who are, to put it plainly, too black.

The notion of acceptable, racially understated, representations of black America was vividly illustrated in a scene from Spike Lee's 1989 film *Do The Right Thing*. In the scene in question, Mookie (a pizza delivery man played by Spike Lee; the African American lead in the film) confronts Pino (the Italian-American son of the pizzeria's owner) about his bigoted but contradictory attitude toward black people. Specifically, Mookie exposes Pino's admiration for particular African American sporting, movie, and music icons (Magic Johnson, Eddie Murphy, and Prince), and his racist vilification of those who dare to challenge mainstream (white) sensibilities by expressing their African Americaness in more overt terms. In this brief interchange, Spike Lee expressed the racial double standards within American society. Many of the white population are *gracious* enough to accept, even adulate, African Americans, but only if they do not explicitly assert their blackness: If you're black you are not expected to harp on it, if you do then you are, to use the racist vernacular, a *"jumped up nigger."* African Americans are tolerated, and even valued, if they abdicate their race and are seen to successfully assimilate into the practices, value system, and hence identity, of white America. Moreover, African American membership in this exclusive club requires constant affirmative renewal. Any fall from grace (ranging from the judicial severity of a criminal misdemeanor, to the tabloidic scandal of sexual impropriety, to even the supposed democratic right of asserting one's racial identity) cancels membership, and re-casts the hitherto American person as a criminally deviant, sexually promiscuous, or simply threatening racial Other, exiled to the margins of American society with the bulk of the minority population. The ability of certain black celebrities to downplay their blackness was the reason for Pino's lauding of Magic Johnson and Eddie Murphy. Spike Lee could have easily substituted Michael Jordan, Bill Cosby, Bo Jackson, or Arsenio Hall, as Pino's favorite stars (Swift 1991). Conversely, the outspoken championing of black civil rights issues by figures such as Reverend Al Sharpton, Minister Louis Farrakhan, and Reverend Jesse Jackson greatly disturbed Pino. These radical black activists with *"chips on their shoulders,"* they were *"niggers."* Like the reactionary color-blind cultural politics that nurtured it, the very notion of racial transcendence, supposedly embodied by Jordan and alluded to by Pino, was a seriously flawed and contradictory concept. Racial discourse is never transcended, it is in a Derridean sense, *always already there* (see Smith 1994). Jordan is not an example of racial transcendence, rather, he is an agent of racial displacement. Jordan's valorized, racially neutered image displaces racial codes onto other black bodies, be they Mars Blackmon, Charles Barkley, or the anonymous urban black male whom the popular media seems intent on criminalizing. Nike's promotional strategy systematically downplayed Jordan's blackness by contrasting him with Spike Lee's somewhat troubling caricature of young, urban, African American males, Mars Blackmon. Borrowing from Pino's discriminatory discourse, Jordan was Jordan, he wasn't *really* black. Mars was a "nigger." The contrast fortified Jordan's wholesome, responsible, All-American, and hence non-threatening persona, and became the basis of his hyperreal identity, which was subsequently embellished by the multiplying circuits of promotional capital which enveloped him.

With specific regard to Nike. Having been deified (initially in opposition to Mars Blackmon) as the All-American paragon of virtue, Jordan assumed the role of centrifuge of a racial sign system which the company subsequently built around him. According to Phil Knight, the Nike chairman, the company compartmentalized basketball into distinct playing styles in order to create an expanding network of ties with the buying public:

> We thought about it, we realized that there are different styles of playing basketball. Not every great player has the style of Michael Jordan, and if we tried to make Air Jordan appeal to everyone, it would lose its meaning. We had to slice up basketball itself. (Quoted in Willigan 1992, 96)

However, the stylistic differences utilized by Nike engaged contrasting elements of embodied racial discourse. In essence Nike mobilized stereotypical racial codes in order to fashion identities for the Air Force and Air Flight endorsers/product lines, which would provide ways of demarcating between them, and also set them apart from the Air Jordan phenomenon. Within Nike's ever expanding economy of larger than life basketball icons (exemplified by the emergence of promotional figures such as Charles Barkley, David Robinson, Scottie Pippen *et al.*), Jordan's identity was continually reasserted out of (racial) difference to predominantly African American figures; once again confirming his imperious racial transcendence, while displacing dominant racial codes onto the bodies of his Nike underlings (see Andrews 1993).

Without question Charles Barkley represents the most problematic of Nike's racial caricatures expounded within their basketball campaigns. Unlike David Robinson, whose physical force and aggression was encased in a veneer of humor and moral fortitude within the parodic "Mr. Robinson's Neighborhood" campaigns, Barkley's image promotes sheer, unadulterated aggression. As Knight enthused, "It's not just Charles Barkley saying buy Nike shoes, it's seeing who Charles Barkley is—and knowing that he is going to punch you in the nose" (quoted in Willigan 1992, 100). In his earliest commercial slot, a black and white commercial inspired by the musical *Hellzapoppin'*, Barkley was initially surrounded by a line of chorus girls. He was then confronted by a group of journalists and photographers, one of which he ends up punching. The ensuing newspaper headline predictably reads "Charles-a-Poppin.'" Even in the renowned Barkley versus Godzilla commercial, the humorous nature of the narrative cannot detract from the fact that Barkley is being portrayed as little more than an overtly physical and aggressive, almost animal-like individual. Likewise, "The Barkley of Seville" commercial, which in lampooning the excesses of operatic expression, still has Charles killing the referee. While these narratives are undoubtedly amusing, they do little but reinforce the popular perception of African American males. Despite their humorous overtones, they merely feed the widespread paranoid hostility created by the media's routine use of stereotypically violent and threatening images of young black males.

The pathological signifiers mobilized by Nike to delineate their embodied racial economy, were negatively reinforced by Michael Jordan without impinging upon (indeed, they augmented) his racially transcendent image. Thus, in stark contrast to Nike's creation of Barkley as an antihero (an image designed to appeal to sizeable sections of the consuming public), Michael Jordan was portrayed as a paragon of American virtue. The positive identification of Michael Jordan's image in opposition to those of Barkley and, to a lesser extent, Robinson, Pippen et al., strategically downplayed his African American identity, by engaging binary oppositions between Jordan and the dominant discursive formations of African American Otherness. In this way, Jordan's atypical black body deflects and reinscribes stereotypical signifiers of racial Otherness onto the pathologized black bodies that dominate the media's representation of African American males; ranging from the demonized black male urbanite (ably represented by Mars Blackmon) to the equally problematic caricaturing of Jordan's Nike basketball brethren.

## "Look, a Negro!": The Devil Inside

The majority of Michael Jordan's tenure in the media spotlight has been characterized by his portrayal as a figure whose singular virtuosity differentiates him from, and hence underscores, the demonized soft body signifiers of African American Otherness. Nevertheless, there have been occasions when Jordan's racially neutered identity has been severely questioned by the popular media. Although explicitly referring to British sporting culture, Kobena Mercer provides insights into the Jordan phenomenon, and explicitly the scrutinizing of his identity:

> As a major public arena, sport is a key site of white male ambivalence, fear and fantasy. The spectacle of black bodies triumphant in rituals of masculine competition reinforces the fixed idea that black men are all "brawn and no brains," and yet, because the white man is beaten at his own game—football, boxing, cricket, athletics—the Other is idolized to the point of envy. This schism is played out in the popular tabloid press. On

the front page headlines black males become highly visible as a threat to white society, as muggers, rapists, terrorists and guerrillas: their bodies become the imago of a savage and unstoppable capacity for destruction and violence. But turn to the back pages, the sports pages, and the black man's body is heroized and lionized; any hint of antagonism is contained by the paternalistic infantilization of Frank Bruno and Daley Thompson to the status of national mascots and adopted pets—they're not Other, they're OK because they're our boys. (Mercer 1994, 178–179)

While Jordan conformed to the role of wholesome, nonthreatening, hard bodied hero, he was deified for being one of "America's boys." However, once his behavior, especially off the court, was deemed to be transgressing the boundaries of what was considered acceptable for the prototypical All–African American male (George 1992), the specter of racial Otherness reared its demonized head.

The interrogation of Jordan's Reaganite hard body was virtually inevitable because, although his very symbolic existence indicated that images of African American athleticism are not necessarily representations of black men misbehaving (Clarke 1991), the new cultural racism was prefigured on the virulent assumption that these *innately* physical males would be misbehaving were it not for the involvement of their natural physical attributes in the disciplinary mores and stringencies imposed by the dominant (sporting) culture. According to this spurious logic, within sporting activity African American males have found salvation (if only temporarily, e.g., Mike Tyson and O. J. Simpson) from themselves. Such reactionary thoughts were echoed by *Chicago Tribune* columnist Bernie Lincicome, in a startlingly offensive summation of the O. J. Simpson case: "Arguments that sports is responsible for O. J. Simpson's present situation must begin with concessions that without sports, O. J. Simpson is sitting in that chair 30 years ago" (1994b, 1). Renouncing such racist diatribes, Giroux (1994) ably illustrated how contemporary American culture is dominated by a fascination with the assumed superior physicality of the black male body, and a simultaneous fear of the ever present threat it poses. Such mass-mediated appeals to middle America's racial paranoia and insecurities dared American popular consciousness to confront the potentiality of Jordan's deviant racial Otherness and, in doing so, posed the unthinkable question, "Perhaps Michael Jordan is black (i.e., pathologically flawed) after all?"

During the 1991–1992 season, and for the first time, Michael Jordan experienced "the underside of stardom" (Isaacson 1992a, 14). As Sullivan noted, "After seven years of nearly perfect marriage with the media and his fans, Jordan endured a season of criticism" (1992, 3). At the hands of a salacious mass media Jordan was: rebuked for failing to attend George Bush's honoring of the Chicago Bulls NBA Championship win at the White House; castigated for gambling large sums of money on his golf game (Jackson 1992); criticized for the ruthless and hypercompetitive side of his nature (outlined in Smith's [1992] controversial book *The Jordan Rules*); attacked for his initial reticence to compete for the United States team in the Barcelona Olympics (Cronin 1991); and chided for his wrangling with the NBA over the commercial rights to his likeness (Banks 1992; Hiestand 1992; Mulligan 1992; Vecsey 1992), which also led to the ignominious "Reebok flap" at the Olympic medal ceremony (Myslenski 1992, 8). In other words, for the first time Jordan's "faults and foibles were chronicled, along with his dunks and doggedness" (Sullivan 1992, 3).

Even though Jordan was able to sidestep the controversies that arose during the 1991–1992 season, media interest had been sparked in a new and seemingly profitable spinoff industry from the Jordan phenomenon. Jordan's new-found human frailties represented big business for the tabloid sections of both the electronic and print media. Much to the delight of the salacious media, within a year the undermine-Jordan industry was given fresh impetus. On May 27, 1993, it was reported that Jordan was seen gambling in Atlantic City late into the night, on the eve of Game 2 of the Chicago Bulls' Eastern Conference Final series against the New York Knicks (Anderson 1993). In light of this incident, and arguably for the first time, the media began to seriously reevaluate Jordan's imaged identity. The catalyst that initiated this reappraisal was undoubtedly his repeated association with gambling, which had first come to national attention in 1992 when it was revealed that Jordan had gambled and lost a considerable amount of money on a golf game played with one Slim Bouler, who turned out to be a drug dealer (Isaacson 1992b). The Atlantic City sighting thrust the open secret of Jordan's love of gambling into a racial discourse with which his image had previously been disassociated (Jackson 1992). In the immediate aftermath of the Atlantic City visit, Jordan's identity as a figure who transcended (displaced) race, was disturbed by the questioning accusations of certain sections of the media. The most inflammable account of the incident, predictably, came from the New York press, and specifically Dave Anderson's intentionally provocative piece "Jordan's Atlantic City Caper" (1993, 11), which first broke the story and pilloried the "best player in basketball history" for letting down his teammates and coaches by gambling until 2:30 AM (an hour later refuted by a variety of sources, including Jordan). In sardonic tone, Anderson identified this display of inappropriate behavior as turning the Knicks "home-court advantage" into their "home-casino" advantage (1993, 11), and conclusively linking Jordan to the NBA's deviant lifestyle:

> Apologists for the N.B.A. lifestyle argue that players are accustomed to staying up until the early hours, then sleeping late or taking a nap after the shootaround. Some N.B.A. players enjoy frequenting the Atlantic City casinos when their teams visit Philadelphia for a game. (Anderson 1993, 11)

The NBA had never been completely separated from its popular, and racially charged, connotation as an aberrant domain. Yet this was the first time that Jordan's imperious image had been tainted with the festering detritus of this implicitly racial discourse. However temporarily, Jordan became an imaged sign whose impending fall from grace appeared destined to reinforce the historically inscribed racial discourses that cast African American males as pathologically deficient individuals, whose weaknesses are manifest in addictive and obsessive lifestyles (see Reeves and Campbell 1994).

Anderson's column not only granted the gambling story a degree of legitimacy because it originated in the august pages of the *New York Times,* it also ignited a furious debate within the popular media. A debate whose underlying current centered on the scrutiny of Jordan's racial identity. In Jefford's (1994) terms, Anderson disrupted the dominant articulation of Jordan's strong and decisive (unraced) hard body à la Reagan, by insinuating that he actually possessed a pathologically weak and corruptible (raced) soft body à la Bernard King, Eddie Johnson, or Terry Furlow, or for that matter Len Bias (see Cole and Andrews 1996; Donohew 1989; and Reeves and Campbell 1994). The *ABC Nightly News* on May 27, 1993, ended with a segment on the story, introduced with a marked solemnity by Peter Jennings. Within the piece, Dick Shaap identified how, in the first quarter of the game against the Knicks, Jordan played like what he was, "The greatest best basketball player who ever lived." By the last quarter, Jordan "looked human, he looked tired." Shaap then asked the audience to consider whether Jordan was worn down by the Knick's aggressive defense, or was he himself to blame for his own demise, "worn down by a visit to this Atlantic City hotel on the eve of the game." Once again, Jordan's iconic stature was questioned for violating "people's expectations," and without condemnation Shaap offered some advice: "The most famous and richest active athlete in the world is not supposed to go to a gambling casino and stay out beyond midnight. He is too easy a target." Jordan's status as an exceptional human being and role model (Mariotti 1993), founded as it was on his imaged identity out of difference to the media's vision of the archetypal black male, was now in doubt. The nation's eyebrows were raised, as the media suggestively implied that Jordan was perhaps human (a less than subtle euphemism for being black) after all (Mariotti 1993; Miklasz 1993).

The raging debate concerning Jordan's gambling habits was given further stimulus in early June with the hastened release of Richard Esquinas's book, *Michael & Me: Our Gambling Addiction . . . My Cry for Help!* (Esquinas 1993). The author maintained the book was circulated sooner than planned because, in the wake of the Atlantic City story, "We wanted to stay in control of information . . . we felt we were losing confidentiality" (Esquinas, quoted in Isaacson 1993, 7). It seemed more likely that the book was distributed in order to take advantage of the popular interest already generated around Jordan's alleged gambling problem. As a result of the popular media's rabid coverage and circulation of the debate over Jordan's alleged predilection for gambling, the story took on "a life of its own," evidencing the "media's apparent inability to put on the brakes when a story is spinning out of control" (Fainaru 1993, 68). In the wake of Jordan's gambling exposé, the media gleefully censured him, and in doing so stimulated popular interest in the story. For this reason, Jordan's attempt to exonerate himself was always likely to elicit a skeptical response from the more avaricious sections of the media:

> I think that was Michael Jordan behind those dark glasses, though it might have been a candidate for the witness protection program. Did he know the camera was on? Was he wired to a polygraph we couldn't see?
>
> Jordan's first step back as icon and wonder symbol looked more like testimony than conversation . . . the network did him no favors, lighting him like a criminal all the while Jordan was insisting a criminal is exactly what he isn't. (Lincicome 1993, 1)

Despite the proliferation of stories related to Jordan's penchant for gambling, the currency of mediated narratives within a postmodern culture engorged by information is unavoidably brief. The gambling story, which temporarily dominated the media's coverage of Michael Jordan and threatened to seriously discredit his All-American image, had within a matter of days become a residual and largely neutral aspect of his mediated identity. This process was hastened by the Chicago Bulls' victory over the Phoenix Suns in the NBA Finals series. Once more Jordan's on-court exploits took center stage, as the Bulls' "three-peat" relegated the gambling issue to the status of a minor problem that was overcome during the course of the team's ultimately triumphant "season of endurance" (Cardon 1993, 5). Jordan's appearance on CBS's *Eye to Eye with Connie Chung* (July 15, 1993) seemed to finally lay the ghost of his gambling problem to rest, as he talked candidly about his life, family, and the gambling controversy. To all intents and purposes Jordan's gambling had become a non-story, and from being packaged as a role model, a "walking image onto which gambling simply does not project" (Fainaru 1993), Jordan had been reinvented as the All-American hero "who loves motherhood, apple pie and *games of chance*" (emphasis added, Heisler 1993, 1).

Question marks surrounding Jordan's personal integrity did not stay dormant for long. The gambling narrative became violently reactivated around the murder of his father in August 1993. Once James Jordan's body had been positively identified, the media immediately and enthusiastically alluded to a connection between the father's murder and his son's gambling, which implied that the murder was a payback for Michael Jordan's gambling debts (Dobie 1994). As Margaret Carlson noted, speaking on an edition of CNN's *Reliable Sources* program which examined the popular media's proclivity for reporting conjecture rather than fact:

> I think there was another thing at work in the Jordan murder which was that people were looking for a reason, and they went back to the last story, the last big story, which was this—these gambling charges, and they took the death, and they took the gambling, and they linked the things without any evidence at all, but there's this human desire, I think, here that newspapers pick up on which is to find a reason. They—we don't want to believe that there's absolute, total, random violence, especially when it's someone famous. (August 28, 1993)

In terms of semiotic analysis, once again the constant erasure and deferral of Michael Jordan's racial signification resulted in the conjunctural re-articulation of Jordan's image. From the relative tranquility of postchampionship euphoria, the signification of Jordan "the obsessive gambler" was exhumed and widely attached to the sign of his murdered father. For example, Michael Janofsky, writing in the *New York Times,* appeared to presume a connection between Jordan and his father's murder, and seemed most disappointed with Sheriff Morris Bedsole's failure to corroborate it: "The absence of clues, Bedsole said, made it impossible for him to speculate on the possibility that Jordan's death was connected to any gambling activities of his son" (1993a, section 1, 25). Writing in the same paper, Ira Berkow added to the speculation:

> [A]nd now that James P. Jordan is dead, we don't know whether the father is paying for his son's celebrity in some bizarre way . . . We don't know all the circumstances behind the death of James Jordan . . . but the police are calling it homicide. (1993a, section 1, 25)

Perhaps the most irresponsible, and certainly the most hypocritical commentary on the murder came from Jay Mariotti. Writing shortly after James Jordan's body had been identified, Mariotti (1993b, 2A) opined, "[I]t would be the height of irresponsibility to start speculating or suggesting factors that may not be factors. Whodunit commentary is impossible until more is unearthed in the Carolinas," and yet, within the same article Mariotti blithely stated, "There are concerns about his gambling habits . . . . Now there is the possibility that his fame may have contributed, in some way, to his father's murder" (1993b, 2A).

The reportage of unfounded conjecture and sensationalist supposition was by no means confined to the print media, as television coverage of James Jordan's murder also revisited and reinscribed the gambling narrative. The *CBS Evening News* of August 13, 1993, covered the breaking news of the Jordan murder as its lead story. A somber Connie Chung opened the program in dramatic fashion:

> Triumph. Turmoil. And now, tragedy. Michael Jordan has seen it all this year. Today police in North Carolina confirmed the worst fears about the basketball star's missing father. James Jordan shot to death. Killer and motive unknown.

The story then moved into a film segment narrated by Diana Gonzalez, a correspondent situated in North Carolina. She described a "devastated" Michael Jordan's return to North Carolina following his learning of the "mysterious" death of his father. Gonzalez then recounted the events leading up to James Jordan's disappearance/murder, and the closeness of the relationship between father and son. She concluded with a revealing commentary on the case:

> The body of James Jordan was found in a area known for a lot of drug related crime, but as of now police say they have no obvious motive. Authorities have not said whether they will consider the *possibility* the killing *might* be connected to the family's gambling activities. Other possibilities include kidnapping for ransom, or simply random crime. (*emphasis added*)

This coverage represented a clear example of what Carlson (CNN's *Reliable Sources,* August 28, 1993) referred to as the media's need for immediate gratification, in terms of instantaneously providing a motive for any action within their gaze. The police may have been unwilling to identify an obvious motive, however CBS News was more than happy to do so. In one fell swoop Gonzalez's less than subtle inferences provided the viewing public with a seemingly compelling rationale for the murder; one that clearly implicated Michael Jordan, without any direct reference to him. Connie Chung, with a picture of James Jordan now providing a backdrop, then contextualized his murder within the narrative of his son's career, "Jordan's murder adds another bitter twist to the darker side of an All-American success story": a narrative that seemed to be realizing Jordan's dreaded metamorphosis from "Michael Jordan the person to Michael Jordan the black guy" (Michael Jordan, quoted in Breskin 1989, 396).

## Back to Basics?: Michael Jordan as Gingrichite America

Media speculation related to Jordan's potentially deviant [racial] identity abated with the arrest of James Jordan's alleged murderers, one of whom was an African American male. In light of this development, the accusatory and racist vectors of the popular media became directed at another black body, that of the indicted African American assailant, Daniel Andre Green. The media's casting of Green as an embodied and highly visible racial sign of "the kind of random violence that all the public was concerned about and afraid of" (Jim Coman, quoted in Janofsky 1993b, 1), neatly absolved Jordan of any responsibility, however indirect, for his father's death. As Janofsky pointed out:

> Today's arrests brought to a swift conclusion a sad and somewhat bizarre case that drew nationwide attention because of the fame of Michael Jordan, the National Basketball Association's premier player, and speculation that the death might be in some way related to Jordan's highly publicized gambling activities. (1993b, 1)

With Daniel Andre Green assuming the mantle of a latter-day Willie Horton (see Feagin and Vera 1995), his demonized racial presence provided a semiotic space for, and inverted unity with, the revitalization of Michael Jordan's All-American sign value. In essence the strategic mobilization of corporeal pathologies associated with the deviant African American Other necessarily resuscitated Jordan's atypical racial persona.

Following the arraignment of his father's alleged murderers, and his subsequent retirement from the NBA in October 1993—which was widely reported as being at least partly attributable to the stress and anxiety resulting from his father's murder and the media's reporting thereof (McCallum 1993)—the articulation of Jordan's simulated existence became infused with a sense of familial sympathy, sorrow, and understanding. As with Wayne Gretzky's "defection" from Canada in 1988 (Jackson 1993, 1994), Jordan's retirement resonated as a catalyst for the popular expression of national loss and mourning (Jones 1993; Madigan 1993; Thomas 1993). In Bill Clinton's funereal terms, "We may never see his like again. We will miss him—here and all around America, in every smalltown backyard and paved city lot where kids play one-on-one and dream of being like Mike" (quoted in *Inside Sports* special issue, "The end of an era," October 1993, 7). However, unlike the

Gretzky scenario—which proved a catalyst for intersecting debates related to Canada's perceived national decline—Jordan's retirement also provided a platform for the national popular celebration of the *American way,* as seemingly vindicated by the very nature of his imperious being. Ira Berkow enthused, "His wholesome image, his broad smile and his basketball achievements made him the embodiment of the American dream" (1993b, 17). John Leland, in the *Newsweek* special issue, "The Greatest Ever," which marked Jordan's retirement, continued this romanticized self-celebratory narrative of contemporary America *through* Michael Jordan; a discourse which for so long had dominated the populist articulation of his career:

> There is a clip of Michael Jordan that we Americans will be replaying in our heads well into the next century. It is a part of our shared cultural experience, a flash of the American Dream bright enough to join us all momentarily in its promise. It begins with Michael swooping toward the basket. His tongue is out, the ball a willing appendage at the end of his long, muscular right arm. He takes one stride, and then he begins to rise.
>
> It is a magnificent thing, his rise, as articulate a refutation of the forces that hold humankind earthbound as the drawings of Leonardo or the joyous music of Louis Artmstrong. His legs start to churn in midair, mocking gravity, and he begins, at his apex, to climb even higher: he begins to fly. Jordan made this move scores of times; television multiplied it a hundredfold. And each time he went up he held out the hope that this time—for the sake of all who believe themselves slaves to gravity—he would never come down. (1993, 9)

Despite the prevalence of such self-satisfied nationalist discourse surrounding the spectacle of Jordan's retirement, some journalists would not let the rumors surrounding Michael Jordan's personal indiscretions dissipate. In the *Newsweek* special issue, Mark Starr resurrected "that gambling thing" (1993, 39) in a particularly indicting manner. After chronicling his varied gambling habits, Starr accused Jordan of being a compulsive gambler; a personality flaw that had rendered his basketball legacy, "sadly, a slightly tarnished one" (1993, 39). Likewise, Harvey Araton's barbed summation of Jordan's career chided him for a hypocritical lack of personal integrity and responsibility:

> For even as Jordan was saying goodbye, his bitterness over his name being dragged through gambling headlines was obvious. He kept referring to the news media as "you guys," you problem makers, as if the news media had dug up Slim Bouler and Richard Esquinas and every other controversy that dogged Jordan the last two years.
>
> That's the troubling part of the Jordan legacy, his lack of public acknowledgement that the persona he marketed so brilliantly, so lucratively, did not come with responsibility, with accountability. (1993, 1)

Evidently in the wake of his retirement, the popular media's representation of Jordan was in a state of flux, polarized by the oppositional signifiers of All-American greatness and African American pathological depravity.

Within four months of his retirement from the NBA Jordan embarked on his highly publicized baseball odyssey. This somewhat improbable venture resolved the semiotic ambiguity and exorcised the specter of racial contamination, implied by the media's prolonged discussion of Jordan's numerous *indiscretions*. Despite the ever increasing presence of African American, Hispanic, and Latino players within the game, baseball continues to be a touchstone of white (sporting) culture. Hence, with Jordan pursuing his, and what is frequently and often uncritically assumed to be *every* true blooded (white) American male's (sporting) dream, the threat posed by his emergent deviant identity to his racially transcendent image almost inevitably subsided. Once again he could be portrayed as the near-mythic All-American hero. Although there were some notable examples to the contrary (for example, Mariotti [1994], and most controversially Wulf [1994]), Jordan's sojourn into minor league baseball was largely characterized as being beneficial to the game as a whole. Perhaps even more important than the direct economic boost that Jordan was expected to bring to the game (Banks 1994; de Lissier and Helyar 1994; and van Dyck 1994a), his very presence in a baseball uniform was felt to have improved the game's image by association (Crain 1994; Lincicome 1994a; van Dyck 1994b; and Verdi 1994a). Jordan was even anointed as the "savior" of the strike-curtailed 1994 Major League Baseball season, "All he has done since putting on a baseball uniform is bring positive attention to a sport in dire need of it, and dignity to himself by risking his athletic reputation on this baseball fantasy" (Burwell 1994b, 3C). As Burwell intimated, the Jordan-baseball couplet proved to be a mutually beneficial alliance. When braced with Jordan's revitalizing All-American aura, baseball's residual identity as the national pastime provided the media with a synergetic narrative context, which almost compelled the discursive appropriation of the valorized personal attributes associated with successful engagement with the American dream; most pertinently, naked innocence, hard-work, commitment, and desire for success (Verdi 1994b). Jordan was valorized for being "just a guy who chased his dream" (Myslenski 1994, 1), and someone who was "not afraid to fail" (Michael Jordan, quoted in *Chicago Sun-Times*, February 8, 1994, 88) in the pursuit of his dream. The discursive emendation of the explicitly American competitive individualism that engulfed Jordan's fledgling baseball career reached its zenith within the crass popular psychology that comprised the inspirational tome, *I Can't Accept not Trying: Michael*

*Jordan on the Pursuit of Excellence* (Vancil 1994). Most of the text for this discussion of Jordan's personal philosophy was garnered from the pictorial coffee table book, *Rare air* (Vancil 1993), which was published the previous year. However, the timing of the later book's release, its very title, and thematic organization, proved an effective intertextual reinforcement of the Algeresque articulation of Jordan's baseball odyssey.

Perhaps wary of the negative publicity that could potentially be accrued if Jordan struggled in baseball (as he plainly did), his coterie of corporate affiliations were initially reticent to develop "Jordan baseball tie-ins" (Jensen 1994). Soon, however, Jordan's baseball trials and tribulations proved too good a marketing opportunity to miss. Having retired the anthemic "Be like Mike" campaign, during Jordan's tenure with the Chicago White Sox' Double-A affiliate Birmingham Barons, Gatorade introduced a television commercial that overtly played on his baseball travail. Over grainy, black and white, nostalgia-inducing sequences drawn from his imperious basketball career, Jordan—bedecked in baseball garb—solemnly declared, "I always wanted the ball, and I got it where it should go. And, I always drank Gatorade because nothing's better." Switching to color, baseball, and the contemporary, the visual narrative displayed images of Jordan diligently practicing his hitting, base running, and throwing, over which he announced, "Now I'm playing baseball. I still drink Gatorade. I still want the ball. I still know where it should go. And sooner or later, I'm gonna get it there [*he smiles*] . . . I hope. Its got to be Gatorade!" This commercial keyed on the self-conscious and whimsical admission of Jordan's fallibility with regard to his baseball abilities and ambitions, and admiration for the strength of character required for putting himself in a position where failure was a very real and public possibility, simply to pursue his dream. Such a theme also provided the impetus for Nike's somewhat belated (especially since the television commercial was made redundant after less than a week, following Jordan's decision to return to the NBA in March 1995) contribution to the fabrication of Jordan's baseball-related identity. Within this television spot, baseball icons Stan Musial, Willie Mays, and Ken Griffey Jr. were shown surveying Jordan's baseball prowess and admitting to the attendant Spike Lee (resurrecting the Mars Blackmon character) that while Jordan cannot be considered their equals in terms of playing ability, there was no doubting his sincerity, or the fact that "he's trying." Following footage of the ball rolling through Jordan's legs, Bill Buckner, the ex–Boston Red Sox player remembered for committing precisely such an error at a crucial point during the 1986 World Series, wryly noted "He ain't no Bill Buckner . . . . But he's trying." Nike pursued this parodic overture within their next Air Jordan commercial which first aired in May 1995. The spot, which Hiestand (1995, 3C) identified as being reminiscent "of your grammar school fiction efforts," reprised images and scenarios drawn from previous Nike commercials, his NBA comeback game against the Indiana Pacers, Bobby Ewing's (Patrick Duffy) resurrection in *Dallas*, and most importantly from Jordan's baseball detour, which was now cast in a surreal light:

> I had this dream . . . I retired . . . I became a weak hitting Double-A out-fielder with a below average arm . . . I had a $16 meal per diem . . . I rode from small town to small town on a bus . . . and then I returned to the game I love, and shot 7 for 28 . . . .Can you imagine it . . . I can't.

This commercial simultaneously brought Jordan's baseball career to a satirical conclusion and effectively announced his return to the NBA. Through the use of parody and self-deprecating humor, it positioned Jordan's relative fail-ure in baseball as a platform for reasserting his humility, steely determination, and desire to realize even the most challenging goals. Despite a .202 batting average at the Double-A level, Jordan's status as an All-American icon was conclusively reaffirmed. As Grant poignantly summarized, Jordan's "improba-ble quest" fell short of his goal, "but it wasn't for lack of effort" (1995, 110).

Evidently, the maturation of Jordan's popular identity in the mid-late 1980s was both influenced by and contributed toward the prevailing climate in popular racial politics. So, his significatory resurrection in the mid-1990s was contingent upon the hyper-reactionary, and necessarily racist, reactionary traditionalism of the new populist Republicanism which engulfed public space. According to John Dempsey, writing in *Variety,* the loss of marquee players, impending contract talks, and the rise of overly physical play, had all contributed to the situation where "the NBA's image dribbles away" (1994, 27). This questioning of the NBA's exemplary image, which Jordan had played such a large part in cultivating, intensified following his retirement from the league in October 1993. Thereby, and by disassociation, Jordan's image was further revitalized. The neo-Reaganite climate of racial retrench-ment—concretized within the Newt Gingrich–orchestrated "Contract with America," which swept the Republicans to a landslide victory in the November 8, 1994, elections for the House of Representatives (see Mollins 1995a, 1995b, 1995c)—rendered the high profile and overt African American constitution of the Jordan–less NBA a semiotic space that inevitably became implicated in the rise to ascendancy of the new New Right's accusatory regime of racial signification. In the wake of the semiotic ambiguity created by Jordan's departure, the NBA became targeted by the reactionary popular media as yet another site for representing African American males as signifiers

of danger and social depravity. The process of honing the NBA into a racially acceptable semiotic space, initiated by Bird-Johnson and consolidated by
the transcendent persona of Michael Jordan (see Cole and Andrews, 1996)
was derailed by reactionary diatribes that condemned the new generation of
NBA stars for being self-centered, spoilt, brash, arrogant, and irresponsible
(Boeck 1994a, 1994b; Burwell 1994a; Dempsey 1994; Diefenbach 1995;
Graham 1995; Swift 1994; Taylor 1995). According to Burwell, here was

> an entire generation of slammin', jammin', no jump-shooting, fundamen-
> tally unsound kids who have bought into the NBA's and Madison
> Avenue's shallow MTV-generated marketing of the game. People with no
> soul for the essence of the game turned the poetry into gangster rap
> (Burwell 1994a, 3C)

The much publicized dissension of players such as Dennis Rodman, Chris
Webber, Derrick Coleman, and Isaiah Rider, became widely characterized as
being indicative of the "league's discipline problems mirror[ing] those of society" (Taylor 1995, 23). Using the NBA as a euphemism for the American
nation, the racial paranoia and insecurity that pervaded popular discourse
depicted the unruly and disrespectful behavior of these *young* African
American males as being as threatening to the stability of the NBA, as the
criminal irresponsibility of the *young* urban African American male was to
American society as a whole. According to Taylor, "A form of insanity is
spreading through the NBA like a virus threatening to infect every team in
the league" (1995, 19). Or, as Diefenbach described it, "In the NBA, at least
for the time being, it is evident: The animals control the zoo" (1995, 31).
Perhaps Graham most succinctly placed the entire debate within its neoconservative political context: "The players are just the most visible example of
what's happening in sports and, in a larger sense, in society: The decline of
old-fashioned values" (1995, 10). Upholding old-fashioned values, and thereby distinguishing the young deviants, were the residual and ever revered
images of Bird, Johnson, and Jordan (Boeck 1994a; Diefenbach 1995). Thus,
despite his commitment to baseball, Michael Jordan's sign-value continued to
influence the racial representation of the NBA. The only difference being his
imperious, but absent, image was now used in an almost nostalgic sense to
distinguish what the league had become. Even *in absentia,* Jordan's image was
a potent agent of racial displacement, which deflected stereotypical racial signifiers away from his atypical black body, and onto those of the youthful
African American miscreants who now dominated the popular representation
of the NBA. This explains the relevance of, and inferences behind, the pointed question asked on the front cover of the December 1994 issue of *Inside
Sports,* "Why Can't Shaq Be like Mike?"

Despite the ubiquitous and intrusive presence of Michael Jordan, his separation from the NBA created the semiotic space for, indeed his physical absence almost necessitated, the creation of a more immediate embodied oppositional referent within the turgid maelstrom the NBA now represented. Grant Hill, the Duke forward, was posited as a future NBA star long before his entry into the league (Wolff 1993). Having debuted in the Jordan-less NBA in November 1994, Hill produced the type of on-court performances that allowed the popular media, and his expectant commercial sponsors, to legitimately capitalize upon the Jordan-like off-court demeanor that had been manufactured for Hill during the course of his successful collegiate career. Almost overnight Hill was sucked into the vortex of promotional culture. This meant that as well as being a regular performer on NBC's, TBS's, and TNT's NBA game coverage, Hill was featured in numerous television (even playing the piano on CBS's *Late Show with David Letterman*), newspaper, and magazine profiles, and appeared in commercials for Fila, Sprite, and General Motors, all of which created an economy of mutually reinforcing texts that expedited the signification of Hill as the new Michael Jordan (DuPree 1994a, 1994b; Feinstein 1995; Junod 1995; Lewis 1995). As a result he became "[e]verybody's new NBA favorite [who] is admired not just for the greatness of his game, but for the content of his character" (Feinstein 1995, 58). In a matter of months, Hill was touted as "the savior" of a league that had become "replete with hoodlums" (Junod 1995, 170, 172) because, like Jordan a decade before him, he had been shrewdly promoted as:

> a harbinger of the day when the value police will finally break down the laws of the locker room and make all those muscled miscreants toe the line in the name of God and country . . . [someone who is] said to "act white" and "play black," he makes a black man's game more palatable to the white folk who have started imputing a connection between "in your face" and "in your house." (Junod 1995, 172)

Or, as Feinstein identified, "To marketers, Hill is a dream come true. He's the anti-Shaq" (1995, 59). The promotional juggernaut that propelled Hill to the top of the 1995 NBA All-Star balloting, and to being co-recipient (with Jason Kidd) of the 1994–1995 NBA Rookie of the Year award, was temporarily interrupted by Jordan's decision to resume his NBA career in March 1995. With the more immediate proximity of Jordan's sign-value actively redeeming the league's tarnished image, Hill was relegated to the status of an apprentice Jordan, the "Heir Jordan" (Johnson 1995, 38), ready to assume the paragonic mantle when his forebear decided to retire once and for all.

Whereas Charles F. Pierce, somewhat prematurely, described Grant Hill as "our first post-Gingrich superstar" (quoted in Junod 1995, 172), Jordan could be considered America's first Gingrichite superstar who epitomized the "back to basics" (to borrow a term from John Major), ideology espoused by the new New Right. Jordan's comeback provided the popular media with a context for accenting the neo-Reaganite personal traits and characteristics that originally framed his mediated identity, implicated him as lustrous vindication of Reagan's color-blind ideology, and thus set him apart from popular stereotypes of the African American male:

> In this season of Jordanmania, we are celebrating excellence, which is all to the good. With his fierce work ethic, his insistence on practices as competitive as games, and his refusal to concede a defeat until the buzzer sounds, Jordan is a role model and then some. Even the ad slogans most widely associated with Jordan—"Be like Mike" and "Just do it"—remind us of how much we can achieve if we simply make a real commitment to our dreams. (Kornbluth 1995, 22)

The reassertion of "SuperMichael" (*Sports Illustrated,* front cover, March 20, 1995) inevitably positioned Jordan in opposition to the NBA's vilified "spoilsports and malcontents" (Leland 1995, 54), thus reinforcing both poles of this racially charged binary opposition. In remarks made during the postgame press conference that followed his comeback game, Jordan obligingly adopted this crusading role:

> I really felt that I wanted to instill some positive things back to the game. You know, there's a lot of negative things that have been happening to the game, and I guess in terms of me coming back, I come back with the notion of, you know, Magic Johnson and the Larry Birds and the Dr. Js— all those players who paved the road for a lot of the young guys. And the young guys are not taking care of their responsibilities in terms of maintaining that love for the game, you know, and not let it waste to where it's so business-oriented that the integrity of the game's going to be at stake. (CNN News, March 19, 1995)

Even Scoop Jackson, writing in *Slam,* the youth oriented and self-styled "In Your Face Basketball Magazine," toed this reactionary line: "Just when the NBA's salvation is in question, *Air Jordan* returns to *save our souls* .... Michael Jordan's return to the NBA is more like Jesus or Dr. King returning to save our souls, rather than a brotha coming back to shoot hoops" (1995, 43). With Jordan engaged in his stated mission of "reclaiming his throne," and righting the wrongs perpetrated by the NBA's "gimme gimme Generation X'ers" (Araton 1995, 6), it remains to be seen whether a series of subpar performances, which eventually led to the Chicago Bulls' second round playoff defeat at the hands of the Orlando Magic, will lead to a serious reexamination and reconstitution of his popular racial identity. There is a distinct possibility that prolonged evidence of Jordan's physical decline, and sporting fallibility, may be couched in terms that mobilize residual and deep-rooted racial anxieties around his imaged persona. However, the only thing that can be conclusively forecast is that the perpetual dynamism and ephemerality of mediated popular culture demands that, as this chapter has hopefully shown, the racial [dis]articulation of Jordan's imaged persona will not achieve any degree of enduring stability or permanence.

In summation, Jordan's conjunctural racial signification will continue to be contingent upon the shifting, and overlapping, terrains of popular culture and popular cultural politics. As a result, the need to bring this analysis to a degree of closure must be tempered by the realization that the rabid dynamism of mediated culture will inevitably, and rather hurriedly, date such a project. Nevertheless, this discussion of Jordan's ongoing simulated metamorphosis can be viewed as signposting "the changing relations of popular culture and daily life, and the changing configurations of our passions and commitments" (Grossberg 1992, 29). More pertinently, this chapter has identified the discursive epidemics that delineate Jordan's evolution as a promotional icon, and act as markers of an American cultural racism that oscillates between patronizing and demonizing representations of African American Otherness. As is the responsibility of any example of critical cultural pedagogy (Giroux 1992, 1994; Kellner 1991, 1995; McLaren 1993, 1994), the goal of this chapter has been to formulate the type of knowledge and understanding that would encourage people to interrogate their engagement with racially oppressive mediated discourses. In framing the articulation of cultural texts such as Michael Jordan, these popular discursive tracts inevitably contribute toward the construction of the multiple inclusions and exclusions through which the American racial formation continues to be structured, disciplined, and experienced. Hence, in excavating and reconstructing the evolution of Michael Jordan as a racial sign, paraphrasing Grossberg (1992), it has been my modest aim to develop a better understanding of the popular politics of racial representation within contemporary culture's "empire of signs" (Dery 1993), which will inform where *we* have been, and where *we* are, in order that *we* can get somewhere better.

# References

Anderson, D. (1993). "Jordan's Atlantic City caper," *New York Times,* May 27, B11.

Andrews, D. L. (1993). "The cult of sporting personality: Nike's affective basketball economy." Paper presented at the annual meetings of the North American Society for the Sociology of Sport, Ottawa, Ontario, Canada.

Andrews, D. (1998). "Excavating Michael Jordan: Notes on a critical pedagogy of sporting representation." In *Sport and postmodern times,* ed. G. Rail, 185–220. New York: State University of New York Press.

Araton, H. (1993). "A legacy as Jordan departs: Stars as corporate heroes," *New York Times,* October 7, A1.

———. (1995). "Be like No. 23, and don't dare say a word," *New York Times,* May 15, C6.

Balz, D. (1994). "The whip who would be speaker: Gingrich sees role as 'transformational,'" *Washington Post,* October 20, A1.

Banks, L. J. (1992). "Powerful Jordan packing plenty of promotional pop," *Chicago Sun-Times,* February 4, 78.

———. (1994). "Baseball can earn, learn from MJ, NBA," *Chicago Sun-Times,* February 6, B14.

Baudrillard, J. (1988). *America.* London: Verso.

Berkow, I. (1993a). "Jordan's haunting words," *New York Times,* August 14, 25.

———. (1993b). "Suddenly, Michael doesn't play here anymore," *New York Times,* October 7, B17.

Blackburn, R. (1988). *The overthrow of colonial slavery, 1776–1848.* London: Verso.

Boeck, G. (1994a). "Spoiled—and rotten? 'Attitudes' of players worry some," *USA Today,* December 1, 4C.

———. (1994b). "Magic: Game needs stars off court," *USA Today,* December 1, 4C.

Breskin, D. (1989). "Michael Jordan: In his own orbit." *Gentlemen's Quarterly,* March, 318–323, 394–397.

Burwell, B. (1994a). "Pacer's victory could end ugly ball," *USA Today,* June 3, 3C.

———. (1994b). "Get real, purists: Jordan is baseball season's savior," *USA Today,* October 7, 3C.

Butler, J. (1993). "Endangered/endangering: Schematic racism and white paranoia." In *Reading Rodney King: Reading urban uprising,* ed. R. Gooding-Williams, 15–22. New York: Routledge.

Cady, S. (1979). "Basketball's image crisis," *New York Times,* August 11, 15.

Cardon, B. (Ed.). (1993). *Chicago Bulls Three-peat!* Chicago: Chicago Tribune Souvenir Issue.

Castle, G. (1991, January). "Air to the throne," *Sport,* 28–36.

Clarke, S.A. (1991). "Fear of black planet," *Socialist Review* 21 (2):37–59.

Callinicos, A. (1993). *Race and class.* London, England: Bookmarks.

Cashmore, E. (1982). *Black sportsmen.* London, England: Routledge and Kegan Paul.

Cobbs, C. (1980, August 19). "NBA and cocaine: Nothing to snort at," *Los Angeles Times,* C1.

Cole, C. L., and H. Denny (1995). "Visualizing deviance in post-Reagan America: Magic Johnson, AIDS, and the promiscuous world of professional sport." *Critical Sociology* 20(3):123–147.

Cole, C. L., and D. L. Andrews (1996). "'Look—Its NBA *ShowTime!*': Visions of race in the popular imaginary," *Cultural Studies: A Research Volume* 1:141–181.

Coontz, S. (1992). *The way we never were: American families and the nostalgia trap.* New York: Basic Books.

Crain, R. (1994). "Baseball to learn to 'Be like Mike,'" *Advertising Age,* February 28, 24.

Cronin, B. (1991). "Olympics don't fit MJ to a tee," *Chicago Sun-Times,* July 31, 114.

Davis, L. R. (1990). "The articulation of difference: White preoccupation with the question of racially linked genetic differences among athletes (review essay)," *Sociology of Sport Journal,* 7(2):179–187.

Davis, M. (1992). *City of quartz: Excavating the future in Los Angeles.* New York: Random House.

de Lissier, E., and J. Helyar (1994). "Is a baseball club with Michael Jordan still minor league," *Wall Street Journal,* April 8, A1, A6.

Dempsey, J. (1994). "NBA's image dribbles away," *Variety,* June 27–July 3, 27–28.

Denzin, N. K. (1991). *Images of postmodern society: Social theory and contemporary cinema.* London: Sage.

Department of Labor. (1965). *The negro family: The case for national action.* Washington, DC: U.S. Government Printing Office.

Derrida, J. (1978). *Writing and difference.* London: Routledge and Kegan Paul.

———. (1981). *Positions.* Chicago: University of Chicago Press.

Dery, M. (1993). "The empire of signs," *Adbusters Quarterly: The Journal of the Mental Environment,* 2 (4):54–61.

Diefenbach, D. (1995). "Disturbing the peace," *Sport,* June, 24–31.

Dobie, K. (1994). "Murder by the roadside in Robeson County," *Vibe,* February, 72–78.

Donohew, L., D. Helm, and J. Haas (1989). "Drugs and (Len) Bias on the sports page." In *Media, sports, and society,* ed. L. A. Wenner, 225–237. Newbury Park: Sage.

Dumm, T. L. (1993). "The new enclosures: Racism in the normalized community." In *Reading Rodney King: Reading urban uprising,* ed. R. Gooding-Williams, 178–195. New York: Routledge.

DuPree, D. (1994a). "Hill has 'em talking: Pistons rookie stirs Jordan comparisons," *USA Today,* October 26, 7C.

———. (1994b). "Impact draws comparisons to Jordan," *USA Today,* December 6, 1–2C.

Dyer, R. (1991). "Charisma," In *Stardom: Industry of desire,* ed. C. Gledhill, 57–59. London: Routledge.

Dyson, M. E. (1993). "Be like Mike: Michael Jordan and the pedagogy of desire," *Cultural Studies,* 7(1):64–72.

Eisenstadt, S. N. (Ed.) (1968). *Max Weber on charisma and institution building.* Chicago: University of Chicago Press.

Entman, R. (1990). "Modern racism and the images of blacks in local television news," *Critical Studies in Mass Communication,* 7:332–345.

Esquinas, R. (1993). *Michael and me: Our gambling addiction . . . My cry for help!* San Diego: Athletic Guidance Center Publications.

Fainaru, S. (1993). "Jordan's actions speak louder than words," *Boston Globe,* June 6, 68.

Fanon, F. (1967). *Black skin, white mask.* New York: Grove Press.

Feagin, J. R., and H. Vera (1995). *White racism: The basics.* New York: Routledge.

Feinstein, J. (1995). "Grant the good," *Inside Sports,* May, 58–59.

Fryer, P. (1984). *Staying power: The history of black people in Britain.* London: Pluto Press.

George, N. (1992). *Elevating the game: Black men and basketball.* New York: HarperCollins.

Gilman, S. (1985). *Differences and pathology: Stereotypes of sexuality, race, and madness.* Ithaca: Cornell University Press.

Gilroy, P. (1991). *There ain't no black in the union jack: The cultural politics of race and nation.* Chicago: University of Chicago Press.

Giroux, H. A. (1992). "Resisting difference: Cultural studies and the discourse of critical pedagogy." In *Cultural studies,* ed. L. Grossberg, C. Nelson, and P. Treichler, 199–212. London: Routledge.

Giroux, H. (1994). *Disturbing pleasures: Learning popular culture.* New York: Routledge.

Graham, S. (1995). "The heroes take a fall," *Inside Sports,* June, 10, 12.

Grant, R.E. (1995). "Running down a dream." In *Beckett Great Sports Heroes: Michael Jordan,* ed. J. Beckett, 110–114. New York: House of Collectibles.

Gray, H. (1989). "Television, black Americans, and the American dream," *Critical Studies in Mass Communication,* 6:376–386.

Grossberg, L. (1988). "The specificity of American hegemony." In L. Grossberg, T. Fry, A. Curthoys, and P. Patton, *It's a sin: Essays on postmodernism, politics, and culture,* 23–34. Sydney: Power Publications.

———. (1992). *We gotta get out of this place: Popular conservatism and postmodern culture.* London: Routledge.

Hall, S. (1981). "Notes on deconstructing 'the popular.'" In *People's history and socialist theory,* ed. R. Samuel, 227–240. London: Routledge & Kegan Paul.

———. (1983). "The problem of ideology: Marxism without guarantees." In *Marx 100 years on,* ed. B. Matthews, 57–86. London: Lawrence & Wishart.

Hall, S., C. Critcher, T. Jefferson, J. Clarke, and B. Roberts (1979). *Policing the crisis: Mugging, the state, and law and order.* London: Macmillan.

Hebdige, D. (1988). *Hiding in the light: On images and things.* London: Comedia.

Heisler, M. (1993). "Jordan's cards under the table," *Los Angeles Times,* May 28, C1.

Henry, W. A. III. (1984). "Faster, higher, stronger." In *Olympic Games 1984: The pictorial record of the XXIII Olympic Games,* 49–51. Upper Montclair, NJ: ProSport.

Herrnstein, R. J., and C. Murray (1994). *The bell curve: Intelligence and class structure in American life.* New York: Free Press.

Hiestand, M. (1992). "Jordan cuts out of N.B.A. apparel deal," *U.S.A. Today,* January 30, 1C.

Hoekstra, D. (1993). "Jordan fed media dose of own medicine," *Chicago Sun-Times,* October 7, 16.

Isaacson, M. (1992a). "2nd world championship is 'more' to Jordan," *Chicago Tribune,* June 15, A14.

Isaacson, M. (1992b). "Jordan leaves gambling story up in air," *Chicago Tribune,* October 17, B1, B5.

———. (1993). "Jordan mum on book's gambling allegations," *Chicago Tribune,* June 4, D7.

Jackson, D. (1992). "Jordan's acquaintances in shadowy world," *Chicago Tribune,* March 29, A1, A16–A17.

Jackson, S. (1995). "The new testament," *Slam,* July, 42–48.

Jackson, S. J. (1993). "Sport, crisis, and Canadian identity in 1988: The issue of Americanisation," *Borderlines: Studies in American Culture,* 1(2):142–156.

———. (1994). "Gretzky, crisis, and Canadian identity in 1988: Rearticulating the Americanization of culture debate," *Sociology of Sport Journal,* 11(4):428–446.

Janofsky, M. (1993a). "Man shot to death is identified as father of Jordan," *New York Times,* August 14, A25.

———. (1993b). "Two men are charged with murder of Jordan," *New York Times,* August 16, C1.

Jeffords, S. (1994). *Hard bodies: Hollywood masculinity in the Reagan era.* New Brunswick, NJ: Rutgers University Press.

Jensen, J. (1994). "Nike, Gatorade resist Jordan baseball tie-ins—For now," *Advertising Age,* March 21, 4, 42.

Jhally, S., and J. Lewis (1992). *Enlightened racism: The Cosby Show, audiences, and the myth of the American dream.* Boulder, CO: Westview.

Johnson, B. (1995). "Adages," *Advertising Age,* April 10, 38.

Jones, C. (1993). "Jordan about to become last year's role model," *New York Times,* October 7, B20.

Junod, T. (1995). "The savior," *Gentleman's Quarterly,* April, 170–175, 238–240.

Katz, D. (1994). *Just do it: The Nike spirit in the corporate world.* New York: Random House.

Kellner, D. (1991). "Reading images critically: Toward a postmodern pedagogy." In *Postmodernism, feminism, and cultural politics,* ed. H. Giroux, 60–82. Albany: State University of New York Press.

———. (1995). *Media culture: Cultural studies, identity, and politics between the modern and the postmodern.* London: Routledge.

Kirkpatrick, C. (1982). "Nothing could be finer," *Sports Illustrated,* April 14, 14–16.

———. (1987). "In an orbit all his own," *Sports Illustrated,* November 9, 82–98.

Kornbluth, J. (1995). "Here comes Mr. Jordan," *TV Guide,* April 22, 22–26.

Langman, L. (1991). "From pathos to panic: American national character meets the future." In *Critical theory now,* ed. P. Wexler, 165–241. London: Falmer Press.

Lanker, B. (1982). "Pieces of '82," *Sports Illustrated,* December 27, 52–69.

Lauter, P. (1995). "'Political correctness' and the attack on American colleges." In *Higher education under fire: Politics, economics, and the crisis of the humanities,* ed. M. Berube and C. Nelson, 73–90. New York: Routledge.

Leland, J. (1993). "Farewell, Michael . . . and thanks . . . for the memories," *Newsweek: Collector's Issue—The Greatest Ever,* October/November, 4–23.

Leland, J. (1995). "Hoop dreams," *Newsweek,* March 20, 48–55.

Lewis, D. (1995). "Who got 'next'?" *Slam,* January, 12.

Lewontin, R. C., S. Rose, and L. J. Kamin (1984). *Not in our genes: Biology, ideology, and human nature.* New York: Pantheon Books.

Lincicome, B. (1984). "Apologetic Bulls 'stuck' with Jordan," *Chicago Tribune,* June 17, D1.

———. (1994a). "Jordan's majesty is safe, despite baseball's efforts," *Chicago Tribune,* March 9, D1.

———. (1994b). "Suspicions, guesses, and knowledge too good to suppress," *Chicago Tribune,* July 8, D1.

Logan, B. (1984). "Bulls hope Jordan's a savior," *Chicago Tribune,* June 17, D1, D6.

Madigan, C. M. (1993). "Gloom in the cathedral of the sneaker," *Chicago Tribune,* October 7, A1, A7.

Mariotti, J. (1993a). "Hoopla: What's up Michael?" *Newsday,* June 4, 181.

———. (1993b). "The ultimate challenge awaits Michael Jordan," *Chicago Sun-Times,* August 15, 2A.

———. (1994). "Michael at the bat was too painful to watch," *Chicago Sun-Times,* February 8, 87.

McCallum, J. (1993). "The desire isn't there," *Sports Illustrated,* October 18, 28–35.

McLaren, P. (1993). "Border disputes: Multicultural narrative, identity formation, and critical pedagogy in postmodern America." In *Naming silenced lives: Personal narratives and the process of educational change,* ed. D. McLaughlin and W. G. Tierney, 201–235. London: Routledge.

———. (1994). "Multiculturalism and the post-modern critique: Toward a pedagogy of resistance and transformation." In *Between borders: Pedagogy and the politics of cultural studies,* ed. H. A. Giroux and P. McLaren, 192–222. New York: Routledge.

Mercer, K. (1994) *Welcome to the jungle: New positions in black cultural studies.* London: Routledge.

Merrill, R. (1988). "Simulations: Politics, TV, and history in the Reagan era." In *Ethics/aesthetics: Post-modern positions,* ed. R. Merrill, 141–168. Washington, DC: Maisonnever Press.

Miklasz, B. (1993). "Jordan gambling with reputation, not poker chips," *St. Louis Post-Dispatch,* June 4, 1D.

Miles, R. (1989). *Racism.* London: Routledge.

Minzesheimer, B. (1995). "Affirmative action under fire," *USA Today,* February 23, 4A.

Mollins, C. (1995a). "The politics of disgruntlement," *Maclean's,* April 17, 34–35.

———. (1995b). "Man of the house," *Maclean's,* April 17, 36–37.

———. (1995c). "Newt's agenda," *Maclean's,* April 17, 38.

Mosse, G. L. (1978). *Toward the final solution: A history of European racism.* New York: Fertig.

Mulligan, M. (1992). "Nike gets rights to Jordan apparel," *Chicago Sun-Times,* January 30, 91.

Murray, C. (1984). *Losing ground: American social policy, 1950–1980.* New York: Basic Books.

Myslenski, S. (1992). "Now you see it, now you don't: Reebok flap finally resolved," *Chicago Tribune,* August 5, D8.

———. (1994). "Jordan: Remember me as just a guy who chased his dream," *Chicago Tribune,* May 1, C1.

Naughton, J. (1992). *Taking to the air: The rise of Michael Jordan.* New York: Warner Books.

Omi, M. (1989). "In living color: Race and American culture." In *Cultural politics in contemporary America,* ed. I. Angus and S. Jhally, 111–122. New York: Routledge.

Omi, M., and H. Winant (1994). *Racial formation in the United States: From the 1960s to the 1990s* (2nd edition). New York: Routledge.

Patton, P. (1986). "The selling of Michael Jordan," *New York Times Magazine,* November 9, 48–58.

Plagen, P. (1993). "Turning hoops upside down," *Newsweek Special Issue: The Greatest Ever,* October/November, 48.

Reeves, J. L., and R. Campbell (1994). *Cracked coverage: Television news, the anti-cocaine crusade, and the Reagan legacy.* Durham: Duke University Press.

Reinerman, C., and H. G. Levine (1989). "The crack attack: Politics and media in America's latest drug scare." In *Images of issues: Typifying contemporary social problems,* ed. J. Best. New York: Aldine de Gruyter.

Ryan, B. (1993). "Courting greatness," *Sport,* December, 26–30.

Sakamoto, B. (1986). "Jordan's glamor fills league arenas," *Chicago Tribune,* December 16, D10.

Smith, A. M. (1994). *New right discourse on race and sexuality.* Cambridge: Cambridge University Press.

Smith, S. (1992). *The Jordan rules: The inside story of a turbulent season with Michael Jordan and the Chicago Bulls.* New York: Simon and Schuster.

Starr, M. (1993). "That gambling thing," *Newsweek Special Issue: The Greatest Ever,* October/November, 39.

Strasser, J. B., and L. Becklund (1991). *Swoosh: The unauthorized story of Nike and the men who played there.* New York: Harcourt Brace Jovanovich.

Sullivan, P. (1992). "MVP Jordan credits Chicago fans," *Chicago Tribune,* June 18, section 4, 3.

Swift, E. M. (1991). "Reach out and touch someone: Some black superstars cash in big on an ability to shed their racial identity," *Sports Illustrated,* August 5, 54–58.

———. (1994). "Hot . . . Not: While the NBA's image has cooled, the NHL has ignited surprising new interest in hockey," *Sports Illustrated,* June 20, 30–40.

Taylor, P. (1995). "Bad actors: The growing number of selfish and spoiled players are hurting their teams and marring the NBA's image," *Sports Illustrated,* January 30, 18–23.

Thomas, R. M. (1993). "Across the globe, expressions of regret and gratitude," *New York Times,* October 7, B21.

Vancil, M. (Ed.). (1993). *Rare air: Michael on Michael.* San Francisco: Harper Collins.

———. (Ed.). (1994). *I can't accept not trying: Michael Jordan on the pursuit of excellence.* San Francisco: HarperCollins.

van Dyck, D. (1994a). "Better believe it: Baseball banking on MJ as 'savior,' " *Chicago Sun-Times,* February 7, 85.

van Dyck, D. (1994b). "MJ's charisma lesson for baseball," *Chicago Sun-Times,* February 25, 108.

Vecsey, G. (1982a). "Dean Smith finally makes the final one," *New York Times,* March 30, B9, B11.

————. (1982b). "Kicking the habit," *New York Times,* March 31, B7, B9.

Vecsey, P. (1992). "Owning a likeness," *USA Today,* November 20, 1C, 4C.

Verdi, B. (1994a). "Question is: Can baseball learn from Jordan style?" *Chicago Tribune,* February 10, D1.

————. (1994b). "Jordan's baseball bid a fantasy, but his work ethic isn't," *Chicago Tribune,* February 15, D1.

Wacquant, L. J. D. (1994). "The new urban color line: The state and fate of the ghetto in postFordist America," In *Social theory and the politics of identity,* ed. C. Calhoun, 231–276. Oxford: Blackwell.

West, C. (1993a). "Learning to talk of race." In *Reading Rodney King: Reading urban uprising,* ed. R. Gooding-Williams, 255–260. New York: Routledge.

————. (1993b). "The new cultural politics of difference." In *Race, identity, and representation in education,* ed. C. McCarthy and W. Critchlow, 11–23. New York: Routledge.

————. (1994). *Race matters.* Boston: Beacon Press.

Wideman, J. E. (1990). "Michael Jordan leaps the great divide," *Esquire,* November, 140–145, 210–216.

Williams, E. (1961). *Capitalism and slavery.* New York: Russell & Russell.

Willigan, G. E. (1992). "High performance marketing: An interview with Nike's Phil Knight," *Harvard Business Review,* July/August, 91–101.

Willis, S. (1991). *A primer for daily life.* London: Routledge.

Wilson, J. Q., and R. Herrnstein (1985). *Crime and human nature.* New York: Simon & Schuster.

Wolff, A. (1993). "The son is shining," *Sports Illustrated,* February 1, 58–64.

Wulf, S. (1994). "Err Jordan: Try as he might, Michael Jordan has found baseball beyond his grasp," *Sports Illustrated,* March 14, 20–23.

# 6

# Safe Sex Symbol?
# Michael Jordan and the Politics of Representation

## Mary G. McDonald

In an era famous for the proclamation that image is everything, Michael Jordan's image also appears to be everywhere. This visibility has been enabled by the marketing power of the National Basketball Association (NBA), commercial sponsors, and Jordan's own promotional savvy—the sum of which has generated over $10 billion for his numerous corporate sponsors and the NBA. Despite his retirement from professional basketball, Jordan continues to be romantically marketed and celebrated. For example, one account hyperbolically proclaims that Michael Jordan is "a 30-something phenomenon. He is a father, he is an athlete, he represents the modern man" (Thomas 1999, E1). And no less a cultural authority than *People Magazine* confered Jordan sex symbol status as one of America's "Best Dressed People" (Toepfer 1996).

Alongside of this hyperbolic praise, there are also personal and professional misfortunes and tragedies. Yet well told narratives surrounding these setbacks often suggest a celebration of triumph over tragedy. For instance, as a high school sophomore Jordan encountered early failure as he was cut from the varsity basketball team. Apparently undaunted, Jordan worked hard (and grew seven inches) eventually earning stardom at the University of North Carolina. The Chicago Bulls' first NBA championship in 1991 solidified Jordan's status as an acrobatic athlete who could endure the "burden" of less-talented teammates. Even father James Jordan's tragic 1993 murder and Michael's subsequent first retirement from basketball garnered a philosophical spin. Jordan exited at the top of his profession and on his own terms: How fitting that James Jordan witnessed his son's last basketball game. After an unsuccessful foray into minor league baseball, Jordan's basketball return was widely proclaimed the "second coming" (Smith 1995). The

Bulls' ensuing fourth championship in 1996 was even secured on Father's Day, a title Michael dedicated to his father's ever present memory (Howard 1996). And months after leading the Bulls to a sixth NBA championship, Jordan announced his second retirement from basketball as a much needed opportunity "to enjoy life and do things I've never done before" (Drell 1999, 8).

Merely describing these narratives fails to explain what they mean and why Jordan apparently means so much to American popular culture. On the one hand there is nothing new about the Jordan phenomenon: Jordan represents the latest, albeit one of the most celebrated, in an extended line of (usually) male athletes who embody long-standing American ideologies: rugged individualism, competitiveness, and the achievement of material success. Equally significant are the ways in which these ideologies have been revised and remolded with changing times. Off the court Jordan embodies masculine strength through domestic sensibilities as a sensitive new age guy (SNAG)—charitable, sexy, approachable, and apparently committed to the joys of family life.

Jordan thus counters the demonic stereotypes of black masculinity circulating in the wider culture. Indeed, Paula Giddings argues in this period of aggravated racial tensions the issues of sexual harassment, date rape, child molestation, and spousal abuse have become national "rituals via Black protagonists" (cited in Gates 1994, 14). And while white President William Jefferson Clinton's sexual harassment scandals have recently taken center stage, there is still considerable evidence to support Giddings's assertions. The most prominent case has been the O. J. Simpson trial for the murder of Nicole Simpson and Ronald Goldman. Via the Simpson spectacle, Americans were fed a dose of titillating, racialized, and often sexualized narratives regarding domestic violence and murder (Morrison and Lacour 1997). This focus has been quite lucrative, generating nearly one billion dollars in Simpson-related media and merchandising sales (Lipsitz 1997).

In contrast, Jordan is portrayed as the consummate family man, thankful for parents James and Deloris's early guidance, and committed to wife Juanita and their children, Jasmine, Jeffrey, and Marcus. Not coincidentally, Jordan's pledge to family occurs at a time when the traditional nuclear family is central to political debates and actions. Much of the debate has been overdetermined by conservative voices, which demand that the nuclear family be fortified. Placed within the nuclear family as a devoted son, father, and husband, Jordan is a "safe sex symbol" who counters historical and contemporary stereotypes of black masculinity as threatening, irresponsible, and hypersexual. These are the very demonic characterizations the New Right argues threaten the nuclear family and by extension the nation. Yet this vision of Jordan also participates in the "family values" climate of contemporary America in ways that support regressive and patriarchal agendas. Thus, while offering contradictory meanings, part of Jordan's iconic status is that his image and various identities—as a man, as an African American, and as a member of the capitalist class—intertwine with historically specific social relations that serve multiple and sometimes conflicting cultural purposes.

Informed by cultural studies sensibilities, in this chapter I explore the public persona of Michael Jordan as an athlete and successful family man in selected sporting and advertising accounts to critique and make visible the notable social relations and economic rationales in which the man and his image are imbedded. This analysis of Michael Jordan is indebted to the insights offered by Stuart Hall (1985; 1986) who argues that cultural meanings are never fixed for all time; rather, meanings are constantly being produced via fluid interactions between ideologies, practices, and historically specific contexts. The theory of articulation acknowledges that meanings are produced as distinctive texts and contexts are linked (articulated) in fresh ways with identifiable consequences. In this chapter I map the contradictory ways in which ideologies of gender, race, class, and sexuality are articulated through the phenomenon of Michael Jordan and the "family values" backlash politics of fin de siècle America.

## The Making of Michael Jordan: Sport, Black Masculinity, and Backlash Politics

Warren Susman's (1984, 146) astute analysis of baseball star Babe Ruth as an "ideal hero for the world of consumption" also illuminates the contemporary Jordan phenomenon. More than a half-century before Jordan, Ruth was promoted by sports writers as the classic American success story, overcoming poverty to achieve sport stardom and numerous endorsement deals, including those for smoking paraphernalia and automobiles as well as Babe Ruth sweaters, caps, and dolls (Sobol 1974). Ruth's masculine persona and athletic prowess offered escapist entertainment in an increasingly standardized and rationalized world (Susman 1984).

Sport has historically offered an especially powerful site for the glorification of masculine bodies. Despite considerable challenges, sport remains a male preserve, a place where masculinity is celebrated and men's larger cultural power is exercised and naturalized (Birrell 1988). Yet this masculine privilege is not shared equally by all men. Michael Eric Dyson (1993a) suggests that Jordan's Ruthian presence is particularly notable given that professional basketball was once "denigrated as a Black man's game and hence deemed unworthy of wide attention or support" (71). Indeed, during the 1970s and early 1980s attendance and commercial support had waned in the NBA because the largely white audience with targeted financial clout grew less interested as African American athletes took over the league's numerical majority. Management-labor disputes and rumors of widespread drug use among the players further beset the league.

During the 1980s the NBA initiated new promotional campaigns attempting to court white and middle-class audiences. According to C.L. Cole and Harry Denny (1994), the NBA constructed and marketed a culturally "acceptable" public face of black masculinity by highlighting glamorous athletic personalities such as Earvin "Magic" Johnson. New promotional narratives marked and marketed the players with classic American ideologies of patriotism, rugged individualism, and racial equality. The (idealized white) spectator's acquired knowledge of the performative personalities and the entertaining character of the NBA functioned to suppress racist suggestions of threat or deviance (Jackson 1994).

Importantly, the timing of the NBA's resurgence and Jordan's position as the most recognizable NBA star parallels the rise of the Reagan-Bush era. This era is not simply a reflection of particular presidents in office, but demarcates a shift in the nation's tenor that continues to define fin de siècle America. Where the 1960s and 1970s were characterized by the persistence of collective activism, social welfare, and emphasis on civil rights battles, at the millennium the national zeitgeist suggests renewed interest in "traditional values" of the nuclear family, corporate dominance, and a heightened preoccupation with mythic and masculine heroism (Jeffords 1994).

While first expressed by the New Right, increasingly socially conservative world views have gained popularity among a broad segment of the American population. These include a growing justification of inequality in the name of economic competition and the belief that social welfare undermines the most cherished ideals of family and nation (Grossberg 1992). While always contested and resisted, supporters position "free market" principles in opposition to federal government "interference." As the scenario goes, state-initiated taxation of individuals and big business, affirmative action policies, and entitlement programs all exert a "deadening" influence on initiative, free enterprise, and personal responsibility. On the other hand, wealth creation and rugged individualism strengthen not only the economy but the nuclear family and, by extension, the very moral fiber of America.

By marketing an "acceptable" face of black masculinity the NBA reaffirms the myth of individualism, a key component of contemporary America that suggests that history is made by the extraordinary acts of unique men (and a few women), irrespective of cultural constraint. As an extension of renewed marketing efforts, the NBA (and an equally invested sport media) offer what Cindy Patton characterizes as an "Africanized Horatio Alger" army of athletes who possess the (new) right stuff with modest beginnings, marketing savvy, skill, and personal determination (cited in Cole and Denny 1994). A recent Nike print and television advertisement echoes these very themes with a pensive-looking Jordan and the accompanying text :

> I've missed more than nine thousand shots in my career. I've lost almost three hundred games. Twenty-six times, I've been trusted to take the game winning shot and missed. I've failed over and over again in my life. And that is why I succeed.

In an era famous for attacks on affirmative action, lukewarm enforcement of civil rights laws, and the dismantling of the welfare state—all of which disproportionately affect people of color—icons of success such as Michael Jordan and the NBA's best players serve an ideological role: they suggest that the achievement of the American Dream is a matter of personal perseverance rather than the province of those born into privilege (McDonald 1996a).

Both Michael Jordan's and the NBA's sustained prominence thus reinforce Jimmie Reeves' (1989) assertion that

> the nation's sport industry, like the entertainment and information industries, must constantly be attuned to changes in the culture or risk losing popularity, relevance and revenues. Those in charge of "regulating" popular sport forms, then, are often required to act as cultural interpreters. (207)

The ideological management of the NBA and the promotion of Jordan reflect and reinforce numerous contemporary themes, albeit in complex ways. Jordan's competitive zeal and powerful slamdunks suggest the larger than life, mythic masculinity that Susan Jeffords (1994) argues is prevalent in some recent Hollywood blockbuster movies. Like Sylvester Stallone as Rambo and Arnold Schwarzenegger as the Terminator, Jordan embodies a "hard body masculinity." These hard bodies presumably fill a void in the patriarchal social body in suggesting a need for masculine assertiveness. The action figure Rambo stands as the iconic masculine hero of the Reagan-Bush era—white, male, and heterosexual—representing the need to squash extreme bureaucratic regulations and government excess (Jeffords, 1994).

As an athlete Jordan is linked with some of these ideologies, as sport can connote the "traditional" values of hard work, teamwork, character building, and discipline. On the court Jordan represents masculine prowess. Indeed, David Halberstam (1991) says that Jordan is

> the athlete personified, ego-centric and single minded, tough and hard—hard on himself, on teammates, on opponents—fearless and unbending, never backing down, eager to put his signature on an opponent, looking for new worlds and teams to conquer. (Halberstam 1991, 81)

Yet when speaking of his own competitive macho persona, Jordan is careful to limit this image to sport.

> When I'm on my game, I don't think there's anybody that can stop me. It's a strong feeling and it has strong implications: Once I get the ball, you're at my mercy, there's nothing you can do about it. I own the ball. I own the game. I own the guy guarding me: I can actually play him like a puppet. I don't do that in life, I don't do that in society. But in a game—when I'm on—yes. (quoted in Breskin 1989, 322)

Off the court and in commercial endorsements Jordan appears as the anti-Rambo—approachable, affable, and often pictured with children and members of his family. The semblance of family, love, and nurturing serves to counterbalance the bravado upon which Jordan's athletic career is based. In one of the first videos (and still among the best sellers) produced by NBA Entertainment, entitled *Michael Jordan: Come Fly with Me* (Sperling 1989), the voiceover further assures Jordan's symbolic worth: "Although Jordan spends a great deal of time in the air his values are firmly in place." The scene then shifts from images of basketball action to Jordan assuring us that

> I was always taught right from wrong. I was always involved in the Boys Club when I was smaller, so I was able to step up and be an outspoken person against things I did not want to be involved in. (Sperling 1989)

This "kinder, gentler" respectability partly explains why an African American man such as Jordan garners mainstream appeal without much white unease.

Complementing a similar dual emphasis on masculine prowess and moral purity, the NBA continues to construct an aura of fantasy, innocence, and escapism. For example, one NBA commercial opens with a variety of exciting highlights of basketball players being cheered by their fans. In the foreground is the indomitable Kermit the Frog singing the song "Happy Feet." The piece is edited so that all the fans and players respond in humorous, uplifting, and emotive ways, apparently dancing and tapping their "happy feet" to the catchy rhythmic beat of the music. The commercial is designed to signify an atmosphere of humor and family enjoyment, and ends with Kermit proclaiming the NBA's slogan: "I love this game."

Long before Jordan's second retirement the league had established basketball games as spectacular entertainment events. An excellent case in point is the 1997–1998 NBA All-Star Game. Entire casts from some of the most prominent Broadway shows helped introduce the players, sang the U.S. and Canadian national anthems, and performed a dramatic halftime show. During intermission, the court was mapped like New York City, with Broadway's prominent cross streets noticeably displayed. Six contemporary Broadway casts performed musical numbers and each ensemble was introduced with a professional basketball player standing by a theater marquee. Indiana Pacers guard Reggie Miller held a cat to introduce a performance by the cast of *Cats.* Los Angeles Lakers star Kobe Bryant emerged from behind a mask to introduce the *Phantom of the Opera.* Even some of the Women's National Basketball Association (WNBA) players were in on the act, including the New York Liberty's Rebecca Lobo and Tamecka Dixon of the Los Angles Sparks standing by the marquee for *Smokey Joe's Cafe.* The Broadway-sport spectacle concluded with Jordan winning the Most Valuable Player award. *Sports Illustrated* writer Phil Taylor (1998) noted that this feat proved that Jordan was "still the best show in sports" (38).

Commissioner David Stern compares the NBA's version of *Showtime* to Disney, noting that while Disney's performers are named Mickey Mouse and Goofy, the NBA's "characters" include Michael Jordan (Swift 1991). That Stern would choose to align the NBA with Disney, the presumed corporate exemplar of wholesome family entertainment, suggests that the NBA's idealized target audience, like Disney's, "relentlessly defines the United States as White, middle-class and heterosexual" (Giroux 1994, 31). With an assist from Nike, and still benefiting from Jordan's marketing reach, the NBA of the twenty-first century has "Disneyfied" into a financially lucrative global entity (McDonald 1996b).

These idealized and glamorous images of both Jordan and the NBA continue to counter renewed criticisms of the league and its players. For example, during the 1997–1998 season, management-labor disputes resurfaced, as did condemnation of several players for dubious actions on and off the court. The greatest attention was directed toward Golden State Warrior Latrell Sprewell, an African American, for his attack on his white coach, P. J. Carlesimo. Sprewell was suspended from the league for choking Carlesimo, yet the dominant construction of this incident did little to interrogate the connection of masculinity to violence, nor the verbally abusive style of many athletic coaches. While whiteness largely remained invisible, dominant renditions of Sprewell's actions once again hailed racist associations of black criminality and deviance (McDonald and Birrell 1998).

These racist assumptions and displays of violent masculinity are repeatedly managed via the marketing of escapist entertainment, unique player personalities, and heroic actions. Furthermore, Cole and Denny (1994) contend that the sanitized public aura of the NBA also obscures a heterosexualized NBA culture displayed through "a 'politics of lifestyle' marked by the semipublic sexual exchange of a conspicuously displayed network of adoring, supporting female fans, girlfriends, and/or wives: it is a masculine lifestyle meant to be embraced, admired, envied, and consumed" (Cole and Denny 1994, 128). This masculinist celebration of heterosexual virility is similarly complicated by racist stereotypes that suggest that African Americans are closer to nature, more sensual and sexual.

During and after his playing career Michael Jordan's persona as a dedicated family man has suggested the league's idealized wholesome image while diffusing lingering impressions of masculine force, black hypersexuality, and deviance. The picture of familial happiness has been a consistent portrait of Jordan throughout the years and now includes wife Juanita and their children. The focus on family is evident in an early Jordan commercial for Coca-Cola. In this ad, a group of boys is playing gleefully until they discover that their tree house contains no Cokes. Instantly the boys realize who can help them, and Michael Jordan is summoned. Jordan runs past his mother, Deloris, who is sitting on the porch, and leaps into the air, elevating in slow motion until he finally delivers the goods to the clubhouse. The spot relies upon a larger cultural awareness of Jordan's athletic skills, most notably his ability to jump and seemingly remain suspended in the air. His mother Deloris emphatically offers her approval by exclaiming, "That's my boy!"

Jordan continues to evoke his parents' guidance as the cornerstone of his personal and athletic successes.

> My mother and father were such good parents that it made me want to be just like them. Mom never used to say much about my basketball, but she would say things like she saw me relating to my boys the way she used to relate to me, then, I knew she was proud of me. In a way, a lot of what you saw in me on the court and off the court—the outgoing personality and the serious side—came from certain genes I adopted and just being around my mother and father. (cited in Krugel, 1994, 227)

In sum, this portrait of Jordan is an enticing image of black masculinity, suggesting "natural" athleticism, an affable personality, and family intimacy. In an era famous for racist assaults on black masculinity as deviant and criminal, Jordan invites "desire without evoking dread" (Jackson 1994, 49).

## Body Fixations

Within the spectacle of the NBA the best basketball players are constantly on display, in arenas, via closeup shots, and in televised slow motion replays. On the court, basketball players are clearly visible, as their mesh uniforms, shorts, and sleeveless shirts reveal much more flesh than baseball, football, or hockey uniforms allow. In sport advertisements, much like televised sport, spectators are encouraged to look intently at the image of the masculine bodies in motion, which, under the logic of consumer capitalism, come with "specific measurable properties that define their value" (Brummett and Duncan 1990, 234). No body in sport has been subject to more intense monitoring than has Michael Jordan's in numerous game telecasts, endorsements, and now via the world wide web.

Jordan's athletic body lies at the core of his cultural appeal. His former Chicago coach, Doug Collins, calls Jordan "the greatest athlete who's ever played any sport: He's changed how basketball's played—that a 6-6, 200 pounder can dominate the game" ("No Bull," 1993). Sportswriter Jack McCallum (1991) speculates that Jordan's uniqueness stems from the anticipation generated on the basketball court by Jordan's merely touching the basketball: "Out comes the tongue, from side to side goes the head and down goes the ball in a hard dribble. What's going to happen? What will he do now?" (68).

Nelson George (1996) calls Jordan the preeminent black athletic sex symbol:

> His wagging tongue, baggy (now standard issue) shorts and 800-watt smile reflects a stylish, idiosyncratic and confident man. By coolly accepting his baldness, he made his glistening Black dome the defining African-American hairstyle of the era . . . (108)

At the end of a long basketball career, Jordan's athletic body was scrutinized in ways imaginable only in a youth culture. Numerous questions arose concerning the productivity of Jordan's aging body. Will Jordan become tired, will his legs "give out" late in a crucial game? Could Jordan still be effective in his mid-to-late thirties? Despite these inquiries, and even once he'd retired from basketball for the second time, most critics conceded that Michael "Air" Jordan could "still take off on some spectacular flights" (Taylor 1998).

Given this relentless fascination, it is not surprising that Jordan's body is also enshrined as a logo. This status ensures that Jordan's expressive physicality will remain etched in popular culture long after his retirement from professional basketball. Nike's Air Jordan Jumpman logo features a sketch of Jordan elevating into the air with legs piked outward and his right hand holding a basketball skyward. This image has replaced the Nike swoosh to sell Brand Jordan, a subdivision of Nike featuring athletic shoes and apparel. The apparel label also features the phrase "distinctive performance products built to dominate." Michael Jordan fragrances, designed and distributed by Bijan Fragrances, offer another logo—a black outline of Jordan's famous bald head and shoulders set against a bright red background. The Jordan fragrance line includes soap, cologne, cologne spray, shower gel, after-shower body oil spray, and alcohol-free deodorant, but Jordan has been quoted as favoring the soap "because it was designed specifically for the size of a big man's hands" (cited in Manning 1998, 36).

This intense focus on Jordan's body represents one more example of America's continued obsession with the physical capabilities of the male body. Despite women's continued presence in sport, dominant constructions of athletic masculinity help to reconstruct and legitimate an ideology of male physical superiority that is often (mis)understood as an ideology of male social superiority (Messner 1988; Theberge 1991). This notion is so persuasive that boys and men are encouraged far more frequently than girls and women to experience their bodies in powerful and space-occupying ways (Connell 1987). Yet these understandings have dubious currency when connected with larger cultural ideologies and images of African American men such as Jordan. There is a long history of white preoccupation with the physicality of black bodies. Rooted in Social Darwinist thought, this focus suggests that African Americans are more physically gifted, closer to nature, and less civilized, with decidedly different constitutions, than whites (West 1993). This dualistic thinking relies upon the presumption of black intellectual and cultural inferiority and has been used by whites to justify racist treatment from the advent of slavery to the current dismantling of social welfare programs.

Sport history is saturated with numerous examples of (mostly) white scientists trying to explain black athletic success in terms of inherent physicality (Wiggins 1989; Harris 1991). In contrast to the portrayal of the black athletic body as physically superior, more recently white bodies are represented as inherently less athletic, hopelessly doomed to corporeal mediocrity. This seems to be the underlying message of a recent *Sports Illustrated* special report that asks, "What Ever Happened to the White Athlete?" On the cover of the issue is a black and white photo of four boyish looking, white male college athletes. Judging from the basketball uniform styles, canvas basketball shoes, and closely cropped haircuts, the nostalgic image suggests the 1950s or the 1960s. The story begins: "Unsure of his place in a sports world dominated by Blacks who are hungrier, harder-working and perhaps physiologically superior, the young White male is dropping out of the athletic mainstream to pursue success elsewhere" (Price 1997b, 30). "Is it in the Genes?" (Price 1997a) regurgitates questionable scientific information exploring the presumed link between racial difference and athletic performance. And while this article appeals to the guise of objectivity by citing evidence that both supports and refutes racially linked genetic explanations, Laurel Davis (1990) argues that the overall framing of this topic downplays human agency and dismisses sociopolitical issues, including the racist preoccupation with the alleged "naturalness" of African Americans (Davis 1990). Similar pseudo-scientific, essentialist logic also informs media constructions of Michael Jordan as an athlete "born to dunk" (Andrews 1996).

Recent commercials play off the complementary portion of this theme by inferring the notion that "white men can't jump." In an advertisement for Tommy Hilfiger a white middle aged man dribbles toward the basket with his tongue protruding, àl la Michael Jordan. He leaps into the air, but smashes his face and tongue against the blackboard before falling back to earth. In another commercial, an advertisement for Snickers, a white player is shown practicing alone with the voiceover stating: "I can't give up, I can't stop trying to fly." After completing a difficult dunk, the athlete's shirt gets caught on the rim, and he exclaims, "I can't get down."

While white physicality is more likely to be subject to ridicule, according to critic bell hooks (1992) the

> commercial nexus exploits the culture's desire (expressed by Whites and Blacks) to inscribe Blackness as "primitive" sign as wildness, and with it the suggestion that Black people have secret access to intense pleasure, particularly pleasures of the body. (hooks 1992, 34)

Nowhere is this more apparent than in the July 1996 issue of *Life* magazine, where a photo essay entitled "Naked Power, Amazing Grace" features seven African Americans and seven white athletes posed naked in separate photos. And while the fifty-fifty representation appears to suggest equality, these athletes are posed and summarily exposed quite differently. The faces of all the white athletes are prominently shown including four (visibly) white members of the U.S. men's water polo team. Rick McNair, Alex Rousseau, Chris Humbert, and Chris Dupanty laughingly defy the camera's gaze while holding water polo balls to shield their penises from view. White diver Mary Ellen Clark is rolled tightly into a fetal-like position reminiscent of a diving pose. Her tightly-closed eyes and tense muscles also infer a general discomfort with her body on display. In contrast, the African American athletes are featured in pensive and serious shots suggesting comfort with the camera's gaze. Track star Carl Lewis reveals the most flesh of all, striking an exaggerated running movement that exposes his buttock. In other shots, black bodies are reduced to mere body parts including 200 meter and 400 meter gold medalist Michael Johnson's bare chest and stomach. Two other photos feature track star Gail Devers's thigh and extremely long fingernails. This objectification is especially pernicious when read with the accompanying text: "The Olympic body is another country, its beauty as exotic and varied as that of any distant terrain" (Grunwald 1996). According to critic Ann duCille this portrait relies upon a history of racist practices and beliefs that suggest that the black body "is an alien land, an exotic continent to be claimed and tamed by the camera in endless low-angle shots that chart the subject's nether regions" (duCille 1997, 308).

Allusions to a presumed natural and exotic makeup rely upon the racist presupposition that people of color are "more prone to be guided by base pleasures and biological impulses" (West 1993, 127). The mythos of black hypersexuality has a long, shifting history that alternatively hails associations of fear and fascination while supporting white cultural and financial privilege. For example, from the Reconstruction Era until the 1930s and beyond, lynchings were often fueled by white racist fears of black hypersexuality and imagined black transgression of proper sexual limits, particularly when the subject was social and sexual interactions between African American men and white women (Levine 1977). As Michael Eric Dyson (1993b) suggests "Fear of black male sexuality is often at root a fear of miscegenation" (169). The threat of violence and the lethal realities of lynching created a climate of intimidation reinforcing ideologies of white domination while providing a supremacist check on black sexuality (Wolf 1992).

In contemporary popular culture this continued fear and fascination has been transformed into a commodity form and black bodies are often coded in ways suggesting a unique worldliness and sensuality. In a culture still influenced by repressive Victorian notions of sexuality, black bodies "are clearly marked as more exciting, more intense and more threatening. The lure is the combination of pleasure and danger" (hooks 1992, 26). And while sexualized images are ever present, according to bell hooks (1992) "It is the young black male body that is seen as epitomizing this promise of wildness, of unlimited physical prowess and unbridled eroticism" (hooks 1992, 34). Yet outside the realm of consumption this same body is often the target of cultural scorn (hooks 34).

Peter Jackson's (1994) analyses of British athletes Daley Thompson and John Barnes helps elucidate the ways Jordan's athletic body negotiates these culturally constructed notions of apprehension and erotic vibrancy. According to Jackson, both Thompson and Barnes are presented in advertising discourses as an amiable vision of black masculinity, as their presumed sensual energy is coupled with impeccable moral reputations and pleasing personalities. This combination also distances Jordan from any suggestion of overt hypersexuality (McDonald, 1996b).

As an athlete and endorser Jordan encourages the targeted male consumer and sport fan to share vicariously in his presumed "natural" energy and sporting achievements (Barthel 1992). Howard White, Director of Athletic Relations for Nike makes this dynamic explicit, noting that the Jordan "brand stands for everything that Michael Jordan is —work ethic, heart, desire—and you can build that into a brand, when people wear that, they get excited about it" (cited in Moore 1997). Jordan's symbolism is also apparent in the Jordan fragrance line. Advertisements suggest that the Michael Jordan cologne "has captured the essence of Michael's personality, character and lifestyle off-the-court" by incorporating distinctive "fragrance" elements. According to the Bijan marketers, Jordan's personality is captured in the separate fragrance components "rare air," cool, home run, fairway, and sensual. The element cool reflects Michael's favorite "outdoor atmosphere"; home run includes scents from Jordan's "baseball glove"; fairway includes essences of lavender and fir needles to capture the scent of Jordan's favorite pastime— golf; sensual suggests that Jordan is "magnetic . . . he's sensual . . . he's unforgettable . . . providing a sensual base that lasts and lasts." This element combines "essences of sandalwood, patchouli and musk."

Jordan's body signifies a glorified upper-class lifestyle—fashionable, sexy, clean, and distinctive—at a time when men of all backgrounds are increasingly being positioned as the "objects of consumer desire" (Mort 1988, 194). In the never-ending capitalist quest to create new desires and anxieties, the promise of "use this to be noticed" is an advertising mantra that, while always present, is now more directly focused at men. This complements advertising's recent historical tendency to direct beauty and fashion products mainly at women. In greater measure than ever, men are offered images of successful African American men such as Jordan suggesting that a given product will enhance action, adventure, occupational status, and sexiness.

Yet this is a complicated process, for just as visual representations of Jordan invite a pleasurable perhaps homoeroticized look, so too do lingering Victorian norms of mainstream (hetero)sexuality and masculine hegemony suggest that this look needs to denied and rendered harmless. Indeed, Jordan and his promoters have taken great care to surround Jordan with an aura of modesty, familial devotion, and playful charm. A recent Hanes underwear commercial offers insight into his cultivated image. The scene opens with two (visibly) white women sitting on a park bench checking out the men who walk by, while trying to determine which style of underwear the men are wearing. They appear as the ultimate "liberated" women who actively express sexual desires. While we never see the men they are rating, we do hear their assessments with the alternating words, boxers, briefs, and bikini (underwear). Michael Jordan then enters the park walking very slowly as the camera pans upward to reveal his face and a suit coat jacket tossed causally over his shoulder. The sight of Jordan leaves the women virtually speechless, seemingly awed at the sight of someone so famous. Jordan immediately takes control of the situation, confessing that he is wearing "Hanes and let's just leave it at that." Jordan laughs sheepishly, shakes his head in disbelief, apparently realizing he has denied these women the chance to overtly objectify him. The women laugh with embarrassment at the discovery of their rating game, especially by someone as famous as Michael Jordan. The interracial heterosexual exchange is contained by Jordan's ability to take control of the situation. Jordan thus exposes the women's game without being exposed: His underwear style may remain a secret, but his affability and modesty are ensured.

Jordan's modesty and friendliness are also apparent in the marketing of his fragrance line. The web page for Bijan fragrances offers eight distinctive sound and visual vignettes of Jordan. Each picture has Jordan in a distinctively different scene away from the basketball court: behind the wheel of his car, speaking to students at an elementary school, with his golf putting iron, at home with his family and the family dog, and singing in the shower, with head lathered and bare chest exposed. This representation of Jordan as a regular guy, devoted husband and father serves to deny any overt association of homoeroticism or hypersexuality (see Jackson 1994; Cole and Denny 1994).

## In the Name of the Family

In a recent interview with Henry Louis Gates (1998), long-time agent, David Falk, suggests that his client Michael Jordan embodies quintessential American beliefs.

> It was clear when you met him that he grew up in a close-knit family . . . . His parents, James and Doloris [sic], had been very, very close to their children, had great family values—they were disciplined, respectful, pretty much color-blind. And obviously, based on his style of play . . . . We felt that he represented something as all-American as apple pie. So the game plan was to get involved with all-American companies like McDonald's and Coke and Chevrolet. Which we did. (cited in Gates 1998, 52)

That Falk would choose to link Jordan to "family values" is not surprising, as both the nuclear family and family values offer an omnipresent preoccupation of fin de millennium America. In the 1990s, Speaker of the House Newt Gingrich promoted the "Contract with America," offering the electorate "a Congress that respects the values and shares the faith of the American family" (cited in Stacey 1996, 4). President Bill Clinton suggested that America would be better off if children were born to married parents. Both Louis Farrakhan's Million Man March in October 1995 and former Colorado football coach Bill McCartney's Christian men's group, the Promise Keepers, implore men to reclaim their "God-given" place at the head of the family (Stacey 1996). October 1, 1996, saw the dedication of "Jordan Institute for Families" at the University of North Carolina. Michael Jordan explained his interest in the project: "I believe that everything that can be done should be done to preserve the family" (Jordan Institute for Families 1998). In 1998 Jordan confessed to talk show host Keenen Ivory Wayans that among his future aspirations: "First and foremost, down the road is being a parent and watching my kids grow up" (*Michael Jordan Says,* 34). And at the time of his second retirement from basketball, wife Juanita Jordan predicted that she would "see Michael doing a lot more car pooling" (Drell 1999, 8).

While never explicitly defined, the term *family values* refers to a conglomeration of ideals suggesting a link between morality and personal responsibility. The entire phrase suggests a nostalgic yearning for a yesteryear in which the traditional nuclear family—composed of the provider/father, stay at home nurturer/mother, and children—was the presumed cornerstone of the nation. The nuclear family's alleged decline continues to be used as the scapegoat for all sorts of "social ills" including welfare dependency, drug addiction, declining educational standards, and sexual "promiscuity" (Stacey 1996). Under the guise of a commitment to family values a whole host of policy changes have been enacted including monetary cutbacks in programs supporting social entitlement as well as funding to the arts and humanities. The family values rhetoric is deployed by conservatives to prevent sex education programs in public schools, the distribution of condoms, the integration of gays into the military, and access to abortion. This rhetoric decrying the nuclear family's demise relies upon privatized and conservative explanations for social conditions which ultimately mask the massive social changes accompanying deindustrialization and globalization (Stacey 1996).

Within the regressive family values climate, poor women have become the ultimate object of ridicule, being blamed both for their own poverty and the alleged collapse of national morality. Because poverty is largely perceived and misunderstood as a black problem, poor African American women are thus positioned as the chief transgressors of fin de siècle America. Under the guise of personal responsibility and family values, lawmakers continue to control poor women's bodies via the imposition of benefit caps on poor women who bear children. Others "use economic coercion to curtail fertility a priori (Norplant)" via compulsory birth control plans (Thomas 1998, 420). These attempts appeal to pathological stereotypes about the poor in which single women have sex and become pregnant for the sole purpose of obtaining a welfare check. As the mythology suggests this dysfunctional behavior is then presumably passed along to impressionable offspring creating a continuous cycle of welfare dependency. Generation poverty thus is the result of a lack of sexual "control" and a lack of commitment to the nuclear family. In constrast, socially constructed ideologies of marriage suggest that fidelity is a commitment designed to tame even the most hedonistic impulse, including (racist images of) excessive black hypersexuality. Dominant representations suggest that a chief danger facing America seems to be that indigent men and women refuse or can not curtail excessive sexual impulses (Thomas 1998).

The Jordan family offers the moral obverse of the most vilified image of single-female-headed households. The Jordans offer an enticing vision of black success and consumer comfort, countering the suggestion that black families are inherently pathological. *Rare Air: Michael on Michael* (Jordan and Vancil 1993) is a testimony to Michael Jordan as a latter-day Renaissance man, handsome, committed to the tough macho world of sport, yet apparently interested in becoming involved in the joys of hearth and home. Photo after photo offers a window into the Jordans' familial bliss and Michael Jordan's apparent status as a concerned husband and caring father. One picture features Jordan reclining in a bathtub with only his head and torso visible among the lather of a bubble bath. At his side are sons Jeffrey and Marcus with expressions of joy and excitement on their faces—not to mention bubbles. Perhaps the most idealistic representations of Jordan are those with his then-infant daughter Jasmine. A series of four pictures feature a bare-chested Jordan holding his daughter who is clad only in a diaper. It is a striking image, one designed to evoke a sentimental reaction at the contrast between Jordan's muscled body, overdetermined with visions of sensual energy, and an infant who represents tenderness, innocence, and vulnerability. The accompanying text notes Jordan's longing to be a hands-on parent:

> My perfect day? I would get up in the morning and go to a pancake house with my wife and kids and have breakfast. If it was summertime, I'd say, "Let's go to Great America." I haven't been to an amusement park since I was 12 or 13 myself. I can't go. I can, but I don't want to go through the whole spectacle. It's not fair to the children. (Jordan and Vancil 1993, 58)

Placed within the nuclear family, the Jordans offer a vision of loving restraint and a commitment to the joys of married family. In contrast to this image of the Jordans' blissful family life, conservatives continue to link black sexuality, crime, and deviance as the source of inner city crime. In the words of one commentator:

> While Black leaders and intellectuals regularly call for gun control to combat the Black crime problem, I rarely hear any of them condemn the sexual irresponsibility that results in the staggering Black illegitimate birth rate, the most significant precursor of that crime problem . . . Until the problems of sexual irresponsibility and illegitimate birth rates in the Black community are seriously addressed, this country will continue to be beset by the resulting and growing crime problem. (Fitzpatrick 1993, cited in Chideya 1995, 31).

This construction refocuses attention away from the structured inequaling resulting from institutional racism and sexism, capital flight, and lack of affordable child care. This regressive sentiment is embodied in numerous public policies including the Person Responsibility and Work Opportunity Reconciliation Act that President Clinton signed in 1996 in an effort "to end welfare as we know it." Among the hallmarks of this legislation are a five-year lifetime limit on benefits, mandatory work requirements after two years of aid, massive cutbacks in the Food Stamp program, and reductions in support directed at legal immigrants, people with disabilities and the elderly poor (McCrate and Smith 1998, 61). Underlying this initiative is the belief that the poor deserve their lot and must be forced by the government to break a vicious cycle of poverty enabled by the welfare state. This perspective ignores the shifting logic of global capitalism, as an increasing number of jobs are part time or temporary, many without health and/or child care benefits. The victim-blaming rhetoric of welfare reform suggests the necessity of a personal attitudinal change toward work rather than the need for structual remedies to alleviate poverty. In the absence of a sustained critique of late-twentieth-century and early twetny-first century, capitalism, poor women, especially African American women, are mistakenly positioned as emblematic of all that's wrong with America.

In contrast, the Jordans reinforce patriarchal gender beliefs with Michael serving as the ultimate breadwinner thanks to his sexual restraint, and lucrative basketball and endorsement earnings. An article in the November 1991 issue of *Ebony* magazine speaks volumes in this regard. Familial bliss to the Jordans is partaking in the good life which Michael has provided for his family, including exciting vacations, dinners, and the promise of greater rewards including future dream homes and numerous automobiles (Norment 1991). The Jordans serve as an enticing vision of the nuclear family at a time when the never-divorced nuclear family with the sole breadwinner father now accounts for only seven percent of the population. The celebrated visibility of the Jordans places the American Dream in a familial context signifying the alleged "fairness" of the American system.

## Concluding Comments

Rather than containing self-evident meanings, the Michael Jordan phenomenon is ideologically coded and affected by larger struggles related to (among others) gender, race, sexual, and class divisions. This analysis of Michael Jordan suggests that social life is always already imbedded in particular relations of power that encourage the production of particular knowledges. And while often misunderstood as a discursive phenomenon, dominant representations of Jordan cannot be artificially separated from their materialist roots. Indeed, representations are constituted and reproduced "by social practices in particular institutional contexts which have histories" (Seidman 1997, 67).

The ubiquitous images of Michael Jordan touting a variety of products occur at a time when men's bodies are increasingly being overtly sexualized in wider culture, especially in advertising. This is an especially powerful occurrence when applied to Jordan, given the white racist propensity to equate black masculinity with hypersexuality. And yet, just as visual representations of Jordan invite both racist connotations and an erotic or homoerotic encounter, so too do lingering Victorian norms of "acceptable" (hetero)sexuality—and white supremacy—suggest that these hypersexualized visions need to be rendered harmless.

Promoters have assisted in projecting Jordan as an incredible athlete and affable family man simultaneously inviting a pleasurable encounter with his presumed "natural" athletic body just as his position within the nuclear family counters stereotypical depictions of black masculinity as dangerously erotic. In doing so, Jordan's public persona also articulates a fresh political project, one that supports the conservative backlash "family values" climate of fin de siècle America. Thus, amid contradictory meanings, mainstream audiences are offered "safe sex," a voyeuristic encounter with Jordan's commodified body.

Critical analyses of the narratives surrounding Michael Jordan offer a unique point of access into the constitutive meanings and power relations of the larger worlds we inhabit. In a political sense, then, what matters most is what Michael Jordan has been made to mean, by whom, and for which material ends (McDonald and Birrell 1999). Conceptualizing the Michael Jordan phenomenon as an important site for understanding complex, contradictory articulations of power thus offers unique insights that ultimately ground progressive engagements within the contested terrain of popular culture.

# References

Andrews, D. (1996). "The fact(s) of Michael Jordan's blackness: Excavating a floating racial signifier," *Sociology of Sport Journal* 13(2):125–158.

Barthel, D. (1992). "When men put on appearances: Advertising and the social construction of masculinity." In *Men, masculinity and the media,* ed. S. Craig, 137–153. Newbury Park: Sage.

Birrell, S. (1988). "Discourses on the gender/sport relationship: From women in sport to gender relations." In *Exercise and Sport Science Reviews,* ed. K. B. Pandolf, 16, 459–502.

Breskin, D. (1989). "Michael Jordan, in his own orbit," *Gentleman's Quarterly* 59, 318–323, 394–397.

Brummett, B., and M. C. Duncan (1990). "Theorizing without totalizing: Specularity and televised sports," *The Quarterly Journal of Speech* 76(3):227–246.

Chideya, F. (1995). *Don't believe the hype: Fighting cultural misinformation about African Americans.* New York: Plume.

Cole, C., and D. Denny (1994). "Visualizing deviance in post-Reagan America: Magic Johnson, AIDS, and the promiscuous world of professional sport," *Critical Sociology* 20(3):123–147.

Connell, R. W. (1987). *Gender and power: society, the person and sexual politics.* Stanford: Stanford University Press.

duCille, A. (1997). "The unbearable darkness of being: "Fresh" thoughts on race, sex and the Simpsons." In *Birth of a nation 'hood: Gaze, script and spectacle in the O. J. Simpson case,* eds. T. Morrison and C. B. Lacour, 293–338. New York: Pantheon.

Davis, L. (1990). "The articulation of difference: White preoccupation with the question of racially linked genetic differences among athletes," *Sociology of Sport Journal* 7(2):179–187.

Drell, A. (1999, February 7). "The most famous dad in the world," *Chicago Sun-Times,* 8.

Dyson, M. (1993a). "Be like Mike?: Michael Jordan and the pedagogy of desire," *Cultural Studies* 7(1):64–72.

———. (1993b). "Reflecting black: African American cultural criticism," Minneapolis: University of Minnesota Press.

Gates, H. L. (1994). "Preface." In *Black male: Representations of masculinity in contemporary art,* ed. T. Golden, 11–14. New York: Whitney Museum of American Art.

———. (1998, June 1). "Net worth," *New Yorker,* 48–61.

George, N. (1996, November 1). "Rare Jordan," *Essence* 27(7):106–108.

Giroux, H. (1994). *Disturbing pleasures.* New York: Routledge.

Grossberg, L. (1992). *We gotta get out of this place: Popular conservatism and postmodern culture.* New York: Routledge.

Grunwald, L. (1996, July). "The soul of these beautiful machines," *Life,* 19(8), 64–66.

Gunther, M. (1997, July 21). "They all want to be like Mike," *Fortune* 136(2):51–53.

Halberstam, D. (1991, December 23). "A hero for the wired world," *Sports Illustrated* 75(27):76–81.

Hall, S. (1985). "Signification, representation and ideology: Althusser and the post-structuralist debates." *Critical Studies in Mass Communication* 2:91–114.

———. (1986). "On postmodernism and articulation: An interview," *Journal of Communication Inquiry* 10(2):45–60.

Harris, O. (1991). "The image of the African American in psychological journals, 1825–1923," *The Black Scholar* 21(4):25–29.

hooks, b. (1992). *Black looks: Race and representation.* Boston: South End.

Howard, J. (1996, December 30). "Father's day," *Sports Illustrated* 85(27):68–69.

Jackson, P. (1994). "Black male: Advertising and the cultural politics of masculinity," *Gender, Place and Culture* 1(1):49–59.

Jeffords, S. (1994). *Hard bodies: Hollywood masculinity in the Reagan era.* New Brunswick, NJ: Rutgers University Press.

Jordan, M., and M. Vancil (1993). *Rare air: Michael on Michael.* San Francisco: Collins.

Jordan Institute for Families (1998). Website, www.unc.edu/depts/family/jif.htm.

Krugel, M. (1994). *Jordan: The man, his words, his life.* New York: St. Martin's.

Levine, L. (1977). *Black culture and black consciousness: Afro-American thought from slavery to freedom.* Oxford: Oxford University Press.

Lipsitz, G. (1997). "The greatest story ever sold: Marketing and the O. J. Simpson trial." In *Birth of a nation 'hood: Gaze, script and spectacle in the O. J. Simpson case,* eds. T. Morrison and C. Lacour, 3-30. New York: Pantheon.

Manning, S. (1998). "The incredible success of Michael Jordan," *Upscale* 9(6):36–40.

McCallum, J. (1991, December 23). "Alone on the mountain top," *Sports Illustrated* 75(27):64–69.

McCrate, E. and J. Smith (1998). "When work doesn't work: The failure of current welfare reform," *Gender and Society* 12(1):61–80.

McDonald, M. G. (1996a). "Horatio Alger with a jump shot: Michael Jordan and the American dream," *Iowa Journal of Cultural Studies* 15:33–47.

———. (1996b). "Michael Jordan's family values: Marketing, meaning and post-Reagan America," *Sociology of Sport Journal* 13:344–365.

McDonald, M. G., and Birrell, S. (1998, August). *Reading sport critically.* Paper presented at the meeting of the International Sociology of Sport Association held in conjunction with the 14th International Sociological Association World Congress, Montreal, Quebec, Canada.

———. (1999). "Reading sport critically: A methodology for interrogating power," *Sociology of Sport Journal* 16(4): 283–300.

Messner, M. (1988). "Sport and male domination: The female athlete as contested terrain," *Sociology of Sport Journal* 5:197–211.

"Michael Jordan says his ultimate dream is to spend more time 'watching my kids grow up.'" (1998, March 9). *Jet* 93(15):34–35.

Moore, T. (1997). "Jordan, inc.," *Slam presents Jordan* (Special Issue), 72–77.

Morrison, T., and C. Lacour (1997). *Birth of a nation 'hood: Gaze, script and spectacle in the O. J. Simpson case.* New York: Pantheon.

Mort, F. (1988). "Boy's own?: Masculinity, style and popular culture." In *Male order: Unwrapping masculinity,* eds. R. Chapman and J. Rutherford, 193–224. London: Lawrence and Wishart.

"No Bull Jordan Quits." (1993, October 6). *Iowa City Press Citizen.* p. 1A–2A.

Norment, L. (1991, November). "Michael and Juanita Jordan talk about love, marriage and life after basketball." *Ebony* 47: 68–76.

Price, S. L. (1997a, December 8). "Is it in the genes?" *Sports Illustrated* 87(3):52–55.

———. (1997b, December 8). "What ever happened to the white athlete?" *Sports Illustrated* 87(3):30–51.

Reeves, J. (1989). "TV's world of sports: Presenting and playing the game." In *Television studies: Textual analysis,* eds. G. Burns and J. Thompson, 205–219. New York: Praeger.

Seidman, S. (1997). *Difference troubles: Queering social theory and sexual politics.* New York: Cambridge University Press.

Smith, S. (1995). *Second coming: The strange odyssey of Michael Jordan—from courtside to home plate and back again.* New York: Harper Collins.

Sobol, K. (1974). *Babe Ruth and the American dream.* New York: Ballentine.

Sperling, D. (Executive Producer). (1989). *Michael Jordan: Come fly with me.* New York: CBS/Fox.

Stacey, J. (1996). *In the name of the family: Rethinking family values in the postmodern age.* Boston: Beacon.

Susman, W. (1984). *Culture as history: The transformation of American society in the twentieth century.* New York: Pantheon.

Swift, E. M. (1991, June 3). "From corned beef to caviar," *Sports Illustrated* 74(27):54–58.

Taylor, P. (1998, February 16). "Hang in there," *Sports Illustrated* 88(6):36–43.

Theberge, N. (1991). "Reflections on the body in the sociology of sport," *Quest* 43:123–134.

Thomas, B. (1999, June 4). "They really want to be like Mike; Jordan's sense of style has turned him into a fashion icon whose name moves merchandise," *Los Angeles Times,* E1.

Thomas, S. (1998). "Race, gender, and welfare reform: The antinatalist response," *Journal of Black Studies* 28(4):419–446.

Toepfer, S. (1996, September 16). "Best and worst dressed people of '96." *People Magazine,* 67–115.

West, C. (1993). *Race matters.* Boston: Beacon Press.

Wiggins, D. (1989). "'Great speed but little stamina:'The historical debate over black athletic superiority," *Journal of Sport History* 16(2):158–185.

Wolf, C. (1992). "The construction of a lynching," *Sociological Inquiry* 62(1):83–96.

# J O R D A N

## and the Global Marketplace

# 7

# The Global Jordanscape

Ben Carrington
David L. Andrews
Steven J. Jackson
Zbigniew Mazur

In the Academy Award–winning motion picture, *Pulp Fiction,* the preco-
ciously talented Quentin Tarantino directs a parodic, if at times
disturbing, depiction of life within contemporary America. Tarantino's narrative mixes gratuitous violence with an understated celebration of mundane popular cultural artifacts: contradictory elements that inhabit, and
thereby constitute, the seamier side of everyday American existence upon
which Tarantino casts his ironic gaze. Yet Tarantino's adroit observations of
popular culture are not reserved for the American context alone. As the following quote ably demonstrates, Tarantino also cleverly alludes to the fact
that the spread of American popular cultural artifacts is not confined by the
geographical boundaries of the forty-eight contiguous states, Alaska, and
Hawaii (it would seem naive in the extreme to think it ever has been).
Indeed, the humorous interplay between Jules (Samuel L. Jackson) and
Vincent (John Travolta) exercises a number of issues pertaining to the
ongoing intellectual debate surrounding the Americanization of global culture, which itself represents a significant armature of the wider process of
globalization:

This chapter is a revised version of "Jordanscapes: A preliminary analysis of the global popular" by D. L. Andrews, B. Carrington, S. Jackson, and Z. Mazur (1996), *Sociology of Sport
Journal,* 13(4):428–457. Reprinted by permission of Human Kinetics Publishers.

Vincent:   But you know what the funniest thing about Europe is?

Jules:     What?

Vincent:   It's the little differences. I mean they got the same shit over there that they got here, it's, it's just there it's a little different.

Jules:     Example.

Vincent:   Alright, well you can walk into a movie theater in Amsterdam and buy a beer. And I don't mean in no paper cup. You're talking about a glass of beer. And in Paris, you can buy a beer in McDonald's. *[Jules looks incredulously]* And you know what they call a Quarter-pounder with Cheese in Paris?

Jules:     They don't call it a Quarterpounder with Cheese?

Vincent:   No, they got the metric system, they wouldn't know what the fuck a quarterpounder is.

Jules:     What do they call it?

Vincent:   They call it Royale with Cheese.

Jules:     Royale with Cheese! *[Jules smiles]* What do they call a Big Mac.

Vincent:   A Big Mac's a Big Mac, but they call it le Big Mac.

Jules:     *[In a pseudo French accent]* Le Big Mac. Ha, ha, ha, ha. What do they call a Whopper?

Vincent:   I don't know, I didn't go into Burger King. You know what they put on french fries in Holland instead of ketchup?

Jules:     What?

Vincent:   Mayonnaise.

Jules:     God damn!

Vincent:   *[Laughing]* I seen 'em do it man, fucking drowning them in that shit.

—Opening scene from *Pulp Fiction,*
directed by Quentin Tarantino 1994

Morley and Robins neatly distinguish globalization as the influence that emergent world markets and products—stimulated by expanding global image industries and supplied by increasingly sophisticated transnational delivery systems—have upon the experience of everyday lives within particular cultural settings (Morley and Robins 1995). This phenomenon has occupied a niche within critical cultural studies at least since Richard Hoggart's (1957) influential scrutiny of what he perceived as the creeping Americanization of postwar British existence. Over the last decade a voluminous debate has evolved around the concept of globalization, prompting Featherstone and Lash (1995) to identify this multifaceted phenomenon as replacing modernity and postmodernity as the central thematic within current cultural theorizing (for example, see Appadurai 1996; McGrew 1992; Robertson 1995; Wallerstein 1990). As Held et al. put it, "Globalization is an idea whose time has come" (1999, 1). Certainly within the sociology of sport community, discussions of globalization have generated an unusually vigorous and insightful body of literature. Without wishing to oversimplify this ongoing, cross-disciplinary debate, *very* broadly speaking interpretations of the cultural impact of globalization can be classified into two distinct theoretical camps: the (economic) homogenizers and the (cultural) heterogenizers. In almost pessimistic resignation, the homogenizers herald the advent of an economically driven era dominated by a creeping global standardization. The heterogenizers, however, repudiate the stultifying influence of global technologies and products in favor of stressing the inherent uniqueness of every localized cultural context. Thus, the adherents of the former framework can be accused of a deterministic universalization, whereas proponents of the latter explanation veer toward an unconvincing romanticization of the ethnic particular.

Distancing itself from the dichotomous nature of much of the globalization literature, this project is underpinned by the need to resolve the interpretative tension between advocates of global homogeneity or global heterogeneity, globalism or localism, sameness or difference. Returning to *Pulp Fiction,* Vincent's droll observation pertaining to the presence of popular American products in Europe, "they got the same shit over there that they got here, its, its just there its a little different" demonstrates a tacit recognition of the cultural dialectic at work within the process and experience of globalization. Such an understanding has been similarly expressed, albeit in a more sophisticated manner, by cultural theorists such as Ang (1996), Appadurai (1996), Bird (1993), Cvetkovich and Kellner (1997), Robins (1990; 1991), Morley and Robins (1995), and Robertson (1995). Despite acknowledged differences in their respective positions and projects relating to the process of globalization, these scholars are all linked by their stated goal of comprehensively articulating the necessary relationship between the global and the local. According to such dialectic thinking, the consumption of global commodity-signs inextricably occurs within localized settings, so the local can only be seen as a "fluid and relational space, constituted only in and through its relation to the global" (Robins 1991, 35). Prompted by

such an understanding, the goal of this project is to examine the interconnections and disjunctures that distinguish the complex relationship between
global media culture and local meaning. Specifically, this chapter uses
Michael Jordan, a vivid example of the "export to the entire world" (Kellner
1995, 5) of much of America's commodity-sign culture, as a suggestive vehicle for critically exploring the relationship between globally mediated cultural products, and the cultural contingencies of three markedly distinct
localized contexts. The task of analyzing Michael Jordan's position and influence as part of what Kellner described as the "global popular" (1995, 5)—
the expanding inventory of prominent forms of globalized media and
consumer culture—will be realized by offering admittedly tentative, but
hopefully informative, reconstructions of Jordan's location and significance
within particular national cultural contexts, namely New Zealand, Poland,
and Britain.

In his "Theory of Political Economy," discussed in the general introduction to the *Grundrisse,* Karl Marx prefigured the reconstructive interpretative
approach adopted within this study; "even the most abstract categories . . . are
by the very definiteness of the abstraction a product of historical conditions as
well, and are fully applicable only to and under those conditions" (McLellan
1977, 355). Understanding the meaning of Michael Jordan within specific
localized cultural contexts demands the reconstruction of the multiple and
interrelated forces that fashion the conjuncture in question (social, cultural,
political, economic, and technological considerations). For, as E. P. Thompson
put it, a cultural product only becomes meaningful "in an ensemble of other
meanings" (1972, 45). Thus, we hope to provide a preliminary analysis of the
position occupied by globally intrusive American sporting icons, such as
Michael Jordan, within contrasting cultural contexts. Our goal is to contribute
to what Chen (1992) proposed as a new internationalist localism within cultural studies, that counters the debilitating introspection of much critical cultural analysis. Following Chen, it is our assertion that critical social researchers
must acknowledge that it makes no political or intellectual sense to refer to
national cultures, national identities, and subjectivities, "without accounting for
these transnational forces flowing into/through our (social) body" (1992, 481).

## Sketching the Jordanscapes: Thinking Globally
## *and* Locally

Our commercials are several things—they're color, they're music, and
they're athletic, and frankly what people learn and know is that we are an
American company. We're selling products that are authentic athletic, and

Michael Jordan is one image that represents that. He is probably the best recognized, best-known American athlete throughout the world.
—Richard J. Donahue, Nike president

We must balance an acceptance that audiences are in certain respects active in their choice, consumption and interpretation of media texts, with a recognition of how that activity is framed and limited, in its different modalities and varieties, by the dynamics of cultural power.
—Morley and Robins

Within an American context Michael Jordan became everybody's All-American commodity sign (see Andrews 1996) due to Nike's—and affiliated corporate concerns, mostly notably those of the National Basketball Association (NBA), McDonald's, and Gatorade—astute manipulation of intersecting economic, cultural, media, and technological forces in "fashioning a commercially viable language of appearances and images" (Goldman 1992, 37). Equally, Nike was at the forefront of the same intertextual corporate coalition that engineered Jordan's global ubiquity: a process motivated by Nike et al.'s desire to exploit largely untapped external markets. This hugely successful transnational stratagem resulted in Jordan's, thereby Nike's and latterly the NBA's, conclusive entry into the inventory of the "global popular" (Kellner 1995, 5). For, to even the most casual observer, Michael Jordan's commodified image can be confronted with startling regularity when strolling through the commercial hyperspaces of the world's major cities, deindustrialized urban wastelands, excessively affluent suburban fortresses, or even rural hinterlands. Moreover, as Griffin noted, "Michael Jordan is not just a sports star; his fame has far exceeded that . . . . He is the most recognized American figure on the planet. It's almost impossible to find someone who doesn't know him" (quoted in Deardoff 1995, 10).

According to one well-respected journalist, Jordan was destined to rise to global fame in the era of the communication satellite, "Since America is the home team in the wired world . . . . It was therefore almost inevitable *given basketball's easy comprehensibility* that the first athletic superstar of the wired world would be a black American basketball player who played above the rim" (Halberstam 1991, 78, emphasis added). Certainly, what is an ever expanding inventory of global cultural artifacts is dominated by the machinations of American mediated popular culture. As Ang noted, the locus of the global media is undeniably America, and there exists a "very substantial Americanness of much 'global' media, not only in terms of corporate ownership and working principles, but also, more flagrantly, in terms of symbolic content: images, sounds, stories, names" (Ang 1996, 161). This cultural phenomenon, exemplified by the global presence of Michael Jordan, has stimulated a virulent strain of anti-Americanization criticism (see Webster 1988, 174–208), built on a pessimistic "vision of the globe flattened into a low-level monoculture, a gigantic K-Mart with no exit" (Buell 1994, 1). Plainly, this one-sided discourse on global Americanization fails to account for the built-in particularity related to the ways in which *American* artifacts are consumed. As Lash and Urry noted:

> [I]t is necessary to take into account not only the global processes of production but also the circumstances in which cultural products are received by audiences. Global programmes, even like *Dallas,* are read differently in different countries and places. Audiences possess skills in reading and using programmes, through talk in households and workplaces and through use of the VCR. At the level of audiences it is inconceivable that there could be global culture. Indeed in some respects there is an increasing contradiction between centralized production (at least in some respects) and more decentralized and fragmented reception. (1994, 308)

Hence, within the remainder of this chapter we intend to build upon the body of work initiated by writers such as Ang (1989) and Liebes and Katz (1990) who have highlighted the processes and practices whereby televised *American* popular culture is differentially located within, and according to, different cultural contexts. In advancing three preliminary vignettes that focus on the popular appropriation of one slice of mediated Americana—namely Michael Jordan—in New Zealand, Poland, and Britain, our goal is to explicate the unavoidable interplay between global and local forces that contributes to the reshaping of cultural spaces of identity within the new global media landscape. It should also be pointed out that although this project represents collaborative research in the truest sense of the term, the three contextual analyses have been written by the authors living and researching in their respective countries, hence the shift between first and third person interlocutor in some sections. As a result there is an unavoidable, and indeed intended, polyvocal nature to this chapter.

### Above the Pacific Rim: Michael Jordan Goes Down Under

In combination, the localized case studies in this chapter confirm the popular references to Michael Jordan as the "everywhere man," not only as an internationally admired sporting hero, but as a global commodity-sign articulated through his ever expanding array of transnational corporate alliances including Nike, the NBA, McDonald's, Coca-Cola, Chevrolet, and Hanes. To some extent one can gauge the veracity of the title "everywhere man" by virtue of his location, despite his recent retirement, within remote cultural contexts. One such "remote" location, at least in geospatial and temporal terms, is New Zealand, or *Aotearoa* ("Land of the Long White Cloud") as it is known by the indigenous Maori. This section uses Michael Jordan as a vehicle for understanding the interconnections and disjunctures that distinguish the complex relationship between global media and local meaning. Specifically, the aim of this section is to: (a) briefly refer to the postcolonial context in New Zealand; (b) identify the popular presence of American popular culture and Michael Jordan in particular within New Zealand; and, (c) initiate a preliminary discussion of what might be referred to as the sporting black Pacific, with respect to the trans-Pacific gaze and identification of New Zealand youth with African American athletes such as Michael Jordan.

## The Postcolonial Context of New Zealand

Throughout its colonization, New Zealand looked to Britain as a source of guidance for almost every aspect of its political, economic, and cultural life. Arguably, its identity was overwhelmingly defined through its love-hate and subordinated relationship with Britain. However, following World War II shifting political, economic, and cultural alliances resulted in a renewed search for symbolic markers of distinction that could transform New Zealand through one of its early phases of postcolonialism.

More recently, New Zealand confirmed its reputation as the social laboratory of the world by virtue of the dramatic changes it has undertaken as it distances itself from a postcolonial past. Indeed, according to New Zealand journalist and television documentary producer Marcia Russell (1996), the transformation of New Zealand between 1984 and 1993 can best be described as a "revolution." For example, in her book of the same name she notes that

> [b]etween 1984 and 1993, New Zealand became a laboratory for an experiment: the transformation of the world's first welfare state into the world's first post-welfare state. Around the world, gurus of market-driven economic theory watched in envy as a tiny nation in the South Pacific did an about-turn and marched in a different direction. (Russell 1996, 9)

In the course of the revolution and its immediate aftermath there were dramatic technological, foreign policy, constitutional, electoral, immigration, and economic changes (Haworth 1994; Kelsey 1996). As Russell (1996, 246) puts it: there was a "convulsive reconstruction" as New Zealand moved from being an isolated, overly regulated, and inward looking nation to one of the most deregulated in the world. In effect, after surviving a market-driven economy it then faced a market-driven government (Russell 1996). Notwithstanding the apparent popularity of the social-democratic model of politics, encapsulated under the "Third Way" rubric, popularized by Blair, Clinton, and Schröder in the late 1990s, the New Zealand model has received a lot of international attention. In fact, several foreign nations, including Canada and several in Europe and Scandinavia are either employing some of the neo-Right New Zealand agenda or seriously considering its potential benefits. However, despite the fact that both free market analysts and political brokers have heralded the apparent "success" of the New Zealand project, highlighted by the state's withdrawal from many areas of social life (Duncan and Bollard 1992), it is clear that "success" has been narrowly defined. The reappearance of food banks for the first time since the 1930s is but one indicator that, in New Zealand, the poor are worse off than ever while the rich are getting richer (Russell 1996). Indeed, the return to power of a center-Left coalition government, in November 1999, is further evidence that the success of the political Right throughout most of the 1990s now appears to be at an end.

In large part, the so-called revolution of the late 1980s and early 1990s was propelled by a multitude of global economic and technological changes that caught this relatively isolated and tranquil little piece of paradise by surprise. Suddenly, New Zealand's future was inextricably linked to an increasingly interdependent and globally wired world. As a consequence there were new questions about the basis and meaning of New Zealand cultural identity within a postcolonial context. Arguably, the renewed search for identity could be described as both inward and outward looking. First, there is a romanticized embracement of what are perceived to be unique traditional cultural practices and symbols, tending to be steeped in nostalgia (Hutchison 1991). And, second, there is a resurgence of political and cultural consciousness among indigenous and other marginalized voices, which seek legitimacy both within and outside of the constraints of the existing national formation. Thus, the postcolonial quest for identity involves a coexisting embracement of, and resistance toward, "otherness." Our particular concern is with New Zealand's dialectic embracement and resistance, or emergent junctures and disjunctures, associated with the global/local nexus of American popular culture, including the NBA and global icons such as Michael Jordan. In our view a key factor in any discussion of global process and local culture in New Zealand requires some reference to its rather rapid deregulation in the late 1980s.

According to Hutchison and Lealand (1996, 7) since deregulation in 1988–1989, "New Zealand has witnessed a radical and revolutionary reshaping of its mediascape . . . that is unprecedented in the rest of the world." For example, the deregulation of New Zealand media has resulted in the possibility of complete foreign ownership—a situation that is unparalleled within the OECD. Thus, while global forces are securing the infrastructure for satellite television and in the face of limited local programming, there are increasing pressures to import foreign, largely American, media products (Spicer, Powell, and Emanuel 1996). It comes as little surprise that the emergence of the twenty-four-hour SKY Sport network in New Zealand virtually demanded the securement of high profile American sport programming such as the NBA.

Basketball in general, and the NBA in particular, already had a small, but avid, following in New Zealand due in large part to weekly NBA highlight programs, weekly sports magazine shows, regular sport news coverage, and a domestic national semiprofessional league. It is through the media that American popular culture in general and one of its icons, Michael Jordan, specifically, emerged within New Zealand. Television in particular provided the platform through which Jordan and his attendant corporate alliances could reach and engage distant audiences. In sum, the shifting domestic mediascape, including the increasing demand for, and availability of, globally produced sports programs, facilitated the NBA's emergence within New Zealand. Next, we outline some of the examples that demonstrate the popular, albeit often superficial, presence of Michael Jordan as an icon of American popular culture in New Zealand.

## The Everywhere Man in the Land of the Long White Cloud

Michael Jordan, by name or by image, has gained increasing popularity in New Zealand over the past ten years. For example, one study of New Zealand high school students revealed that Michael Jordan was by far the number one choice as regards sports role models (see Melnick and Jackson 1993; 1996). In a more focused analysis of the popular identification of Michael Jordan among New Zealand university students, another study indicated that every person at least knew who he was (Jackson and Andrews 1994). Perhaps the most striking result from this study was the fact that just under 50 percent identified Jordan with respect to his Nike sponsorship while another 18 percent linked Jordan with McDonald's. Numerous other corporate affiliations were noted but even for those students who failed to name a specific sponsor mention was often made of his role as an imaged commodity. These results confirmed our initial suspicions that Jordan's popular presence is predicated on his intertextual corporate alliances. An example may help illustrate the

intertextual presence of the NBA in the local context of New Zealand. The
NBA gains most of its media visibility through SKY TV, the local rendition
of the Murdoch-owned global media company. While actual games, both live
and tape-delayed, are often direct feeds, the negotiation for advertisements is
often done on a more regional basis.

During the 1995 playoffs one particular sequence of commercials aired
on New Zealand's SKY TV effectively illustrates the global promotional
culture of the NBA. The advertisements, in unedited order, were: a Nike ad
featuring Michael Jordan doing a slow motion dunk to the spiritual sound
of a choir, a Hong Kong–based Chinese-language ad for NBA merchandise,
a Sprite soft drink ad that, ironically, tells us that "Image is nothing," a Nike
soccer commercial popularly known as "the wall," which features a soccer
ball circulating the globe being passed between globally recognizable soccer stars, and, finally, a Reebok (Planet Reebok) commercial that illustrates
the global world of sport and includes images of NBA star Shaquille
O'Neal. In light of the cross-promotional strategies previously alluded to,
most of the intertextual links between the NBA and Jordan, O'Neal, Nike,
and Reebok are fairly evident. The Chinese NBA merchandise ad, which
uses an image of Michael Jordan, appears completely out of place within a
New Zealand context, and is obviously part of a larger Asia-Pacific regionally based campaign. The Sprite commercial (produced by Coca-Cola,
which formerly sponsored Jordan) features basketball star Grant Hill and
identifies the product as the "official drink of the NBA." No doubt the
overall intertextual presence and influence of the advertisements could be
interpreted much more broadly. However, at the very least these advertisements promote a variety of American cultural products including: the
NBA, Sprite (Coca-Cola), Nike, and Reebok. In addition, the ads also construct Jordan, O'Neal, and Hill as commodity-signs, both directly as sport
heroes and, indirectly, through their other commercial affiliations (e.g.,
Jordan and McDonald's, Chevrolet, Gatorade). An important question that
emerges from this discussion is the nature and extent to which these intertextual mediated images are incorporated into the everyday lives of New
Zealand youth.

By chance, I had the opportunity to discuss the popular cultural impact
of Michael Jordan and the NBA with three young males in New Zealand,
aged seven, eight, and eleven. I was intrigued by their desire for NBA clothing, but what really astounded me was the depth and intensity of their interest in NBA collectors' cards. Not only did they possess a genuine business
savvy in relation to the exchange and market value of their collections but

also a broad knowledge base with respect to the players themselves, including personal anecdotes and performance statistics. Although these youth certainly held an interest in other players, particularly Shaquille O'Neal, the return of Michael Jordan in 1996 restored his center stage position. For example, after drawing my attention to his shiny new shoes I questioned seven-year-old Simon about why he chose Nike, especially given his love of Shaq and his Orlando Magic baseball cap. In an admittedly leading question, I asked him if it was because of Michael Jordan's return and he said "yes." When I asked him what shoes he would have bought if Jordan had not returned he said, "Reebok," and when asked why he simply said, "Shaq." The interviews with the young children highlight an important point. In many respects the fascination of these Kiwi kids with the NBA and Michael Jordan parallels that of youth in many other countries. However, the fascinating point about these kids' identifications is that they had never actually seen an NBA game; indeed, due to transmission and reception barriers where they reside they are unable to even subscribe to SKY Television (the main source of NBA coverage). Hence, while direct media coverage of a particular sport is important in cultivating a mass market of consumers, the available advertisements that employ particular cultural practices such as basketball, and high profile global icons such as Michael Jordan, to sell their commodities are equally important in establishing a discourse that popularizes their mutually reinforcing intertextuality.

While the previous examples touch upon what could be described as embracement of Michael Jordan, there is certainly some evidence of more ambiguous, sometimes resistant responses to American popular culture in general and the global sporting hero in particular. For example, in 1995, New Zealand's national sport, rugby, was in the midst of a crisis, or what Peter Fitzsimons (1996) characterized in the title of his book: *The Rugby War*. To put the situation into context, rugby, as New Zealand's national sport and an increasingly global game, had for years been struggling through a conspicuously slow transformation from pseudo amateurism to professionalism. Suddenly, at least in relative terms, rugby's labor force found itself in the midst of a bidding war between two rival organizations. The first, known as the World Rugby Corporation (WRC), was being backed, though to a lesser extent than many believed, by Australian media kingpin Kerry Packer. The second, and eventual victor, was a group consisting of the three premier Southern Hemisphere national rugby unions (New Zealand, Australia and South Africa). The latter group was being backed by media mogul Rupert Murdoch. The highly secretive global battle between these two organizations, particularly on the part of the WRC, resembled international espionage. Of primary concern for our interests however, was the dramatic shift in thinking and philosophy among the players, who suddenly realized that they were indeed a form of athletic labor, for all intents and purposes commodities that had been making, and would now more than ever make, other parties very wealthy. Fitzsimons (1996) recounts a particularly symbolic moment in 1995 when representatives of the Murdoch-subsidized New Zealand Rugby Football Union (NZRFU) met with representatives of the current All Blacks. Much to their surprise and perhaps chagrin, the highly respected elders of the national game encountered the new breed of soon-to-be professional All Blacks. Fitzsimons contrasts the two generations of All Blacks noting that those of the past had played for pride and honor alone, whereas:

> The younger generation, on the other hand, while just as honoured to wear the famous jersey, were part of the Jordan Generation of sportsmen around the world: not necessarily avaricious or greedy, but simply wanting a fair share of the wealth that they knew they were creating. Just as Michael Jordan had done, with such enormous success. (Fitzsimons 1996, 143)

The "Jordan Generation" could, in fact, be considered a response to global forces, not unlike those that were taking the NBA to the far corners of the earth and making Michael Jordan one of the most recognized figures on the planet. There was a tacit recognition of the new media technologies, the potential global audiences, and the corresponding rewards available through corporate sponsorships and advertising.

This very point was confirmed in 1995 by Ian Robson (CEO of the Auckland Warriors, a new rugby league franchise and arguably the first professional sport team in New Zealand), during a roundtable discussion on the future of rugby in light of the globalization of sport. According to Robson:

> [W]e're in a time now where for the young lads behind us, the most admired recognised and acknowledged sporting hero is not a New Zealander he's a black American by the name of Michael Jordan . . . and if we, as sporting administrators . . . don't use the resources that men like Murdoch are now placing before us . . . to reestablish and create heroes, create role models . . . we stand still at our own peril. (*Fraser*, TV1 1995)

Notably, Robson recognizes both the threats and the opportunities linked to the influence of the likes of Rupert Murdoch, who was at least indirectly instrumental in creating global sport and global icons such as Michael Jordan. Specifically, it would appear that Robson gauges the impact of Michael Jordan as a threat via his standing as New Zealand youths' most popular sporting hero. Conversely, he is acutely aware that New Zealand sport could and should harness the newly emergent media technologies in order to survive and thrive within the global marketplace. A final small, but conspicuous, point made by

Robson that warrants attention concerns Michael Jordan's racial identity. Specifically, he notes that: "the most admired, recognised and acknowledged sporting hero is not a New Zealander he's a black American by the name of Michael Jordan." Though it may seem trivial, to the extent that Michael Jordan is indeed black, it raises a few questions about the representation and meaning of black, particularly American, athletes or celebrities within a New Zealand context. For example, how do New Zealand audiences identify with foreign athletes such as Michael Jordan? Given the overwhelmingly negative media portrayals of blacks in other realms do negative racial/ethnic stereotypes become articulated to specific individual identities? Do Maori and/or Polynesian youth hold a special affinity for African American athletes and celebrities by virtue of perceived shared social struggles? Clearly, it is beyond the scope of this analysis to address all of these issues. Nevertheless, some pre-liminary discussion of the trans-Pacific relationship between local audiences and popular cultural sporting heroes is provided.

## The Sporting Black Pacific

In his analysis of Jordan's location within the popular imaginary of black British youth, Ben Carrington (Andrews, Carrington, Jackson, and Mazur 1996; see this chapter too) provided an insightful examination of the transnational framework within which black sporting identities need to be understood. Extending Paul Gilroy's (1993) notion of the "black Atlantic," Carrington interrogated the specific "sporting black Atlantic," in order to reveal the new intermediary spaces of identity that have emerged between the global and the local, in this case Britain. For Carrington, the sporting black Atlantic represents

> a complex cultural and political space, unhindered by the constraints of national boundaries, whereby migrations and/or achievements of Black athletes have come to assume greater significance for the dispersed peoples and cultures of the Black diaspora—the sports arena, thus operates as an important symbolic space in the struggle of Black peoples against the ideologies and practices of White supremacy. (Andrews, Carrington, Jackson, and Mazur 1996, 449)

Through his essay Carrington notes how black athletes, regardless of whether they are from Africa, the Caribbean, or America, tend to be defined in terms of their "black" identity by black British males. This occurs largely because of the exclusionary definitions of British national identity which have historically failed to accommodate black and other racial/ethnic identities. The result is a particular type of diaspora, whereby black Britons look "across the Atlantic," and elsewhere in order to appropriate the "raw materials for creative purposes which redefine what it means to be black, adapting it to distinctly British experiences and meanings" (Gilroy 1987, 154).

Without question, the context of the black British diaspora is unique and it is not our intention to suggest that direct comparisons could or should be made with New Zealand. However, there are some indications that New Zealand youth do identify with American popular culture and particular aspects of African American culture, including: music, fashion, and sport (Allison 1990; Jackson and Andrews 1996; Lealand 1994). In all likelihood Kiwi youth are attracted to the hype and glamor of American styles and trends because they express a form of difference (Jackson and Andrews 1996; Lealand 1994). Moreover, the identification of Maori and Polynesian youth in New Zealand may have another dimension. As Wilcox (1996, 123) notes:

> Maori and Polynesian youth . . . tend to identify with the music, dress, and styles of their African-American counterparts [where] they find . . . a focal point of resistance, a means of challenging the hegemony of New Zealand's overwhelmingly white power structure through membership in a transnational tribe.

Thus, identification with what they perceive to be their oppressed, trans-Pacific "brothers" and "sisters" may be exhibited through consumption of American popular culture but it may also reflect a more serious agenda linked to racial politics. No doubt this would be a fruitful area for future analyses. Moreover, in conjunction with the notion of a "sporting black Pacific" it would be useful to examine the nature and extent to which African American identities and practices are resisted within particular factions within the New Zealand community. For example, it may be that concerns about American televisual violence may be exacerbated by local articulations of street gang culture and perceived rising levels of violence in general. The recent New Zealand banning of NBA basketball star Shawn Kemp's Reebok Kamikaze advertisement is a case in point. Confirming its reputation for employing one of the world's most conservative, yet contradictory, media broadcast policies regarding violence, New Zealand's Television Commercial Approvals Bureau has prohibited the airing of the commercial. The ban has surprised many people and Reebok in particular, given that the same ad is shown all over the world without controversy, the physical contact displayed is between Shawn Kemp and an imaginary, animated opponent, and, finally, there are many similar ads featuring New Zealand athletes that have been approved. Until further analysis is undertaken the picture remains unclear. However, one possible interpretation is that local state censorship regulations could be interpreted as a form of resistance against threatening images of America, constructed through the intersection of sport, technology, and commodified images of violence and racial otherness.

On January 13, 1999, Michael Jordan retired from the NBA for the second and final time. Yet his legacy within New Zealand (and no doubt elsewhere) lives on. And while his first retirement was defined in terms of his athletic accolades his second departure appears to be more of an economic postmortem officially referred to as "the Jordan effect." As one New Zealand newspaper headline put it, "Mike money dries up" (Wharton 1999). And while the accountants and economists complete their analyses of how much impact Jordan has had on a number of global industries, stock is being taken with respect to his effect on places such as New Zealand. On the one hand the amount of NBA coverage via satellite television is unparalleled and 1998 saw a major milestone achieved when Sean Marks became the first Kiwi to be drafted by the NBA (Hinton 1998; South 1998). However, at the same time the local National Basketball League (NBL) continues to struggle, with no television contract and fading attendance at live games. Chances are the "everywhere man" will maintain his global presence through his network of commodities and sponsorship for years to come. And, in New Zealand, where Adidas is set to launch its multimillion-dollar sponsorship of the All Blacks, Jordan may increasingly become both the popular and economic benchmark by which local icons such as Jonah Lomu are measured.

## Michael Jordan and Youth Culture in Postcommunist Poland

During the 1990s, and as the vanguard of the globalizing Nike, Inc. and the National Basketball Association, Michael Jordan has become a sports superhero for many young people in Poland; the first basketball player to enjoy the status in the past reserved for soccer stars. As in many other—seemingly peripheral—parts of today's globally wired community (Lash and Urry 1994), broadcasts of Jordan's sporting prowess, his almost superhuman physical excellence, and the artistic quality of his play, have proven to be tremendously appealing to Polish youth. The words of the noted Polish poet Stanislaw Baranczak demonstrate that, as well as securing a significant degree of popular appeal among the youth population, Jordan's influence has permeated even the more respected echelons of Poland's cultural hierarchy:

> Basketball . . . is an unrepeatable element of American mass culture and—
> you can't hide it—art, art to the backbone and in the full sense of the

word. One day . . . I will prove that basketball at the top level is essentially poetry. If the latter is defined by scholars as such a form of language
organization which constitutes a "superimposed" arrangement, serving its
own purposes only and not the trivial need of communicating—what else
is Jordan doing, when, hanging in the air when doing a lay-up, he is not
just putting the ball into the basket with his right hand, which he could
easily do and score two points for his team without any risk, but he is putting the ball over the basket to his left hand and only then throwing it?
This is the same as rhyme in poetry . . . (Stanislaw Baranczak, quoted in
Okonski and Szostkiewicz 1994)

Of course, Michael Jordan's imaged identity has made similar incursions
into indigenous cultures around the world. However, as this chapter hopes
to demonstrate, it is wrong to assume that the globalization of his image
leads to uniform processes and practices of localized production and consumption within distinct cultural settings. For example, the Polish articulation and appropriation of Michael Jordan can only be understood within
the context of the centuries-long Polish fascination with America and its
culture, and the recent collapse of communist rule in the country. Both of
these sociopolitical phenomena will be addressed within this suggestive
preliminary analysis of Michael Jordan's appropriation by Poland's postcommunist youth culture.

## Poland's American Dreaming

Poland's popular national imaginary has historically looked yonder (Webster
1988) to the United States as a bastion of freedom, justice, economic success,
personal achievement, and happiness. This relationship can be traced back at
least to the American War of Independence, which was viewed with much
interest in Poland largely due to the heroic exploits of the Polish war heroes,
Kazimierz Pulaski and Tadeusz Kociuszko. The American Revolution coincided with the period when Poland gradually lost its independence, so
America became closely identified with the ideals of freedom and justice,
which were suppressed in the Old World by the absolutist monarchies of central Europe. The other key elements present in Polish thinking about America
are the notions of economic success, personal achievement, and happiness.
The Polish version of the American Dream was created against the backdrop
of mass-scale emigration to the United States in the nineteenth and twentieth centuries, the last significant wave of migrants arriving in the 1980s. In
Poland, the adjective *amerykaski* (American) came to mean "the best," "of
superior quality." Even today the proverbial *wujek z Ameryki* (an uncle from

America), stands for the enormous opportunities for achieving personal success that America represents to Polish people.

With the political reformation of Eastern Europe following the conclusion of hostilities in 1945, Poles were effectively cut off from direct contact with their simulated American paradise, and from the desired products of the American cultural economy. For the newly installed communist government, American culture represented an ideological threat to its attempts at totally controlling all aspects of social, economic, and political life. This proved to be a legitimate concern, as many Poles became enthralled by the rare colorful images of America to which they had clandestine access, and developed an even stronger fascination with the goods and ideas from which they were barred. Although such sentiments have recently been turned into promotional clichés by the advertising initiatives of particular transnational corporations, it should not be overlooked that for many Poles living under the communist regime, "Coca-Cola," "rock'n'roll," "blue jeans," and hence, the sign, "America," stood for personal liberation. With the spread of such acts of cultural resistance—however covert and symbolic—America was effectively turned into an ever more powerful and seductive popular mental construct; a simulated cultural space that provided a stark contrast to the drab and de-individualizing economic realities of life in Eastern Europe (Wawrzyczek and Mazur 1994); regardless of what the real socioeconomic conditions of America were actually like.

The setting of Polish-American cultural contact changed drastically with the collapse of communist rule. The Solidarno trade union, created by Lech Walesa after successful industrial action in 1980, was outlawed with the imposition of martial law in December 1981. As the communist regime, headed by General Wojciech Jaruzelski, lacked political legitimacy and was subsequently unable to deal with the country's perpetual economic crisis, it was eventually forced to open the "Round Table" negotiations with the opposition. In June 1989 the first partly democratic elections were held and brought an overwhelming victory to the Solidarity movement. The creation of a new government under Tadeusz Mazowiecki effectively put an end to the communist rule, and initiated a series of changes in the other East European countries, which ultimately led to the collapse of the Soviet bloc. In the wake of the overthrow of forty-five years of communist rule, Poland's newly ensconced and democratically elected power elite sought direction, in terms of political and economic initiatives, from the capitalist democracies and free market economies of Western Europe and North America (Krzysztofek 1992–1993; Reykowski 1994a, 1994b, 1994c).

The period 1989–1995 marked the birth and rapid development of a
Polish consumer culture, as Poles enthusiastically embraced the commodified popular cultural artifacts that now invaded their borders. The rise of
mass consumerism—the development of identities and aspirations associated with the possession of material goods, which serve as important status
indicators—has been perhaps the most conspicuous social change within
postcommunist Poland. Finally being able to realize their American dreaming (Wawrzyczek and Mazur 1994), Poles wholeheartedly embraced
Western commercial products. Thus, consumer decisions were to a large
extent the open expression of the pro-American popular sentiment that, for
four decades, had been suppressed by the communist regime (Pakula 1992;
Zagrodzka 1994).

That is not to assert that there has not been some widespread resistance
to the insurgent presence of American cultural artifacts within everyday Polish
existence. At the heart of this cultural, political, and economic anxiety was the
ideology of liberation through individual pleasure seeking with which
America is closely identified. As expressed within debates in the Polish parlia-
ment, among certain more reactionary circles the flood of American popular
culture products and commodities is identified with the vulgarization and
degradation of native cultural values and with the propagation of unrestrained
consumption, hedonism, and immorality (Proceedings of the Parliamentary
Committee of Culture and Mass Media 1992). In the complex political landscape of postcommunist Poland, where several political ideologies compete in
the struggle to give new form and direction to the developing system, the
preservation of national culture against the apparent invasion of threatening
influences of aggressive corporate capitalism became an issue for parties both
on the Left and the Right. Although the influence of American media culture
is open to debate, it does appear to have had an influence on furthering inter-
generational conflict within contemporary Poland. Increasingly, young people
form their identities outside the traditional subject positions offered by the
family and nation. Older generations focus on macroeconomic scale, they
measure the successes of rapidly changing Polish governments against the standards of Western Europe, and they almost uniformly support Poland's ambition of integrating with Europe by joining the European Union and NATO.
Conversely, young people seeking a point of reference look not to Western
Europe but to their simulated vision of America. It is not the mediated image
of the well-ordered, affluent, but confined life of Germans or Belgians, it is
what they see as the unlimited, colorful, bizarre lifestyle of Americans that they
wish to emulate (Adamski 1994).

## Satellite S(t)imulation

One of the achievements of the Solidarno revolution most appreciated by the Polish public, and a profound catalyst in the evolution of modern Poland, was the newly acquired and unbridled access to mass communications technology, especially to direct televisual networking. It has been persuasively argued that the ability of the Polish populace to participate in the consuming pleasures of the rapidly globalizing mass media proved a significant factor in the downfall of communist rule. According to Appadurai, in 1980s Poland "the lifestyles represented on both national and international TV and cinema (the mediascape) completely overwhelmed and undermined the rhetoric of national politics (the ideoscape)" and resulted in "the inability of the Polish state to repress its own working class" (1990, 308). The rise of the democratic movement in Poland can be seen as an example of the radical disjuncture between mediascapes and ideoscapes, which created popular dissension. The intensification of information fluxes and international communication—no longer impeded by political restrictions—made it possible to enthusiastically incorporate American popular culture into the Polish world view. The residual practice of viewing America as a cultural, economic, and political dreamland was now reinforced by glossy American programming and advertising campaigns for American companies, both of which offered novel and colorful packages of American commodity-signs that made even more compelling the popular associations between America and youthfulness, humor, postmodernity, personal freedom and, most of all, the world of leisure. Increasingly, the category of "Americana" (things American) has become intrinsically associated with the realm of pleasure, by providing a beguiling alternative to the mundane concerns that continue to plague everyday life in postcommunist Poland.

It was in this complex context, and via the newly deregulated mass media networks, that youth interest in Michael Jordan in particular, and the NBA in general, became an emergent popular cultural phenomenon, with no perceivable antecedents. With the exception of some enthusiasts, knowledge of the NBA in Poland during the late 1980s was virtually non-existent. The collapse of communism in Poland coincided with both the NBA's and Nike's concerted efforts to increase their presence within—and hence share of—the global marketplace. Thus, in recent years, regular television broadcasts, increased newspaper and magazine coverage, and the circulation of allied commercial messages, have significantly increased the popular presence of the NBA within Polish culture. Today, the NBA is an aspect of American popular culture that is, in some sense, familiar to most people in Poland, and most enthusiastically followed by the young. The first NBA games reached Polish audiences through satellite TV, with Poles picking up the satellite TV intended for German and other West European audiences. The somewhat relaxed attitude to licence fees meant that housing estates were fitted with their own cable networks. These relayed satellite broadcasts received via a huge disk installed on one of the buildings on the estate.

The ability to capture Eurosport, and especially the German sports channel DSF, broadcasts immediately stimulated interest in NBA basketball. Seizing on the game's burgeoning popularity, the public Polish Television 2 (TVP2) soon introduced its own regular weekly basketball programs. The TVP2 buys TBS (Turner Broadcasting System) Thursday night NBA matches and shows them on Friday afternoons. The package comes complete with commercial breaks "furnished by the NBA and its players," so the editing of the program is limited to Polish language commentary. Interestingly, the two Polish commentators developed a new unique style of sport reporting within this program. The opening words are always "*Hej, tu NBA*" ("Hi, this is the NBA") and the commentators would rather use the direct "you" form when addressing the viewers instead of the more usual form *prosz pa stwa* ("ladies and gentlemen"). The use of the players' nicknames—Hakeem the Dream, Sir Charles—further confirms the contrived intimacy offered by the broadcast. Given the hip informality espoused by the commentators, which is itself identified with being "American," it is evident that the program is directed at a young audience. As well as television coverage, there are also three national magazines devoted entirely to basketball *(Tygodnik Koszykarski Basket, Magic Basketball, Koszykówka),* and the NBA is also intensively discussed within the sports sections of national, regional, and local newspapers. Graphically illustrating the not insignificant attention paid to the NBA by the Polish media was the fact that Michael Jordan's return to basketball in 1995 made the news of the day on national TV, and received front-page coverage in most newspapers.

More than anything else, it is the carefully fashioned stars of NBA basketball that make it so alluring for young Polish viewers. The broadcasts present NBA games as duels between the respective stars of teams, set against each other in fierce combat. Polish viewers very often admit to watching games primarily to enjoy the superhuman exploits of the sport's stars, rather than caring about the final result of the contest. Certainly, Michael Jordan has been the most important character in popularizing the NBA televisual drama. Jordan's articulation within the Polish media, and his appeal to the Polish populace, can be attributed to his status as a marker of difference from instabilities within Polish society. Many young people have rejected a Polish reality wracked with political crises, falling governments, party competition, and personal scandals, in favor of the American hedonistic hyperreality fashioned around Michael Jordan by Nike, the NBA, and other transnational concerns. Reading the intertextually fabricated narrative of Michael Jordan, the Polish consumer is encouraged to view him as the latest reincarnation of the hyper-individualistic ideology most closely associated with American culture. The constant exploitation of Jordan's athletic abilities—repeated slow-motion pictures of his moves, shots, passes, and slam dunks—have produced seductive and powerful positive associations for Polish audiences. The fantastic ease with which he moves on the court and above it, apparently defying the laws of gravity, suggests that it is possible to break boundaries of human achievement that were deemed impenetrable. As such, Jordan represents the apotheosis of such American values as freedom, independence, lack of restrictions, informality, optimism, wealth, and entrepreneurial skills. Jordan is thus cast as a self-made man, possessing God-given talent, who worked his way up from anonymity and was allowed to flourish thanks to the existence of the NBA. Jordan is not presented as being exploited by ruthless capitalists (as communist ideology would demand); rather, he is portrayed as exuberantly exploiting the possibilities opened by corporate capital.

## Subcultural Youth Formations: Jordanki and Lodziarze

The images produced by Michael Jordan, and other NBA commodity-signs, are desired and eagerly awaited by young consumers. These acts of consumption, even if only symbolic in nature, help substantiate the reality of the world that many young people are trying to create for themselves in the new Poland; a reality that would make them as free and as "Western" as the Solidarno revolution promised them. The hyperreal world of American professional basketball provides access to freedom, excellence, entertainment, variety, and vitality. These signifieds of the NBA-produced pictures are nothing new: Michael Jordan et al. stand for those elements of the Polish version of the American Dream that have been present in the popular imagination for centuries. What the joint working of basketball broadcasts, and commercial messages using scripted basketball imagery, seem to say is that access to the mythical existence signified by America can be easily gained through consumption of the commercial products—Nike shoes, NBA apparel, Coca-Cola, or McDonald's hamburgers—which have seemingly been made an integral part of the game itself.

The fascination with basketball is manifested in youth fashion. "Basketball style"—a baseball cap with an NBA team logo, a T-shirt, shorts, and basketball sneakers—is a norm rather than an exception in the casual wear of young Poles. Obviously, clothing serves as one of the easiest ways of identifying oneself with a particular basketball idol. Number 23 T-shirts (Jordan's number) were sellouts in 1993 and 1994. Furthermore, the appearance of the word *jordanki* in youth slang, as the name used to refer to basketball sneakers in general, and to Air Jordan Nikes in particular, shows how easily and eagerly American commodity signs associated with Michael Jordan are incorporated into the lives of young Poles. The basketball imagery is used side by side with other elements of the media-created hyperreality pertaining to be America in the promotion of other American products, and it contributes to the development of lifestyles imitative of the "American way of life."

The greatest barrier for circulation of American goods in Poland is undoubtedly their price. Being popular in terms of the demand that exists, such products are hardly part of popular culture in terms of their accessibility. As much as McDonald's is not exactly a chain of cheap restaurants, similarly both Nike and Reebok sneakers are too expensive for most young people to purchase. In 1995, a pair of Nike basketball sneakers cost approximately $100 in Poland, while the average monthly salary amounted to little more than $250. Thus, American goods become markers of social distinction, and largely disassociated from their primary use values. *Jordanki,* original and authentic Chicago Bulls caps, No. 23 T-shirts, and other basketball paraphernalia are purchased to be worn as status indicators; streetwise fashions that identify the owner as someone who knows what's "in" and does not settle for substitutes.

Basketball-related commodities are also used in the creation of distinct subcultural youth styles. Within some rituals of consumption, the elements taken over from the basketball world are not only put to new uses, but they also form new systems of connection, to generate new meanings in a variety of improvised combinations (Hebdige 1979, 102–106). This process of subcultural bricolage is well evident in the case of a group that bears the slightly scornful name of *lodziarze* (ice cream sellers). The name refers to the preferred clothing style of the group—white or bright loose clothes, with characteristic calf-length pants, baseball caps, and other elements of the basketball costume described above. Such groups appear to be largely made up of working-class males in their early teens. The selection of a sport as a source of distinctive subcultural style is by no means a new development. For years there have existed subcultural groups centered around soccer (the so-called *szalikowcy* or "scarf-bearers"). However, the *lodziarze* take the appropriation

of sport culture a stage farther. The intentional transformation of sport clothing into everyday style shows how youths want to distance themselves both
from the standards of the older generation, and from other subcultural youth
groups such as skinheads or punks. The clothes, not always appropriate for the
Polish weather, also speak to a certain California dreaming and the longing
for more personal liberation.

Clearly, and despite the warnings issued by some Polish institutions wor-
ried about the integrity of a native culture threatened by rampant consumerism, many young people see Michael Jordan and other American
corporate icons as embodiments of their own desires and yearnings. American
icons such as Michael Jordan are seductive because they not only seem to
offer a break from the totalitarian past, they also apparently bring one closer
to the idealized America of the Polish popular imaginary. The presence of
Jordan's commodified image in Poland celebrates the economic effectiveness
of free market capitalist economics, and inalienably promotes an American
ideology of freedom, individualism, and competition. Thus, when appropriated and re-articulated by contemporary Polish youth, American popular sport
culture, including NBA basketball and specifically Michael Jordan, becomes a
prominent reservoir of ideas and an important source of reference for
expressing the limits/possibilities, pleasures/pains, and fascinations/fears that
delineate postcommunist Poland.

## The Sporting Black Atlantic: Sport, Diaspora, and Michael Jordan

For more than a decade, Michael Jordan has figured prominently within the
British popular imagination as a supreme athlete. For the black British audience at least, Jordan embodies a sense of black agency, enabling him to transcend his sporting significance, and giving him a cultural status as high as any
pop or film star. Black expressive culture in Britain, and particularly black
youth culture, has been culturally dominant, shaping the forms, style, and
content of white British youth culture for more than fifty years, thus the
prominence of Jordan within black vernacular cultures means that he occupies a correspondingly central role within British culture more generally.[1]

It is suggested in this section that the notion of the sporting black
Atlantic provides a useful transnational framework for mapping the cultural significance of athletes such as Jordan. That is, in order to appreciate the
role that Jordan occupies within black British culture, we must understand
the ways in which black sports stars generally have been incorporated within the vernacular cultures of the black diaspora. What is offered, then, is not

a definitive framework for analyzing the significance and significations of
global stars such as Jordan, but rather a suggestive formulation of the sporting black Atlantic that can be used to analyze such contemporary transnational sporting figures; as well as the wider historical movement,
importance, and signification of black athletes over the past two hundred
years between Africa, Europe, and the Americas.

The notion of black transnational sporting identifications has a longer
history than many of the schematic chronologies of the "rise" of globalization allow for. The sociology of sport in particular, in adapting current social
theory debates to the analysis of sport, has tended to neglect the concept of
diaspora as a way of conceptualizing and understanding these issues. This section attempts, therefore, to interrogate some of the silences within accounts
of globalization by the use of the concept of diaspora, and subsequently to
intervene in the theoretical debates around diaspora itself that have so far
failed to fully acknowledge sport's central place in discussions of cultural politics within the black diaspora.

This is done by providing a brief historical sketch and theoretical conceptualization of the sporting black Atlantic, before locating Jordan within
this genealogical map. Finally, some problematics are raised in relation to the
politics of cultural representations and identifications that figures such as
Jordan engender. It is suggested that although Jordan offers an important site
for many black British youth, and male youth in particular, in presenting
notions of empowered black physicality, the ultimate reduction of an identification with black community politics (evident in previous radical black athletes such as Muhammad Ali and others) to black identity politics situated on
"the (male) body" presents worrying developments for future black emanci-
patory politics.

## Diasporizing Sociology

There are problems with even some of the more self-reflexive accounts of
globalization (whether theorized in terms of the modernity or capitalist axis),
which in their periodization and conceptualization adopt a Euro-centered
viewpoint, disavowing the complex relationship between globalization and
imperialism. Such an account, it has been argued, is simply "a theory of
Westernization by another name, which replicates all the problems associated
with Eurocentrism: a narrow window on the world, historically and culturally" (Nederveen Pieterse 1995, 47; see also Hesse 1999). Further, one of the
central problems in attempting to think through the issues of global cultural

formation and identifications across and beyond national borders is that sociology itself has been so closely linked with the development of nation-states. That is, sociology has too often taken (sometimes uncritically) the nation as its main object for analysis, equating society unproblematically with the nation, thus neglecting the fact that the academic production of knowledge and the theories produced are as much tied to the nation-state formation process as the world such theories tried to explain. Increasingly, attempts are being made to reposition sociology in such a way that it problematizes the nation/society couplet and takes a wider, historical approach. As Nederveen Pieterse argues:

> [A] global sociology is taking shape, around notions such as social networks (rather than "societies"), border zones, boundary crossing and global society. In other words, a sociology conceived within the framework of nations/societies is making place for a post-inter/national sociology of hybrid formations, times and spaces. (1995, 63)

One such attempt has been to utilize the notion of diaspora as a way of conceptualizing current sociological concerns around "the global" and "the local." One of the effects of the "turn to diaspora" has been that in trying to understand the processes of global cultural formations, our conceptualizations of space—whereby disconnected people can communicate ideas and shared interests, and (re)establish relations and identities (real and imagined)—has been radically redefined. Space here operates between and within the outer-national, national, regional, and local—occupying all of these spaces at once. These radical critiques of uncritical accounts about "natural," territorially fixed, notions of the relationship between culture, community, and place can be seen in the attempts by various authors to rethink these categories in terms of the flows and routes through which space is constructed. Such conceptualizations can be seen in numerous contexts, from Massey's (1994) notion of a "global sense of place," through Nederveen Pieterse's (1995) use of the concept "translocal space," to Brah's (1996) "diasporic space." What all of these accounts try to do, is to loosen notions of space and place from necessarily being tied down to specific bounded notions of geographical location, and to show how space is itself constructed through political and ideological discourses, and is a site for the maintenance and challenging of power relations. As Gilroy observes, our understanding of space is transformed "when it is seen less through outmoded notions of fixity and place and more in terms of the ex-centric communicative circuitry that has enabled dispersed populations to converse, interact and even synchronize significant elements of their social and cultural lives" (1994a, 211).

The claim to diasporic identifications as part of local cultural politics can therefore be seen as an articulation of wider political struggles in claiming "discrepant histories," meaning that the term *diaspora* becomes "a signifier, not simply of transnationality and movement, but of political struggles to define the local, as distinctive community, in historical contexts of displacement" (Clifford 1994, 308). The need to write diasporic histories of global culture (Nederveen Pieterse 1995, 63) can be seen in the writings of Paul Gilroy, who has attempted to transcend the national(ist) paradigm that dominates so much of the cultural studies field (despite its claims to embrace "difference") and to posit instead a history based on the intercultural and transnational formations of what he calls "the black Atlantic" (1993). Seeking to introduce "new intermediate concepts, between the local and the global" (1992, 188), he takes the Atlantic as a unit of analysis in order to "produce an explicitly transnational perspective" (1992, 192) and uses the metaphor of the ship as the link between the African continent, Europe, and the Americas. In attempting to extend "existing formulations of the diaspora idea" (1996, 22), Gilroy formulates the idea of the black Atlantic as "a deterritorialised, multiplex and anti-national basis for the affinity or 'identity of passions' between diverse black populations" (1996, 18):

> [T]he black Atlantic provides an invitation to move into the contested spaces between the local and the global in ways that do not privilege the modern nation state and its institutional order over the sub-national and supra-national networks and patterns of power, communication and conflict that they work to discipline, regulate and govern. (1996, 22)

Gilroy's concerns, up until now, have been with the intellectual exchanges within the black Atlantic (DuBois, Wright, and Delaney in particular), and within the cultural sphere, music. I want to suggest, however, that the notion of the black Atlantic can be productively adapted as a model to comprehend the lives, travels, migrations, and significances of black athletes over the past two hundred years or so, via the concept of the sporting black Atlantic.

## Toward a Genealogy of the Sporting Black Atlantic

The most substantial increase in the numbers of blacks (that is African and African Caribbeans) living in Britain dates from the postwar period when Britain, along with many other Western European countries, actively sought to redress its labor shortages by recruiting skilled manual laborers from its colonies. The symbolic moment for this migration occurred when, in June 1948, the *Empire Windrush* docked in Tilbury with 492 Jamaicans on board, starting a process that was to markedly change the nature and size of the black community in Britain, and the cultural landscape of Britain itself. However, it is important to remember that there has been a longer and extensive, if unacknowledged, black presence in Britain. Indeed, as Peter Fryer points out, there were Africans living in Britain during the third century, as part of the Roman imperial army, long before the "English" arrived (1984, 1). Later, during the sixteenth century, as British imperialism and the mechanisms of slavery gathered pace, a sizeable, though disparate, black population began to emerge—most working as servants—as it became fashionable in some quarters to have black slaves among the household servants (1984, 9). By the middle of the eighteenth century, particularly in the slave-ports of Liverpool, Bristol, and London, it was possible to talk of an emerging self-conscious, and politicized, black community living and working in Britain and engaged with radical working-class politics of the time.

It is into this history of migration and involvement that we need to locate black Atlantic athletes, as they formed a central part of these emerging communities. As Linebaugh and Rediker observed, during the eighteenth century black men and women arrived in increasing numbers in London, where they found various forms of work as "cooks, boxers, writers, and especially domestic servants, day labourers, and seamen" (1990, 243). Black athletes, primarily as boxers, and normally as freed slaves, became central icons in publicly symbolizing the transition of black people from slave subjects to public citizens. Sport within black communities has therefore long been a crucial site for black political mobilization, at both the local level (in terms of black sporting clubs and leagues functioning as cultural spaces as part of wider community politics), to the international level (for example, the politics manifest within the anticolonial politics of West Indian cricketing success) (see Carrington 1998; Edwards 1969; Hartman 1996; James 1963; Race and Class 1995). Extending this notion, Fryer makes an interesting connection between the political significance of black radicals such as William Cuffay, William Davidson, and Robert Wedderburn, and black pugilists of the eighteenth century: "It is hardly surprising that, of the black people living in Britain in this period whose names are known, so many were fighters of one sort or another: political activists or prize-fighters" (1984, 227).

The arena of sports, and in particular boxing, enabled these black men to momentarily transgress some of the racial constraints imposed on their lives. By publicly challenging Western racial sciences' beliefs about the inherent degeneracy and weaknesses (physical, moral, and intellectual) of the "black race," and by performing on an international stage that was largely unattainable for blacks

in any other cultural sphere at that time, their sporting activities acquired a
political significance that transcended the sporting arena. The Atlantic, and the
role of ships, remained central for this emerging "transnational" athlete. As a
mode of transportation, sometimes as a form of early employment, and as a way
of practising the skills needed to compete in Europe's boxing arenas, these black
men literally fought their way across the Atlantic to their freedom.[2] Indeed, the
hidden history of not only black boxers, but footballers, rugby players, crick-
eters, cyclists, and athletes in Britain, from the eighteenth century through to
the Victorian and Edwardian periods, is only now beginning to become recognized (for example, see Fryer 1984; Green 1998; Vasili 1996, 1998). This is
important in helping to relocate the centrality of imperialism to the cultural,
political, and economic development of modern Britain and the positioning of
blacks as agents within that history. The intriguing and fascinating life history
of Arthur Wharton, the first black professional footballer, the first African professional cricketer, and the first athlete to run the 100 yards in ten seconds (an
AAA record he held for nearly forty years) is another that deserves to be better known and understood within this context (Jenkins 1992; Vasili 1998).[3]

Arguably, however, it was the complex figure of Jack Johnson who
became the most well-known of the early sporting black Atlantic stars. When
Johnson beat Tommy Burns for the World Heavyweight Championship its
international significance (which attracted front page headlines around the
world, including Britain) could be seen not only in the riots that took place
across many American cities as jubilant blacks were attacked by whites, but
throughout many of the British colonies too, where Johnson's constant beat-
ings, both symbolic and literal, of the "white man" caused "unrest" within the
Caribbean and Africa (Green 1998). Such was the fear of Johnson that an exhibition match between Johnson and the British boxer William "Bombardier
Billy" Wells in London in 1911 was cancelled, due to fears about the effects
that this might have on undermining the social and racial order not only in
the British colonies but within Britain too. As Vasili notes, the success of sporting black Atlantic figures, such as Johnson and others, struck directly at the
core concerns and fears of white supremacist logic, namely that:

> Black athletic success as symbolic expression of the degeneracy of the
> White "race"; the consequent rewards of this success as a threat to White
> economic (and social) superiority; that the collective confidence and spir-
> itual sustenance given to black communities by Johnson as an heroic
> model may inspire emulation. (1998, 185)

Thus, the sporting black Atlantic can be defined, on one level, as a complex
cultural and political diasporic space, which transgresses the boundaries of

nation-states, whereby the migrations and achievements of black athletes have come to assume a heightened political significance for the dispersed cultures and peoples of the black diaspora—the sports arena thus operates as an important symbolic space in the struggles of black peoples against the ideologies and practices of white supremacy.

For black Britons in particular these "cosmopolitan" cultural formations and outer-national diasporic identifications can be seen as a powerful counter to nation-state nationalisms and conservative monocultural ideologies, with their associated assimilationist drives. Such self-consciously selected cultural expressions and identifications cut across national borders, reconfiguring what it means to be a national subject, and providing transnational routes of identity formation. The diasporic identifications with transnational sporting stars thus challenges narrow prescriptive accounts of national identity, and re-articulates the elements of the black Atlantic cultural world for a specifically black British sensibility:

> [T]he black diaspora culture currently being articulated in postcolonial Britain is concerned to struggle for different ways to be "British"—ways to stay and be different, to be British *and something else* complexly related to Africa and the Americas, to shared histories of enslavement, racist subordination, cultural survival, hybridization, resistance, and political rebellion. (Clifford 1994, 308, emphasis in the original)

Thus, exported from their "countries of origin" and adapted into signifiers of expressive black physicality, black Atlantic athletes (such as Jesse Owens, Arthur Ashe, Althea Gibson, Muhammad Ali, Viv Richards, Pele, Jackie Joyner-Kersee, Brian Lara, and Ronaldo) form part of the cultural resources of black Britons.

## Situating Jordan

It is within this broad framework that we can best "locate" Jordan within the black British consciousness. Jordan's undoubted ability, together with his physical presence, intellectual artistry, and sublime aesthetic, provide images of an assertive and emancipated black masculinity that embody many of the aspirations of black men in Britain. Although notions of Jordan's "Americanness" cannot be dissociated from his image—indeed, it is partly integral to it—it is the diasporic imagined community that allows Jordan to figure so prominently within black British vernacular culture (and by default, given black Briton's hegemonic position within British youth cultures, within youth culture in Britain per se), aided also by the close and increasing connections and crossovers between sport (particularly basket-ball) and music (particularly hip-hop).

It is interesting to note both the dominance of African Americans with-in the sporting black Atlantic world and the fact that it is those countries out-side of the United States that are more likely to embrace sporting figures from beyond their particular national "location"—before the 1998 Football World Cup, Jordan apparently confessed that he had never heard of the world's most famous soccer player, Ronaldo (Kettle 1998). This is, in part, due to the insu-larity of American culture more generally, which often fails to comprehend that America (despite the best efforts of Hollywood constructions) is not, in fact, the world. It could be argued, then, that the sporting black Atlantic is more readily found in London or Soweto than it is in Chicago or New York. Hence, although a transnational phenomenon, the sporting black Atlantic can only be expressed in, made sense of, and experienced through, the particu-larities of the local.

Within the sporting black Atlantic the strong prominence of American sports stars appears, at first glance, to be a direct result of America's dominant economic position within the capitalist world order. However, this would be to (mis)read such cultural connections as an example of "cultural imperialism," which sees such "flows" as essentially unidimensional (emanating from America "to the rest") and culturally homogenizing ("McDonaldization"). The cultural configurations of the sporting black Atlantic are not, merely, a reflection of an underlying economic determinant of the circuits of global capitalism, as such diaspora formations move between and beyond such processes—though they can never, of course, be entirely divorced from them. As Clifford (1994, 302) notes, "[C]ontemporary diasporic practices cannot be reduced to epiphenom-ena of the nation-state or of global capitalism. While defined and constrained by these structures, they also exceed and criticize them."

## Jordan, Commodification, and Body Politics

It is impossible to discuss the global circulation of Jordan, as a mass-mediated and commodified form, without also discussing the growth in visual spectac-ularization of the black (male) form within the Western media. These con-tradictory processes are played out within the sign economy where "blackness," and the black body (and particularly the sporting black body), has become a highly valued commodity, while at the very same time, within the "real economy" actual black people (divorced from the surplus sign value of their own bodies) struggle within the material effects of global late capitalism.

Black people, once literal commodities during Atlantic slavery, have, via the processes of the global spectacle of mass-mediated sexualization and objectification of the black body, been transformed into commercial commodities to be bought and sold throughout the globalized media market. As Carby notes:

> In these days of what is referred to as "global culture," the Nike corporation produces racialized images for the world by elevating the bodies of Michael Jordan and Tiger Woods to the status of international icons. Hollywood too now takes for granted that black bodies can be used to promote both products and style worldwide . . . . But despite the multi-million-dollar international trade in black male bodies, and encouragement to "just do it," there is no equivalent international outrage, no marches or large-scale public protest, at the hundreds of thousands of black male bodies languishing out of sight of the media in the North American [and indeed British] penal system (1998, 1).

Carby, suggests, that despite the hyper-visibility of blacks within media culture, we have seen no concomitant developments within the public sphere of black political mobilization. Indeed, some have argued that the allure of the "spectacle of the black body" has not only served to obscure the "real" condition of many black peoples, but has simultaneously diminished the space for progressive politics itself.

This can be seen in what Gilroy has referred as the development of a "bio-politics," "in which the person is defined as the body and in which certain exemplary bodies, for example those of Mike Tyson and Michael Jordan, Naomi Campbell and Veronica Webb, become instantiations of community" (1994b, 29). The effect of such politics means that whereas previous attempts to transform the condition of black communities articulated around the "liberation of the mind," today's bio-politics is only expressed via modalities of the body. Racialized bio-politics, therefore, establishes the boundaries of the authentic racial community through "the visual representation of racial bodies—engaged in characteristic activities—usually sexual or sporting—that ground and solicit identification if not solidarity" (Gilroy 1994b, 29). For Gilroy this is problematic, as:

> it marks the racial community exclusively as a space of heterosexual activity and confirms the abandonment of any politics aside from the ongoing oppositional creativity of gendered self-cultivation . . . . If it survives, politics becomes an exclusively aesthetic concern with all the perils that implies . . . . (Gilroy 1994b, 29)

While Gilroy's pessimistic reading of this as signaling the end of political dialogue and interaction may be a little premature, the ability to conceive of political possibilities beyond the body has certainly resulted in a substantial reconfiguration of that dialogue. It is not surprising, given the claims I have tried to make for the political significance of black Atlantic athletes, that sports stars, and Jordan in particular, are so often used by current radical black writers such as Gilroy and Carby, to support their own arguments about the shifts within contemporary black culture and politics.

The changing significance and signification of black athletes over the past two hundred years has not only mirrored, but in many cases actually constituted, the form and formation of black politics more generally. It appears that we have moved from a position of black athletes embodying a politics of social transformation to politics itself being reduced to the body of individual athletes—the agency encapsulated within the images of Ali "speaking out" during the 1960s and 1970s is now transposed to the static and voiceless icon of a Michael Jordan figure stuck in midair clutching a ball. This is the point that bell hooks alludes to when she suggests the need to differentiate between previous black athletes, such as Jack Johnson and Joe Louis, who symbolized, at least for some black men, a resistance to the racial oppression of their era, to those of today (such as Jordan) who allow their black bodies to be commodified for capitalist (and racist) exploitation:

> Appropriated by market forces, the subversive potential of the black male body is countered. This has been especially the case for black male bodies whose radical agency is often diffused by a process of commodification that strips those bodies of dignity. The bodies of Johnson and Louis were commodified, yet that process was one that exploited and sensationalized political issues like racial separatism and economic inequality. Rather than oppose those forms of commodification that reinvent the black male body in ways that subordinate and subjugate, today's black male athlete "submits" to any objectified use of his person that brings huge monetary reward. Black male capitulation to a neo-colonial white supremacist patriarchal commodification signals the loss of political agency, the absence of radical politics. (hooks 1994, 133)

Perhaps, then, it may be necessary to make a distinction between those figures who have consciously used their sporting abilities as a means for wider political ends, such as Ali, Carlos and Smith, and Viv Richards, to those who have lacked an explicit progressive political agenda, but who, nevertheless, have come to symbolize an empowered black physicality through their sheer physical achievements, for example, Jordan. However, the advances, and conflation, of transnational capitalism, global financial networks and marketing, and media culture have developed so far and extensively that it is increasingly difficult to argue that stars such as Jordan offer scope for counterhegemonic readings. Jordan, both as a referent and as a signifier, is now virtually synonymous with Nike and many other capitalist corporations, to the extent that

Jordan as a sign cannot easily be disentangled from the conservative neo-liberal capitalist values (such as "free-born" individualism and competition) that he so eagerly endorses.[4] As one British commentator put it, Michael "the human billboard" Jordan, "is one of the best friends white American capitalism ever had" (Landesman 1998, 1).

If this is the case what "space" is left for any alternative reading other than that of Jordan as the silent messenger of global capitalism? Contrary to the more reductionist "cultural industry" theorists, it is important to remember that, especially within the black diaspora, cultural consumption, identifications, and practices are never totally about either capitulation and complicitness, nor resistance and critique. That is, such dialectical processes are always contradictory. As Dyson notes:

> There is also the creative use of desire and fantasy by young blacks to counter, and capitulate to, the forces of cultural dominance that attempt to reduce the black body to a commodity and text that is employed for entertainment, titillation or financial gain. Simply said, there is no easy correlation between commodification of black youth culture and the evidences of a completely dominated consciousness. (1993, 69)

bell hooks too concedes that "Jordan's image has subversive potential" (1994, 134), thus it could be argued that it is within the sporting black Atlantic that this space for oppositional readings exists. Within the black British imaginary, Jordan figures as a confident, articulate, and gifted black athlete, complicit, to a degree, with the economic demands of American capitalism, but not totally so. Black British youth, it could be argued, actively reappropriate some of the dominant ideologies that surround Jordan and adapt them for a set of images displaying empowered black physicality and agency; buying into the "presence," but not necessarily the "products," of Jordan.

## Conclusion

The ending of Jordan's athletic career does not seem to have adversely affected his global presence, and he remains as popular with British (and indeed, Polish and New Zealand) youth as at any time during the 1980s and 1990s. Indeed, he seems to have a presence as large as before, both within and outside of the sports arena. From the front covers of *Fortune* (August 1998) to *Vanity Fair* (October 1998) magazines and beyond, Jordan, aligned as always to American corporate sponsorship, appears omnipresent and shows little sign of diminishing. Given this, it is often difficult to truly comprehend Jordan's global significance, and what this has said, and continues to say, about racial politics within America, Europe, the Caribbean, and elsewhere. Henry Louis Gates has argued that "Jordan has rewritten the rules. In one magical package, Michael Jordan is both Muhammad Ali and Mister Clean, Willie Mays and the Marlboro Man" (1998, 61). But has Jordan really changed the rules upon which black athletes are supposed to perform/conform? To compare Jordan's apolitical, racially nonthreatening, "All-American" image to Ali, is a gross misrepresentation of the political significance of Ali's (pre-1980s, at least) pan-Africanist, anticolonial, and anti-American imperialist stances (for a more convincing analysis of Ali's global significance see Marqusee 1999). And magical for whom? Certainly for the NBA and corporate America.

The history of the sporting black Atlantic has shown that, for more than two hundred years, black athletic achievement within white supremacist societies has always carried a wider symbolic resonance. The achievements of black athletes was always, therefore, a political statement (whether expressed explicitly or not) on the racial order of the day: a public critique of racial injustice and subordination, often allied to a critique of the social-economic determinants of that exploitation. While Michael Jordan's achievements on the basketball court are now beyond doubt (that is one area at least where he has "re-written the rules," or at least the record books), his uncritical endorsement of, and personal complicitness with, corporate America represents, in the final analysis, a negation of the critical positioning to systems of economic exploitation that millions of blacks in the West, and beyond, continue to face. The same, so-called, "Third World" workers, with whom Ali, symbolically at least, identified, now make the goods (under grossly exploitative conditions) upon which Jordan himself, and corporate America even more so, profit, and this is the greatest paradox about Jordan's "achievements."

That Jordan has majestically mastered the boundaries of his sport is undoubted. Less clear is whether Jordan has significantly transcended the racial and political boundaries of the master's rules.

# Notes

1. As Stuart Hall has remarked, black British youth are "the defining force in street-oriented British youth culture. Without them, it often seems, white British youth culture simply would not exist" (1998, 40).

2. Early figures who exemplified many of the key characteristics of the sporting black Atlantic world would include figures such as Bill Richmond, Tom Molineaux, and James Wharton. Born in New York in 1763, the son of Georgia-born slaves, Richmond was brought to England by a British general after the American Revolution, eventually becoming a well-known figure in London's social circles before finishing his days as a

publican in London's West End. Following Richmond in winning his freedom through boxing, Tom Molineaux, born in Virginia in 1784, came to England in 1803, where he met Richmond, who helped to establish him on the boxing circuit, where record crowds turned out to see him fight. He eventually died in poverty, aged only thirty-four, in Ireland. James Wharton, born in Morocco in 1813, became known as "The Moroccan Prince" or "Jemmy the Black." Wharton came to England in 1820, where, working as a cabin boy on ships plying to India, he learned to box and fought in one of the longest bouts in the history of boxing (going 200 rounds and lasting more than four hours). Wharton taught boxing and gave exhibition fights after he retired, eventually settling in Liverpool before his death in 1856 (see Fryer 1984).

　　3.　Another early-twentieth-century figure whose life exemplifies the passage and movement of black Atlantic athletes is the boxer Larry Gains. Born in Toronto, Canada, at the turn of the twentieth century, Gains traveled to Europe to pursue his career as a boxer (after being inspired by meeting Jack Johnson when he was a teenager). He moved throughout Europe, fighting in Paris (where he met the young Ernest Hemingway), Stockholm, Milan, and Berlin, before he finally settled in England, where he became British Empire Champion (he was prevented from fighting for the British Heavyweight Championship because of his color). Ironically, despite being inspired to become a boxer after meeting Johnson, it was Johnson's very success in challenging the ideology of white supremacy, and the subsequent drawing of the "color line," that prevented Gains competing for the official World Heavyweight Championship. In Gains autobiography, he provides an interesting account of how the passage across the Atlantic was more than just a means of transportation and a chance to practice the skills he would later require, but importantly a way of gaining acceptance into the male working-class Atlantic world through his ability and status as a boxer. In a chapter headed, "Slow Boat To England," Gains writes, "every time I trained on deck, a big, tough-looking stoker who had done a bit of fighting would stand watching me .... Well, eventually he came over and said he would like to spar with me. I was grateful for the chance of a work-out. But I soon realised that this was to be little more than that. All work on the boat came to a standstill, and everyone came crowding around .... His intention quite clearly was to knock me out. He came in, swinging with both hands. He was really a brawler and nothing more. I couldn't miss him and eventually I stretched him out on the deck. They carried him below. After that, the attitude of the crew changed drastically. Overnight, I became everybody's friend, a man of respect. Their judgements were simple, almost primitive. If you were the best fighting man aboard, the boat belonged to you" (Gains, N.D, 27–28).

　　4.　The extent to which the sign economy and the real economy have merged in unprecedented ways within contemporary media culture (and that Jordan is perhaps the key icon of this) was evident when Jordan appeared on the front cover of *Fortune* magazine as an industry in his own right, which is estimated to have generated in excess of ten billion dollars during his career (Johnson 1998).

# References

Adamski, W. (1994). "Strukturalno-kulturowe i edukacyjne przeslanki transformacji systemowej" ("Structural, cultural and educational premises of the system transformation"), *Kultura i Spoleczenstwo* 1:13–22.

Allison, P. (1991). "Big Macs and baseball caps: The Americanisation of Auckland," *Metro*, 124–130.

Andrews, D. L. (1996). "The fact(s) of Michael Jordan's blackness: Excavating a floating racial signifier," *Sociology of Sport Journal* 13(2):125–158.

Andrews, D. L., B. Carrington, Z. Mazur, and S. J. Jackson (1996) "Jordanscapes: A preliminary analysis of the global popular," *Sociology of Sport Journal* 13(4):428–457.

Ang, I. (1989). *Watching Dallas: Soap opera and the melodramatic imagination.* London: Routledge.

———. (1996). *Living rooms wars: Rethinking media audiences for a postmodern world.* London: Routledge.

Appadurai, A. (1996). *Modernity at Large: Cultural dimensions of globalization.* Minneapolis: University of Minnesota Press.

Bird, J. (Ed.). (1993). *Mapping the futures: Local cultures, global change.* London: Routledge.

Brah, A. (1996). *Cartographies of diaspora: Contesting identities.* London, Routledge.

Buell, F. (1994). *National culture and the new global system.* Baltimore: Johns Hopkins University Press.

Carby, H. (1998). *Race men: The W. E. B. DuBois lectures.* London: Harvard University Press.

Carrington, B. (1998) "Sport, masculinity, and Black cultural resistance," *Journal of Sport and Social Issues* 22 (4):275–298.

Chen, K. H. (1992). "Voices from the outside: Towards a new internationalist localism," *Cultural Studies* 6 (3):476–484.

Clifford, J. (1994). "Diasporas," *Cultural Anthropology* 9(3):302–338.

Cvetkovich, A., and D. Kellner (Eds.) (1997). *Articulating the global and the local: Globalization and cultural studies.* Boulder: Westview Press.

Deardoff, J. (1995). "MJ's overseas popularity hardly foreign." *Chicago Tribune (Home Again Section),* March 24, 10.

Duncan, I., and A. Bollard (Eds.) (1992). *Corporatization and privatization: Lessons from New Zealand.* Auckland: Oxford University Press.

Dyson, M. (1993) "Be Like Mike?: Michael Jordan and the pedagogy of desire," *Cultural Studies* 7 (1): 64–72.

Edwards, H. (1969). *The revolt of the black athlete.* New York, Free Press.

Featherstone, M., and S. Lash (1995). "Globalization, modernity, and the spatialization of social theory: An introduction." In *Global modernities,* ed. M. Featherstone, S. Lash, and R. Robertson, 1–24. London: Sage.

Fitzsimons, P. (1996). *The rugby war.* Sydney: HarperSports.

Fryer, P. (1984). *Staying power: The history of black people in Britain.* London: Pluto Press.

Gains, L. (no date). *The impossible dream: An autobiography by Larry Gains.* London: Leisure Publications.

Gates, H. L. (1998). "Net worth: How the greatest player in the history of basketball became the greatest brand in the history of sports," *The New Yorker,* June 1, 48–54.

Gilroy, P. (1992) "Cultural studies and ethnic absolutism." In *Cultural studies,* ed. L. Grossberg, C. Nelson, and P. A. Treichler. London: Routledge.

———. (1993). *The black atlantic: Modernity and double consciousness.* London: Verso.

———. (1994a). "Diaspora," *Paragraph* 17(3):207–212.

———. (1994b). "After the love has gone: Bio-politics and etho-poetics in the black public sphere," *Third Text* 28/29:25–45 (Autumn/Winter).

———. (1996). "Route work: The black Atlantic and the politics of exile." In *The post-colonial question: Common skies, divided horizons,* ed. I. Chambers and L. Curtis. London: Routledge.

Goldman, R. (1992). *Reading ads socially.* London: Routledge.

Green, J. (1998). *Black Edwardians: Black people in Britain 1901–1914.* London: Frank Cass.

Guttman, R. J. (1993). *Richard J. Donahue: Nike's president* (Interview), *Europe* (July-August), 30–.

Halberstam, D. (1991). "A hero for the wired world: In the satellite age, Michael Jordan has become the global hero of a global show," *Sports Illustrated,* December 23, 76–81.

Hall, S. (1998). "Aspiration and attitude . . . Reflections on black Britain in the nineties," *New Formations,* Spring, 33, 38–46.

Hartman, D. (1996). "The politics of race and sport: Resistance and domination in the 1968 African American Olympic protest movement," *Ethnic and Racial Studies* 19 (3):548–566.

Haworth, N. (1994). "Neo-liberalism, economic internationalisation, and the contemporary state in New Zealand." In *Leap into the dark: The changing role of the state in New Zealand since 1984,* ed. A. Sharp, 19–40. Auckland: Auckland University Press.

Hebdige, D. (1979). *Subculture: The meaning of style.* London: Methuen.

Held, D., A. McGrew, D. Goldblatt, and J. Perraton (1999) *Global transformations: Politics, economics, and culture.* Cambridge: Polity Press.

Hesse, B. (1999). "Reviewing the Western spectacle: Reflexive globalization through the black diaspora." In *Global Futures,* ed. A. Brah, M. Hickman, and M. Mac An Ghail, 122–143. London: Macmillan.

Hinton, M. (1998). "Why basketball's cock-a-hoop," *Sunday Star Times,* August 23, B2.

Hoggart, R. (1957). *The uses of literacy.* London: Chatto and Windus.

hooks, b. (1994). "Feminism inside: Toward a black body politic." In *Black male: Representations of masculinity in contemporary American art,* ed. T. Golden, 127–140. New York: Whitney Museum of American Art.

Hutchison, V. (1991). "The planetary Pakeha." In M. King Pakeha, *The quest for identity in New Zealand,* 129–145. Auckland: Penguin Books.

Hutchison, I., and G. Lealand (1996). "Introduction: A new mediascape," *Continuum: The Australian Journal of Media and Culture* 10 (1):7–11.

Jackson, S. J., and D. L. Andrews (1996). "Excavating the (Trans) National Basketball Association: Locating the global/local nexus of America's world and the world's America," *Australasian Journal of American Studies,* 15:57–64.

Jackson, S. J., and D. L. Andrews. (1994, May). *Mapping the meaning of Michael Jordan: A survey of New Zealand university undergraduate students.* School of Physical Education, University of Otago, New Zealand.

James, C. L. R. (1963[1994]). *Beyond a boundary.* London: Serpent's Tail.

Jenkins, R. (1992). "Salvation for the Fittest?: A West African sportsman in the age of the new imperialism." In *The cultural bond: Sport, empire, society,* ed. J. Mangan. London: Frank Cass.

Johnson, R. S. (1998). "The Jordan effect: The world's greatest basketball player is also one of its great brands. What is his impact on the economy?" *Fortune,* June 22, 124–126, 130–132, 134, 138.

Kellner, D. (1995). *Media culture: Cultural studies, identity, and politics between the modern and the postmodern.* London: Routledge.

Kelsey, J. (1996). *Economic fundamentalism: The New Zealand experiment—a world model for structural adjustment?* Auckland: Pluto Press.

Kettle, M. (1998). "Bulls land another title as sublime Jordan walks on air," *The Guardian,* June 16, 8.

Krzysztofek, K. (1992–1993). "Applicability of the theories of modernization for the development of post-socialist countries: The Polish case and the East European perspective," *Polish Political Science,* XXII–XXIII:11–27.

Landesman, C. (1998). "Half man, half logo," *The Independent, Wednesday Review,* June 24, 1.

Linebaugh, P., and M. Rediker (1990). "The many-headed Hydra: Sailors, slaves, and the Atlantic working class in the eighteenth century," *Journal of Historical Sociology* 3(3):225–252.

Lash, S., and J. Urry (1994). *Economies of signs and space.* London: Sage.

Lealand, G. (1994). "American popular culture and emerging nationalism in New Zealand," *National forum: The Phi Kappa Phi Journal* 74 (4): 34–37.

Liebes, T., and E. Katz (1990). *The export of meaning: Cross-cultural readings of Dallas.* New York: Oxford University Press.

Marqusee, M. (1999). *Redemption Song: Muhammad Ali and the spirit of the Sixties.* London: Verso.

Massey, D. (1994). *Space, place, and gender.* Cambridge: Polity Press.

McGrew, A. (1992). "A global society?" In *Modernity and its futures,* ed. S. Hall, D. Held, and A. McGrew, 61–116. Cambridge: Polity Press.

McLellan, D. (1977). *Karl Marx: Selected writings.* Oxford: Oxford University Press.

Melnick, M. J., and S. J. Jackson (1993). *Study of sport heroes/heroines, villains, and reference idols among New Zealand teenagers.* Unpublished Research Study: School of Physical Education, University of Otago, Dunedin, New Zealand.

Melnick, M., and S. Jackson (1996). *Globalization, the mass media, and reference idol selection: The case of New Zealand adolescents.* Paper presented at the annual meeting of the North American Society for the Sociology of Sport, Birmingham, Alabama, November 13–16.

Morley, D., and K. Robins (1995). *Spaces of identity: Global media, electronic landscapes, and cultural boundaries.* London: Routledge.

Nederveen Pieterse, J. (1995). "Globalization as Hybridization." In *Global modernities,* ed. M. Featherstone, S. Lash, and R. Robertson, 45–68. London, Sage.

Okonski, M., and A. Szostkiewicz (1994). "Poeta w krawacie" ("The poet wears a tie"): Interview with Stanislaw Baranczak, *Tygodnik Powszechny,* December 18–25, 12–13.

Pakula, A. (1992). "Amerykanizacja kultury" ("Americanization of culture"), *Dialog* (1–2).

Race and Class (1995). "All in the Game? Sport, race, and politics," April-June, 36(4).

Reykowski, J. (1994a). "Transformacja ustrojowa" ("The transformation of the political system"), *Zycie Gospodarcze* (18), 9.

———. (1994b). "Transformacja ustrojowa" ("The transformation of the political system"), *Zycie Gospodarcze* (20), 9.

———. (1994c). "Transformacja ustrojowa" ("The transformation of the political system"), *Zycie Gospodarcze* (22), 9.

Robertson, R. (1995). "Glocalization: Time-Space and homogeneity-heterogeneity." In *Global modernities,* ed. M. Featherstone, S. Lash, and R. Robertson, 25–44. London: Sage.

Robins, K. (1990). "Global local times." In *Society and social science: A reader,* ed. J. Anderson and M. Ricci, 196–205. Milton Keynes: Open University.

———. (1991). "Tradition and translation: National culture in its global context." In *Enterprise and heritage: Crosscurrents of national culture,* ed. J. Corner and S. Harvey, 21–44. London: Routledge.

Russell, M. (1996). *Revolution: New Zealand from fortress to free market.* Auckland: Hodder, Moa, Beckett.

South, B. (1998). "Making mark in NBA out of this world," *Sunday Star Times,* June 21, B5.

Spicer, B., M. Powell, and D. Emanuel (1996). *The remaking of Television New Zealand 1984–1992.* Auckland: Auckland University Press.

Thompson, E. P. (1972). "Anthropology and the discipline of context," *Midland History* 3:41–55.

Vasili, P. (1996). "Walter Daniel Tull, 1888–1918: Soldier, footballer, black," *Race and Class,* 38 (2):51–70.

———. (1998). *The first black footballer—Arthur Wharton 1865–1930: An absence of memory.* London: Frank Cass.

Wallerstein, I. (1990). "Culture as the ideological battleground of the modern world-system," *Theory, Culture, and Society* 7:31–55.

Wawrzyczek, I., and Z. Mazur (1994). "Do Polish youth dream American? The penetration of American cultural values in Poland." In *The American dream, past and present,* ed. A. Salska and P. Wilson, 14–22. Lodz, Poland: Wydawnictwo Uniwersytetu Lodzkiego.

Webster, D. (1988). *Looka yonder!: The imaginary America of populist culture.* London: Comedia.

Wharton, D. (1999). "Mike money dries up," *Sunday Star Times,* January, 17, B8.

Wilcox. L. (1996). "Saatchi Rap: The 'worlding of America' and racist ideology in New Zealand," *Continuum: The Australian Journal of Media and Culture* 10:121–135.

Zagrodzka, D. (1994). "W pogoni za grzesznym" ("Chasing the sinful world"), *Gazeta Wyborcza.* Magazyn, December 30, 6–9.

# 8

# Michael Jordan, Sneaker Commercials, and Canadian Youth Cultures

## Brian Wilson
## Robert Sparks

Retailers were booking orders as fast as Nike could take them. By March, Air Jordan was a retail sellout. Nike sold in three months what had been projected for the entire year . . . . Little kids lined up in stores to get the shoes worn by America's latest hero. Most of the time, they couldn't find them because Air Jordans were in such short supply. Scarcity created a demand never before seen in the athletic shoe business . . . . At [a] Nike sales meeting a month later, surprise guest Michael Jordan ran onto the court of Linfield College through the spotlight of a darkened court . . . and dribbled the ball to the basket at the far end. Then he took off through the air, moving more like a glider than a man, and jammed the ball. Nike sales rep and employees cheered and clapped in the longest standing ovation in Nike history. "We made history together, Nike and myself and all of you," Jordan said into a microphone. "It was a good team victory for all of us."
—Strasser and Becklund

In 1984, Nike and then NBA rookie Michael Jordan formed one of the most profitable relationships in endorsement history. Nike's ingenious marketing of their attractive, well-spoken, hard-working, and supremely talented spokesperson, particularly in ultra-appealing television commercial formats that connected Jordan's style and performance with the Nike logo, was a template for other athletic apparel companies and became the standard in athletic apparel marketing. Today, the Nike-Jordan relationship is still unmatched. Jordan has become one of the most recognizable people (athlete or not) on the planet, and Nike one of the most recognizable brand names. With this brilliant promotional strategy, Nike (and Jordan) have successfully

This chapter is adapted, by permission, from B. Wilson and R. Sparks, 1996, "'It''s gotta be the shoes':Youth, race, and sneaker commercials," *Sociology of Sport Journal,* 13(4): 398-427.

defined what is "cool" for vast segments of the youth consumer market. This
is a marketing success story of nearly unprecedented proportions.

However, there is an ugly side to this story and other athlete-sponsor
success stories, according to many critics. Athletic apparel manufacturers in
general, and Nike in particular, have been criticized for "outsourcing" production overseas to exploit cheap labor in the developing world, while promoting their products domestically to markets of impressionable youth.
Jordan and other celebrity athlete icons, the feature attractions in athletic
apparel advertising, have been denounced for irresponsibly "pimping" expensive shoes and apparel to youth who idolize these athletes and are ill-
equipped to resist the urge to "Be Like Mike." Furthermore, athletic apparel
commercials are believed to insidiously promote social mobility through
sport over other (more realistic) forms of social mobility by showing exceptional athletes in accessible commercial formats. Other critics argue that these
commercials lead youth, "the audience with the greatest gullibility and the
least amount of money," to think that they can "achieve their dreams by putting out good money" (Buchignani 1990, A4; see also Alert 1997). For some
youth, this means stealing in order to attain the "right shoes," as Telander
(1990) reports:

> For 15 year old Michael Eugene Thomas, it definitely was the shoes . . . .
> Thomas was found strangled on May 2, 1989. Charged with first degree-
> murder was James David Martin, a basketball buddy who allegedly took
> Thomas's two-week-old Air Jordan basketball shoes and left Thomas's bare-
> footed body in the woods near school. Thomas loved Michael Jordan, as well
> as the shoes Jordan endorses, and he cleaned his own pair each evening. He
> kept the cardboard shoe box with Jordan's silhouette on it in a place of
> honor in his room. Inside the box was the sales ticket for the shoes. It
> showed he paid $115.50, the price of a product touched by deity. (37)

Although journalistic reports of youth violence (such as Telander's
above) are often criticized for their tendency to sensationalize isolated inci-
dents and to blame someone or something for the "problems with society's
youth" (see Acland 1995), there is no denying that athletic apparel companies
and celebrity athletes are extremely influential players in the popular culture
industry and do have far-reaching impacts (negative or otherwise). Athletic
apparel television commercials, in particular, have become a cultural reference
point for many North Americans. They have a distinct vernacular of catch
phrases such as "Just Do It," "Bo Knows," "It's Gotta be the Shoes," and "Life's
Short, Play Hard." They have unique personalities such as "superfan Mars
Blackmon" (Nike promoter and filmmaker Spike Lee who appeared in a
series of commercials with "his idol" Michael Jordan), and "Little Penny" (a

ventriloquist's doll replica of, and outspoken sidekick of former Orlando Magic star, current Phoenix Suns player, and Nike promoter "Penny" Hardaway). They have uniquely defined zones of cultural production such as "Mr. Robinson's Neighborhood" (the "paint" on a basketball court under the defensive basket where San Antonio Spur and Nike promoter David Robinson blocks opponents' shots) and "fun police" headquarters (where the "fun police force," including NBA players and Nike promoters Kevin Garnett, Tim Hardaway, and Gary Payton coordinate their efforts to make sure basketball games are never boring). This commercial culture has been embraced by large segments of youth and is interwoven into other elements of youth culture—dress codes, street vernacular, dramatic styles of self-presentation, modes of address, and authorized subjects of discourse.

Since the early 1990s, Michael Jordan and Nike have played key roles in the evolution of this cultural movement.[1] While early Nike ads (mid-late 1980s) showed the young "Air" Jordan as a gravity-defying slam dunk artist in more conventional (but still effective) athletic apparel commercial formats, it was his 1991 association with filmmaker Spike Lee that launched Jordan and Nike well beyond sport and into mainstream popular culture. In a renowned commercial featuring Spike Lee as superfan "Mars Blackmon," Lee's "cinematic alter ego" from the film *She's Gotta Have It* (Andrews 1996), "Blackmon" is shown contemplating whether Jordan's performance can be attributed to his Nike shoes. Blackmon concludes finally, along with a cast of fans and NBA players who are shown throughout the commercial chanting the commercial's tagline "it's gotta be the shoes." While this commercial likely had a powerful appeal in itself, it was Spike Lee's elevation of "style" within and deriving from his films such as *Do the Right Thing* (a well-known scene from the movie shows an angry black male challenging a white male who scuffed his new "Air Jordan" sneakers) and *Malcolm X* (millions of dollars have been made from hats and clothing with the unmistakable patented "X" on it) that confirmed the marketing genius of Jordan-Lee ads for Nike. Considering the notoriety of these commercials and related popularity of advertised shoes and apparel with youth consumers, it is reasonable to suggest, as many social critics have, that youth are influenced by these commercials in sometimes negative ways. However, there is also a tendency for critics to make presumptuous and oversimplified claims about the impacts of these commercials and athletes on youth. For example, it is often implied that all youth interpret these ads (and the athletes featured in them) in similar ways, that youth are uncritical consumers of these commercials and athletes, and that commercials (in isolation from other conditions) "cause" youth to react in certain ways.

Most often, youth audiences are considered to be a "mass audience," not audience "segments" with distinct interpretive capacities and critical capabilities.
A testament to this point is that previous research in this area has failed to
consider empirically how different audiences (for example, black and white
youth, or Canadian and American youth) interpret the same messages or how
different genres of messages (for example, television commercials as opposed
to NBA coverage) might be understood by the same audiences. In many
cases, however, the audience is not considered at all.

What follows is the report of a study undertaken to investigate the complexities of interpretation and consumption as they relate to race, advertising,
and youth. The focus of this research is on the positioning of athletic footwear
commercials and celebrity black athletes in the cultures of middle-class black
and nonblack male youth in two Canadian cities, Toronto and Vancouver. In
this context, a series of study questions will be addressed, including: to what
extent do athletic apparel commercials featuring athletes such as Michael
Jordan "create" popular culture by defining youth's awarenesses of what is
"cool" and socially desirable at the same time that they stimulate product
demand; to what extent are youth active consumers (that is, do youth play a
more active role in the creation of sneaker culture than the critics think);
what are the lines of separation between the interests of and the interpretive
capacities of different groups of youth; are these lines freely made or do
youth's differing national backgrounds, social locations, peer cultures, and
personal interests in some way shape their understandings and appreciations
of, for example, athletic apparel commercials and celebrity black athletes?

The position taken in this chapter is that the influences of television
advertising (and other forms of programming) cannot be "read" from the
message, and that audience research is necessary for understanding what
audiences do with advertising. At the same time, however, this chapter is cautious about what can be gained from audience research. It does not assume
that a "snapshot" view of peoples' interpretations of a televisual text is some-
how generalizable to "real life" circumstances. Audience research can give
only a partial view of the dynamics of message assimilation and use at any
given time. Not only is it "incomplete" in terms of the range of interpretations that are possible within a given population at a given moment in time,
it also provides only a limited indication of what the assessed audience "will
do next," and no indication at all of what the audience "could do" if given
the chance (Hartley 1994). Nevertheless, by studying audiences' interpretations of television contents, and particularly by assessing the meanings that
various audiences give to the same contents, a kind of normative "map" can

be made of the plausible range of interpretations, adaptations, and uses of the contents. In this way, a partial picture of the impacts of media contents can be developed.

The purpose of this chapter is to develop just such a picture. The following format was adapted for this task. First, relevant theory and research is reviewed, focusing on audience research, youth consumption, black athlete media portrayals, minority portrayals in Canadian media, and race relations in Canada. Second, a methodological rationale for using focus groups as a form of audience ethnography is proposed. Third, key findings from a study of youth audiences are summarized, and the implications of these results are discussed with reference to theory and method.

## A Brief History of Audience Research

Contemporary research perspectives on media audiences owe a common debt to work conducted by David Morley at the Centre for Contemporary Cultural Studies (CCCS) at the University of Birmingham in the late 1970s and the 1980s. Of particular significance historically was Morley's (1980) use of "ethnographic" methods (in Morley's original research, this meant group interviews) to determine how viewers of different classes and education levels interpreted media texts. These methods were later extended to include observations of and interviews with people in their homes, their "natural" television watching environment (Morley 1986). These were attempts to empirically account not only for viewer interpretations, but also the importance of social context and place of reception. In essence, Morley (and those who followed, including Ang 1985; Buckingham 1987; Hobson 1982; Lull 1990; Tulloch and Moran 1986) effectively showed qualitatively how the activity of media use cannot be separated from the interpretations people make of media texts. These methods were a reaction to previous research that used either experimental studies or survey methods to measure the attitudinal and behavioral consequences of media texts on viewers (while often ignoring or underestimating the interpretive capacities of viewers), or textual analysis studies that attempted to identify the meanings embedded in different media texts (without actually talking to audience members).[2]

Perhaps the most notable of Morley's contributions was his empirical "test" of Stuart Hall's (1980) encoding-decoding model of media production and consumption. Hall's model showed the media communication process to be a whole, with the moment of program making at one end of a continuum and the moment of audience interpretation at the other. In his model,

Hall acknowledged that intended meanings that are "encoded" into various media (e.g., television program, newspaper article) by media producers, might be interpreted ("decoded") in unintended and unanticipated ways by some audiences. For Hall, viewers bring their own interpretive frameworks to media texts and, in this sense, the encoded message is not guaranteed to be decoded in accordance with its producers' intentions (Hall 1980). Hall distinguished what he called the "preferred" reading of media texts, a reading that conformed with the dominant cultural order and a reading therefore that the "ordinary" viewer would make. Those readings that displayed the basic premise of the preferred reading but varied in other ways were "negotiated" readings, while those readings that in no way conformed to the "preferred" reading were "oppositional." It was the researcher's responsibility to define these types of reading, and to examine how they compared to viewer interpretations of the media text.

Critics of the encoding-decoding model (and Morley's "test" of the model) (see Lewis 1983; Morley 1981; and Moores 1993) argued that the notions of encoding and "preferred readings" wrongly implied a correspondence between the broadcaster's personal (ideological) intentions in producing a message, and the (preferred) reading that resulted. Practically speaking, Hall's conditions have not stood up to scrutiny. Moores (1993), for example, has confirmed that broadcasters operate more on a taken-for-granted basis using professional conventions than they do with deliberate biases and purposes (although this does not preclude the possibility that "professional conventions" might systemically reproduce the beliefs and ideologies of the media producers). The notion of the "preferred reading" itself has been shown to be little more than the researcher's own interpretation of the text (Lewis 1983), while analyses of viewer interpretations were shown to require sensitivity to genre preferences (e.g., some viewers' preferences for certain programs might influence their interpretations of these programs).

Despite these shortcomings, Morley's work provided critical insights (in part, through the shortcomings of his research) into the complexities of the interpretative process. Nightingale (1996) summarizes the contributions made by Morley and others that followed the British audience research tradition:

> The projects challenged the separation which had divided audience research from the study of texts—films, television programs, books—and promised to consolidate a new era of "balanced" cultural criticism, in which equal weight was to be accorded to text and audience. The research took the concept "audience" and tried to shake it loose from "mass audience" preconceptions and general survey methodologies. It tried to make

room for the audience as "real" people engaged in the production of their culture, rather than as abstract generalities, and each tried to integrate the audience in a critique of popular culture. (viii)

A useful alternative to Morley's (and Hall's) original class-based understanding of audience interpretations is Janice Radway's conception of the "interpretive community," which she developed (drawing on Fish 1979) at the University of Pennsylvania in the late 1970s and early 1980s. Radway held that the meaning of an activity for an individual is related to one's "social location," and that people with similar locations would give similar meanings to their activities. For example, in Radway's (1991, originally published in 1984) ethnography of romance readers, the "community" of female readers she studied made explicit connections between their reasons for reading romance novels (escape from the monotony of day to day activity) and their daily social situation as housewives in "patriarchal marriages." Radway's attention to social location with respect to gender and class, her focus on viewer uses of (as well as interpretation of) media texts and her emphasis on the importance of genre allowed her to effectively avoid many of the shortcomings of Morley's early work (although unintentionally—she was unaware of the developments at the CCCS at the time of her research). Despite these advances, critics of Radway's work have been skeptical about dividing people into "clear" demographic categories because these distinctions do not account for the flow of social life (Ang 1991; Radway 1988). Radway herself noted that her work failed to adequately describe how membership in the romance-reading community was composed or explain how "social determination operate(d) with respect to the larger activity of reading romance" (1991, 8). These limitations of Radway's work, however, were for the most part methodological and not structural in that she did not adequately operationalize the concept of social location as a context of meaning construction.[3]

## The Battle for Cultural Power:
## Youth Subcultures, Interpretive Communities, and Taste Cultures

Radway's "interpretive community" framework has unique potential for advancing research on the interpretive process, particularly if used in combination with the body of work on youth subcultures that already has a well-defined theory of social position and meaning construction (see Lull 1992; Willis 1990; Hebdige, 1979). Radway's framework lends itself to this sort of adaptation and could extend youth subculture research by providing a tentative bridge with theories of media interpretation (1991, 8). According to

Radway, similarities in a group's interpretations of media texts can be attributed to specific "cultural competencies" (e.g., the ability of sport enthusiasts to
appreciate the narrative styles, modes of discourse, drama, and oral histories of
their sport) that are acquired as a consequence of the group's social location.
This understanding of the "interpretive community" can be used to examine
how youth audience interests and interpretations are related to the social and
cultural circumstances of everday life. By maintaining this intersection
between "taste" and "interpretation" within youth groups, it is possible to
avoid the determinist and reductionist pitfalls that result from grouping audiences into "interpretive communities" based on arbitrary research criteria such
as ethnicity, age, gender, social class, occupation—an approach that wrongly
and "artificially isolates individuals into categories that may have little reality
in the flux and flow of social life" (Machin and Carrithers 1996, 343; Ang
1991; Radway 1988).

Willis (1990) has noted that youth actively construct meaning, identity,
and lifestyle through their interpretation and consumption of television,
advertising, music, and clothes. Willis refers to this active construction as
"symbolic creativity." He argues that these creativities are negotiated within
structural constraints (such as memberships of race, class, gender, age, and
region) in order to give meaning to one's consumptions and experiences.
However, as McGuigan (1992, 117) points out, when youth "consume" culture there is "constant interaction and borrowing, complicating ethnic differences and to some extent gender differences as well." Hebdige (1979)
explored some of these "negotiations" in his landmark work on spectacular
British subcultures. He used the term *bricolage* to describe how "basic elements can be used in a variety of improvised combinations to generate new
meanings" (1979, 103). Moores (1993) contended that Willis's symbolic creativity, while similar to bricolage, helps to explain how all youth actively construct meaning, identity, and lifestyle, not just the spectacular groups
(Hebdige's focus).

Lull (1995) used the concepts of "cultural power" and "symbolic power"
to help explain how and why people use cultural resources to construct identities. Lull (1995, 71) defined cultural power as the "ability of groups and individuals to construct (usually partial and temporary) ways of life . . . that appeal
to the senses, emotions, and thoughts of self and others." He followed
Thompson (1994) in his definition of "symbolic power" as "the capacity to
use symbolic forms . . . to intervene in and influence the course of action or
events" (Lull 1995, 71). According to Lull, cultural power is exercised when
individuals and groups symbolically construct and "declare" their cultural

identities and activities. Lull (see also Hebdige 1979; Willis 1990) draws joint-ly from the work of both Willis and Hebdige, suggesting that people (as "active scavengers and bricoleurs") exercise cultural power by symbolically exploring aspects of culture (e.g., fashion, language, and hairstyle). Lull acknowledges, however, that cultural power is exercised both by the individ-uals and by institutional "sponsors." For Lull, the most profound social con-sequences of popular culture, whether these be resistive to or supportive of preferred or dominant modes of thinking, lie in people's use of media imagery to express themselves and influence others.

"Cultural power" and "symbolic power," which encompass the more specific notions of "symbolic creativity" and "bricolage," are helpful concepts for explaining the "use" of the running shoe in adolescent street culture. Feniak (1991, F7) discusses how "sneakers," made by such companies as Nike, Converse, and Reebok were initially popular in American "paved over, graf-fiti filled playgrounds." However, with the sneakers' ascension to iconic status in mass media imagery in films such as Spike Lee's *Do the Right Thing* and in athletic apparel commercials featuring popular basketball stars, a new passion for the shoes was developed among many youth (Reilly 1991; Feniak 1991). Sneakers have since become a widely recognized social artifact that is often associated with youth culture. Present symbolic and practical uses of the sneaker might be considered examples of symbolic creativity for youth who negotiate and create meaning with sneakers and the athletic apparel com-mercials that shape their "brand identities."

Lull (1995, 75) refers to the athletic shoe phenomenon as an "extraordi-nary example" of the correspondence between ideological representation and social interpretation, and between symbolic power and cultural power. Lull describes the athletic apparel commercial as the "basketball-star/black cul-ture/athletic shoe commercial," suggesting that athletes such as Michael Jordan project such awesome cultural power that culture itself is "extended" to a range of youthful "cultural agents" that cross gender, race, and class barriers:

> Jordan is not a media creation; he is strategically re-created for commer-cial purposes . . . every detail is managed to perfection—from the slow motion, high flying slam dunks on TV to the broad, disarming smile star-ing at us from the Wheaties box. His bigger than life persona is part of an inviting pool of contemporary symbolic resources used to fashion cultur-al power . . . the cultural agents range from inner-city black boys whose lifestyle is glorified by the commercial media to suburban white girls who high-five and call each other "homegirls." (Lull 1995, 78)

Significantly, Lull identifies here and in his other work the potential for certain forms of popular culture "to transcend boundaries of social class, race, gender, educational level, and nearly every other demographic marker" (Lull 1985, 215). He notes how the compelling range of influences that mass media provides increases the potential for audiences to "cross over" (consume another group's culture) by giving people from differing social strata access to each other's cultural artifacts, symbols, and narratives. However, it is crucial to note that crossover interests and consumption patterns (the cultural activities that are enjoyed and participated in by different audiences) do not necessarily coincide with common interpretations made by audience members (referring to the socially shared meanings that these activities have for their participants). For example, both black youth and white youth might be interested in a sneaker endorsed by Michael Jordan in a television commercial, however, each of these elements—Michael Jordan, the commercial, and the shoe—could have manifestly different meanings for the youth. In this way, the "social impacts" of these cultural elements might also be quite different even though the youth shared a common interest in and enthusiasm for basketball and basketball celebrities, apparel, and footwear.

## Cultural Power and Black Resistance

It would also make sense, using Radway's framework, that interpretations of commercials promoting athletic shoes would be similar for members of groups that are "similarly located." The difficulty is to find a nonreductionist way of defining social location so that the intricacies of taste and interpretation can be understood in a useful way, but are not oversimpified in the process. Willis (1990, 8) illustrates some of the complexities associated with doing research on race and youth culture in his study of young blacks' experiences in Britain as follows:

> often young black people are engaged in a doubly creative task. They are trying to negotiate what it means to be a black person in a white culture at the same time they are engaged in the same creative activities as their white peers, through which they explore aspects of their black identities. The balance that young people strike between these things differs from culture to culture and from individual to individual.

Majors (1990) described this process of "negotiation" in his research on black masculinity and sport. He suggests that black males cope with their frustration, alienation, and social impotence within an institutionally racist society by "channeling their creative energies into the construction of unique, expressive, and conspicuous styles of demeanor, speech, gesture, clothing, hairstyle, walk, stance, and handshake" (1990, 111). This phenomenon, which Majors calls "cool pose," can be seen in the sport of basketball in the emergence of an expressive style among black basketball players that encompasses creativity, grace, and agility, embedded in an aggressive assertion of masculinity. Of particular importance is that these behaviors are considered to be uniquely "black" and act as resistance to the dominant white culture. Dyson (1993, 66) stresses this point, suggesting that "black sport" has become a way of "ritualizing racial achievement against socially imposed barriers to cultural performance . . . [and] as a means of expressing black cultural style, as a means of valorizing craft as a marker of racial self-expression, and as a means of pursuing social and economic mobility." There is evidence to suggest that "cool pose" holds similar meanings for black Canadian youth (in a Canadian society characterized by predominantly subtle but still pervasive forms of discrimination—see later section in this chapter). Ethnographic research in an inner city Toronto school conducted by Solomon (1992) showed "black" forms of symbolic resistance to be asserted by two groups of black youth, the "jocks" and the "rastas." The groups had distinct patterns of dress, hairstyle, communication, and demeanor that acted as race-based resistance against the expectations of their high school—expectations that these youth considered to be insensitive to their distinct racial background and experiences. For these youth, sport was also a primary means of achieving a race-based identity and a sense of "manliness." Solomon draws on Willis's (British) model to suggest that sport allowed them to preserve "a degree of machoism from the real and imputed degradation of their conditions" (Willis 1976, 176).

Although not focused on sport, Hunt's recent research (1997) on diverse audience reactions (black, Latino, and white) to news media coverage of the Los Angeles "riots" provides useful insights into the relationship between audiences, race, and (black) resistance. Hunt's analysis was the basis for developing a balanced and sophisticated understanding of black resistance as it relates to the media. Hunt's study highlighted the critical/resistive potential of audiences (particularly black audiences) to hegemonic media texts—texts that (according to Hunt's reading) contained deceiving ideological messages about race relations. Of particular significance was Hunt's necessarily cautious attempt to explain his respondents' interpretations as examples of "audience resistance" in both theoretical and practical terms. Hunt (1997) explains:

> In the crudest terms, what I have described in this book as informant opposition to the text's assumptions might be seen in one of two ways: either as acts of resistance, or acts of pseudo-resistance. I argue for the former interpretation. My finding that KTTV framed these events largely in accord with the status quo . . . and that many study groups (Black-raced groups in particular) challenged this framing, is my rationale.

> Indeed, consistent with audience powerful and in-between perspectives
> that acknowledge the ability or tendency of individuals to resist the ide-
> ologies inscribed in media texts . . . several study groups managed to sub-
> vert the hegemonic meanings encoded in the KTTV text, to turn the text
> to uses other than those intended. In this sense, I cautiously celebrate
> instances of viewer opposition to the assumptions embedded in the
> KTTV text; we might see these as either constituting meaningful acts of
> resistance in their own right, or contributing to a consciousness necessary
> for meaningful social action at some later moment in time. (161–162)

An important addendum to Hunt's discussion was that "Black raced-inform-
ants exhibited a consciousness [about the subtle deceptions embedded in
news media texts] qualitatively different than from that exhibited by Latino
and White-raced informants" (163; see also Jhally and Lewis 1992; Lewis
1991, for similar findings of "raced" interpretations). These relationships
between interpretation, media consciousness, genre, and race that were identified by Hunt's (and Jhally and Lewis's) research are central to the current
study and will be revisited later in this chapter.

Recent journalistic accounts also provide some evidence of the ways
that youth communities interpret and consume Michael Jordan and athletic
apparel. Informal interviews conducted by a news reporter with a small sample of black Chicago youth showed that these youth resent Jordan for
"spend(ing) all his time golfing, living high and everything and doing commercials," and for not helping clean up inner city neighborhoods. However,
the author noted an important contradiction between the youths' critique of
Jordan and the Jordanesque style they had adopted:

> Their avowed distaste notwithstanding, Jordan has exercised considerable
> influence on these kids. The players wear oversized shorts, a point of style
> popularized by Jordan, though well before their time. All dream of jam-
> ming the ball like him too . . . . Jordan and his advisors would recognize
> these young men as a thin slice of the demographic pie chart—under 18,
> Black and inner city males. (Joyce 1998, A26)

A similar journalist account of youth style reported in a Canadian
newsmagazine suggested that Toronto youth uncritically embrace the hip-
hop styles promoted by Nike and other designers such as Tommy Hilfiger and
Ralph Lauren. However, the meanings given to these "black" styles by youth
of different races were shown to be complicated by racial tensions related to
the appropriation of these styles by nonblack youth groups. In particular, the
author discussed the racial politics surrounding the question, "why a White
kid would want to look Black, act Black, [and] talk Black," finding that most
of the "wiggers" (white youth who adopt "black" style and/or demeanor)
either didn't want to discuss the topic or "would just shrug their shoulders

and say they dress hip-hop because they're bored or 'cuz it's comfortable' or 'I feel like it'" (Baines 1997, 81). It was proposed that, for these nonblack youth, "expressing themselves through a style that doesn't belong to them could be seen as a radical act, a way of testing to see if racial identity, in a world increasingly preoccupied with difference, can be fluid" (Baines 1997, 81). Baines (1997, 80) also found that black youth "end up feeling more powerless as White youth play around with hip-hop culture." Although this journalistic research is not as methodologically rigorous as conventional ethnography or audience studies, it is useful as a theoretical and empirical reference point considering the overall lack of grounded research on the meanings of sneaker-style in the everyday lives of youth.

## Race, Representation, and the Mass Mediated Black Athlete

Although there are few studies focused on the ways that audiences interpret and consume media images of the black athlete, there is a larger body of textual and content analysis research examining the ways that these images are constructed by media producers. These studies provide important context for audience studies by showing generally what images are available for audience consumption. With this type of background, potential audience interpretations can be theorized and media production patterns can be understood. Research in this area shows that black athlete portrayals are either stereotypical and demeaning (Lule 1995; Wonsek 1992), or nonstereotypical and misleading (McKay 1995; Wenner 1994), as Andrews outlines clearly in his article in this volume. Recent research in the Canadian context supported these findings. In particular, a study of black athlete portrayals during Toronto Raptor NBA game telecasts in 1996 showed how black portrayals fell into the contradictory categories of "good black" and "bad black" (Wilson 1997). Nonstereotypical ("good") blacks were shown to have a work ethic, to demonstrate courage, and to have persevered in their successful rise from poverty to NBA stardom. Stereotypical ("bad") blacks were shown to be intimidating, ominous figures in promotional contexts, while being associated with crime and labeled as "undisciplined" in news-related coverage. These portrayals were believed to support an ideology that attributes black success or failure to an ability or inability to take advantage of available opportunities that exist in the (apparent) absence of structural barriers to mobility.

In other research on television advertising during Canadian telecasts of Toronto Raptor games (Wilson 1999), it was argued that the commercialization of black culture was potentially disempowering for blacks because the creative and resistive potential that black culture holds for young black males (see Majors and Billson 1992; Majors 1990) had been appropriated by big business to sell products. The promotion of black culture was also believed to potentially reinforce the myths of social mobility through sport, to emphasize the negative stereotypes that underlie the inequalities that exist in Canadian society (see next section), and to exclude (black) women. In general, the research highlighted the unintentional consequences of promotional strategies used by Nike and other athletic apparel companies.

## Globalization, Americanization, Canadian Media, and Canadian Culture

To understand the social impacts of media portrayals of African American cultural icons broadcast from American-based media on Canadian youth, we have adopted Lull's (1995, 147) theory of globalization, a theory that emphasizes how mass media messages and ideologies are modified by the local context of reception. Lull draws on Appadurai (1990) to criticize claims of global homogenization (the "global village"), suggesting that, while current developments in communication and culture have impacted societies worldwide, these cultural forces have produced "heterogeneous dialogues" between the mass mediated messages and the particular culture (see also Maguire 1999). In this sense, to understand the impacts of widely transmitted cultural messages, an understanding of the "place of reception" is required.

Although the complexity of the globalization process poses difficulties for those attempting to identify transnational media impacts, it is still generally accepted that American culture (through the media) impacts Canadian culture. Winter and Goldman (1995, 205–206) provided the following examples of these (potentially) media-related impacts: (a) Canadians who attended to U.S. media "identif(y) more closely with anti-government sentiment that is more in keeping with the American free-enterprise system than the more mixed Canadian economy"; (b) first-year university students "knew as much, and in some cases more, about American personalities than Canadian ones—a result that could reasonably be attributed to media effects"; and (c) knowledge of Canadian judicial process "was inversely related to reliance on U.S. TV programs involving lawyers as characters" (Baer and Winter 1983; Tate and Trach 1980). A study conducted by Winter (1985) showed that his sample of 275 Windsor residents (Windsor is a border town immediately across from Detroit, Michigan) had more knowledge about many aspects of American culture than they did of Canadian culture. Winter and Goldman explain (1995, 208–209):

While 57 percent could name the first U.S. president, George Washington, only 38 percent could name Sir John A. MacDonald [Canada's first Prime Minister]. While 34 percent could identify Michigan governor James Blanchard, only 5 percent could identify premier Howard Pawley [Ontario's Premier at the time]. Eighty-two percent were unable to name the last Canadian film they had seen; 78 percent were unable to name the author of the last Canadian book they had read; 69 percent were unable to name one Canadian author; 56 percent couldn't name their favorite Canadian TV program, or didn't have one; 36 percent said they had never bought a Canadian album or audiotape; and 30 percent were unable to name one Canadian vocal/instrumental artist or group.

Although these findings do not "prove" media "effects," they do suggest that American media and television are powerful cultural conditioners. These results are not surprising considering the widespread dissemination of American mass media throughout Canada. For example, in 1987–88, U.S. stations commanded 31.9 percent of the English-speaking Canadian audience compared to a Canadian program share of 26 percent (Canada 1992; Canada 1990), while 78 percent of Canadian households subscribe to cable television systems that offer a minimum of three U.S. commercial networks (Canada 1991). Although quotas for Canadian content in domestic programming and guidelines restricting foreign ownership of national media enterprises are in place, the Free Trade Agreement between Canada and the United States (signed January 1989) and the North American Free Trade Agreement (NAFTA—signed December 1992) essentially neutralize any Canadian control of the "real world of broadcasting industry" (Raboy 1989, 74).

This should not be taken to mean that American programming "obliterates what is distinctively Canadian" (Feldthusan 1993, 45–46). On the contrary, the complexity of this relationship between Canadian viewers and American media should usefully highlight the distinct ambiguity of Canadian culture, as Wernick (1993, 297–298) suggests:

America, the incarnation of centralizing and modernizing industrial progress, is still modernity. But Canada, a dispersed society of margins without a centre, now becomes a figure of post-modernity. Even with its hint of national self-flattery, the result is intriguing. It is as if, through a paradox of its cultural absorption, Canada, not the United States, is the most contemporary—that is, the most post-modern—of nations; and this because, precisely in that subordinated context, its national identity is founded in the determined absence of any such thing.

Wernick's understanding of postmodernism is based on his view of "local cultures" reflecting global developments, without needing to think about the specific relation of those developments to their national context. Although

Wernick's point appears excessive in his overstatement of a diffuse Canadian "postmodern" culture, he accurately clarifies the need to understand media reception and creation outside the American context and within a theory of globalization (such as Lull and Appadurai's) that accounts for "heterogeneous dialogues" between mass media and local (but not necessarily national) cultures.

## Media Reception in the Canadian Racial Climate

Theorizing the potential meanings of (American) black athlete portrayals for Canadian audiences within Lull's framework on globalization—a theory that emphasizes the ways that media interpretation is dependent on the context of reception—requires a sketch of the distinct racial climate and history of Canada. Canada has traditionally supported an ideology of "multiculturalism" (in contrast to the American "melting pot"), a commitment that was official-ly established at a constitutional and legislative level in 1971. These policies led to the establishment of agencies and funded programs that attempted to promote and manage racial and ethnic diversity. More recently, there has been a shift in multicultural directives "from an initial focus on culture and eth-nicity ('celebrating differences') to one which emphasizes antiracism and equity ('managing diversity')" (Fleras 1995, 409). The Multiculturalism Act of 1988 in Canada required institutions under federal control "to make appro-priate adjustments for minority accommodation through improved entry, access, representation and treatment" (Fleras 1995, 409). This act was intend-ed to reinforce, reflect, and promote the reality of multiculturalism in Canada.

For many critics, Canada's movement against ethnic inequality is ineffec-tive and illusory.[4] Research has shown consistently that there are comparatively fewer educational and economic opportunities for visible minorities in Canada compared to those of European (mainly British or French) descent (Agocs and Boyd 1993; Boyd 1992; Henry 1994; Satzewich and Li 1987). Evidence of unequal treatment, systemic barriers, and failure to accommodate diversity have been well documented in studies of occupations (Agocs and Boyd 1993; Boyd 1992; Collinson et al. 1990; Fernandez 1988; Henry and Ginzberg 1993).

An ethnographic study of the experiences of racism for those of "black and Caribbean origin" in Toronto revealed perceptions of racism in, among other areas, employment, the justice system, and education (Henry 1994). Racism in employment appeared to be subtle but tangible, with Henry (1994) finding that "on the whole, entry level jobs and 'stay put' jobs were easier to obtain, but the real employment problem came about because of a lack of promotional opportunities for people of color" (199).

In education, youth in Henry's study (1994, 134–136) felt that teachers in their schools tend to treat them "as an undifferentiated Black rather than individuals." There was also "a widespread feeling that Black students are generally expected to excel in sports but not in academic subjects" (Henry 1994, 136).

While less pervasive than the American media, Canadian-owned media have also been shown to subtly support racism by positioning minorities in limited ways. Racial minorities (not exclusively blacks) have been shown to be underrepresented or portrayed stereotypically in places such as billboard advertising and in major magazines, as well as on television—as characters in dramas, as news anchors, as news reporters, as guests on news features, and as product spokespersons in commercial advertising (Canada 1988; Canada 1984; Quill 1990).

Overall, this evidence revealing discriminatory practices and institutional and structural disadvantages for blacks in Canada (see also Cannon 1995, Henry et al. 1995) is still in contrast with an American system that is characterized by segregation and racial violence (see Connolly 1995; Dyson 1995; Omi 1989; Omi and Winant 1994). It is noteworthy, for example, that the respondents in Henry's (1994) study of minority experiences and perceptions in Toronto had found an economic niche for themselves in either wage labor or self-employment. This condition contrasts with the widespread poverty and unemployment of the black underclass in the United States.[5]

## Audience Ethnography, Interpretive Communities, Taste Cultures, and Athletic Apparel Commercials

This literature review has demonstrated that previous research has begun to empirically examine audience interpretive processes as they relate to race, the media, and consumer culture. Nevertheless, this program of research is not yet well developed. To understand the potential range of influences of television advertising on different youth cultures (nationally, regionally, locally) and especially the implications of particular genres of advertising (such as athletic apparel commercials), more focused research is necessary. The present study examines these implications, and the "heterogeneous dialogues" surrounding athletic apparel commercials (the related processes of interpretation) by describing the reactions of racially distinct Canadian youth audiences to these commercials. The study builds on previous research by addressing television commercials as a distinct genre, and youth audience segments as "interpretive communities." An important goal of the study is to assess the interplay of social location and the social construction of meaning. This area is not well theorized in media research (Radway 1991), and has been undervalued in both text-based and audience-based research. As Lewis (1991) warns:

> [I]n audience research ... there has been a tendency to dismiss the impor-
> tance of crude materialities like class and race, to question the power of
> these materialities to shape people's perceptions of television, popular cul-
> ture and the world in general. While it would be foolish to ignore the
> complexity of these causal relations, it is equally foolish to ignore causali-
> ty altogether. (193)

While critics suggest that ethnographic and media-specific interviews frag-ment "lived experience" (McGuigan 1992; Radway, 1988), it makes sense that if we are to understand the dynamic impacts of the mass media we have to take seriously the varied and detailed ways in which media are consumed. The latter of itself constitutes a basis for an ethnography of television view-ing, and for a commitment to ethnography as an empirical method.

## Research Method

The empirical component of this study was designed to capture recent exam-ples of athletic footwear commercials from sports programming, and then evaluate youth readings and interpretations of these commercials in light of their peer culture(s). A subsample of six representative athletic apparel com-mercials featuring black athletes was selected from an overall sample of com-mercials recorded during the 1994 NCAA men's basketball tournament and the 1994 NBA playoffs. These were chosen with the intention of prompting discussion about the cultural impacts of the commercials and the celebrity black athletes featured in the commercials by groups recruited to preview the segments. The subsample was viewed by seven groups of youth (with between two and eight subjects in each group) who routinely watch televised basket-ball. Three groups were comprised of fifteen- to nineteen-year-old black males and four of fifteen- to nineteen-year-old nonblack males (a mix of whites, Asians, two East Indians, and one Israeli). These sessions were video-taped and later transcribed for analysis.

The black subjects (n=14) were recruited in Toronto, a city with a sig-nificant black population. The nonblack subjects (n=23) were recruited in Vancouver to comprise a segment that had little experience with blacks (based on the demographic makeup of the city).[6] Group members were drawn from the same school, and typically were friends (and in most cases played basketball together). All groups shared an interest in basketball and were regular or occasional viewers of televised basketball. The goal of the recruitment strategy was to find groups of adolescents with similar interests and a common youth "culture." These stipulations did not strictly control for socioeconomic class, although consistencies were likely. The study was intended to examine how social location (with a focus on race as a demographic feature), interests, and "interpretive strategies" interacted. The black male subjects who participated in the study were recruited in the same way as the nonblack subjects, that is, from a common school and from among friends.[7] Using groups of friends was intended to put the respondents (especially the mixed group of nonblacks) more at ease when talking about a sensitive issue such as race. All indications were that this method worked, as the groups did not exhibit any signs of polarization or dissonance when discussing racial topics and issues.

A focus group methodology was used based on the understanding that "directed" interaction within a homogeneous group can bring out ideas and points of view that would not come out in casual conversation (ethnography) or in one-to-one interviewing (Morgan 1988). Also, to study "group" culture and "group" reactions to and interpretations of media texts, it is preferable to observe these interpretations in a group setting. Focus group research is also preferable to structured survey research for deriving "understandings" and interpretations that could not be discovered without interaction among peers and probing by the interviewer. The small focus group approach was modeled after Jhally and Lewis's (1992) study of audience responses to *The Cosby Show*. This kind of research requires balancing multiple points of view and interpretations yet trying to achieve a coherent picture of the interplay of text, audience, and culture.

Two moderators were used in the research. A white interviewer (the primary investigator) interviewed the nonblack groups and a black interviewer (a contact in Toronto) interviewed the black groups. This approach was also based on Jhally and Lewis's (1992) method, where same race moderators were used to ease the discomfort people might feel talking about race. Ethnographic and content analysis methodologies were used to analyze the cumulative focus group data (Stewart and Shamdasani 1990). The analysis was mainly ethnographic in its reliance on direct quotation and interpretation of general ideas and themes.

The limitations and assumptions inherent to this sort of research are well stated by Jhally and Lewis in the preface to their book:

> We assume that the significance, or meaning, of television in popular culture is a product of the interplay between a television program and the attitudes the viewer brings to it. We accept, therefore, that television is influential. But we also accept that the precise nature of its influence is

unpredictable: it will depend upon viewers who have thoughts, interests, and opinions before they sit down in front of the screen . . . . Establishing connections between attitudes and perceptions is technically difficult and demanding. It is a little like a trial in which the jury can only reconstruct events from evidence and testimony presented to it after the fact. So it is with this kind of investigative audience research inasmuch as we cannot perch inside people's brains and watch ideas and opinions forming. Like the prudent jury, we must use our knowledge and skill to interpret what people tell us rather than accept all testimony at face value. (9)

## Results

Distinct racially based themes emerged in the analysis of the black and nonblack youths' responses to questions that dealt with the influence of celebrity black athletes, the realism of the previewed athletic footwear commercials, and the significance of athletic apparel in the youths' daily lives. While all youth displayed an enthusiasm for basketball and basketball culture, their perspectives on various issues were "race-specific." That is to say, the youths' accounts of the commercial messages and their life experiences were characterized by multiple opinions, themes, and understandings that were "woven" together, often within the same statements. Within the various studied topic areas, the groups' similar and distinct positionings as television audiences, as consumers of popular culture, as negotiators of their social situations, and as "readers" of media text were revealed. Overall, black respondents appeared to identify with, support, and adulate the celebrity athletes, at times seeing the athletes as role models. The nonblacks "admired" the athletes and enjoyed the apparel commercials, but did not appear to be influenced in the same way or to the same extent.[8]

Since the commercials were not the essential focus of the group response component of the study (they were used to cue discussion about issues of race and cultural consumption, not to cue discussion about the contents of the commercials themselves), a detailed analysis of their structure and contents is not provided here. However, two of the six commercials warrant a brief explanation and description because they were referred to considerably more often than the others, and they prompted some of the most differentiated responses between groups. They were taken from a series of Nike "Barber Shop" commercials that showed various NBA players (all black) "hanging out" in a barber shop, talking and laughing. One commercial showed NBA star Chris Webber and his teammate (at the time) Latrell Sprewell joking and reminiscing about a well-known "slam dunk" that Webber had done on superstar Charles Barkley in an NBA game. The commercial ended with Webber joking that Barkley told him after the dunk that he (Webber) was his role model, an ironic statement since Barkley is well known for public statements suggesting that athletes have no responsibility to be role models for kids, and also because Webber, at the time, was a first-year NBA player and Barkley was an established veteran. A notable aspect of this commercial was the emphasis on basketball "style" and "attitude," evident from the status given to the "great move" and the playful self-promotion that followed it. A viewer with background knowledge of Chris Webber would associate his "trash talk" and "attitude" with his former college team at the University of Michigan where he played with a trend-setting flamboyant group of players known as the Fab Five. The other commercial reinforced the style component, as former and present NBA players "hung out" in the barber shop, talking about the well-known "finger roll" move used to perfection by NBA legend George "Ice Man" Gervin.

## Celebrity Influence, Critical Consumption: Black Youth Responses

For the black respondents, the focus group questions were used as a departure point for discussions about the influence of the black athlete on popular culture and style, the place of the athlete as a cultural icon and for more racially oriented discussions of youth culture and sport culture. Many of the black adolescents gave responses acknowledging the celebrity black athletes' definitive influence on popular style through athletic apparel and the athletic apparel commercial. This influence was manifested most often in the respondents' desire to look like the celebrity athlete, as the following statements show:

> I didn't have anything else [referring to Michael Jordan sneakers]. I know when I was in grade eight, I had every single pair from the first one that came out. I had snakeskin ones, I had the black ones, I had the ones with the little design under. I remember Reebok Pump when they first came out, I was like, ya, they can't make you do that. But when I saw Dee Brown in the dunk off, and he pumped up [pretends to pump up shoes] and he did this [respondent pretends to slam dunk], I was like, "I want that shoe" [respondent smiling and clapping hands][another respondent smiles and nods in response to the last statement] I'm guilty, I'm guilty. After Dee Brown in the dunk off, the day after, I went and paid one hundred and eighty-five dollars for the Reebok.

Not all respondents indicated that they were compelled to "be like" the celebrity athletes. Some were critical of people they knew who idolized and imitated celebrity basketball players. One black respondent described this sentiment explicitly:

> Like if you go to the Y [referring to the YMCA] . . . I saw this one guy,
> "Garry," the guy with the dreads, always wears a Shawn Kemp jersey, or
> that guy from the Y who wears his Larry Johnson shirt. I think some peo-
> ple fantasize too much. [respondent pretends to be one of the people who
> wears the jerseys] "Ya, like if I wear my Michael Jordan shirt I'll be just
> like Michael Jordan" . . . I think some people don't know where TV ends
> and real life begins.

These youth were critical of people they knew who "idolized" the athletes. Their criticisms reflected an awareness of the influence of the celebrity
athlete in the respondents' cultural environment. However, the conditional
role of celebrity athletes in shaping or framing the popularity of certain
clothing items and footwear (as discussed above) indicates that celebrity athletes are part of these youth's cultural environment and that they do influence
some (if not most) youth in the groups. All black groups agreed that athletic
wear, and specifically the basketball sneaker, was a necessary part of the socially acceptable "look" within their peer group The following statements
demonstrate this sentiment:

> You need to get within a certain crowd, or in some cases maybe you like
> this girl or something. When you want to impress her, so, "Oh ya, I have
> the shoes, maybe she'll think I have money" . . . just cause it has that little
> thing on there that says "Air" or "Nike" or something. You gotta have it,
> man. It's just the way people put it in your head. You gotta have Nike
> shoes. You can't come to camp wearing grubby shoes.

One respondent described the social pressure to have the shoes while addressing the implications of not being able to afford the shoes:

> If you're wearing Mike's [Jordan] stuff, Starter stuff, the crowd of people,
> that's the kind of people you hang with. But there's another class that can't
> afford that. You have to buy another brand that's not known . . . all the peo-
> ple like that will be in another crowd.

There was also evidence that the celebrity black athlete had role model
importance for some respondents. The athlete appeared to be a reference
point, defining a style that further influenced their masculine identity. For
these respondents, what the athlete says and does on and off the court
appeared to be influential. The following statements referred to outspoken
basketball superstar Charles Barkley and basketball great Michael Jordan:

> Look at Charles Barkley, his attitude on the court. He'll speak his mind,
> just tell you, get on your case, whatever. And I like that. He's not afraid to
> tell you, "Well, I'm going to do this to you if you keep doing this, if you
> keep going over my back," and he'll do it too. And a lot of the people in
> the commercials are different from the way they are in real life, just like a
> cover up of who they really are. And Charles, he does the commercials the
> way he wants to do them, that's just who he is, that's how the commercial

goes. A lot of people don't do that . . . a guy like Michael Jordan, you can say he plays basketball, this and that, right. But his personality's good too.

The youths' excitement and interest in the "real life" depictions of black celebrity athletes in the athletic apparel commercials was also indicative of their adulation of these athletes:

> I think the one in the barber shop, even though it doesn't relate to any-thing on the court, but you get to see a different side of the players, you don't just see guys dribbling, shooting on the court. You can see like they're people too. They're not illiterate, they're not stupid. You know, they're people, they can talk. It shows a different side of the players, not just like on-court perspective . . . when they showed Tim Hardaway [black celebrity athlete shown in a Nike barber shop commercial], he was just asking George Gervin a question about the finger roll, and when I saw him, I was like [respondent pretends to look in awe, or very impressed], cause I love Tim Hardaway, so when I saw him it was like, yes, you have to show his face in there, you know.

Many black respondents explained how their identification with the black athlete was based on the athlete's preferable playing style as well as cultural role. Although one group seemed to favor playing style over the athlete's cultural identity, the other groups suggested that both playing style and cultural identification were important:

> You have to remember, when you do a commercial, you want something that catches the eye . . . and if there were basketball commercials with stuff like that, for example, that Chris Webber commercial, if it was like Rony Seikaly, and John Paxson and Larry Bird and Kevin McHale [all white players] [other respondents are laughing at the idea], I don't think that people would look at that commercial. You wouldn't see like Larry Bird crowning [slam dunking over] Chris Webber or anything like that man. Like when you see dunks and stuff . . . all you see is black people. I would rather see twelve black people play. The basketball looks different. When you see white people play it's so fundamental.

Although these respondents showed respect for "good" white basketball play-ers, the more prevalent condition was that black respondents tended to "iden-tify" with black basketball players and not with white basketball players. These respondents appeared to feel that there was a distinctly black "style" of dress and demeanor, as well as basketball playing style. Several remarks from black respondents distinguished their own black style and "dress code" from that of white adolescents:

> If you . . . see a white guy . . . [interrupted by another respondent who finishes sentence], wearing "black" clothes, people call him a wigger. [Note: "wigger" means "white nigger."] . . . [other respondent continues from last statement] and if you see a black guy with the same clothes as a white guy you say, "What's going on, what's wrong with that guy, go home

and take that off and don't wear it"....white kids always try and copy the
black kids [pretending to be a white adolescent], "Oh, that looks cool,
where did you get that?" And then they'll go out and buy that the next
day, and then you don't want it no more.

These perceived cultural differences between black and white youth went
beyond just clothing and shoes according to the respondents:

In everything, the girls you go for, the clothes you wear, the music you
like, the way you act, the way you talk, sports, everything. You get laughed
at if you're talking to a white girl. You get laughed at if you're playing a
white sport. You get laughed at if you're dressing like a white person. You
get laughed at if you're listening to heavy metal, everything. It's all the
same. Black people and white people judge too much.

Inherent in these statements was the acknowledged importance of peer
acceptance. Although race was not emphasized in all instances, the importance of being "black" appeared to be unquestioned, particularly with respect
to being in a black peer group (as was the case with these respondents) that
valued basketball as a cultural form, and that viewed the celebrity black athlete as a cultural icon. These respondents appeared to use fashion to help
define their masculine identities, emphasizing the social pressures to wear
"Mike's stuff" and other acceptable clothing in order to "hang with" "the girl
you like" or to "get within" the desired crowd. Also, it seemed that underlying the respondents' explanations about why blacks and whites were different
was an understanding that racially and culturally based differences were negotiated in everyday life, a negotiation that encompassed fashion as well as more
socially inscribed factors. In essence, their identities within their own peer
groups were shaped by the style of clothes they wore, a distinctly "black" style
that was influenced by celebrity athlete–endorsed athletic apparel. This differentiation was reinforced by other culturally based distinctions that were
drawn between black and white music, sports, talk, and "the girls you go for."
In this sense, the youth were negotiating their adolescence, their masculinity,
and their racialized identity while living in a predominantly white society.

### Relatively Ambivalent Consumption: Nonblack Responses

Whereas the black respondents appeared to use the focus groups as a forum to
express important views about relevant cultural issues with little to no prompting from the moderator, the nonblack respondents appeared to be commenting on a subject that was of interest to them as basketball players, but not as
something that significantly impacted their lives. The respondents in the black

and nonblack groups used similar language to describe the commercials and appeared to enjoy the same commercials, but appeared to interpret and relate to the commercials in distinct ways. Athletic apparel and celebrity black athletes were not as influential for the nonblack adolescents (compared to the black adolescents) and there was no evidence of "significant" cultural identification with the black athletes. In this case, what the adolescents did not say was often as important as what they did say. The following comments are typical of those made by respondents in nonblack groups about the role of the black athlete:

> We go for a dunk, we want to look like Michael Jordan. It's true. Everybody wants to look like Michael . . . sometimes we copy how the commercials are. We talk like they talk.

Respondents who did not comment appeared to be uncertain (or unconcerned) about the influence of the black athlete. It seemed evident by their lack of interest and input that this topic had limited meaning for several of the respondents. This comparative lack of enthusiasm was evident from the nonblack comments about the Nike barber shop commercials:

> I like the fact that they are just hanging around talking . . . they were funny and they had action in there . . . [in response to the question "What was it that you liked about the barber shop commercials?"] the style and the way they told the story . . . [other respondent continues] they have good guys . . . [other respondent continues] they have good lines too . . . [other respondent continues] ya, a lot of creativity in them.

Although the respondents had favorite athletes, their descriptions of these athletes and of why they liked them demonstrated little personal identification with the athletes beyond the fact that they played basketball well:

> [referring to Larry Bird, a white basketball player] I like him as a player, he's a good player . . . [when asked what it was about the athletes that makes them appealing] because they're good and flashy, and I guess people look up to them. They score a lot of points . . . good players, great players.

Comments such as these, while favorable, do not match the striking enthusiasm shown by the black groups for the same commercials. In all the nonblack groups, some respondents indicated that they could not relate to the black athletes as portrayed in the commercials. Usually two or three group members in each group made specific comments while other group members would nod or not react. Their comments contrast the cultural identification demonstrated by the black respondents:

> I didn't like those ones, a bunch of bald guys in a barber shop . . . maybe black guys sit around in a barber shop like that . . . the Nike ones they said

how great they were back in their day . . . [other respondent continues]
'cause they're like Webber bragging about dunks and stuff . . . [other
respondent continues] it's more on looks, the other one's [the Starter commercial with white athletes Larry Bird and Lenny Dykstra and black
female athlete Florence Griffith-Joyner] more on practice.

Similar to the black groups, some nonblack respondents were also critical of people they knew of who copied the characters in the commercials
and tried to "be like" the celebrity athletes. An important difference, however, was that the nonblack respondents did not recognize this "modeling" to
be a widespread phenomenon, at least among their peer group. This would
likely explain why only a few respondents commented on this phenomenon
at all when asked about the realism and the impacts of the commercials.
Furthermore, one group of nonblack respondents felt that the athletic apparel commercials and celebrity athletes had a greater influence on black adolescents (which is especially interesting given the groups' admittedly limited
exposure to "real life" blacks):

I think they [blacks] copy a lot, like they'll get on a basketball court and
they'll act like that because of the commercials. Like they see a guy on the
commercials and they go to court and trash talk. I don't think it's part of
their game . . . [other respondent continues] I think a lot of people from
Canada pick that up, trash talking and stuff, so they do it.

Some respondents (one or two in each group) indicated that it made no
difference to themselves whether the athletes in the commercials were black
or white:

If you like basketball, black people play basketball, so it's no big thing. No
I don't see any black people there. You're still going to buy the thing even
though a black person wears it . . . [when asked if it would make a difference if the athletes in the barber shop commercials were white] as long as
they were good, or like Chris Mullin [white basketball star].

In sum, the most marked trend was the limited influence that the athletes appeared to have on the nonblack respondents. These adolescents were
"literate" in basketball and basketball culture, had seen the commercials, were
familiar with the players, wore the shoes, and enjoyed watching game highlights of the celebrity athletes, but rarely indicated/demonstrated that the
commercials influenced their "style," peer culture, or masculine identity. The
primary difference between these youth and the black youth in this respect
was that the shoes were not a crucial part of the nonblacks' style and that the
race of the celebrity athlete appeared to be of little consequence for these
nonblack adolescents.

## Summary and Conclusion

The research findings showed that the black and nonblack focus groups had racially distinct "appreciations" and understandings of the footwear commercials and the celebrity black athletes featured in the commercials. While both groups were interested in basketball-related culture and style, and were regular viewers of televised basketball, their interpretations and uses of the artifacts, personalities, and narratives of the commercials were defined by their social location as racially distinct "interpretive" communities. Although the black and nonblack youths' shared interest in basketball culture is partially supportive of Lull's (1985) view that certain popular culture phenomena may transcend demographic markers such as race, the meanings that these youth groups gave to these cultural affiliations and involvements were differentiated by race. In this way, the celebrity black athletes, athletic footwear commercials, and athletic apparel were seen to occupy distinctive cultural spaces for the black youth versus the nonblack youth.

Retrospectively, it can be conjectured that the "style" of play (the graceful, high flying style associated with the black players and the fundamental, "mechanical" style associated with the nonblack players), the modes of interpersonal communication, and the dress codes exhibited in these commercials were derived more from black forms of basketball culture than nonblack forms. The nonblack participants were therefore positioned as voyeurs of black culture with respect to the commercials and were forced into the role of "crossing over," a role with which they were not altogether comfortable (similar to Baines's (1997) findings in Toronto). The distinctive interpretations and appreciations of commercials by the black and nonblack groups can be seen as emanating from distinctive "cultural competencies" (Radway 1991; Bourdieu 1984) derived from their differing cultural experiences. The results showing blacks to be influenced in their everyday "style" and to have a culturally based identification with and support for black celebrity athletes (that nonblacks did not show) informs Lull's (1985) work by showing how distinctly "raced" understandings of a popular culture text can mix with shared tastes and interests (in basketball programming and basketball heroes). The black groups' responses also provide insight into the "negotiations" (Willis 1990) that these adolescents make as a result of their social positioning as blacks in a white culture. The black respondents' identification with the "style" and attitudes demonstrated by the celebrity black athletes, the respondents' pride in their distinctly "black" clothing, and the animosity shown by some respondents toward white adolescents who try to appropriate this black style (akin to Baines's (1997) findings), supports Majors's (1990; Majors and Billson 1992) views on the "cool pose" as resistance through distinctiveness. The black respondents' perceptions of society as inherently racist toward black people were also consistent with Majors's (1990) and Solomon's (1992) positions that black "style" is symbolic opposition to the dominant white culture. Further, the sometimes critical stance taken by the black youth, while limited in scope, might be interpreted as "viewer resistance" (in Hunt's [1997] terms) if we consider the youths' tendencies to be conscious of and resist some of the ideologies inscribed in media texts, and, on this basis, their potential for "meaningful social action at some later moment in time" (Hunt 1997, 162). However, bearing in mind these youths' underlying consumption patterns ("you gotta have Nike shoes") and their often uncritical acceptance of their favorite celebrity athletes, this "resistance thesis" should be adopted conditionally and cautiously. It should also be noted that the black youths' critiques were at no time focused on the celebrity athletes who promote the shoes (unlike Joyce's (1998) finding that some black youth in Chicago are critical of Michael Jordan). This finding could suggest that the Canadian youth, who at the time of the study (before the Raptors and Grizzlies expansion franchises in Toronto and Vancouver) were far removed from any potential contact with NBA players who sometimes participate in local community-based initiatives, might be less sensitive to Jordan's absence. Further, the hypothesis that Jordan has been overexposed such that his popularity has decreased in recent years (Gates 1998) might have been evident if the research was conducted after the expansion of the NBA into Canada.

This research also demonstrated how important having "athlete endorsed" apparel ("Mike's stuff") was for the black youth, and how owning this apparel gave these youth a sense of cultural power and belonging. For the nonblack youth, who owned the celebrity athlete–sponsored apparel and who had a cultural understanding of the commercials, there seemed to be some cultural power associated with owning the shoes and being "literate" in basketball culture, although there was not the same symbolic meaning for these youth as with the black groups. This evidence supports Lull's conception of cultural power, where these youth, although more notably the black youth, "symbolically explored" apparel as style to express themselves and their masculinity as a means of exercising cultural power. Also, the apparent impacts of black athlete- and apparel company–sponsored style lends support to Lull's (1995) understanding that cultural power is exercised by individuals (such as Michael Jordan) and by institutional sponsors (such as Nike). In this sense, Michael Jordan has "helped seize upon the consequences of black preoccupation with style, and the com-modification of black juvenile imagination at the site of the sneaker," and reflects the position of athletic apparel as an icon for "the culture of con-sumption" (Dyson 1993, 70). These findings also provide further evidence of the race-based distinctions between the youths' consumption patterns (all youth buy the shoes and watch basketball) and the cultural meanings given to consumption (the different-raced youth groups assigned different meanings to the shoes, apparel, and the celebrity athlete spokespersons).

Some black respondents indicated that the high price for athletic appar-el is a problem for some adolescents. Although this was not expanded upon by the respondents, the acknowledged pressure to own athletic apparel was the sort of social pressure referred to by those who see popular culture-ori-ented commercial messages leading to violence and crime among youth (Feniak 1991; Buchignani 1990; Hickey 1989). However, there was no tangi-ble evidence in these interviews to directly support these allegations. In fact, the respondents, although influenced by the commercials, were not ignorant of how the commercials are designed to target youth. They made specific ref-erences to "what they are trying to do" in the commercials, and the associa-tions the advertisers are trying to make. The nonblack respondents admitted to buying the shoes advertised in the commercials as well as to mimicking the celebrity athletes on-court style. Although the running shoe appeared to be part of their culture, it did not appear to have the same distinct meaning for them as it did for the black respondents. In this instance, the commercials appeared to be influential for the nonblack youth (as well as black youth), but not to the point where the "value" of the athletic shoe (i.e., symbolic, cultur-al, and economic value) might inspire violence or crime. An important caveat to these findings, however, is that both populations (black and nonblack) were recruited from middle-class neighborhoods and middle-income strata, and the affordability of the footwear featured in the commercials was therefore not as much an issue for them as it might be for groups from lower income brackets living in an inner city context.

Although this chapter has focused on negotiations of race and culture, issues of masculinity are undeniably woven within the adolescents' com-ments. The symbolic resistance associated with the distinctly black "style" that was expressed by the black groups, according to Majors and Billson (1992) and Solomon (1992), is a strategy to cope with marginality, to adapt to envi-ronmental conditions, and to neutralize stress—to negotiate their masculini-ty and race. For the nonblack males, this "style"-based coping mechanism was not evident. This is not to say that nonblack males as youth (and in some cases, minority group members) do not negotiate their identities and cope in other ways with the difficulties associated with their own social location, but this adaptation does not appear to be associated with the black athlete or athletic apparel. Although differences in the groups' masculinities were not clearly articulated here because the negotiations made by the nonblack groups were not explicit, the study findings support Majors and Billson's work, reinforcing their contention that "cool" has been exported "out of the ghetto" and into the lives of middle-class black males. Importantly, the incorporation of black culture by athletic apparel companies (see Wilson 1999), while giving all suburban youth (black or white) access to a repackaged form of "cool pose," has created a tension for the black youth interviewed in this study, who resent the ways that "wiggers" have demeaned and diminished the resistive capacities of "black style and culture."

The study's finding that the youths' interpretations and appreciations were differentiated along the lines of their respective ethnic backgrounds and social locations supports Radway's conception of the "interpretive community" and helps clarify Radway's question of how "social determination operates" (1991, 8) with respect to the processes of interpretation. In essence, and based on the discussion of race and media portrayals of blacks above, it would appear that differences in cultural experience connected with race served to shape two different interpretive groups within the study (blacks and nonblacks). However, it would be deterministic to suggest that the black and nonblack groups comprised two unconditionally distinct interpretive groups. There is no evidence to suggest that all the commonalities related to the youth's similar ages, socioeconomic backgrounds, and most of all their "taste" culture (as basketball enthusiasts) were negated by their racial identifications. On the contrary, both black and nonblack groups used a common idiom (basketball vernacular), were conversant about the players and commercials, and shared a common understanding of the styles associated with basketball. At the same time—and although we recognize the difficulties associated with linking social location and cultural competencies and affinities—it was apparent that the black respondents, unlike the nonblack respondents, had a particular interest in cultural issues surrounding the black athlete and at times identified with these athletes. In this sense, the youth in the study comprised two distinct interpretive communities defined by cultural differences that, in turn, were defined by their distinct social locations and racial identities. In saying this we recognize that these individuals are simultaneously members of an array of interpretive communities, memberships that are contingent upon the context of media consumption.

By situating these results in the context of youth culture in Canada, a broader understanding of the impacts of American culture on Canadian culture can be achieved, and the findings can be used to assess the globalization theories proposed by Lull (1995), Appadurai (1990), Wernick (1993), and Feldthusan (1993). Although this study does not build on a comparable project in Canada, the support for Majors's (1990) work on "cool pose" noted above suggests that similar "cool pose–like" stylistic coping mechanisms are also at work in Canada and that they are influenced by the mediated images of athletic apparel and celebrity athletes that emanate from the United States. This research, while specifically focused on the relationship between the media and youth style, provides some confirmation for work showing Solomon's (1992) findings that style-related subcultural identification was crucial for black Canadian youth in a Toronto high school (e.g., Solomon 1992). Further, the black respondents' apparent identification with and sometimes adulation of the celebrity black athlete suggests that American black sports figures do have meaning for these blacks in the Canadian context. It appears, then, that the way that the sneaker's symbolic affiliation with "black cultural nuances of cool, hip and chic" (Dyson 1993, 72) in the broader American cultural landscape applies equally to the Canadian cultural landscape. In this sense, despite Lull's (1995), Wernick's (1993), and Appadurai's (1990) emphasis on the importance of the context of reception, the apparent widespread impacts of American media in this study lend credence to Feldthusan's (1993) understanding of Canadian receptivity to American populism. Feldthusan's observation undoubtedly needs some caveats. The cultural diversity across Canada and within the metropolitan centers defies such a simplistic generalization, as Wernick (1993) suggests in his characterization of Canada as a postmodern nation. Nevertheless, further audience work on race is warranted to establish how different "interpretive communities" react to American media contents.

This research has demonstrated that athletic footwear commercials featuring celebrity black athletes such as Michael Jordan influence youth culture and style, and that the commercials' apparent impacts are mediated by racial differences and differences of cultural experience. These findings also highlight some pressing issues in audience research regarding the impacts of minority portrayals and television commercial advertising more generally. Athletic apparel companies make lucrative profits by using celebrity black athlete spokespersons and by "capitalizing on the images and myths of basketball" (Wonsek 1992, 457). These companies actively and purposefully work to construct a segment of mass consumer culture through their advertising campaigns (Strasser and

Becklund 1991; Katz 1993) that influences popular culture and social conditions. Many argue that it is unreasonable to hold athletic apparel companies responsible for their customers. As social psychologist Harold Kassarjian of UCLA queries, "[I]s what the shoe companies are doing any different than Mattel selling toys on Saturday morning television . . . the world doesn't need $200 sneakers, but it doesn't need Hostess twinkies either" (Barrett et al. 1989). Nike representatives are supportive of this view, arguing that they are not trying to promote a black basketball player specifically, but that black athletes, at this period in time, are the primary high-profile athletes in basketball. As Nike advertising representative Dan Wieden indicated when discussing the racial implications of using celebrity black athletes to sell apparel, "I'm not going to put a lawyer in basketball shoes and try and sell you basketball shoes" (York 1991).

Also implicated in this potentially exploitive process are the athletes themselves. Michael Jordan, in particular, has been criticized for his apolitical, "ineffectual," and "defensive" (Dyson 1993, 70–71) stance toward social issues pertaining to Nike. Jim Brown, Hall of Fame football player and now a renowned worker with inner city youth gangs, has argued:

> Just by stepping forward and engaging the community, Michael Jordan could put an end to gang violence . . . . But like so many of today's athletes, he allows his agent to do the thinking for him. And for an agent, everything is driven by the dollar. (quotes in Joyce 1998)

Other black activists such as Jesse Jackson have defended Jordan's apolitical stance, asking, "Why is it expected of a ballplayer or a boxer to be an astute sociopolitical analyst?" suggesting that athletes (because of their busy schedules) are not "in the best position to be social interpreters" and arguing that "it isn't right to shift the burden to [Jordan] because he is a high profile spokesperson" (quoted in Gates 1998, 58). On one hand, Jackson's argument appears to make sense in the contemporary conservative political context where these stances appear to be "out of style" and often met with disdain. For example, former Chicago Bulls player and Jordan teammate Craig Hodges, an outspoken advocate of black rights and worker for inner city youth, was apparently "blacklisted" by the NBA for his critical position on social issues. Alert (1997) described Hodges's actions:

> In 1992, after the Bulls won their second championship, the team made an obligatory trip to the white House to receive congratulations from then-President George Bush. While the rest of the team wore one of their fine $1,000 Armani suits, Hodges showed up in all-white Kente cloth outfit, a testament to his African heritage. He also dropped off a self-written

letter criticizing the government for its policies, their ignorance of inner city matters and international strong-arm tactics. Hodges hasn't played in the NBA since. (72).

On the other hand, Jackson's argument is flawed. If we consider the history of effective black resistance through sport, where athletes such as John Carlos and Tommie Smith (both of whom raised their fists in a "black power salute" on the medal podium during the 1968 Olympic Games) and Muhammad Ali, who publicized issues related to the exclusion, segregation, and degradation of blacks socially and economically, a stance by Jordan, another exceptional athlete and charismatic individual, does not seem so exceptional or radical—even in a conservative political climate. It seems unlikely that the problems experienced by Hodges would be experienced by Jordan, the superstar of superstars. Jim Brown observes, "The agent and Jordan are afraid of the backlash if Michael took up a cause, but would anyone really question his intentions. There wouldn't be a backlash. He'd just grow up in people's eyes."

In addition to these crucial (and popular) arguments about "who is responsible" and "what should be done" is the central issue of this chapter: what are the impacts of these athletes on youth and youth culture? That there are serious impacts on youth is generally taken for granted. The complexity of these impacts on different interpretive groups, as demonstrated in this research, gets ignored. On this basis, while acknowledging the responsibilities for Nike, Jordan, and other apparel companies and athletes in the production of popular cultural commodities, it is also necessary to support programs and initiatives that emphasize critical media consumption, and research that exposes the mythologies, stereotypes, and sensationalism common in media discourse. Not only would this be useful for youth, who could gain a more critical understanding of advertising production strategy, and about the differences between reality and the media's portrayal of reality; it would also provide media literacy skills for adults and youth who, in some cases, uncritically consume journalistic reports that portray "society's youth" as both troubled (e.g., needing sneakers to define their undeveloped, insecure identities) and troubling (e.g., violent, hedonistic consumers who will "do anything" to get what they want). In this context, further research that highlights the different ways that (interpretive) youth communities make sense of apparently influential popular cultural phenomena is crucial for responsibly understanding the complexities of youth interpretation, a process that is too often described in the simplest of terms.

# Notes

Portions of this paper have been taken from an unpublished master's thesis entitled *Audience reactions to the portrayal of black in athletic apparel commercials,* University of British Columbia, 1995 (Wilson 1995).

1. The market of the 1980s was a competition between Nike and then-rival Converse, who had Larry Bird, "Magic" Johnson, and Julius "Dr. J" Erving promoting their shoes. In recent years, Reebok and Adidas, despite their signings of Shaquille O'Neal and the supposed "heir(Air) apparent" to Jordan, teen star Kobe Bryant, still fall well short of Nike and Jordan.

2. Experimental studies, often referred to as "effects" research, have been extensively criticized, most notably for a) using short term studies to measure long term effects; b) attempting to create "controlled" conditions for an event (television viewing) that cannot be reproduced outside of the actual site of consumption; and c) focusing on the impact of the television message on the passive television viewer (that is, treating the television viewer as an "empty vessel") (Lewis 1991, 9). Survey research on audiences has been criticized largely for "disguising television's many subtleties beneath a facade of arithmetic precision" (Lewis 1997, 89), while textual analysis work has been denounced for making assumptions about audience interpretation without the benefit of empirical audience research.

3. Machin and Carrithers (1996) have proposed a useful revision to the interpretive community framework. The researchers suggested that more participant observation based research would allow analysts to capture the improvisation that takes place when people discuss social texts, and the changes in opinion over different conversations. They explained how "ethnography is never ethnography of a culture in general, out of time, but of a particular set of people at a particular time" (1996, 352).

4. Although not pursued here, it is worth mentioning that multiculturalism's emphasis on diversity has drawn criticism from those claiming that the creation of the "hyphenated Canadian" (e.g. African-Canadian) is a symbol of internal weakening and divided loyalties (Bissoondath 1994).

5. Henry (1994), Franklin (1991), and Glasgow (1980) refer to the black underclass that populate certain areas of the United States. The black underclass is defined here as "a permanently entrapped population of poor persons, unused and unwanted" who live in areas highly segregated from whites and middle-class blacks, and "are unemployed, and may be engaged in petty criminal activity" (Henry, 1994, p. xv).

6. Census data were used to contextualize the ethnic makeup, education levels, occupations, and income levels of the neighborhoods where the participants lived. The statistics showed that the black adolescents (Toronto) interviewed in this study lived in a middle-to upper-income area where the representation of black people was about 5 percent of the population compared to a majority of people of Anglo-European descent (Statistics Canada 1991a). The nonblack adolescents (Vancouver) also lived in and/or went to school in middle-income areas but had only limited exposure to blacks. People of black origin made up less than 0.5 percent of the population in these areas compared to a majority of people with British or Chinese origin (Statistics Canada 1991b). The nonblack participants in the study confirmed these observations, universally indicating

that they had little exposure to blacks with comments such as, "I don't really know any black people", "we've got one black guy in our school," and "[I know] a couple [of blacks], not that many." There were no notable exceptions to this pattern of responses.

7. The race of the participants was defined by the subjects themselves on the biographical questionnaire using Fuller's (1992) method from her cross-cultural survey of *The Cosby Show* that put "race" as an open-ended question. A "regular" viewer of televised basketball was defined as someone who watched one or more games (or part games) each week during basketball season. All participants were regular viewers according to this definition. The goal in this instance was to assess how a "taste culture" (Bourdieu 1984) of black and nonblack basketball enthusiasts interpreted the same media text and related to background issues of race. By drawing both groups of participants from similar income areas, we could compare interpretive strategies for groups that were drawn from similar social strata and who shared a common interest in watching televised basketball but occupied a different "social location" with respect to race.

8. In describing these themes, "typical" comments were defined as those that were supported by "most" members of the noted groups (whether this be all groups, the black groups or the nonblack groups). In other instances, if there was no disagreement within a group about a topic and a few comments appeared to represent the group's perceptions (if others nodded or gave affirmative words), these comments were considered "representative." "Other" comments were defined as those mentioned by one or more respondents, but were not indicative of the group's sentiments. These general definitions of "typical," "representative," and "other" varied depending on how many of the group members commented and the nature of the conversation. In some instances, groups members made gestures or brief comments, while in other situations all respondents were fully involved in the conversation. In the discussion that follows, these variations are clarified by describing the particular circumstances of the case and identifying the coding strategies used. Also, a sample of group discussion is provided (representing several individuals) with the intention of making any research bias more readily recognizable. In this way, the methods used to describe the results are made as explicit as possible.

# References

Acland, C. (1995). *Youth, murder, spectacle: The cultural politics of "youth in crisis."* Boulder: Westview Press.

Agocs, C., and M. Boyd (1993). "The Canadian ethnic mosaic recast for the 1990's." In *Social inequality in Canada,* ed. J. Curtis, E. Grabb, and N. Guppy, 330–352. Scarborough, ON: Prentice Hall.

Andrews, D. L. (1996). "The fact(s) of Michael Jordan's blackness: Excavating a floating racial signifier," *Sociology of Sport Journal* 13(2):125–158.

Alert, C. (1997). "Truth and consequences," *Shield* 9(2):67–75.

Ang, I. (1991). *Desperately seeking audience.* London: Routledge.

———. (1985). *Watching Dallas: Soap opera and melodramatic imagination.* London: Methuen.

Appadurai, A. (1990). "Disjuncture and difference in the global cultural economy." In *Global culture: Nationalism, globalization, and modernity,* ed. M. Featherstone, 295–310. London: Sage.

Baer, D., and J. Winter (1983). "U.S. media imperialism in a Canadian community: The inclusion of anti-government sentiment," *Canadian Journal of Communications* 10(1).

Baines, A. (1997). "Black like me," *Toronto Life,* January, 78–81.

Barrett, T., R. Pyrillis, and L. Davenport (1989). "Has sneaker madness gone too far?" *Newsweek,* December 18, 51.

Bissoondath, N. (1994). *Selling illusions: The cult of multiculturalism in Canada.* Toronto: Penguin Books.

Bourdieu, P. (1984). *Distinction.* London: Routledge.

Boyd, M. (1992). "Gender, visible minority, and immigrant earnings inequality: Reassessing an employment equity premise." In *Deconstructing a nation: Immigration, multiculturalism, and racism in 90s Canada,* ed. V. Satzewich, 279–321. Halifax, NS: Fernwood Publishing.

Buchignani, W. (1990). "Big name footwear has parents running scared," *Montreal Gazette,* October 28, A1, A4.

Buckingham, D. (1987). *Public secrets: Eastenders and its audience.* London: BFI.

Canada. (1992). *Viewing 1990 culture statistics.* Ottawa: Statistics Canada.

———. (1991). *The year in review, 1990–91.* Ottawa: Canadian Radio-Television and Telecommunications Commission.

———. (1990). *Canadian broadcasting corporation annual report 1987–88.* Ottawa: Canadian Radio-Television and Telecommunications Commission.

———. (1988). *Reflections from an electronic mirror: Report of a National Forum on Multiculturalism and Broadcasting.* Ottawa: Minister of Supply and Services.

———. (1984). *Equality now!: Report of the Special Committee on Visible Minorities in Canadian Society.* Ottawa: Queen's Printer.

Cannon, M. (1995). *The invisible empire: Racism in Canada.* Toronto: Random House.

Collinson, D., D Knights, and M. Collinson (1990). *Managing to discriminate.* London: Routledge, Chapman and Hall.

Connolly, W. E. (1995). *The ethos of pluralization.* Minneapolis: University of Minnesota Press.

Deatrick, J., and S. Faux (1989). "Conducting qualitative studies with children and adolescents." In *Qualitative nursing research: A contemporary dialogue,* ed. M. Morse, 185–203. Rockville, MA: Aspen Publishers.

Dyson, M. (1995). *Making Malcolm.* New York: Oxford University Press.

———. (1993). "Be like Mike?: Michael Jordan and the pedagogy of desire," *Cultural Studies* 7(1):64–72.

Feldthusan, B. (1993). "Awakening from the national broadcasting dream: Rethinking television regulation for national cultural goals." In *The beaver bites back?: American popular culture in Canada,* ed. D. Flaherty and F. Manning. Kingston, ON: McGill-Queen's University Press.

Feniak, P. (1991). "Air it! Pump it! Worshipping the running shoe," *Toronto Star,* June 29, F1–F7.

Fernandez, J. (1988). *Racism and sexism in corporate life.* Englewood Cliffs, NJ: Prentice Hall.

Fish, S. (1979). *Is there a text in this class? The authority of interpretive communities.* Cambridge, MA: Harvard University Press.

Fleras, A. (1995). "'Please adjust your Set': Media and minorities in a multicultural society." In *Communication in Canadian society,* ed. B Singer, 406–430. Scarborough, ON: Nelson Canada.

Franklin, R. (1991). *Shadows of race and class.* Minneapolis: University of Minnesota Press.

Fuller, L. (1992). *The Cosby Show: Audiences, impact, and implications.* Westport, CT: Greenwood Press.

Gates Jr., H. (1998). "Net Worth," *New Yorker,* June 1, 48–61.

Glasgow, D. (1980). *The black underclass: Poverty, unemployment, and entrapment of ghetto youth.* San Francisco: Jossey Bass Publishers.

Hall, S. (1980). "Encoding/decoding." In *Culture, media, language: Working papers in cultural studies,* ed. S. Hall, D. Hobson, A. Lowe, and P. Willis, 1972–79. London: Hutchison.

Hartley, J. (1994, August). *Audience research and communications studies.* Presentation given at Simon Fraser University, Vancouver, Canada.

Hebdige, D. (1979). *Subculture: The meaning of style.* London: Methuen.

Henry, F. (1994). *The Caribbean diaspora in Toronto: Learning to live with racism.* Toronto: University of Toronto Press.

Henry, F., C. Tator, W. Mattis, and T. Rees (1995). *The colour of democracy: Racism in Canadian society.* Toronto: Harcourt Brace and Company.

Henry, F., and E. Ginzberg (1990). "Racial discrimination in employment." In *Images of Canada,* ed. J. Curtis and L. Tepperman, 302–309. Toronto: Prentice Hall.

Hickey, P. (1990). "If the shoe fits," *Montreal Gazette,* Oct. 28, A3.

Hobson, D. (1982). *Crossroads: The drama of a soap opera.* London: Methuen.

Hunt, D. (1997). *Screening the Los Angeles "riots": Race, seeing, and resistance.* New York: Cambridge University Press.

Jhally, S., and J. Lewis (1992). *Enlightened racism: The Cosby Show, audiences, and the myth of the American dream.* Boulder: Westview Press.

Joyce, G. (1998). "Facing the court of appeal," *Globe and Mail,* May 9, A24, A26.

Katz, D. (1994, August). "Triumph of the swoosh," *Sports Illustrated,* 54–73.

Kellner, D. (1995). *Media culture.* New York: Routledge.

Lewis, J. (1997). "What counts in cultural studies," *Media, Culture, and Society,* 19:83–97.

———. (1991). *The ideological octopus.* New York: Routledge.

———. (1983). "The encoding/decoding model: criticisms and redevelopments for research on decoding," *Media, Culture, and Society* 5:179–197.

Livingstone, S. (1994). "Watching talk: gender and engagement in the viewing of audience discussion programs," *Media, Culture, and Society* 16:429–447.

Lule, J. (1995). "The rape of Mike Tyson: Race, the press, and symbolic types," *Critical Studies in Mass Communication* 12:176–195.

Lull, J. (1995). *Media, communication, culture: A global approach.* New York: Columbia University Press.

———. (1992). *Popular music and communication.* Newbury Park, CA: Sage.

Lull, J. (1990). *Inside family viewing—Ethnographic research on television's audiences.* London: Routledge.

———. (1985). "The naturalistic study of media use and youth culture." In *Media gratifications research,* ed. K. Rosengren, L. Wenner, and P. Palmgreen, 209–224. Beverley Hills: Sage.

Machin, D., and M. Carrithers (1996). "From 'interpretive communities' to 'communities of improvisation,'" *Media, Culture, and Society* 18:343–352.

Maguire, J. 1999. *Global sport: Identities, societies, civilisations.* Cambridge: Polity Press.

Majors, R., and J. Mancini Billson (1992). *Cool pose: The dilemmas of black manhood.* New York: Lexington Books.

Majors, R. (1990). "Cool pose: black masculinity and sports." In *Sport, men, and the gender order,* ed. M. Messner and D. Sabo, 109–114. Champaign, IL: Human Kinetics Books.

McGuigan, J. (1992). *Cultural populism.* New York: Routledge.

McKay, J. (1995). "'Just Do It': Corporate sports slogans and the political economy of enlightened racism," *Discourse: Studies in the Cultural Politics of Education* 16(2):191–201.

Moores, S. (1993). *Interpreting audiences: The ethnography of media consumption.* Thousand Oaks, CA: Sage.

Morgan, D. (1988). *Focus groups as qualitative research.* Newbury Park, CA: Sage.

Morley, D. (1986). *Family television—Cultural power and domestic leisure.* London: Comedia.

———. (1981). "The Nationwide audience-A critical postscript," *Screen Education* 39:3–14.

———. (1980). *The "Nationwide" audience: Structure and decoding.* London: BFI.

Nightingale, V. (1996). *Studying audiences: The shock of the real.* New York: Routledge.

Omi, M. (1989). "In living color: Race and American culture." In *Cultural politics in contemporary America,* ed. Angus and Jhally, 111–122. New York: Routledge.

Omi, M., and H. Winant (1994). *Racial formation in the United States: From the 1960's to the 1990's* (2nd ed.). New York: Routledge.

Quill, G. (May 19). "The Canada I know is not inhabited by people I see on beer commercials," *Toronto Star,* 1990 H6.

Raboy, M. (1989). "Two steps forward, three steps back: Canadian broadcasting policy from Caplan-Sauvageau to Bill-136," *Canadian Journal of Communication* 14(1):70–75.

Radway, J. (1991). *Reading the romance: Women, patriarchy, and popular literature.* Chapel Hill: University of North Carolina Press.

———. (1988). "Reception study: Ethnography and the problems of dispersed and nomadic subjects," *Cultural Studies* 2(4):359–376.

Reilly, R. (1991). "He's gotta pitch: Filmmaker and superfan Spike Lee has thrown some new curves into sport advertising," *Sports Illustrated,* May 27, 74–78, 80, 82, 84–86.

Satzewich, V., and P. Li (1987). "Immigrant labor in Canada: The cost and benefit of ethnic origin in the job market," *Canadian Journal of Sociology.*

Solomon, P. (1992). *Black resistance in high school: Forging a separatist culture.* Albany: State University of New York Press.

Statistics Canada. (1991a). *Profile of census tracts in Toronto(Part A).* *(Publication No. 95 353).* Ottawa: Industry, Science and Technology, Canada.

———. (1991b). *Profile of census tracts in Vancouver (Part A).* *(Publication No. 95 388).* Ottawa: Industry, Science and Technology, Canada.

Strasser, J., and L. Becklund (1991). *Swoosh: The unauthorized story of Nike and the men who played there.* Orlando, FL: Harcourt, Brace and Jovanovich.

Stewart, D., and P. Shamdasani (1990) *Focus groups: Theory and practice.* Newbury Park, CA: Sage.

Tate, E., and L. Trach (1980). "The effects of United States television programs upon Canadian beliefs about the legal procedure," *Canadian Journal of Communication* 6(4):1–16.

Telander, R. (1990). "Senseless," *Sports Illustrated,* May 14, 36–38, 43–44, 46, 49.

Thompson, J. B. (1994). "Social theory and the media." In *Communication theory today,* ed. D. Crowley and D. Mitchell. Cambridge: Polity Press.

Tulloch, J., and A. Moran (1986). *A country practice: "Quality soap."* Sydney: Currency Press.

Wenner, L. (1994). "The dream team, communicative dirt, and the marketing of synergy: USA basketball and cross-merchandising in television commercials," *Journal of Sport and Social Issues,* 18(1):27–47.

Wernick, A. (1993). "American popular culture in Canada: Trends and reflections." In *The beaver bites back?: American popular culture in Canada,* ed. D. Flaherty and F. Manning, 293–302. Kingston, ON: McGill-Queen's University Press.

Willis, P. (1990). *Common Culture.* Buckingham, UK: Open University Press.

———. (1976). *Profane culture.* London: Chalto and Windus.

Wilson, B. (1995). *Audience reactions to the portrayal of blacks in athletic apparel commercials.* Unpublished master's thesis, University of British Columbia, Vancouver, BC.

———. (1997). "'Good blacks and bad blacks': Media constructions of African-American athletes in Canadian basketball," *International Review for the Sociology of Sport* 32(2):177–189.

Wilson, Brian. (1999). "'Cool pose' incorporated: The marketing of black masculinity in Canadian NBA coverage." In *Sport and Gender in Canada,* ed. P. White and K. Young, 232–253. Toronto: Oxford University Press.

Winter, J. (1985, May). *National and binational ramifications of the free press marketplace: A Canadian perspective.* Paper presented to the annual conference, International Communication Association, Honolulu, Hawaii.

Winter, J., and I. Goldman (1995). "Mass media and Canadian identity." In *Communication in Canadian Society,* ed. B Singer, 201–220. Scarborough, ON: Nelson Canada.

Wonsek, P. (1992). "College basketball on television: a study of racism in the media," *Media, Culture, and Society* 14:449–461.

York, S., (Prod.). (1991). *Selling the dream.* Television Broadcast. Washington, DC: Smithsonian Institute.

# part V

# J O R D A N

## and Critical Pedagogy

# 9

# Be Like Mike?:
# Michael Jordan and the Pedagogy of Desire

## Michael Eric Dyson

Michael Jordan is perhaps the best, and best-known, athlete in the world today. He has attained unparalleled cultural status because of his extraordinary physical gifts, his marketing as an icon of race-transcending American athletic and moral excellence, and his mastery of a sport that has become the metaphoric center of black cultural imagination. But the Olympian sum of Jordan's cultural meaning is greater than the fluent parts of his persona as athlete, family man, and marketing creation. There is hardly cultural precedence for the character of his unique fame, which has blurred the line between private and public, between personality and celebrity, and between substance and symbol. Michael Jordan stands at the breach between perception and intuition, his cultural meaning perennially deferred from closure because his career symbolizes possibility itself, gathering into its unfolding narrative the shattered remnants of previous incarnations of fame and yet transcending their reach.

Jordan has been called "the new DiMaggio" (Boers 1990, 30) and "Elvis in high-tops," indications of the herculean cultural heroism he has come to embody. There is even a religious element to the near worship of Jordan as a cultural icon of invincibility, as he has been called a "savior of sorts," "basketball's high priest" (Bradley 1991-92, 60), and "more popular than Jesus," except with "better endorsement deals" (Vancil 1992, 51). But the quickly developing cultural canonization of Michael Jordan provokes reflection about the contradictory uses to which Jordan's body is put as a seminal cultural text and ambiguous symbol of fantasy, and the avenues of agency and resistance

This chapter was originally published in 1993 in *Cultural Studies,* 7(1): 64-72. It is reprinted by permission.

available especially to black youth who make symbolic investment in Jordan's body as a means of cultural and personal possibility, creativity, and desire.

I understand Jordan in the broadest sense of the term to be a public pedagogue, a figure of estimable public moral authority whose career educates us about productive and disenabling forms of knowledge, desire, interest, consumption, and culture in three spheres: the culture of athletics that thrives on skill and performance, the specific expression of elements of African-American culture, and the market forces and processes of commodification expressed by, and produced in, advanced capitalism. By probing these dimensions of Jordan's cultural importance, we may gain a clearer understanding of his function in American society.

Athletic activity has shaped and reflected important sectors of American society. First, it produced communities of common athletic interest organized around the development of highly skilled performance. The development of norms of athletic excellence evidenced in sports activities cemented communities of participants who valorized rigorous sorts of physical discipline in preparation for athletic competition and in expressing the highest degree of athletic skill. Second, it produced potent subcultures that inculcated in their participants norms of individual and team accomplishment. Such norms tapped into the bipolar structures of competition and cooperation that pervade American culture. Third, it provided a means of reinscribing Western frontier myths of exploration and discovery-as-conquest onto a vital sphere of American culture. Sports activities can be viewed in part as the attempt to symbolically ritualize and metaphorically extend the ongoing quest for mastery of environment and vanquishing of opponents within the limits of physical contest.

Fourth, athletic activity has served to reinforce habits and virtues centered in collective pursuit of communal goals that are intimately connected to the common good, usually characterized within athletic circles as "team spirit." The culture of sport has physically captured and athletically articulated the mores, folkways, and dominant visions of American society, and at its best it has been conceived as a means of symbolically embracing and equitably pursuing the just, the good, the true, and the beautiful. And finally, the culture of athletics has provided an acceptable and widely accessible means of white male bonding. For much of its history, American sports activity has reflected white patriarchal privilege, and it has been rigidly defined and socially shaped by rules that restricted the equitable participation of women and people of color.

Black participation in sports in mainstream society, therefore, is a relatively recent phenomenon. Of course, there have existed venerable traditions of black sports, such as the Negro (baseball) Leagues, which countered the exclusion of black bodies from white sports. The prohibition of athletic activity by black men in mainstream society severely limited publicly acceptable forms of displaying black physical prowess, an issue that had been politicized during slavery and whose legacy extended into the middle of the twentieth century. Hence, the potentially superior physical prowess of black men, validated for many by the long tradition of slave labor that built American society, helped reinforce racist arguments about the racial regimentation of social space and the denigration of the black body as an inappropriate presence in traditions of American sport.

Coupled with this fear of superior black physical prowess was the notion that inferior black intelligence limited the ability of blacks to perform excellently in those sports activities that required mental concentration and agility. These two forces—the presumed lack of sophisticated black cognitive skills and the fear of superior black physical prowess—restricted black sports participation to thriving but financially handicapped subcultures of black athletic activity. Later, of course, the physical prowess of the black body would be acknowledged and exploited as a supremely fertile zone of profit as mainstream athletic society literally cashed in on the symbolic danger of black sports excellence.

Because of its marginalized status within the regime of American sports, black athletic activity often acquired a social significance that transcended the internal dimensions of game, sport, and skill. Black sport became an arena not only for testing the limits of physical endurance and forms of athletic excellence—while reproducing or repudiating ideals of American justice, goodness, truth, and beauty—but it also became a way of ritualizing racial achievement against socially imposed barriers to cultural performance.

In short, black sport activity often acquired a heroic dimension, as viewed in the careers of figures such as Joe Louis, Jackie Robinson, Althea Gibson, Wilma Rudolph, Muhammad Ali, and Arthur Ashe. Black sports heroes transcended the narrow boundaries of specific sports activities and garnered importance as icons of cultural excellence, symbolic figures who embodied social possibilities of success denied to other people of color. But they also captured and catalyzed the black cultural fetishization of sport as a means of expressing black cultural style, as a means of valorizing craft as a marker of racial and self-expression, and as a means of pursuing social and economic mobility.

It is this culture of black athletics, created against the background of social and historical forces that shaped American athletic activity, that helped produce Jordan and help explain the craft that he practices. Craft is the honing of skill by the application of discipline, time, talent, and energy toward the realization of a particular cultural or personal goal. American folk cultures are pervaded by craft, from the production of cultural artifacts that express particular ethnic histories and traditions to the development of styles of life and work that reflect and symbolize a community's values, virtues, and goals. Michael Jordan's skills within basketball are clearly phenomenal, but his game can only be sufficiently explained by understanding its link to the fusion of African-American cultural norms and practices, and the idealization of skill and performance that characterize important aspects of American sport. I will identify three defining characteristics of Jordan's game that reflect the influence of African-American culture on his style of play.

First, Jordan's style of basketball reflects the will *to spontaneity*. I mean here the way in which historical accidence is transformed into cultural advantage, and the way acts of apparently random occurrence are spontaneously and imaginatively employed by Africans and African-Americans in a variety of forms of cultural expression. When examining Jordan's game, this feature of African-American culture clearly functions in his unpredictable eruptions of basketball creativity. It was apparent, for instance, during game two of the National Basketball Association 1991 championship series between Jordan's Chicago Bulls and the Los Angeles Lakers, in a shot that even Jordan ranked in his all-time top ten (McCallum 1991, 32). Jordan made a drive toward the lane, gesturing with his hands and body that he was about to complete a patent Jordan dunk shot with his right hand. But when he spied defender Sam Perkins slipping over to oppose his shot, he switched the ball in midair to his left hand to make an underhanded scoop shot instead, which immediately became known as the "levitation" shot. Such improvisation, a staple of the will to spontaneity, allows Jordan to expand his vocabulary of athletic spectacle, which is the stimulation of a desire to bear witness to the revelation of truth and beauty compressed into acts of athletic creativity.

Second, Jordan's game reflects the *stylization of the performed self*. This is the creation and projection of a sport persona that is an identifying mark of diverse African-American creative enterprises, from the complexly layered jazz experimentation of John Coltrane, the trickstering and signifying comedic routines of Richard Pryor, and the rhetorical ripostes and oral significations of rapper Kool Moe Dee. Jordan's whole game persona is a graphic depiction of the performed self as flying acrobat, resulting in his famous moniker "Air Jordan." Jordan's performed self is rife with the language of physical expressiveness: head moving, arms extending, hands waving, tongue wagging, and legs spreading.

He has also developed a resourceful repertoire of dazzling dunk shots that further express his performed self and that have garnered him a special niche within the folklore of the game: the cradle jam, rock-a-baby, kiss the rim, lean in, and the tomahawk. In Jordan's game, the stylization of a performed self has allowed him to create a distinct sports persona that has athletic as well as economic consequences, while mastering sophisticated levels of physical expression and redefining the possibilities of athletic achievement within basketball.

Finally, there is the subversion of perceived limits through the use of *edifying deception,* which in Jordan's case centers around the space/time continuum. This moment in African-American cultural practice is the ability to flout widely understood boundaries through mesmerization and alchemy, a subversion of common perceptions of the culturally or physically possible through the creative and deceptive manipulation of appearance. Jordan is perhaps most famous for his alleged "hang time," the uncanny ability to remain suspended in midair longer than other basketball players while executing his stunning array of improvised moves. But Jordan's "hang time" is technically a misnomer and can be more accurately attributed to Jordan's skillful athletic deception, his acrobatic leaping ability, and his intellectual toughness in projecting an aura of uniqueness around his craft than to his defiance of gravity and the laws of physics.

No human being, including Michael Jordan, can successfully defy the law of gravity and achieve relatively sustained altitude without the benefit of machines. As Douglas Kirkpatrick points out the equation for altitude is $1/2g$ x t2 $=$ VO x t ("How Does Michael Fly?" 1990). However, Jordan appears to hang by *stylistically* relativizing the fixed coordinates of space and time through the skillful management and manipulation of his body in midair. For basketball players, hang time is the velocity and speed with which a player takes off combined with the path the player's center of gravity follows on the way up. At the peak of a player's vertical jump, the velocity and speed is close to, or at, zero; hanging motionless in the air is the work of masterful skill and illusion ("How Does Michael Fly?" 1990). Michael Jordan, through the consummate skill and style of his game, only appears to be hanging in space for more than the one second that human beings are capable of remaining airborne.

But the African-American aspects of Jordan's game are indissolubly linked to the culture of consumption and the commodification of black culture. [1] Because of Jordan's supreme mastery of basketball, his squeaky-clean image, and his youthful vigor in pursuit of the American Dream, he has become, along with Bill Cosby, the quintessential pitchman in American society. Even his highly publicized troubles with gambling, his refusal to visit the White House after the Bulls' championship season, and a book that purports to expose the underside of his heroic myth have barely tarnished his All-American image. [2] Jordan eats Wheaties, drives Chevrolets, wears Hanes, drinks Coca-Cola, consumes McDonald's, guzzles Gatorade, and, of course, wears Nikes. He and his shrewd handlers have successfully produced, packaged, marketed, and distributed his image and commodified his symbolic worth, transforming cultural capital into cash, influence, prestige, status, and wealth. To that degree, at least, Jordan repudiates the sorry tradition of the black athlete as the naif who loses his money to piranha-like financial wizards, investors, and hangers-on. He represents the new-age athletic entrepreneur who understands that American sport is ensconced in the cultural practices associated with business, and that it demands particular forms of intelligence, perception, and representation to prevent abuse and maximize profit.

From the very beginning of his professional career, Jordan was consciously marketed by his agency ProServ as a peripatetic vehicle of American fantasies of capital accumulation and material consumption tied to Jordan's personal modesty and moral probity. In so doing, they skillfully avoided attaching to Jordan the image of questionable ethics and lethal excess that plagued inside traders and corporate raiders on Wall Street during the mid-eighties, as Jordan began to emerge as a cultural icon. But Jordan is also the symbol of the spectacle-laden black athletic body as the site of commodified black cultural imagination. Ironically, the black male body, which has been historically viewed as threatening and inappropriate in American society (and remains so outside of sports and entertainment), is made an object of white desires to domesticate and dilute its more ominous and subversive uses, even symbolically reducing Jordan's body to dead meat (McDonald's McJordan hamburger), which can be consumed and expelled as waste.

Jordan's body is also the screen upon which is projected black desires to emulate his athletic excellence and replicate his entry into reaches of unimaginable wealth and fame. But there is more than vicarious substitution and the projection of fantasy onto Jordan's body that is occurring in the circulation and reproduction of black cultural desire. There is also the creative use of desire and fantasy by young blacks to counter, and capitulate to, the forces of cultural dominance that attempt to reduce the black body to a commodity and text that is employed for entertainment, titillation, or financial gain. Simply said, there is no easy correlation between the commodification of black youth culture and the evidences of a completely dominated consciousness.

Even within the dominant cultural practices that seek to turn the black body into pure profit, disruptions of capital are embodied, for instance, in messages circulated in black communities by public moralists who criticize the exploitation of black cultural creativity by casual footwear companies. In short, there are instances of both black complicity and resistance in the commodification of black cultural imagination, and the ideological criticism of exploitative cultural practices must always be linked to the language of possibility and agency in rendering a complex picture of the black cultural situation. As Henry Giroux observes:

> The power of complicity and the complicity of power are not exhausted simply by registering how people are positioned and located through the production of particular ideologies structured through particular discourses. . . . It is important to see that an overreliance on ideology critique has limited our ability to understand how people actively participate in the dominant culture through processes of accommodation, negotiation, and even resistance. (Giroux 1992, 194-95)

In making judgements about the various uses of the black body, especially Jordan's symbolic corporeality, we must specify how both consent and opposition to exploitation are often signaled in expressions of cultural creativity.

In examining his reactions to the racial ordering of athletic and cultural life, the ominous specificity of the black body creates anxieties for Jordan. His encounters with the limits of culturally mediated symbols of race and racial identity have occasionally mocked his desire to live beyond race, to be "neither black nor white" (Patton 1986, 52), to be "viewed as a person" (Vancil 1992, 57). While Jordan chafes under indictment by black critics who claim that he is not "black enough," he has perhaps not clearly understood the differences between enabling versions of human experience that transcend the exclusive gaze of race and disenabling visions of human community that seek race neutrality.

The former is the attempt to expand the perimeters of human experience beyond racial determinism, to nuance and deepen our understanding of the constituent elements of racial identity, and to understand how race, along with class, gender, geography, and sexual preference, shape and constrain human experience. The latter is the belief in an intangible, amorphous, non-historical, and raceless category of "person," existing in a zone beyond not simply the negative consequences of race, but beyond the specific patterns of cultural and racial identity that constitute and help shape human experience. Jordan's unclarity is consequential, weighing heavily on his apolitical bearing and his refusal to acknowledge the public character of his private beliefs about American society and the responsibility of his role as a public pedagogue.

Indeed it is the potency of black cultural expressions that not only have helped influence his style of play, but have also made the sneaker industry he lucratively participates in a multi-billion dollar business. Michael Jordan has helped seize upon the commercial consequences of black cultural preoccupation with style and the commodification of the black juvenile imagination at the site of the sneaker. At the juncture of the sneaker, a host of cultural, political, and economic forces and meanings meet, collide, shatter, and are reassembled to symbolize the situation of contemporary black culture.

The sneaker reflects at once the projection and stylization of black urban realities linked in our contemporary historical moment to rap culture and the underground political economy of crack, and reigns as the universal icon for the culture of consumption. The sneaker symbolizes the ingenious manner in which black cultural nuances of cool, hip, and chic have influenced the broader American cultural landscape. It was black street culture that influenced sneaker companies' aggressive invasion of the black juvenile market in taking advantage of the increasing amounts of disposable income of young black men as a result of legitimate and illegitimate forms of work.

Problematically, though, the sneaker also epitomizes the worst features of the social production of desire and represents the ways in which moral energies of social conscience about material values are drained by the messages of undisciplined acquisitiveness promoted by corporate dimensions of the culture of consumption. These messages, of rapacious consumerism supported by cultural and personal narcissism, are articulated on Wall Street and are related to the expanding inner-city juvenocracy, where young black men rule over black urban space in the culture of crack and illicit criminal activity, fed by desires to "live large" and to reproduce capitalism's excesses on their own terrain. Also, sneaker companies make significant sums of money from the illicit gains of drug dealers.

Moreover, while sneaker companies have exploited black cultural expressions of cool, hip, chic, and style, they rarely benefit the people who both consume the largest quantity of products and whose culture redefined the sneaker companies' raison d'etre. This situation is more severely compounded by the presence of spokespeople like Jordan, Spike Lee, and Bo Jackson, who are either ineffectual or defensive about or indifferent to the lethal consequences (especially in urban black-on-black violence over sneaker company products) of black juvenile acquisition of products that these figures have helped make culturally desirable and economically marketable.

Basketball is the metaphoric center of black juvenile culture, a major means by which even temporary forms of cultural and personal transcendence of personal limits are experienced. Michael Jordan is at the center of this black athletic culture, the supreme symbol of black cultural creativity in a society of diminishing tolerance for the black youth whose fascination with Jordan has helped sustain him. But Jordan is also the iconic fixture of broader segments of American society, who see in him the ideal figure: a black man of extraordinary genius on the court and before the cameras, who by virtue of his magical skills and godlike talents symbolizes the meaning of human possibility, while refusing to root it in the specific forms of culture and race in which it must inevitably make sense or fade to ultimate irrelevance. Jordan also represents the contradictory impulses of the contemporary culture of consumption, where the black athletic body is deified, reified, and rearticulated within the narrow meanings of capital and commodity. But there is both resistance and consent to the exploitation of black bodies in Jordan's explicit cultural symbolism, as he provides brilliant glimpses of black culture's ingenuity of improvisation as a means of cultural expression and survival. It is also partially this element of black culture that has created in American society a desire to dream Jordan, to "be like Mike."

This pedagogy of desire that Jordan embodies, although at points immobilized by its depoliticized cultural contexts, is nevertheless a remarkable achievement in contemporary American culture: a six-foot-six American man of obvious African descent is the dominant presence and central cause of athletic fantasy in a sport that twenty years ago was denigrated as a black man's game and hence deemed unworthy of wide attention or support. Jordan is therefore the bearer of meanings about black culture larger than his individual life, the symbol of a pedagogy of style, presence, and desire that is immediately communicated by the sight of his black body before it can be contravened by reflection.

In the final analysis, his big black body—graceful and powerful, elegant and dark—symbolizes the possibilities of other black bodies to remain safe long enough to survive within the limited but significant sphere of sport, since Jordan's achievements have furthered the cultural acceptance of at least the athletic black body. In that sense, Jordan's powerful cultural capital has not been exhausted by narrow understandings of his symbolic absorption by the demands of capital and consumption. His body is still the symbolic carrier of racial and cultural desires to fly beyond limits and obstacles, a fluid metaphor of mobility and ascent to heights of excellence secured by genius and industry. It is this power to embody the often conflicting desires of so many that makes Michael Jordan a supremely instructive figure for our times.

## Notes

1. I do not mean here a theory of commodification that does not accentuate the forms of agency that can function even within restrictive and hegemonic cultural practices. Rather, I think that, contrary to elitist and overly pessimistic Frankfurt School readings of the spectacle of commodity within mass cultures, common people can exercise "everyday forms of resistance" to hegemonic forms of cultural knowledge and practice. For an explication of the function of everyday forms of resistance, see James Scott (1990), *Domination and the Arts of Resistance.*

2. For a critical look at Jordan behind the myth, see Sam Smith, *The Jordan Rules* (New York: Simon and Schuster, 1992).

## References

Boers, T. (1990). "Getting Better All the Time," *Inside Sports,* May, 30–33.

Bradley, M. (1991–1992). "Air Everything," *Basketball Forecast,* 60–67.

Giroux, H. (1992). *Border Crossings: Cultural Workers and the Politics of Education.* New York: Routledge.

"How Does Michael Fly?" *Chicago Tribune,* February 27, 1990, 28.

McCallum, J. (1991). "His Highness," *Sports Illustrated,* June 17, 28–33.

Patton, P. (1986). "The Selling of Michael Jordan," *New York Times Magazine,* November 9, 48–58.

Scott, J. (1990). *Domination and the Arts of Resistance.* New Haven: Yale University Press.

Vancil, M. (1992). "Playboy Interview: Michael Jordan," *Playboy,* May, 51–164.

**10**

# Just Do It:
# What Michael Jordan Has to Teach Us

## Michael Hoechsmann

[Michael] Jordan's powerful cultural capital has not been exhausted by narrow understandings of his symbolic absorption by the demands of capital and consumption. His body is still the symbolic carrier of racial and cultural desires to fly beyond limits and obstacles, a fluid metaphor of mobility and ascent to heights of excellence secured by genius and industry. It is this power to embody the often conflicting desires of so many that makes Michael Jordan a supremely instructive figure for our times.

—Michael Eric Dyson

All good things must come to an end, and it appears that Michael meant it in '98; he has retired once and for all. Even though Jordan himself is unlikely to fade into quiet retirement, the Michael Jordan "moment" has passed. That moment in history—when globalization, media culture, the fetishization of Afro-American culture, the marketing and popularity of the sneaker, the growth of a new global corporation (Nike), and the need in the United States for a squeaky clean black role model coalesced—will be forever Michael's. Of course, a whole host of pretenders wait in the wings, hoping to carry Michael's mantle of greatness, but it is unlikely—even impossible—that any of them will achieve the heights of Air Jordan, either on or off the court. Michael is, after all, more than a great basketball player and a successful businessman. Rather, he is an icon of a moment in history. Yes, there will be heirs. Even "Airs," as the Toronto Raptors' Vince Carter, also a product of the University of North Carolina, is known. (Carter's gravity-challenging moves have earned him the respect of the NBA and the moniker "Air Canada," which, not ironically, neatly mirrors the name of the corporate sponsor of Toronto's home court, The Air Canada Centre). But the Jordan "moment" will not repeat itself.

For the Chicago Bulls, the glory years are over and the absence of Michael's impact on the game is apparent. Following closely on his heels, Scottie Pippen, Phil Jackson, and Dennis Rodman moved on to greener pastures, and, at the dawn of the third millennium, the "rebuilding" Bulls stood dead last in the NBA. But while the Bulls may have collapsed without Michael's dominating performances, Jordan's cherubic visage continues to occupy a place in the public sphere (whether displayed in television and magazines or on billboards) and his extraordinary fame ensures that he will remain part of the popular imaginary for a very long time. On the one hand, Michael shows no signs of wishing to fade from the public imaginary. He continues to prominently endorse Nike sneakers, he has bought his way back into the NBA—as a part-owner of the Washington Wizards—and he has formed a strategic partnership with John Elway and Wayne Gretzky to launch mvp.com, an Internet marketing initiative bent on dominating the online shopping market for sporting goods. But, on the other hand, when Jordan sank the winning shot in the 1998 NBA championship series, a monumental story in professional sports history came to an end and a brief, but significant, chapter in contemporary cultural politics came to a close.

Now is the time for reflecting upon the Michael Jordan moment. So what have we learned from this instructive tale?

The notion that Michael Jordan is a "supremely instructive figure for our times" may appear ironic to the many educators who are struggling to carry out their pedagogy against the great motivational weight of the culture of consumption. If anything, the culture of consumption, with its foregrounding of the fleeting and the ephemeral, would seem profoundly anti-educational. The pedagogy of consumption plays a powerful role in the self- and group identity formation of young people, but it grates at many of the traditional objectives of schooling (which, of course, have never been uniformly realized in societies structured by the inequities of class, race, and gender): the cultivation of an informed citizenry, the development of a skilled and compliant workforce, the transcendence of self-interest for a greater sense of the social good, and an inculcation of the desire for personal and intellectual growth. Despite the profound disjunctures between the pedagogy of mass schooling and the pedagogy of consumption, they must both be recognized as powerful ideational forces, which combine, however ironically, to form the attitudes and world views of young people. And this is where "the supremely instructive figure" of Michael Jordan, one of the best-known celebrities in the world—even in retirement—and an iconic force in contemporary popular culture, can lend us a hand.

The remarkable story of Michael Jordan, a superlative sports star and the quintessential corporate pitchman of the 1990s, draws together cultural, social, and economic questions into a dynamic interplay. Air Jordan embodies personality, performance, prowess, and—in his status as a commodity-sign—a branded consumer product. Jordan stands in metonymic relationship to Nike sneakers; despite his endorsements with the likes of consumer heavyweights such as Coca-Cola, McDonald's, and Chevrolet, it is the sneaker that Jordan has helped to reconsolidate as the youth commodity par excellence. To borrow Roman Jakobson's distinction between metaphor and metonymy, the cultural attributes associated with Jordan stand in metaphorical relation to him. On the vertical plane of metaphor, dissimilar elements are yoked together, while on the horizontal plane of metonymy like elements stand in direct relation, just as a part stands for a whole (i.e., the crown for the empire). Thus, raise the name or image of Michael Jordan and a litany of qualitative characteristics on the plane of metaphor are invoked; raise his name or image on the plane of metonymy and Nike running shoes are invoked. Conceptually speaking, Nike and Jordan are one. While Nike has a great number of endorsers on board, it is only now, with the emergence of Tiger Woods, that the Nike sign has bifurcated to include a newcomer. Hardly has there been a commercial tie so intimate. (Unlike the Quaker, Betty Crocker, Aunt Jemima, Mickey Mouse, and Ronald McDonald, Jordan is not a fictional character but a real figure around which multiple fictions circulate.)

On the surface, Jordan is simply "the quintessential role model in the twin worlds of sports and advertising" (Feschuk 1993a, A20), someone who has emerged from humble roots to the pinnacle of celebrity status, both as sports superstar and commercial icon. In sport, few can dominate their game the way Jordan does, but his promotional attributes transcend his remarkable ability to take flight with a basketball in his hand and seemingly hang in the air. Jordan's "hang time" was successfully crafted into Nike's "Air Jordan" shoe, which grossed $130 million in its first year on the market (Andrews 1996, 137). While it may be "hang time" that makes Jordan unique and marketable, it is his qualities as hard working (neatly complementing Nike's "Just do it" slogan), personable, and talented (hence, Gatorade's "Be like Mike" slogan) that make him attractive to advertisers and consumers alike. Yet there is more to Jordan than simply a hard sell to the culture of consumption.

The resonance of the Nike "Air Jordans" shoes and Chicago Bulls jackets, hats, and T-shirts in contemporary youth culture goes far beyond any simplistic pronouncements of "sold-out" youth. At bare minimum, the ever-increasing speed of consumer culture, into whose path virtually all social and cultural meanings must fall, creates the conditions where it is impossible to imagine a social self outside of the domain of commodities. In other words, within the great store of cultural and social repertoires from which a given youth can select the elements of their own identity—a domain that encompasses historical memories as enacted through popular culture, family, education, community, etc.—a growing number of elements have been commodified. As George Lipsitz remarks: "It is not so much that youth cultures are under the 'thrall' of commodities, but rather the power of commodities inevitably shapes the contours of personal and collective identity . . . at a time when consumer culture and media representations play a more powerful role than ever before in defining individual and group identity . . ." (1994, 26). This is not to say that youth do not rework, often in very ironic ways, and resist the symbolic resources made available to them by the culture of consumption. Rather, commodities and commodity-signs are simply dominant forces in the discursive fields of youth, powerful symbolic resources to negotiate in their own journeys towards self- and group identity formation.

In the marketplace of everyday meanings, the sneaker has long played an important role in youth cultures. In a study of teenager consumption patterns, *Business Week* reported that the primary consumer item for teenagers was "athletic shoes," which accounted for twice the spending on blue jeans and 50 percent more than "general clothing" (Zinn 1994, 79). Lightweight and versatile, the sneaker combines style and recreation into one rugged package. A practical shoe, it is also resonant with social significance. Dyson makes a forceful point on the cultural significance of this seemingly superficial artifact of contemporary popular culture, which is worth quoting at length:

> At the juncture of the sneaker, a host of cultural, political, and economic forces and meanings meet, collide, shatter, and are reassembled to symbolize the situation of contemporary black culture. The sneaker reflects at once the projection and stylization of black urban realities . . . and reigns as the universal icon of consumption. The sneaker symbolizes the ingenious manner in which black cultural nuances of cool, hip, and chic have influenced the broader American cultural landscape. (Dyson 1994, 125)

Given the continuities between mass media imagery, consumer culture, and self-identity, the wearing of a sneaker by contemporary youth is not just a utilitarian act, but also a stylized performance. It is an investment of cultural and social significance into a material good that stands in, however fleetingly, as a totemic marker of contemporary youth cultures. Advertisers have recognized the cultural significance of sneakers to contemporary youth and with the help of figures such as Michael Jordan have facilitated both "sneaker companies' aggressive invasion of the black juvenile market" (Dyson 1994, 125) and an appeal to a broader white mainstream youth market. As Toronto advertiser Brian Harrod remarks, "The white middle-class kid may want to be as black as he can in his attitude. He finds excitement there" (quoted in Christie 1995, D2). Of course, the ambivalence of race in Jordan's image—the visibility/invisibility of Jordan's race in white mainstream culture and the significance of his race to black youth culture(s)—constitutes a dynamic site of contemporary youth identity formation.

The dialectic of fear and desire that has characterized the long and diverse history of the appropriation of black culture by the dominant mainstream in North America is replayed in the case of the sneakers. At worst, Jordan is just the point guard for what was Reagan and Gingrich's version of America, a black man stripped of racial connotations who "proves" that hard work and determination are the keys to the American Dream. Certainly, one element of the celebration of Jordan is a victim-blaming response to the impoverished conditions of many African Americans. That race seems to disappear whenever a black man or woman enacts a middle- to elite-class lifestyle and sensibility certainly signals the entanglement of race and class in the United States. But Jordan does not just transcend race in the United States, rather, he transforms race for white viewers, providing a desired alignment for white folks with a black personality who does not appear to pose a threat. Basketball, a game associated with inner city—read "black"—America, has been subject to an astute marketing effort which has raised it to All-American status with baseball and football. Jordan, as the most dominant player in basketball, has seen his stock rise with that of the game. Racial displacement or not, Jordan is on one level simply a superlative athlete who attracts crowds wherever he goes. Thus, in terms of the broadest reception of Jordan, there are no smokescreens; he has got what it takes, and he uses it ("Just do it!"). Jordan is a complex phenomenon. Depending on the reading, he can be seen to displace or enact his racial heritage. Arguably, the reality is a dialectical rendering of both.

In a media era, commodities are not simply joined to signs, but "commodities get produced as signs and signs become produced as commodities" (Goldman 1992, 37). The question that must be raised about the role of advertising in commodity fetishism, however, is whether the commodity itself has changed in the process of its mediation by advertising. Clearly, it is important to identify the various guises of the commodity: its status as a material object, its representation in advertising, and the new ascribed values and connotations that are associated with the object through its representation and its reception (this latter category often coalesces around a key theme or figure, as is the case with a celebrity endorser such as Michael Jordan). What we are looking at is the need for a definition of commodity fetishism that goes beyond the material item to also include its representation in the media, predominantly, as it were, by advertisers. In other words, it is the value added in advertising that is coming to be consumed, not simply the use-value, however fetishized, of the material object.

Jordan and other celebrity endorsers stand on the cusp between production and consumption. Clearly, Jordan's role is to compel potential consumers to buy Nike, but he represents a cost that must be embedded into the product's price, along with the actual costs of production, prior to its sale. Of course, marketing and promotion are integral costs of merchandising in a consumer culture, but the proportion of Nike's costs that are spent on celebrity endorsements dwarfs the cost of production. Given that Nike has a number of celebrity endorsers at any given time, and that the princely sums paid to them do not include the costs of the high-end television and magazine ads in which they appear, it appears that Nike spends more money on promoting the consumption of their products than on producing them. Nike speaks to the madness of our consumer culture; from the value-enhancing image of the Quaker on a Quaker Oats box in the late nineteenth century to the present, we can witness a progression away from the assumption that the value of material goods is intrinsic to their formal qualities. More often than not, the value added by advertising can be more important than those intrinsic formal qualities.

Why do kids like Nike "Air Jordans"? Because Michael Jordan is the embodiment of cool, a vehicle for youth dreams and desires. What is cool? Well, that emerges from popular culture and social practice. His image may be packaged and sold by Nike, but his resonance with young people emerges as his image is integrated into their lives. In other words, what compels young people toward certain commodities involves the recognition of elements of youth culture reified in the commodity and the commodity-sign, not as the result of advertisers' creative genius but through social practice, be it on the basketball court, in the school halls, or on the street corner. In the case of Nike, "Air Jordan" shoes, and Michael Jordan, we have to consider them as a set of equivalent commodities (or commodity-signs) that stand in metonymic relationship to one another. It is almost impossible to discern which commodity (or commodity-sign) is bought when a pair of these shoes is purchased. Is it the shoes themselves? Is it Michael Jordan? Is it the Nike swoosh? In the case of Max, my seven-year-old son, it is clearly the commodity-sign "Michael Jordan" that he is consuming (thankfully, we purchased the shoes secondhand, so Nike hasn't hit us in the wallet—at least, not yet). As for what the commodity-sign "Michael Jordan" means to Max, I can only venture to observe that it involves qualities such as being "cool," "strong," and the "best."

As educators, we miss these lessons at our own peril. Is it possible to carry on teaching the inherited curriculum when youth are under the thrall of media-era celebrities such as Air Jordan? Yes, perhaps. Clearly, mass mediated culture depends on superficiality; its depth is in the metaphorical realms it taps into. Spending precious classroom moments on the Michael Jordan "moment" is not going to solve the educational "crisis" brought on by globalization. Educational "crises" come and go, more often than not on the coattails of significant cultural, social, economic, and technological changes. But for educators to recognize the role of commodities and commodity-signs as significant symbolic resources in the self- and group-identity formation of young people is a first step toward a critical pedagogy that interrogates consumption and commodification while recognizing the ongoing resonance of commodities and commodity-signs in the lives of youth.

If we are to draw on the ideas and examples elaborated here and to begin (or continue) to read the popular "against the grain," while recognizing the powerful resonance of popular culture in everyday life, then we must get "in the paint" ourselves. There is no privileged place outside of the circuits of contemporary culture for critical theorists to rest on their laurels while reading the popular. This is particularly true in relation to the classroom, where the cultural divide between youth as consumers and instructors as critical theorists is most acute. If we are going to make a difference, to change some ways of thinking, then we must be learning all the while. Given the profoundly changing times in which educators and their students find themselves, where the pedagogy of consumption is ascendant in the struggle over the identities and desires of young people, it is imperative that educators make a greater effort than ever before to take youth culture(s) seriously, just as their counterparts in advertising have been doing for the balance of the century.

Consumption may hold increased significance for young people, but it does not preclude alternative world views. Youth may be "buying in" to the culture of consumption, but this does not mean that they are "selling out." As much as the Michael Jordan story demonstrates the ruptural social, cultural, and economic changes of the end of the millennium, there are many residual sites of stability such as schools, families, communities, workplaces, youth organizations, and the like that continue to educate and influence young people. Furthermore, it is vital to point out that many of the artifacts and meanings promoted through the pedagogy of consumption are recirculated directly from the practices of youth cultures. In other words, the commodity-sign, which is marketed to youth, already incorporates the desires and experiences of youth themselves. As Paul Willis states, "[C]ommerce keeps returning to the streets and common culture to find its next commodities" (1990, 19). Yes, Jordan is "cool," he's "hype." But while he may have "hang time," he's just one of us. Word.

# References

Andrews, David. (1996). "The fact(s) of Michael Jordan's blackness: Excavating a floating racial signifier," *Sociology of Sport Journal* 13:125–158.

Christie, James. (1995, Feb. 13). "Bad behaviour can prove profitable," *Globe & Mail,* D2.

Dyson, Michael Eric. (1994). "Be like Mike?: Michael Jordan and the pedagogy of desire." In *Between borders: Pedagogy and the politics of cultural studies,* ed. H. Giroux and P. McLaren, 119–126. New York: Routledge.

Feschuk, Scott. (1993, June 4). "Basketball's bad boy makes good," *Globe & Mail,* A21.

Goldman, Robert. (1992). *Reading ads socially.* New York: Routledge.

Lipsitz, George. (1994a). "We know what time it is: Race, class, and youth culture in the nineties." In *Microphone fiends: Youth music and youth culture,* ed. A. Ross and T. Rose, 17–28. New York: Routledge.

Willis, Paul. (1990). *Common culture: Symbolic work at play in the everyday cultures of the young.* Boulder: Westview Press.

Zinn, Laura. (1994, April 11). "Teens: Here comes the biggest wave yet," *Business Week,* 76–86.

# Contributors

**David L. Andrews** is Associate Professor of Sport and Cultural Studies in the Department of Kinesiology at the University of Maryland, College Park and a visiting research fellow at De Montfort University, UK. He is also an assistant editor of the *Journal of Sport and Social Issues,* and has published on a variety of topics related to the critical analysis of sport as an aspect of contemporary commercial culture.

**Edward G. Armstrong** teaches sociology at Murray State University. He is the author of *Black Consciousness: A Conceptual And Empirical Analysis.*

**Ben Carrington** teaches sociology and cultural studies at the University of Brighton.

**C. L. Cole** is Associate Professor of Kinesiology, Sociology, and Women's Studies at the University of Illinois, Urbana-Champaign. She is editor of the *Journal of Sport and Social Issues,* coeditor with Michael Messner of SUNY series, Sport, Culture, and Social Relations, and she is on the editorial board of *Cultural Studies Critical Methodology* and the advisory board of *GLQ.* She is currently completing a book on embodied deviance, sport, and national identity in post World War II America.

**Norman K. Denzin** is Distinguished Professor of Communications, College of Communications Scholar, and Research Professor of Communications, Sociology, and Humanities at the University of Illinois, Urbana-Champaign. He is the author of numerous books, including *Interpretive Ethnography; The Cinematic Society; Images of Postmodern Society; The Research Act; Interpretive Interactionism; Hollywood Shot by Shot; The Recovering Alcoholic;* and *The Alcoholic Self,* which won the Charles Cooley Award from the Society for the Study of Symbolic Interaction in 1988. In 1997 he was awarded the George Herbert Award from the Study of Symbolic Interaction. He is the editor of *The Sociological Quarterly,* coeditor of *The Handbook of Qualitative Research,* coeditor of *Qualitative Inquiry,* and series editor of *Cultural Studies: A Research Annual,* and *Studies in Symbolic Interaction.*

**Michael Eric Dyson** is an African-American, religious, and cultural studies scholar, and presently holds an Ida B. Wells Barnett University Professorship at DePaul University, having previously served as professor of communication studies at the University of North Carolina, Chapel Hill. His books include *I May Not Get There With You: The True Martin Luther King, Jr.; Between God and Gangsta Rap; Race Rules: Navigating the Color Line; Making Malcolm: The Myth and Meaning of Malcolm X;* and *Reflecting Black: African-American Cultural Criticism.* His writing has also appeared in numerous journals and magazines, including *The New York Times, Vibe Magazine, Current Biography, The New Yorker,* and *Rolling Stone.*

**C. Keith Harrison** is Assistant Professor at the University of Michigan, in Ann Arbor. He has published extensively on race relations and sport, black athletic identity, and mass media images of sport. He is founder and director of the Paul Robeson Research Center for Academic and Athletic Prowess in the Division of Kinesiology, Department of Sports Management and Communication. In 1997–1998, he was the recipient of the Teaching Excellence Award in the Division of Kinesiology, and recently awarded the Victor P. Dauer Distinguished Lecturer Award at Washington State University. His forthcoming book will focus on the images of African American athletes in American culture.

**Michael Hoechsmann** completed his Ph.D. thesis, "Consuming School in the 90s: Youth, Education, and Popular Culture," at the Ontario Institute for Studies in Education, University of Toronto. He is the Director of Education at Young People's Press, and an Adjunct Professor in the Cultural Studies Program at Trent University. He has published numerous articles on youth and the media and served for six years on the editorial collective of *Border/Lines: Canada's Magazine of Cultural Studies.*

**Steven J. Jackson** is Senior Lecturer in the School of Physical Education, University of Otago, New Zealand, where he teaches courses in Sport, Media, and Culture, and Sociology of Sport. His research interests include sport media, globalization and sport, and sports advertising. A member of the editorial board for the *Sociology of Sport Journal,* Steve is coeditor of *Sport Stars: The Politics of Sporting Celebrity,* and *Sport, Culture, and Advertising.*

**Douglas Kellner** is George Kneller Chair in the Philosophy of Education at UCLA and is author of many books on social theory, politics, history, and culture, including *Herbert Marcuse and the Crisis of Marxism; Critical Theory, Marxism, and Modernity; Jean Baudrillard: From Marxism to Postmodernism and Beyond; Postmodern Theory: Critical Interrogations* (with Steven Best); *Television and the Crisis of Democracy; The Persian Gulf TV War; Media Culture;* and *The Postmodern Turn* (with Steven Best).

**Zbigniew Mazur** is Associate Professor at the Institute of English Studies, Maria Curie-Sklodowska University, Lublin, Poland, where he lectures on British and American history and culture. He also teaches cultural theory at the University of Warsaw. In 1997–1998 he was Visiting Fulbright Professor at the University of Pennsylvania. His research concentrates on American history, popular culture, and the theory of cultural studies. He is the author of *Settlers and Indians: Transformations of English Culture in Colonial Virginia.* His research interests include the problems of Americanization and globalization of culture. He is a coauthor of "Do Polish Youth Dream American? The Penetration of American Cultural Values in Poland," in *The American Dream: Past and Present.* He is currently working on a study of popular recreations in colonial America.

**Mary G. McDonald** is Associate Professor in the Department of Physical Education, Health, and Sport Studies, and an affiliate with the Women's Studies program at Miami University in Ohio. Her scholarship focuses on feminist and cultural studies of sport, the media, and popular culture, and explores power relations as constituted along the axes of race, class, gender, and sexuality. Her research has appeared in the *Sociology of Sport Journal, American Studies,* and the *International Review for the Sociology of Sport.* She is coeditor of *Reading Sport: Critical Essays on Power and Representation.*

**Robert E. Sparks** is Associate Professor of Human Kinetics at the University of British Columbia. His research interests span the areas of mass communication, consumer culture, social identity, and public health, with emphasis on the processes of social communication in advertising and the mass media, and theories and methods in audience research and reception analysis. In previous research, he has examined the information needs and priorities of sports journalists, the audience strategies of all-sports cable television, active lifestyle messages in consumer brand advertising, and youth awareness of tobacco marketing and sponsorship. His essays have appeared in sociology, communications, policy, and marketing periodicals, including: *Sociology of Sport Journal; Canadian Journal of Communications; Policy Options; Quest; Asia-Australia Journal of Marketing; International Journal of Advertising and Marketing to Children;* and *International Marketing Review.* His articles include: "Youth Awareness of Tobacco Sponsorship as a Dimension of Brand Equity," *International Journal of Sport Marketing and Sponsorship;* "Tobacco Control Legislation, Public Health and Sport Sponsorship," *Asia-Australia Journal of Marketing,* and "'Delivering the Male': Sports, Canadian Television, and the Making of T.S.N.," *Canadian Journal of Communication.*

**Brian Wilson** is Assistant Professor in the School of Human Kinetics at the University of British Columbia, having previously been a SSHRC postdoctoral fellow in the School of Communication at Simon Fraser University. His research interests include media representations of race and gender, audience studies, youth culture, social movements, and the sociology of sport. His most recent research focuses on the production and consumption of alternative media by youth subcultural groups, with a concentration on the "anti-jock" (cyber)movement. Brian's ongoing research includes studies on the rave subculture, youth culture in recreation/drop-in centers, and grassroots movements to revive/save troubled professional sport franchises.

# Index

United Center, 17, 23, 24, 30, 41
United Kingdom, xviii. *See also* Britain, Great Britain
United States Department of Justice, 68, 80
United States Secretary of Commerce, 16
United States Women's National Soccer Team, 81
University of California-Los Angeles (UCLA), 248
University of Birmingham, 221
University of Colorado, 167
University of Maryland, 68
University of Michigan, xi, 237
University of North Carolina, xiii, 119–122, 153, 167, 269
University of Pennsylvania, 223
University of Utah, 17
Unseld, Wes, 49
UpClose, 31
urban underclass, 126
urban youth, 75, 77, 86, 93, 97
Urry, J., 182, 191
*USA Today,* 17–19, 22–26, 28–39, 43, 61
USA Track and Field Junior Olympics, 80
Utah Jazz, 5, 11

Vaccaro, Sonny, 123
van Dyck, D., 139
Van Standifer, G., 97
Vancil, M., 8, 9, 10, 61, 140, 168, 259, 265
Vancouver, 220, 234, 250
Vancouver Grizzlies, 244
*Vanity Fair,* 209
*Variety,* 141
Vasili, P., 204
Vecsey, G., 10, 121, 132
Ventura, Robin, 26
Vera, H., 117, 137
Verdi, B., 139
vernacular cultures, 199

Vester, H-G., 25
Victorian, 164, 165, 170, 204
Vietnam, 55, 56
viewer resistance, 244
*Village Voice,* 56, 59
Virginia, 211
Voss, D., 25

Wacquant, L., 98, 116, 119
Walesa, Lech, 193
*Wall Street Journal,* 16
Wallerstein, I., 179
Washington Wizards, xiii, 270
Washington, D.C., 82, 97
Washington, George, 231
Wawrzyczek, I., 193, 194
Wayans, Keenan Ivory, 115, 167
Webb, Veronica, 207
Webber, Chris, 236, 237, 239, 242
Webster, D., 182, 192
Wedderburn, Robert, 203
welfare state, 157, 169, 183
Wells, William "Bombardier Billy", 204
Wenner, L., 229
Wernick A., xiv, 231, 232, 247
West Indian, 203
West, C., xiv, 118, 162, 164
West, Jerry, 60
Western Europe, 193, 194, 196, 202
Western racial science, 203
Westernization, 200
Wharton, Arthur, 204
Wharton, D., 191
Wharton, James ("The Moroccan Prince", "Jemmy the Black"), 210, 211
Wheaties, 4, 46, 47, 225
White House, 28, 132, 264
White, Howard, 165
White, J., ix
whiteness, 111
Whiteside, K., xiv
Wideman, J. E., 126
Wieden and Kennedy, 3, 45, 53, 75, 80, 90, 125